THE FAITH OF THE CHRISTIAN CHURCH

THE FAITH OF THE CHRISTIAN CHURCH

An Introduction to Theology

Tyron Inbody

WILLIAM B. EERDMANS PUBLISHING COMPANY

GRAND RAPIDS, MICHIGAN / CAMBRIDGE, U.K.

Wm. B. Eerdmans Publishing Co.
255 Jefferson Ave. S.E., Grand Rapids, Michigan 49503 /
P.O. Box 163, Cambridge CB3 9PU U.K.
www.eerdmans.com

Printed in the United States of America

10 09 08 07 06 05   7 6 5 4 3 2 1

ISBN 0-8028-4151-1

To
Tyler Patrick
Mark Edward

Contents

Preface

I. A New Entry into the Field

In 1961 William Hamilton, the earliest voice in the "radical theology" of the 1960s, announced the demise of the search for "the essence of Christianity." He declared that we cannot "deliver *the* essence [of the Christian faith], once and for all, but rather *an* essence here and now for us."[1] From now on the style of theological writing can only be "fragmentary"; there can be no comprehensive statements of the meaning of the Christian faith. "We must accept," he said, "our subjectivity and partial visions, and save ourselves from the errors of the earlier essence-of-Christianity tradition simply by not claiming permanent validity for what we see."[2]

Few theologians today dare — or even care — to deny the limited perspective of every theology and the contextual nature of faith itself. Many major theologians in the second half of the twentieth century, such as John Cobb, have declined to write a systematic theology "because as an individual of limited perspective, he was always engaging new material. So, any systematic theology one can write would be limited in scope, and fail to encompass as many viewpoints and concerns as possible."[3] Nevertheless, I can account for at least 150 texts since 1961 that attempt to introduce students to the breadth of the Christian vision of reality or to provide a systematic statement of the truth of the gospel.

1. William Hamilton, *The New Essence of Christianity* (New York: Association Press, 1961), p. 12.

2. Hamilton, *The New Essence of Christianity,* p. 19.

3. J. R. Hustwit, "Whitehead and Schleiermacher: System and Life," *Process Perspectives* (Winter 2002-2003): 5.

Following this four-decade flurry of texts, why place another entry into the horse race of textbook sales? Will a new text not have to be something completely novel, or, better, notorious, in order to gain the attention of a saturated market? There may be no more pent-up demand for a new text than there is for sauerkraut ice cream. My reply to this caution is not that I have something scandalous to say or something that has never been said before by any other theologian. Rather, after more than a quarter of a century of teaching Christian doctrine in introduction and systematic theology courses (I have taught each course twenty-eight times!), I am writing a book with the students whom I teach in mind. My audience is not an idealized student of an earlier generation, but the actual students with whom I deal everyday.

Today's student is significantly different from the students of my generation in college and seminary. We were (almost) all male, white, young, first-career, attended small denominational colleges, had an extensive church background, and were liberal arts majors with leisure time to study. Although today's students are in some ways more ready for serious theological study than we were at that stage in our life, they differ significantly from the student I was familiar with in college, seminary, and graduate school — not least of which is they are much more harried. When I left my residency at the Divinity School at the University of Chicago in 1969, prepared to teach theology in the secular world of modernity, I found that the world up and changed on me within a couple of years.

II. Today's Theology Student

I can detect at least four distinct changes in these decades that distinguish today's theology students from the students of my generation.

Diversity within the Student Body

There is, of course, no such thing as "today's student" or the "typical contemporary student." Today's college and seminary students are a very diverse, not a homogeneous group. They differ in any number of ways. Although the proportion of female to male students in undergraduate study has remained constant for many years, the number of women who now study in fields historically dominated by men has increased, and so our awareness of gender issues has become prominent in humanistic studies. The same can be said about racial and ethnic issues. These have not only become distinct fields of academic study, but the concerns of these fields have shaped and reshaped the approaches and subject matter of the social sciences and the humanities. All of this has profoundly affected our awareness of the role of context, perspective, and ideology in almost every field of study, including theology. Although many students do not know the term "postmodern," or could not define the term for my glossary, they have an intuitive sense of context and perspective, even of relativity, and consequently assume diversity as part of the context of their study.

Relatively Traditionless Students

There is a large number of students who have very little familiarity with the Bible or the church, or whose exposure is so highly selective as to be virtually useless for serious theological work. This is often as true of students of ministerial studies as it is for students of the study of religion. Most of today's students were raised in a culture, in families, and in some cases even in churches, where they did not learn even the most rudimentary things about the Scriptures. This hole in their knowledge extends to the history of the church and to the range of Western religious and theological traditions. One can account for this in the seminaries in part by the significant number of students who are "recent converts" or "re-converts" to the Christian faith, either by way of a new experience of faith itself or as a reappropriation of their childhood faith. The notable fact is that many students have serious theological interests, more so, indeed, than many of the "lifetime Christians" in my student days.

The reality is that most of my students have deep life commitments to the Christian faith and to the church, but they enter seminary with an astonishing lack of knowledge of the Scriptures, hermeneutics, the history of the church, and of the theological traditions of the church. Unlike my generation, which knew the Bible and much of the tradition, and who had our own set of modern problems with the Scripture and tradition, this generation hungers for some basic knowledge of Scripture and tradition and a perspective to bring to these which will engage them at the level of their own formation and the formation and vitality of the religious life of congregations. But one cannot assume anymore that students know even the primary biblical stories (such as Abraham, Moses, the prophets, and Jesus), or key biblical passages (such as the Gospels and Romans), or basic theological words (such as image of God, atonement, and justification), or important names in the tradition (such as Augustine, Luther, Calvin, or Wesley).

Absence of a Liberal Arts Background

There is a large number of students who have very little background in the liberal arts throughout their undergraduate studies. Because of the period they attended a college or university, the increasingly professional or occupational orientation of degree programs, the absence of general education requirements that would have provided them with some understanding and even mastery of the liberal arts, and the large number of requirements in their major fields of studies, many have only the most superficial acquaintance with humanistic studies, either its perspectives, goals, methods, or content. They are not uneducated; they simply lack any general knowledge of religion and philosophy, and even studies in history, literature, and the social sciences. The result is that many of the intellectual issues and resources that the liberal arts cultivated in earlier years as preparation for theological studies are new to them, and therefore unexplored and undeveloped. Philosophical problems, historical perspective, the comedy and tragedy of life conveyed through literature, and insights into human nature from psychology and sociology have to be introduced into theological studies. Furthermore if some did pursue religious and philosophical studies in university settings, their focus was primarily on the goals and methodologies of the "religious studies" agenda of the university instead of the "theological studies" which most seminary students who are heading toward some form of Christian ministry need. The one caveat is that most students are familiar with and responsive to popular culture, especially as conveyed by the electronic media, such as movies and television.

Demographic Shift in the Population

This is, in my opinion, one of the most fortunate shifts in the population of theology students in the last four decades. A large percentage of students enrolled in seminaries today are women and second-career students. These students are interested in theological matters both for personal and for professional reasons. This means the majority of students today come to theological problems with an intensity and practicality that is different from the more theoretical interest I brought to my seminary studies. The result is that, although most second-career students are bright, motivated, and serious about the questions and answers of the Christian faith, they are less interested in the way these questions are formulated and explored in older theology textbooks. When I entered seminary, the "bite" to theological questions had not yet been

felt for most of us. Our interest was primarily a mixture of intellectual titilla-
tion, professional preparation, and passing the courses. But there is an immediacy to questions bearing on personal and pastoral identity and practice
among this generation of theological students.

The demographics of my own seminary indicate how and why this shift
has occurred. In 2004, 51% of our masters students were female, 49% were
male; 74% were Caucasian, 19% were Black, and 6% were Asian, Hispanic, Native American, and International; 13% were 22-30, 24% were 31-40, 34% were
41-50, 24% were 51-60, and 5% were 61-70. The largest age cohorts were 41- to
50-year-old females and males (26). Twenty-one denominations were represented, the largest being United Methodist but more than one from AME,
Baptist General, CME, Disciples of Christ, Episcopal, National Baptist,
PCUSA, Roman Catholic, UCC, and non-denominational. Seventeen different
states were represented, from California to New York.[4] It is no mystery why
such demographic shifts have also shifted the agenda for students of theology.

III. The Context for the Book

No consensus exists today among theologians either about the proper subject
matter or about the proper method to employ in theological thinking. There
are a number of reasons why this is so, and together they establish a new context for theology in contrast to the consensus that dominated almost all Protestant theology when I was a theology student in the 1960s. At that time, the
debate was between liberal theologians (more philosophically oriented toward religion) versus neoorthodox theologians (more oriented toward the
creeds and traditions of the church), and neo-orthodoxy had won the day
hands down. Today, there are so many voices that the style is not as much a
"crossfire" or "hardball" debate as it is a "town hall forum" in which each
voice is trying to be recognized in order to be heard.

The Increasing Gap between the Universities and the Seminaries

One of the most significant developments in theology in the last four decades — and one which I decry with great nostalgia — has been the expanding gap, indeed, gulf between the "religious studies departments" of the uni-

---

4. For a new profile of all seminarians today, see Barbara Wheeler, "Fit for Ministry?"
Christian Century, April 11, 2001, pp. 16-23.

versities and colleges and the "theology departments" of the seminaries. As one religious studies advocate puts it, "If the academic study of religion wishes to be taken seriously as a contributor to knowledge about our world, it will have to concede the boundaries set by the ideal of scientific knowledge that characterizes the university. . . . A study of religion directed toward spiritual liberation of the individual or of the human race as a whole, toward the moral welfare of the human race, or toward any ulterior end than that of knowledge itself, should not find a home in the university; for if allowed in, its sectarian concerns will only contaminate the quest for a scientific knowledge of religions and eventually undermine the very institution from which it originally sought legitimation."[5] Even though state university departments of religion are restricted to the academic study of religion because of the first amendment clause to the Constitution, the religion departments of most liberal arts colleges, even those colleges with past or present connections to a church, are equally committed to the study of religion only and not to theological reflection.

Two generations ago this gap was not so pronounced, as the giants in the field of religious studies were North American theologians who taught in seminaries (Paul Tillich and Reinhold and Richard Niebuhr, for example). The same was true in biblical studies. Today even those who teach in seminaries find that their "constructive" as well as their "descriptive" work is deeply affected by the questions, norms, and goals of the religious studies departments outside the seminaries. Or they live part of their lives within the seminary and the church, and the other part of their lives within the academy. Thus, there is an increasing divide between people who understand theology as the church's thinking for itself (for example, Stanley Hauerwas, Duke Divinity School) and those who understand theology as "public theology," a way of thinking about the resources of religion in our culture (for example, Victor Anderson, Vanderbilt Divinity School). This gap between the church and the academy places at stake the very definition of theology among contemporary theologians.

The Shattered Spectrum

The death of the theological giants in the 1960s, such as Barth, Bultmann, Tillich, and Niebuhr, was also the death of the neo-orthodox consensus

---

5. Donald Wiebe, *The Politics of Religious Studies: The Continuing Conflict with Theology in the Academy* (New York: St. Martin's Press, 1999), p. xiii.

throughout the middle half of the twentieth century. To be sure, there were major differences between the liberal and conservative forms of neo-orthodox theology (Tillich verses Barth), but there was a consensus among all of them that theology dealt with the Christian revelation, with the Word of God, and with salvation. The significance of the public pronouncement of "the death of God" in the 1960s was in part a declaration of the waning authority of neo-orthodox theology[6] and a revival of "God the problem" for late modern theology.[7] We entered a time which Lonnie Kliever called "the shattered spectrum,"[8] when a new generation of voices clamored to be heard (radical, secular, process, liberation, eschatological, political, play, narrative, Black, feminist, Latin American). If one approved of this shattering, it was considered a time of creativity and excitement; if one disapproved, it was a time of dissolution, disillusion, and chaos. For almost everyone, however, it meant that theology consisted of "tracking the maze"[9] instead of engaging in theological construction.[10]

The Blurred Lines between Premodern, Modern, and Postmodern Culture

There is a large number of "postmodern" students who are enrolled in theological seminaries today. They may not know the term but they know the context — although even *Time* and *Newsweek* now use the word freely. The term, of course, is one of the most amorphous words in our current jargon.[11] Yet it points to some deep shifts in the sensibilities of our culture since I began teaching in a seminary. Postmodernism entails, in part, a shift from the book to the screen, from the word to the image, from logic to engagement — shifts which shape the sensibilities and thought of the contemporary student.

---

6. The first hint of this demise can be found in an essay by Langdon Gilkey, "Cosmology, Ontology, and the Travail of Biblical Language," *The Journal of Religion* 41 (July 1961): 194-205.

7. Gordon Kaufman, *God the Problem* (Cambridge: Harvard University Press, 1972).

8. Lonnie Kliever, *The Shattered Spectrum: A Survey of Contemporary Theology* (Atlanta: John Knox Press, 1981).

9. Clark Pinnock, *Tracking the Maze: Finding Our Way through Modern Theology from an Evangelical Perspective* (San Francisco: Harper & Row, 1990).

10. The most creative book for interpreting this period in theology and for attempting to lay the groundwork for a reconstruction within the liberal and neoorthodox traditions in late modern theology was Langdon Gilkey, *Naming the Whirlwind: The Renewal of God-Language* (Indianapolis: Bobbs-Merrill, 1969).

11. Tyron Inbody, "Postmodernism: Intellectual Velcro Dragged Across Culture?" *Theology Today* 51/4 (January 1995): 524-38.

These, in turn, hint at a profound shift away from the modern agenda of Western philosophy and theology. What theology is to do, who is to do it, and how it is to be done (its sources and norms) are once again controversial. The modern Enlightenment quest of clarity and certainty (for foundations), based on an appeal to reason or to science, is completely foreign to the experience, formation, or agenda of many contemporary theological students.

Every theology is addressed as an answer to the particular set of questions, problems, dilemmas, and needs of a particular time and place. We live in a period of transition in which it is not utterly clear what is our situation to which the gospel must speak its word. What is clear, I think, is that at the beginning of the twenty-first century in North America we are living in a time of perceptible transition from one cultural era to another. Specifically, we live in a time of great tensions and anxieties and conflicts caused by a shift from the modern world to a postmodern world. We do not know yet what to call this "postmodern" world because we do not even know yet what this new world will look like in contrast to modernity. All we know is that the modern world has revealed huge faults of delusion, injustice, and failure, and that some of the characteristics of the postmodern world can be described as uncertainty, loss of confidence in reason and science, relativism, loss of identity, narcissism, and nihilism. We inhabit a cultural Disneyland, a consumer culture in which the self is constructed on an ad hoc and individualistic basis. The consequences of this cultural shift have been enormous for theology.

Indifference to Modernity

One of the most notable characteristics of the postmodern context is the relative indifference of today's students to modernity, especially to its foundationalism, its commitment to reason and science, and its reductionism. There are, to be sure, staunch defenders and proud representatives of modernity in the church, such as Bishops John Shelby Spong (Episcopal) or Joseph Sprague (United Methodist), who feel themselves as exiles from the church because so many in the church resist the modern world. And they do attract a significant group of enthusiastic followers. But equally significant is the strong rejection by traditionalists within their own churches and the postmoderns who do not sympathize with their agenda — and these are not all right-wing reactionaries. Although the dilemma often is more intuitive and unarticulated than explicit and overriding, many students are in a quandary about what authority to give to modernity and its challenges to traditional Christian faith. Should it be embraced unequivocally (as in modernism), worked within (as in liberalism), resisted (as in fundamentalism), challenged (as in evangelicalism), or ignored and moved beyond (as in postmodernism)?

Most theological students today are bright. Some of those who seem at first glance to be more modest in their intellectual endowment or to be poorly educated prove to be, on closer exam, simply not formed by the agenda that shaped modern theology. The modern sources of belief and practice, norms of meaning and truth, and purpose of theology itself, whether in its liberal, postliberal, or fundamentalist forms of modernity, seem foreign to their experience or life projects. I simply do not have many students whose agenda is even deeply affected let alone determined by the modern quest for detached objectivity and absolute certainty. The Enlightenment project affects them in their religious life, if it affects them at all, only at the fringes and then only hidden and unconscious ways. Except for a few rare atypical students, both modernism and fundamentalism seem equally odd to them. My perception is that the modernity agenda of unequivocal clarity and absolute certainty exists today only among more fundamentalist colleges and seminaries.

There are, to be sure, some premodern students for whom the modern notions of meaning and truth seem never to have challenged their beliefs and practices in the first place. It is almost as if they had leapfrogged the Enlightenment, similar to the way in which some third world countries have jumped from the world of archaic technology to the world of advanced technology. But there are many postmodern students who have abandoned the questions, the procedures, the criteria, and the agenda for theological thought set by modernity and decided that to be a Christian is more to adhere faithfully to a Christian view of the world than it is to give reasons to the modern world for believing the Christian view of the world. When they read Hodgson and King's *Christian Theology: An Introduction to Its Traditions and Tasks*,[12] a book primarily oriented to contemporary responses to the Enlightenment project, they simply have no idea what most of the authors are talking about, not because they are not intelligent but because their own questions are more postmodern than modern. It never occurs to them that modern doubt and the quest for clarity and certainty should negate, control, or shape their beliefs and practices. They are products of a world in which the Enlightenment project has come to an end or is being radically challenged and transformed before their eyes.

Making absolute claims about the truth, which was so dear both to liber-

---

12. Peter Hodgson and Robert King, eds., *Christian Theology: An Introduction to Its Traditions and Tasks,* second ed. (Philadelphia: Fortress Press, 1985).

als and fundamentalists in the modern era, is unappealing to them. Instead, they are concerned about knowing Christ by faith and commitment with the purpose of their being transformed and participating in the transformation of the world. While I was raised at the end of the modern era and found the church's teachings and practices so laced with adjectives like "absolute" and "objective," and tied to the myth of neutrality, that I experienced many of the church's beliefs and practices to be intellectually dishonest, coercive, and re-pressive, many of my students, on the other hand, were raised in a culture of relativity, uncertainty, cynicism, and lack of conviction and structure, and they are searching for something to believe in and to follow which will give structure and meaning to their lives of uncertainty and instability. Though a few students retreat to another form of modernity, namely, fundamentalism, and search for absolute truth through fideism or rationalistic arguments, most are indifferent to any form of foundationalism, whether it be modern or fundamentalist. As Brian McLaren says, "Arguments that pit absolutism versus relativism, and objectivism versus subjectivism, prove meaningless or absurd to postmodern people: They're wonderful modern arguments that backfire with people from the emerging culture."[13] Today's student of theol-ogy lives in this time of transition from modern to postmodern sensibilities.

Heterogeneity

It is common today to refer to the "culture wars" which dominate our society and our politics, and the church stands at the center of those conflicts. We do not live in a homogeneous culture. For some this is the decline and ultimate death of our culture. They long for the (presumed) good old days when Christianity, Protestantism, and European values shaped our society. Others are proud of the pluralistic past and present of the country and the church. It is a source of strength, and, indeed, represents the life in the kingdom of God more faithfully than a monoculture does.

One dilemma for the church, and a source of tension within many churches and denominations, is that the church growth movement has estab-lished rather clearly on the basis of its research that "the principle of homoge-neity" is the primary principle in the growth and stability of churches. People like to go to church with people who look and act like themselves. But this principle fits neither the mission nor the reality of Protestant seminaries to-

13. Quoted by Lon Allison and Rick Richardson, "Emergent Evangelism: The Place of Ab-solute Truths in a Postmodern World — Two Views," *Christianity Today*, November 2004, p. 44.

day. They base their guidelines and agenda not only on the reality that homogeneous seminaries are not sustainable by mainline denominations (most students attend for reasons of convenience rather than reasons of ideology). Even more important is their conviction that the gospel of Jesus includes all sorts of people within God's kingdom. Although every religion, denomination, church, and person shares a set of symbols and practices in common with others, or there would be no identity at all, each, nevertheless, shares different contexts for interpretation and different understandings of the meaning of those shared symbols and practices.

IV. The Author's Framework

Every book is written from a particular point of view. Even "objective" books are shaped by the interests of the author — what subject is selected, what topics within that subject matter are treated and what are not, how it is organized, what is emphasized and how, and the judgments made by the author on that subject. The roles of perspective and agenda are especially apparent in the world of religion and theology. Consequently, the reader of an introduction to theology has every reason to know right off the bat something of the background and interests of the author. No theologian ever declares dogma or even writes in the name of the church. The church in its various councils speaks through its creeds, articles of religion, confessions of faith, and statements of faith. Theology is done by individual theologians from their point of view. Thus theology always entails items from the canon, the history of theology, the context of the times, and the background and interests of the individual theologian. What are the background and perspectives which shape this book?

No theology is ever final, neither the creeds of the church, nor confessions of faith, nor Barth's nor Tillich's theology, nor this one. The proud pretensions of modernity to have certain foundations of knowledge and certainty are rejected here. The postmodern emphasis on "perspectivalism" is affirmed. One postmodern theologian puts it in a way many premodern Protestants would have put it: "Atheistic postmodernism says that we are not God because there is no God. Christian thought says we are not God because only God is God."[14]

My finite limitations (of awareness as well as knowledge) also prevent me

---

14. Mark Westphal, "Blind Spots: Christianity and Postmodern Philosophy," *Christian Century,* June 14, 2003, p. 33.

from including the perspective of every theology that has been written in the past or is being written today. In the first place, I do not and cannot read everything that is published in theology today. Although I read widely, try to engage new perspectives and interpretations, and remain open to what I can learn from as many perspectives as possible, I cannot take in and digest everything, nor do I pretend to do so here. I have to start from and write from within my own knowledge and experience, which include, first of all, my background, and then, what I have learned over the last forty years from reading and talking with other theologians and students.

My background and agenda, therefore, may be of some interest to the reader. No one, of course, fully comprehends the mix of motives behind their work. Subjects of interest and attention, agendas, and approaches to anything are a complex blend of intellectual, professional, temperamental, and biographical influences. I was raised in a small, conservative, evangelical (essentially a fundamentalist) church in Elkhart, Indiana, in the late 1940s and 1950s. This church dominated my life until I went to a small, denominational, liberal arts college in 1958. Family and friends gathered in this close-knit church about a half mile away from my house. Jesus Christ, and a special "born again" relationship with him, was the center of every service, not simply the semi-annual two-week "revival meeting." Although I tried many times at these meetings "to have a born again experience," it never happened. To this day I have never had such an experience, and do not know what it would feel like to have what William James called a "twice born" experience.[15] Although there are many Christians who know in the depths of their self what it means to have such an experience, I believe there are many deeply committed Christians, including many Protestant evangelicals, who know exactly what I am describing.

Nevertheless, at the same time I knew everything I believed most deeply and was most committed to was defined by the church, especially its Scriptures and hymns, much of which I still say and sing from memory without the benefit of book and hymnal. Once a quarter we had the Eucharist — we called it "communion Sunday" — and although it was preceded by an evangelistic sermon, the last part of that service was like no other time in the life of my church. I knew there I was a Christian, I knew I knew Jesus Christ, and I knew that that reality determined my view of the world, how I constructed it, what I valued, what I wanted to be and to be like. I wondered how I could be this kind of Christian, whose life is defined by the reality of Christ, and yet

---

15. William James, *The Varieties of Religious Experience* (New York: Mentor Books, 1958; originally published 1902), Lectures IV-VII.

not a "real Christian" because I had not "had a born again experience." Although I have acquired many sacramental, liberal, and postliberal views in the meantime, I still to this day am an evangelical Protestant who is convinced that if one knows God in Christ that knowledge must be "of" and not simply "about." It must go to the depth of who one is, shaping all one's life if it is genuine faith.

Unlike many students today, however, college was the other "most important thing" in my life. If I ever had a new reshaping experience, it was not in my church but in my college, under the influence of Bob McBride and Marvin Henricks, who deconstructed much of my former beliefs, feelings, and practices, and set me on the path of reconstructing my life. Indiana Central (now University of Indianapolis) was a small, denominational school in University Heights — the kind of place and time when new worlds were opened up to many adolescents raised in small midwestern towns.

The experience remade me in ways that seem not to happen to many students today. I confronted modernity head on and have never been the same since then. I never lost my faith; the matters of faith were always my "ultimate concern" (Paul Tillich), but I questioned many of my beliefs and practices from childhood. Liberalism was alive in those times and places, even in small midwestern colleges, and I imbibed of it deeply. Basic questions about faith and reason and the reality of God were at the forefront of the philosophy and religion courses. This was true even when I went to seminary. Although neo-orthodoxy held sway over the theology, Bible, and homiletics departments at United, liberal theology remained powerful through the influence of the theology of Tillich, Bultmann, and the Niebuhrs. It had been in college in the late 50s and early 60s that I was introduced to the process theology of Whitehead, Wieman, Loomer, and Meland. This attraction was renewed when I went to the bastion of twentieth-century liberal theology, the Divinity School of the University of Chicago, for my graduate work with the late Langdon Gilkey. Those days at Chicago were focused on matters of theological method and the question of the reality of God. These preoccupations with theological method and with "God the problem" followed me into my first teaching appointment at Adrian College in Michigan in 1969.

And then the world up and changed on this newly minted graduate. Almost overnight, secularism was challenged by a revival of religion, especially in its conservative forms, all over the world. We were in a new situation where religion, spirituality, and even fundamentalism were again on the agenda of any cultural critic, religion scholar, and theologian.

When I moved back to my seminary to teach in 1976, a move which I welcomed even though I relished teaching in undergraduate college, I rediscovered, in addition to the revival of religion, the whole range of classical Christian teachings I had ignored for some time, beginning with the Trinity and christology, and I discovered the whole new emerging world of postmodernism and postliberal theology. Although to this day I remain convinced that there is much good to affirm about modernity, and that one can be a modern person and a Christian at the same time, I am also convinced by postmodernism of the many great faults in modernity and in liberalism, and have been deeply influenced by postliberal themes about the language of faith and the role of the community in defining and sustaining the life of faith.

The criticisms of liberalism by the various postmodern theologies, notably the liberation and postliberal theologies, provide a new context and direction for much of what is said in this book. Modern foundationalism, with its search for clear and distinct ideas and absolute certainty rooted in the ideal method, is bankrupt. Modernism, the attempt to translate both the teachings and the symbols of the church into some other mode of discourse, is defunct. Nevertheless, I remain convinced that the Christian can engage the modern world (or late modern world, if you prefer) as a Christian. We do not need to disavow the insights and every value of modernity in order to be postmodern in our context and agenda.

All of this means, for understanding this book, that there is no one label to attach to this interpretation of Christian doctrine. One reason is that the old labels simply do not stick any longer; the glue is dried up. Furthermore, in some ways they are irrelevant or inapplicable. What do left, center, and right, or conservative and liberal mean anymore? The second reason is that for postmodern or late modern thinkers, the various temperaments, perspectives, and styles summarized in these labels are not mutually exclusive. In some ways this book is conservative in temperament and in other ways it is liberal; it is shaped both by modern and postmodern perspectives; the content is evangelical and it is catholic and reformed. Resources are mined from the church fathers (Irenaeus, Augustine, Athanasius), the various Protestant Reformers (notably Calvin, Luther, and Wesley), and modern evangelicalism and liberalism. The interpretation of doctrines is also deeply shaped by the various feminist, Black, and Latin American liberation theologians. Some characteristic themes of process theology are also apparent throughout. Methodological purists (methodologists who engage in methodolatry) might say that the book, therefore, does not have a single and pure point of view. That accusation meets with my approval. I prefer to draw on the insights of a variety of perspectives to interpret the range of Christian teachings than to describe myself as a methodological purist.

I consider myself, then, to be something of an anomaly today, although I believe that many theologians and students of theology find themselves on the borders of many different perspectives. I am a blend of evangelicalism inherited from childhood and adolescence, of classical liberalism adopted during my college and graduate years, and of postliberal sensibilities which gradually but deeply have changed my mind on many theological issues and interpretations throughout my years of teaching. Most college and seminary students today do not inhabit all of these worlds sequentially as I have, for they do not personally live in a world which is as rich as the complex worlds of evangelicalism, liberalism, and postmodernism all wrapped up in one person. Being shaped, past and present, by each of them makes it impossible for me to adopt an ideological label for my thinking. Although I have less and less sympathy with fundamentalist forms of Christianity (or of any religion, for that matter), I increasingly am fascinated by the developments which have occurred among the new generation of evangelical theologians. I have a love/ hate relationship with classical liberalism, as I am convinced that we are not and should not be beyond some aspects of the Enlightenment, while I am also convinced of the weaknesses, even some of the destructive and demonic qualities, of classical liberalism. Not only do I not fit an ideological label; I am not even much interested in one anymore. So the book which follows is my conversation with a number of voices who are engaged in an ongoing conversation about the traditional loci of Christian teachings.

V. The Content of the Book

Main Features of the Book

The book is an introduction to the major teachings (doctrines) of the Christian church. The twelve chapters deal with twelve of these primary doctrines of the faith. It begins with theology as such, and moves from there to matters of criteria and revelation and faith, then to God, creation, suffering and evil, human nature, Jesus Christ, salvation, church, sacraments, and finally to eschatology. My first letters from and discussions with my editor, Allen Myers, Senior Editor at Eerdmans, came in October and November, 1992, the contract was finally signed in 2000, and the chapters were completed in October 2003.

Each chapter is written on the basis of twenty-five years' experience teaching students the basic doctrines of the church. They include a discussion of the classical doctrines filtered through a predominantly Protestant lens. Each provides a summary of problems, issues, and contemporary interpretations of each doctrine. The book moves between a survey of the history and problems of each of the doctrines and my constructive commentary on each doctrine. When finished reading the book, students should be familiar with the primary images, symbols, and doctrines of the church and, if my example is compelling, enthused to try their own hand at constructive interpretation — "What do you understand to be the faith of the Christian church?" The book introduces just enough questions to stimulate reflection and just enough answers to enable students to move on to their understanding of the faith of the church.

The book appeals to a wide range of readers. It is usable both by more conservative and more liberal students across the broad mainstream of Protestant Christianity. I often discuss a variety of viewpoints on a controversial topic, not in order to provide a smorgasbord from which to pick and choose, but rather to provide a tool box from which the student can select tools with which to carry on their theological interpretation. Thus, a dialectical style often characterizes the chapters. By this I mean, first of all, that often the student will encounter the argument that the answer to a theological question is both/and rather than either/or. I mean, also, that lines of arguments are often two-way streets in which the traffic goes in both directions. Often arguments do not have to be separated as either/or choices but rather properly distinguished while they overlap or depend on each other for a fuller truth. Often in theology there is some truth on each side of an argument, and the task is how to state these in such a way as to not have to choose between two half-truths or to deny the truth of the other side of the argument.

The book includes many illustrations from popular culture within the text. I also provide short quotations in each chapter for visual impact and thought stimulation. These range from Barth to bumper stickers, from popular magazines to theological tomes. The book represents enough of a consistent point of view that the student will know where the author stands and why, but is open enough and inclusive enough of different ideas that the student will know there are other interpretations which he or she can pursue. One potential criticism, I think, might be that the book does not represent a singular, "hardball" point of view, but, rather, introduces issues and options, leaving the student without an unequivocal answer.

What Is Unique about the Book

Several things are unique about this book. The format of highlighted quotes embedded within the text and the use of many examples from popular culture should appeal to students because of their familiarity with this format in their everyday reading and viewing. Also, although the book is a textbook, it is written in a relatively informal style to appeal to people shaped by contemporary media.

The book is irenic in tone and style, disavowing the "crossfire" screaming at each other which is the style characteristic of so much of our culture from politics, television, and, indeed, our churches. It is addressed to students who are less interested in labels and ideological conformity than in simply thoughtful reflection on the meanings of Christian teaching. As described by a student in a paper for my introduction to theology course, "Like a combination of boxing referee and professional mediator, Inbody seeks the high ground of dialogue and cooperation rather than the 'bare-knuckle' approach."[16]

As another notable difference from many introduction to theology texts, this text includes sections of chapters on topics not regularly discussed in other widely used textbooks (and I would not have included if I had been writing this book only for myself). Over the years students in my introductory course and others have insisted I discuss topics which were troublesome for them — regardless of whether I wanted to talk about them or not — such as creationism, the Devil, miracles, intercessory prayer, shame, the virgin birth, and the end times rapture. Finally, I also provide an extensive glossary for students who initially may be dismayed by some of the words theologians use.

While the book is an introduction, it is neither as "thin" as some introductory texts nor as "thick" in content as some other books in systematic theology. The balance between "accessibility" and "substance," I believe, will make this an attractive and usable introductory text for many students of theology today.

It is impossible to recognize, let alone to acknowledge, everyone who helped me on this project. Three groups, however, deserve special recognition. First, my wife, Fran; my two sons, Mark and David; their wives, Mia and Karen; and my grandsons, Tyler and Mark, deepen every day my awareness of how much we depend on love and grace in our lives. Second, the large number of students who have taken my introduction to theology and systematic theology courses over a quarter of a century have prompted and shaped much of what is written in this book. Because of them, I have never lost my interest in and love of theology. Finally, the staff at Eerdmans, beginning with Allen Myers, Senior Editor, who recruited me and supported me for over a decade; Hannah Timmermans, who did meticulous editing of the manuscript; and Jennifer Hoffman, Associate Managing Editor, who brought the production to completion. I am grateful beyond any words I can put on paper.

16. Dennis Williams, Reflection Paper #4, November 4, 2003, 1.

CHAPTER ONE

Thinking about Faith

I. The Faith of the Christian Church

The Christian faith is rooted in a community of believers. Although that faith must be personally appropriated to be authentic, it is not derived from the private experience of Christians. Paul reminds the church at Corinth, "For I handed on to you as of first importance what I in turn had received" (1 Cor. 15:3). His mystical encounter with the living Christ on the road to Damascus made him an apostle, but it did not generate the content of his faith. He embraced the preaching of the primitive church, which proclaimed that God has used Israel and Israel's son, Jesus, to renew the creation (Acts 2:14-39; 3:13-26; 5:30-32; 13:17-41). That apostolic witness has been formed and reformed in the doctrines (teachings) of the church for twenty centuries. Every Christian's faith begins as an engagement with the church's witness to Christ. Regardless of how preoccupied we are with our own experience, we do not begin with our own experience but with "the faith of the Christian church."

Your use of — or discomfort in using — the definite article ("the") will tell you something about your understanding of faith. If you speak only of "Christian faith," you might think of faith as a private experience to which you apply "Christian" as an adjective. If you speak of "the Christian faith," you are more likely to think of faith as the shared language of the community, a tradition of practices and beliefs with which you identify. One of my purposes throughout this book is to show how the Christian faith is both objective and subjective. Christian faith is not merely generic faith (our common human spirituality), but is a way of life that entails a dialectic between, on the one hand, specific stories, symbols, practices, and beliefs that you learn (*the*

Christian faith) and, on the other, your experience of the living Christ within your life as a believer (Christian *faith*).

This is an offensive claim to some modern Christians. Many North Americans believe Christian faith is the unique way I, as a private consumer, assemble my own spiritual meanings from the shopping mall of religious choices. Faith consists of my experiences and beliefs. "Christian" is simply the adjective I apply to my own inner voice.[1] "Christian" does not necessarily designate specific practices or beliefs. To set such boundaries would deny me the uniqueness of my own religious experience. It would suppress the authenticity and authority of my religious feelings. Such reaction to boundaries is instinctive in our culture. No one has the authority — or the audacity — to define boundaries to anyone's faith, including her or his Christian faith. With the collapse of the authority of traditions, each person is left with only the authority of her or his own religious experience. Many Christians are (mis)led by our culture to believe that when they speak of real faith they refer to their private inner experiences. *When does it fit in Vhon?*

If we are Christians, however, our faith is derived from and measured by the faith of the Christian church. There is a dialectic between our living faith as believers and the faith we inherit from past generations and share with a living community today. I intend this as both a descriptive and a normative claim. We are deluded when we deny that what we practice, feel, and believe is not transferred to us from a living community. A collection of stories, a network of rituals, a system of beliefs, and socially shaped feelings are transmitted to us from a community of people who practice the Christian faith. Every modern Christian lives within a dialectic of a Christian form of inner experience and a set of symbols, practices, and beliefs long before she or he begins to think theologically. Theologians have long recognized this dialectic between objective and subjective components of faith. The word "faith" in its confessional form, *credo* (I believe), points both to something we inherit and to our own personal appropriation of the reality to which it calls attention. This polarity is formulated in the ancient Latin distinction between *fides quae creditur,* "the faith which is believed," and *fides qua creditur,* "the faith through which [it] is

---

1. One of the best books on contemporary American religion is Robert Bellah, Richard Madsen, William Sullivan, Ann Swidler, and Steven Tipton, *Habits of the Heart: Individualism and Commitment in American Life* (Berkeley: University of California Press, 1985). The centerpiece in this study is Sheila Larson, who dubs her faith "Sheilaism." "My faith has carried me a long way. It's Sheilaism. Just my own little voice" (p. 221). See also Harold Bloom, *The American Religion: The Emergence of the Post-Christian Nation* (New York: Simon and Schuster, 1992), and David Lyon, *Jesus in Disneyland: Religion in Postmodern Times* (Malden, Mass.: Blackwell, 2000).

believed." This book, then, is about what constitutes *the Christian* faith and how it creates Christian *faith* in the life of each believer. It is itself an example of one way we transmit the Christian faith of previous generations to the present one by interpreting that faith in our contemporary context.

Faith, then, as I use the term, has two distinct meanings. The intrinsic relationship between them — that is also part of the meaning of dialectic — shows how both the objectivity of an inherited tradition and the subjectivity of individual appropriation are essential to authentic faith. This polarity describes the creative tensions in most Protestant theology since the Enlightenment. Faith has a deeply personal quality to it, as when we say earnestly to a friend, "I have faith in you." Faith goes to the center of the self and defines the inner core of our being. It deals with what we most depend on, what we most deeply trust in, what we are most deeply concerned about. Faith also has a linguistic and social dimension to it, as when we say instinctively, "I believe the faith of the church." Faith cannot be Christian faith without a community of people who practice a way of acting, feeling, and thinking. Before we have "faith" we learn about "the faith." There is no authentic Christian existence without both ingredients. To affirm Christian faith is to say I believe what the church believes. Simultaneously, it is to say these beliefs are mine, they go to the center of who I am, and refer to what I take to be most trustworthy about life.

The Christian, then, is called to witness to her faith both as content and experience. She is, also, summoned to "give an account" of it (cf. 1 Peter 3:15) — to describe, explain, and interpret her faith as clearly as possible to herself, to the church, and to the world. Christian faith involves "thinking about faith." This is what Christians call "theology." We are challenged to explain what we mean or why we believe what we say. We are asked to interpret what the church practices, believes, and teaches, how this shapes what the community and each individual does, and what this requires for our life in and for the world God loves. Theology moves beyond witness to the task of thinking with the church in our context about God and the meanings of the Christian faith.

This is a troublesome task for some Christians. They do not see that thinking about faith is intrinsic to the life of faith. They consider faith as having to do with doing rather than believing, with feeling rather than thinking. Therefore, the case has to be made for some beginning students that thinking about faith is important in a living faith. A few have to be convinced that, as Donald Luck put it, "even though theology is 'believing thinking' as much as it is 'thinking about believing,' it still remains thinking. It is an academic subject even when pursued by the church for the sake of the church."[2]

2. Donald Luck, *Why Study Theology?* (St. Louis: Chalice, 1999), p. 40.

II. Why Complicate Things?
Some Preliminary Questions about Theology

When I began teaching theology I discovered, to my amazement, that many of the students in my "Introduction to Theology" class were seniors. The curriculum at my school, like that of most mainline Protestant seminaries in those days, was "progressive": since students are adult learners, they should take courses only when they are convinced they need them. I quickly discovered that some students delayed taking a course in theology because they were not convinced that theology was important. Some students would say, "I don't do theology; I practice my faith. Christians are not called to explain their beliefs but to change the world." Why, how, and to what they were called to change the world was seldom discussed beyond vague notions of "justice" or "doing good" or "helping people." I also discovered, however, that every student had a wide range of beliefs already in place (even though they didn't call them theology). When they said, "I am not a theologian and I don't want to waste my time doing theology," some actually meant, "I do not want anyone 'messing around' with the beliefs with which I am very comfortable."

Facing Intimidation

Some students of theology feel intimidated in their first course. There are several reasons for this.

First, some are in a theology course because they have to fulfill a requirement in the curriculum. While many students take courses in theology because they have hard questions they want to answer, others are more oriented toward people than ideas, or are more interested in spiritual formation than in intellectual problems.[3] Some students today have a meager background in the liberal arts. While almost all come to seminary well trained in some field of learning, these fields often are not the liberal arts. Frequently, students have had few courses in history, philosophy, literature, the arts, and the sciences, and as a result, they have not been trained in the liberal arts way of thinking. But they soon discover that theological thinking is akin to the way of thinking in the liberal arts. Indeed, the liberal arts arose in the Middle Ages as preparation for theological studies. Their fundamental purpose was to train for analytical and critical thinking. Theological thinking has been shaped by the

---

3. For a discussion of this challenge, see Virginia Samuel Cetuk, *What to Expect in Seminary: Theological Education As Spiritual Formation* (Nashville: Abingdon, 1998).

kind of critical analysis and reflection developed through the study of history, philosophy, literature, psychology, and sociology. Unfortunately, some have not learned to be comfortable with and enjoy this way of thinking. Deprived of this experience in their undergraduate programs, some are ill equipped, disoriented, and intimidated by this approach to thinking about faith.

Second, beginning students have to deal with an onslaught of new terms they have never heard before. Starting with the frightening word "theology," they soon encounter such pretentious sounding terms as hermeneutics, soteriology, ecclesiology, and eschatology — and all those "ology" words sound so esoteric. They even confront some Hebrew, Greek, and Latin words and phrases like *chesed* or *esse* or *sola Scriptura*. All of this seems so elitist (and tedious). In *A Month of Sundays*, John Updike describes the boring seminary education of the Reverend Thomas Marshfield, who was sent from his Midwestern parish in disgrace to a desert retreat in the West for some enforced rest and relaxation. During one of the mornings when the errant cleric is writing his confessions, he describes one of his seminary professors, the Reverend Wesley Augustus Chillingsworth:

> His course epitomized everything I hated about academic religion: its safe and complacent faithlessness, its empty difficulty, its transformation of the tombstones of the passionate dead into a set of hurdles for the living to leap on their way to an underpaid antique profession. The old scholar's muttering manner seemed to acknowledge this, as without mercy he dragged us, his pack of pimply postulates, from Hottentot tabus and Eskimo hospitality . . . on to the tedious Greeks and the neo-Platonists . . . and further on to the rollicking saints, knitting their all-weather spacesuits of invisible wool, Augustine and his *concupiscentia*, Bonaventura and his *gratia*, Anselm and his *liberum arbitrium*, Aquinas and his *synderesis*, Duns Scotus and his *pondus naturae*, Occam and his razor, and Heaven knows who else.[4]

Some theologians, indeed, are tempted to exhibit their learning by using arcane terms in order to impress their audience. This is unfortunate, even scandalous. Every field of knowledge or practice has its technical terms, however, from the chimney sweep who recently cleaned out our dryer exhaust pipe to the astrophysicist. The seamstress employs a technical language (a ham, boning, point pins, bobbins, stitch witchery, cording, pinking shears, transfer pencil, interfacing, stabilizer, ring thread, slash, and rotary cutter), as

---

4. John Updike, *A Month of Sundays* (New York: Alfred Knopf, 1975), pp. 50-51.

does the soccer coach (touchlines, wall pass, upper ninety, overlapping run, sweeper, stopper, marking back, target player, and striker). The electronic engineer, the architect, the business administrator, the psychotherapist, the computer programmer, the conflict resolutionist, the sociologist, and the carpenter all have a vocabulary distinctive to their particular field. Their words are tools that enable those in very abstract or very concrete fields to communicate with each other in shorthand ways that are clear and precise. Every one of these languages is esoteric to me until I master it enough to use the language to communicate or to accomplish a task. Theology is the precise language people of faith use to talk about how they practice and understand their faith.

A third hurdle is that a few students think of theologians as absent-minded, self-absorbed, contentious academics. Unfortunately, some theologians do think of themselves as individual competitors who use words to win battles of the mind. Theological discussion is concluded when you determine a winner, which means, the one who is right. Indeed, this polemical style is an old model for theology. The great theologians of the schools in the Middle Ages conceived of theology as a "dispute." Antagonists put forward proposals for a debate, and the sides contended with each other until a winner was declared, because one's capacity to reason destroyed the other's arguments.

But there is another way to do theology, and that is the spirit that underlies this book. This alternative format is more conversational than confrontational. Although rational argument is in the foreground, the "argument" is more a long-standing conversation between people of faith than a dispute among contestants.[5] It is more a dialogue than a showdown. The purpose is to enrich the depth and breadth of faith rather than to win points. It is more irenic in manner than polemical. This style assumes that many people have many truths to bring to a living faith, that more win when the understanding of faith is deepened than when someone is proven wrong. Irenic theology desires and welcomes a plurality of voices. As an advocate of this kind of theology, I will describe different perspectives, modes, and traditions of theology throughout the book even while I promote my own. I hope you will detect that an irenic spirit may discover the truth more effectively than a capacity to defeat an adversary in an argument.

---

5. For a discussion of theology as conversation, see Clark Williamson, *Way of Blessing, Way of Life: A Christian Theology* (St. Louis: Chalice, 1999), pp. 22-27.

Two Objections

There remain, however, two substantive challenges to the importance of theology for the life of faith.[6] They are similar in that each implies that faith is not about thinking but about feeling, believing, and acting. Faith is feeling the presence of Jesus in your heart and trusting in God to guide your life; faith is believing the truth of the Bible and the creeds of the church; faith is acting through the power of the Spirit to live the Christian life, and bringing justice and well-being to society. Introducing critical thinking into your faith is like introducing cholesterol into your arteries: it will cut off the blood supply to the heart of true religion. Theology promotes skepticism about faith, not its enrichment. Some college, university, and seminary students are discouraged when they walk out of the classroom they entered expecting their faith to be confirmed and strengthened, and leave finding instead that their beliefs are more unsettled than they expected them to be. They see theology as an attack upon their faith, an effort to force them to revise, denude, or abandon their faith for secular ways of thinking. Such objections, however, misunderstand the purpose and nature of theology.

The first objection, based on a misunderstanding of the *purpose* of theology, is that theology is *unnecessary* for the life of faith. The Bible is the proper ground for faith and practice. The Christian life is built on the bedrock of Scripture. The presence, nature, and will of God are communicated to us through the Bible. We do not need anything more than the Bible to know God and to know about God. "Holy Scripture," the *Book of Common Prayer* tells us, "containeth all things necessary to salvation: so that whatsoever is not read therein, nor may be proved thereby, is not to be required of any man, that it should be believed as an article of the Faith, or be thought requisite or necessary to salvation."[7] Regardless of whether we honor the "inerrancy of Scripture," or the "primacy of Scripture," or Scripture as the "unnormed norm," or Scripture as the "primal

> "Even if I have a warm personal relationship with Jesus, I also need an account of what's so special about Jesus to understand why my relationship with him is so important. If I think about dedicating my life to following him, I need an idea about why he's worth following."
>
> **WILLIAM PLACHER**

---

6. For a much more extensive discussion of these objections to theology, see Luck, *Why Study Theology?* chaps. 1-3.

7. *Book of Common Prayer,* "Articles of Religion," VI.

document" of our faith, most Protestants consider Scripture to be the authority for faith and practice. Therefore, since all we need is the Bible, theology is redundant.

But this claim is misleading. No Christian reads the Bible as if all parts are of equal authority and clarity. We omit entire books from the canon, at least in practice. We have to evaluate and to prioritize what ideas in the Bible we should believe and practice. Almost all Christians worship on Sunday rather than the Sabbath, in direct disobedience to the fourth commandment (Exod. 20:8). Most churches allow women to pray in church with their heads "unveiled" and to teach males in Sunday school, defying 1 Corinthians 11:4-7 and 1 Timothy 2:11-12. Few Christians would advocate capital punishment for adultery or homosexual behavior, even though these are included in the list of offenses for such punishment in Leviticus 20. Few would require an unmarried rape victim to marry her assailant, though Deuteronomy 22:28-29 does. Even fundamentalists are "literalists" only about what they choose to be. All Christians have a "canon within the canon." They have criteria — a theology — by which to choose certain verses or books or biblical themes over others.

Furthermore, no one reads the Bible without interpretation. No text interprets itself. Someone has to determine what certain words and ideas mean. Even translation is guided by interpretation. Some of my students insist on using the NIV instead of the NRSV because the former translates certain key passages "correctly." They know Isaiah 7:14 prophesied that a "virgin," not a "young woman," would conceive because their theology tells them how the passage must be properly translated. No one can exegete such texts without a hermeneutic (a theory of interpretation about how to read the Bible). In addition, most of us find the Bible's defense of slavery, subordination of women, hatred of enemies, and anti-Judaism in the New Testament deeply problematic. Finally, when we read the Bible we have to reconcile its claims with other beliefs we hold, such as the scientific theory of evolution. No one depends on a simple reading of the Bible for faith and practice. Everyone approaches the Bible with a theology in hand.

The second objection, which misunderstands the *nature* of theology, considers theology to be an *abstract theory* that diverts the believer away from the primary purpose of the Christian life. The goal of faith, according to such an understanding, is to trust in God through committed discipleship to Jesus. Faith rests in our direct experience of God, the intensity of our relationship with Christ. Thinking about faith, some Christians argue, diverts the believer from genuine faith. Christians are called to love God and their neighbor. Love calls for obedience to God and the search for justice, not analysis of our beliefs. Far more important for the Christian life are spiritual humility, mystical insight, religious experience, and the committed life of love. Some Christians, unfortunately, think theology moves us away from the immediacy and simplicity of faith toward subtle distinctions, arid definitions, hair-splitting analysis, and speculation. It is a dangerous game that can cause paralysis and controversies that divide the church. Theology, like cable television and talk radio, displays a morbid craving for controversy and dispute over words.

This is an unfortunate, indeed, disastrous perception of theology. Just as we cannot live as human beings without thinking about our world, so we cannot live as Christians without thinking about our faith. No world exists apart from language, ideas, and theories. All experiences and actions occur within a "worldview" (a framework of understanding what the world is like and how it works) and a "perspective" (the position from which one views the world). Feeling apart from a framework of meaning is merely bodily sensation. Acting apart from a framework of purposes and goals is merely random motion. Experience without theory is empty of meaning; practice without theory is blind flailing. Disciplined thinking within the life of faith is necessary for clarity, new insights, and direction. World construction (a linguistic framework) is necessary to understand the Bible and the faith of the church. It contributes to a vital and open faith by enabling us to make new connections. If your faith cannot stand a little shaking (some new questions and new insights), perhaps there is not much faith there in the first place. Real faith is like Weebles: "Weebles wobble, but they don't fall down." It is not like dominoes: if one article of faith falls, it doesn't mean that all the rest will fall as well.

> "The heart may be more important in the long run than the mind, supposing them to be distinguishable. But a heart with a stupid or crooked mind will find its good intentions dissipated in banalities."
>
> **ROBERT NEVILLE**

At this stage of our exploration of theology, I can only plea for you to be patient and see whether by the end your experience is like mine and that of most of my students. No one had to convince me in college to take as many liberal arts courses as I could, especially religion, philosophy, history, and sociology courses. I have always had an inordinate interest in "the perennial questions." I did, however, complain when the curriculum required me to take a "Music Appreciation" course. My family background had not introduced me to "high" music and art (my family called it "long hair" in the forties and fifties). I was certain that taking these required courses would be a waste of time. Something changed, however, as I gradually began to understand the different styles of music throughout Western history. I learned to enjoy them. I have savored twenty-five seasons attending the Dayton Philharmonic. My purpose in recounting this homely example is to indicate that a similar transformation usually happens to theology students who take their first required course and refuse to be intimidated by the complexity of theology; they discover not only that they have been thinking theologically about faith for a long time but that they now appreciate new ways of thinking that add depth, vitality, and even joy to their faith.

III. Making Sense of Faith: The Task of Theology

Theology does not belong to the *esse* (being) of the church; it belongs to its *bene esse* (well-being). Let me explain the difference. The heart of Christian discipleship is loyalty to Jesus Christ, not academic discussion. A sophisticated theology is not required for salvation. To be sure, all Christians are theologians in a broad sense simply because they use Christian language and have some capacity to talk about their faith. In *this* sense theology belongs to the essence of the church. But many faithful disciples have a fairly unreflective way of saying what they do and believe and feel. I think, however, that the health of the church depends, in part, on our giving a *reflective* account of our faith. The well-being of the church relies on some formal, focused, disciplined reflection on the meaning and truth of the Christian faith. After worship the church must instruct and give an account of what it believes and why. The Bible must be interpreted; the creeds must be explained; experience must be illuminated.

> "There is no man who does not have his own god or gods as the object of his highest desire and trust, or as the basis of his deepest loyalty and commitment. There is no one who is not to this extent a theologian."
>
> **KARL BARTH**

To be a Christian, then, is to be a theologian in the broader sense of being a "thinking Christian."[8] In this larger sense, theology is simply the conversation of all Christians with each other about what is vital to the Christian pathway.[9] It is the ongoing discussion we have with those who have gone before us, and those who are among us now, as well as with our contemporary

---

8. For a statement of this role of the pastor and professional theologian, see John Cobb, *Can Christ Become Good News Again?* (St. Louis: Chalice, 1991), part II, "A Thinking Church," chaps. 4-8.

9. Williamson, *Way of Blessing,* pp. 22-24.

context of our faith. Theology is the thinking and talking all Christians engage in so they can learn and grow in the scope of their experience and understanding of their faith.

Theology in the narrower sense, however, is a particular kind of conversation. When a Christian asks a question, or explains what she means in making an affirmation, or clarifies an ambiguous statement, or interprets Scripture to mean one thing instead of another, or defends a belief in the face of criticism, or critiques a belief of another person, or evaluates the practice of another Christian, or correlates her beliefs about creation with evolution, or proposes a new understanding of a biblical story, she is doing theology in the narrower sense. These verbs all imply an effort to understand. Although theology in this narrower sense can be done by the "average Christian," pastors and professors are by their profession theologians in this narrower sense. They ask, "What is the gospel and what is its meaning and truth today?" "What does it mean to say God created heaven and earth?" "How can Jesus be divine and human at the same time?" "What is it that Christians can hope for?" Theology narrowly defined is faith seeking understanding.

How Theology Arises

Beginning students in theology will encounter a long history of theology about which they may know little. This history begins with the Christian "apologists," followed by late antiquity, the High Middle Ages, the Protestant Reformation, the Enlightenment, modern liberalism and fundamentalism, and the current transition from a modern to a postmodern context. Many students will learn the details of this history, while others will only hear in passing the "big" names — Justin Martyr, Origen, Irenaeus, Augustine (perhaps the premier theologian of all Christian history), Athanasius, Thomas Aquinas, Anselm, John Calvin, Martin Luther, John Wesley, Friedrich Schleiermacher, Charles Hodge, Karl Barth, Paul Tillich, Rosemary Radford Ruether, and the latest important theologian to read if one wants to be informed. Most will find these thinkers informative, even fascinating. They may broaden, even change, your theology.

For some students, however, theological questions will not heat up until they experience some sort of crisis in their "embedded theology"[10] (the deeply rooted set of beliefs they already have before they encounter theology

---

10. Howard Stone and James Duke, *How to Think Theologically* (Minneapolis: Fortress, 1996), pp. 13-16.

as a formal discipline). It is very important for you to recognize that you are not without a theology. You already have a set of beliefs bred into your heart and mind by learning the primary language of faith. In hearing Scripture read, in practicing the liturgy, in Bible study and sharing groups, in seeing and hearing the images, metaphors, and stories of the community, and in emulating the lives of the saints in your congregation, you have already absorbed an embedded theology. It is "in your bones" as well as your head, an interpretation and explanation of the faith you learned from your pastors, Sunday School teachers, "Disciple Bible Study," InterVarsity counselors, and "Emmaus Walk" instructors.

Some element of your embedded theology may become unclear, seem to be inadequate, or even seem uncertain in the light of some new ideas. Beliefs may get challenged. Unless you conclude that doubt about the certainty of those beliefs is unacceptable, you may gradually become more curious, open, and reflective about your beliefs. You may conclude that you are honoring God with your mind as well as your heart and soul when you think about the faith of the church. When you discover why the Bible is not uniform, how to distinguish the worldview of the first century from medieval or modern views, you may become excited and confident in your own capacity to enter into this two-thousand-year-old conversation.

The Object of Theology

The primary object (or subject matter) of theology is God. This is evident in the meaning of the word itself. In its roots it means *logos* (discourse) about *theos* (God). Theologians, however, do not think only about the doctrine of God. Most of the time they think about nature, human nature, and human history — but all of it in relation to God. That is what makes it theology. Modern theologians have debated whether God's revelation in Jesus Christ as witnessed in Scripture is the primary object of theology (Karl Barth) or whether theology is the description of the consciousness of God in human experience as it is shaped by the Christian community (Friedrich Schleiermacher). But theologians do not write descriptively about why people believe in God or what good or bad effects belief in God has had throughout history. They write normatively about nature, history, and all of the features of human experience as they relate to the reality, character, purposes, and power of God.

Christian language works on two levels. Our "first-order" language is the language of address to God and witness to the world. The primary language of the church is to witness to the significance of Jesus Christ. It consists of telling the gospel story and making its primal affirmations, such as "Jesus Christ is Lord." Theology, on the other hand, is a "second-order" language. It is, to quote Schubert Ogden, "the fully reflective understanding of the Christian witness of faith as decisive for human existence."[11] The language of theology, therefore, is dependent upon and interprets the first-order language of faith. Theologians ask, What is the gospel? What is the wholeness and consistency of the gospel? What does it mean to be responsible to the gospel in our context? It is helpful to notice the close connection between the terms "disciple" and "discipline." Theology is one dimension of discipleship.[12] It is discipleship as disciplined thinking about faith.

Theology, then, is one particular kind of conversation among many in which Christians engage. Christians talk "to" or "with" God in worship, prayer, liturgy, and charismatic ecstasy. They talk "for" or "on behalf of" God in witness, proclamation, testimony, prophetic pronouncement, and evangelical witness. Theologians talk "about" God when they tell us who God is, what God is like, what God wills, how God works in our lives, and what God will do at the end of history. In short, *theology is reflective talk about God.*

The Nature of Theology

Theology is a particular way of thinking about God. Modern theologians describe it as "the rational account given of the Christian faith."[13] The concept of a "rational account," however, means two different things among modern theologians. Because faith itself has become problematic in the modern world as a result of the Enlightenment worldview, some modern theologians think it is necessary to know basic theological truths independent of faith in order to make faith possible or plausible. They move from knowledge grounded in general human experience or reason to faith in God. Liberal philosophical theologians and evangelical apologists thus search for the "foundations" of faith independent of faith itself.

Other modern theologians understand a rational account to be "faith seeking understanding," a phrase formulated by Anselm, the eleventh-century archbishop of Canterbury. Their approach is not "fideistic"; it is not,

11. Schubert Ogden, *On Theology* (New York: Harper and Row, 1986), chapter 1.

12. Douglas Hall, *Thinking the Faith: Christian Theology in a North American Context* (Minneapolis: Augsburg, 1989), pp. 58-66.

13. S. W. Sykes, "Theology," in *Westminster Dictionary of Christian Theology,* ed. Alan Richardson and John Bowden (Philadelphia: Westminster, 1983), p. 566.

"I simply believe — that's it!" Rather, these theologians begin with the faith of the church and seek to give a rational account of it: "For I do not seek to understand that I may believe, but I believe in order to understand," Anselm wrote. "For this also I believe — that unless I believe, I should not understand."[14] Anselm began with the faith he inherited, affirmed it, and then attempted to understand it. He did not assume he had no right to believe until he could prove the truth of faith on some independent grounds. He tried to explain what he inherited and accepted.

I think Anselm was basically correct. Very few people are ever argued into faith. They do not affirm a tradition or live in trust because they are compelled by a logical argument. Either they already know faith as an existential reality, or they are converted to faith apart from any theological arguments. But when for some reason — an anomaly, a crisis, or an intellectual conflict — questions arise, they seek to understand faith more fully in order to see whether and how it is still plausible. They seek to understand faith's "logic." Theology as faith seeking understanding desires to see that faith is reasonable to the mind as well as the heart, at least so far as the natural temperament and endowments and the training of the believer require or permit.

Theology is the Christian faith subjected to critical thought. This could be a disconcerting definition to offer some new students. In our culture the word "critical" usually means to find fault or to denigrate or to repudiate. Some might conclude, instinctively, that their theology professors are attempting to ridicule, question, or negate their deepest beliefs, which they take to be essential to their faith. Consequently, students could be turned off of theology because they want to protect themselves from an onslaught on their faith — an onslaught that seems to come, ironically, from the very people who claim to speak for the church.

I hope, however, you can overcome the assumption that "critical reflection" primarily means finding fault with your faith. The word "critical" comes from the Greek word *kritikos,* which means "skilled in judging," as in the law court.[15] A critic was a judge who was thought to be discerning, capable of making wise decisions in cases brought before him because he operated with good criteria or standards of judgment. To think critically about Christian faith is to be able to make judgments about one belief or another in the light of the arguments given for or against the meaning and adequacy of a belief. Sometimes, to be sure, critical reflection means rejection. Some-

---

14. *Saint Anselm, Basic Writings,* "Proslogion," trans. S. N. Deane with an introduction by Charles Hartshorne, second ed. (LaSalle, Ill.: Open Court, 1968), p. 7.

15. Luck, *Why Study Theology?* p. 121.

times it leads to affirmation. More frequently, it means reinterpretation of a symbol or doctrine.

This critical process consists of giving arguments for or against an idea, defending an idea, amending it in the light of new ideas, and "in general making the best case that can be made."[16] You might begin to understand the goal and strategy of theology by comparing the theologian to an attorney who "builds a case" before the court of law. Or, the theologian might be compared to a movie critic; the critic may give a scathing denunciation or a glowing recommendation of a given movie, but she is a good critic if she can give a sound, convincing judgment about the movie derived from her wealth of knowledge about the hundred years of movie history and cinematic technique.

Who Does Theology?

The well-being of the church is strengthened by the work of three kinds of theologians. First, I have already shown the way in which all Christians are theologians. The hymns we sing declare much about the character and will of God, about human nature and destiny, about the way of salvation, and about human responsibility. Whether through an oratorio from Handel's "Messiah," or Isaac Watts's and Charles Wesley's hymns, or Fanny Crosby's gospel songs, or contemporary praise tunes, Christians affirm a set of beliefs about the nature of God, the two natures of Christ, a renewed humanity, and Christian hope. These are sources and expressions of our embedded theology. Even if persons come to study for some kind of Christian ministry primarily because their "hearts are filled," they do not come empty-headed. They come with a rich inheritance.

Most Christians have also learned their inherited theology from a second kind of theologian. The church designates leaders with responsibility to proclaim the Christian witness and to teach and interpret the language of faith. For most Christians this person is the priest or pastor of the local congregation or the leader of a parachurch organization. One of the major tasks of this person is to teach the local congregation through preaching and instruction in the content of the Christian faith. The pastor is a theologian with

> "All who believe and think about what they believe are theologians."
>
> **JÜRGEN MOLTMANN**

16. Robert C. Neville, *A Theology Primer* (Albany: State University of New York Press, 1991), p. 10.

responsibility to think critically with the members of the congregation about faith. When a leader is authorized through ordination or consecration, the church charges the representative to expound the faith of the church. Clergy are the resident theologians of the congregations, in the sense that they both teach the doctrines of the Christian faith and lead other members of the congregation to think about the faith. This is one of the goals in studying theology in seminary.

There is, also, a small cadre of professional theologians. They are persons sponsored by the church to devote their lives to critical thinking about the Christian faith. Their professional lives are pledged to theological reflection. Professional theologians are usually scholars and teachers who are professors in departments of religion in colleges and universities or in seminaries. They earn their salaries by scholarly research, writing books and articles, and teaching courses in schools and churches. They reflect on Christian identity, the conundrums of the faith, and the meaning, truth, and practice of faith in our contemporary context. The greatest threat to professional theologians is that their language becomes so specialized that they address only other theologians through an esoteric language. Unlike the language of the seamstress, whose customers simply want a product or a skill and not a theory, the language of theology is inherently abstract and so involves hairsplitting. However, in the sense that the pastor is like the seamstress, pastors can become effective leaders by helping the church understand its faith and think about the practical but difficult intellectual, moral, and cultural problems of our time.

The Audience for Theology

To whom do theologians speak? This question goes back at least to the twelfth century. Bernard of Clairvaux thought theology should be located in the monastery. His reason was that there is no thought without commitment, no neutral standing place. Therefore, since Christian believers do theology, theology belongs in the church. Peter Abelard, on the other hand, believed a kind of objective detachment is possible in thinking about theological questions. Theology is a kind of critical study of faith apart from the church. Theology, therefore, is a discipline of sacred learning based in the university rather than the monastery. This debate raged throughout the eighteenth-century Enlightenment and up to our day. It came to a head in the twentieth century in the argument between those who understand theology to be solely a church discipline (such as Karl Barth) and those who retain the Enlightenment ideal of theology as a study of religious phenomenon (of which Christian faith is an example) and who believe that theology can and should be carried on as public discourse in the context of the academy and the larger culture as well as the church (such as David Tracy).[17]

If you have had courses in religion in a college or university in the last twenty-five years, you know something about how this debate is carried on today. Most people engaged in religious studies are neutral about the truth or falsity of what they study. Religious studies reflect a scientific approach that seeks to understand religion, not to defend it or to advocate it. Scholars study the social, psychological, and aesthetic functions of religion.[18]

Nevertheless, a few scholars in the academy understand religious studies as a form of theology. Theology belongs in the university as "public theology" as well as in the church as "dogmatic theology."[19] Public theologians think of theology as an analysis of religious experience and of the religious symbols of a culture which can serve the well-being of the larger culture. In this context, theology is an analysis of religious consciousness, practices, and symbols.

My view is that church is the *primary* context for theology. The objective of the theologian is to examine the meaning and truth of the faith of the Christian community. At the same time, I want the academy and the public involved in my reflection on Christian faith. So I embrace elements of both sides in this debate.

An either-or choice is unnecessary for two reasons. First, Christian faith *is* one form of human religious consciousness and practice. No talk of special revelation or the church as a unique faith community can deny that fact. Therefore, Christian faith is a legitimate object for study in the university as well as in the church. Faith seeking understanding needs these insights in order more adequately to understand our faith. Second, the stories and symbols of the Christian faith do not belong solely to the church. These symbols and practices continue to have an impact in our culture — in art, literature, mov-

17. For a defense of all three "publics" as the appropriate context for theology, see David Tracy, *The Analogical Imagination: Christian Theology and Christian Pluralism* (New York: Crossroad, 1981), especially chapter 1.

18. A clear and consistent representative of this point of view is Donald Wiebe, *The Politics of Religious Studies: The Continuing Conflict with Theology in the Academy* (New York: St. Martin's, 1999).

19. For a defense of public theology, see William Dean, *The Religious Critic in American Culture* (Albany: State University of New York Press, 1994); Linell Cady, *Religion, Theology, and American Life* (Albany: State University of New York Press, 1993); Sheila Davaney, *Pragmatic Historicism: A Theology for the Twenty-First Century* (Albany: State University of New York Press, 2000); and Victor Anderson, *Pragmatic Theology: Negotiating Intersections of an American Philosophy of Religion and Public Theology* (Albany: State University of New York Press, 1998).

ies, and rituals — and not always in distorted forms. Therefore, public theologians are important for the church's understanding of its faith. Nevertheless, the church remains the primary context of theology because it is the community responsible for transmitting those symbols and because it is the primary audience for thinking about the meaning and truth of Christian faith.

The Criteria for Theology

As critical thinkers, theologians think according to criteria. The two primary criteria that guide theological thought are *appropriateness* and *credibility*.[20] Are our claims appropriate to the gospel, and are they credible in terms of their inner coherence and their consistency with our other beliefs about the world and human existence? These two criteria determine what are the "right affections" (orthopathy),[21] the "right beliefs" (orthodoxy),[22] and the "right practice" (orthopraxis)[23] the church must teach if it is going to be the church today. These criteria distinguish good theology from bad theology. This by no means implies there is only one right theology. There are many appropriate and credible theological perspectives on the gospel. But it does mean that any theology that claims to be Christian must be judged as appropriate to its gospel and credible to the church and others willing to listen.

When I introduce the notion of "ortho" into my discussion, I inject a concept that is offensive if not intolerable for many Christians today.[24] "Ortho" suggests the possibility of "heresy" in our affections, beliefs, and practices. It suggests it is possible to feel, believe, or practice things incompatible with the gospel. Not only can theological ideas be judged to be inconsistent, they can be judged to be "incorrect" or "inappropriate" to Christian faith. One might be a "heretic" as much by setting one's heart upon Caesar's kingdom instead of the coming reign of God, or by ignoring the stranger and

---

20. Ogden, *On Theology,* chapter 1.

21. Ted Runyon, *The New Creation: John Wesley's Theology Today* (Nashville: Abingdon, 1998), pp. 147-69.

22. G. K. Chesterton, *Orthodoxy* (San Francisco: Ignatius, 1908).

23. Gustavo Gutiérrez, *A Theology of Liberation* (Maryknoll, N.Y.: Orbis, 1973), p. 10; Juan Segundo, *The Liberation of Theology* (Maryknoll, N.Y.: Orbis, 1976), pp. 83-85; Andrew Park, "Theo-Orthopraxis," *United Theological Seminary Journal of Theology* (1993): 59-72.

24. For a stimulating debate between two important theologians who differ on the appropriateness of "talk about heresy" in the church today, see Thomas Oden, "Can We Talk about Heresy?"; Lewis Mudge, "Gathering around the Center: A Reply to Thomas Oden"; and Thomas Oden, "Can There Be a Center without a Circumference? A Response to Lewis Mudge," all in *Christian Century,* April 12, 1995, pp. 390-96.

the oppressed, or by failing to live in utter confidence in God and the assurance of God's grace, as by denying the doctrine of the Trinity or rejecting the doctrine of the resurrection.

Friedrich Schleiermacher defined heresy as any affection, practice, or belief that preserves the appearance of Christianity but contradicts its essence. This essence consists of views of God, Christ, and humanity consistent with the redemption experienced through Jesus Christ.[25] James Cone defines heresy as any teaching or activity that contradicts the liberating gospel of Jesus Christ. It is the refusal to speak or live the truth of freedom and justice in the light of the One who is the Truth.[26] These liberal criteria could be replaced by more conservative criteria, such as a conversion experience, substitutionary atonement, or exclusivism. Liberal and conservative theologians differ on what these "orthos" are. But both judge our passions, beliefs, and behaviors as right or wrong in light of their understanding of the gospel.

I want to be extremely vigilant here. I do not introduce the idea of heresy in order to suggest that theology is an effort to sniff out heresy among those who do not agree with the theology of my community or with me. The church has an appalling history of oppressive theologies. Some of the most demonic actions of the ancient, medieval, and modern church resulted from efforts to identify, condemn, and turn over victims to various inquisitions for silencing or extermination. There is a good reason why most Christians have a visceral reaction to the word "heresy" and avoid using it like the plague. Most of us, however, do not presume that Christians can feel, believe, and do just anything they want if they are Christians. Even if we are more skittish about using the word than Schleiermacher or Cone, we are, nevertheless, involved in making judgments about affections, beliefs, and practices in light of our understanding of the gospel. All thinking about faith involves criteria by which to evaluate the appropriateness of the passions, beliefs, and actions of the Christian life. I will discuss in some detail the question of what these criteria are in Chapter Two.

IV. The Limits of Theology

Any discussion of criteria suggests that theology is as perilous as it is exciting. Is it not the height of arrogance to speak about God, to judge people's affec-

25. F. D. E. Schleiermacher, *The Christian Faith*, vol. 1 (New York: Harper Torchbooks, 1963), paragraphs 23-24, 95-101.

26. James Cone, *God of the Oppressed* (New York: Seabury, 1975), p. 36.

tions, beliefs, and practices by specific norms, to claim to know who is a Christian? In one sense the answer obviously is "yes." Theology is the foolish attempt to speak about God, the ultimate mystery, who is beyond the grasp of all human categories. The dangers posed by theologians who think they understand God are so deep in the history of the monotheistic faiths that it seems wise to many people, even inside the church, to suspect theology. The appropriate alternative answer, however, is not "no."

Although theologians think about God, they are not thinking God's thoughts after God thinks them. Theology is our task, not God's! It is always a human, finite, limited work. Our thinking is continually susceptible to distortion, pretension, even abuse. One way to remind ourselves of our limits is to understand theology as a form of play. The analogy is helpful here. Remember, play is serious business for children. Play is the way they learn, grow, and mature. When children become adults they continue to play. They imaginatively construct and reconstruct the world in which they live through their stories, myths, and rituals. Theology is a way to re-imagine and reconstruct our world as Christians. Theology is a form of adult play for Christians.

Context

Every theology is *contextual* in the sense that it arises out of, is shaped by, and addresses the context of the contemporary believer. Even if our questions and God's answers may be transcultural, what we ask, how we ask it, and the answers we find are formed by the context of the theologian. Our temperament, family background, community, nation, race, ethnic origin, social class, and gender shape our perceptions, agendas, and conclusions. Every theology throughout history, therefore, has employed, either explicitly or implicitly, a "method of correlation." Paul Tillich made this dialectic explicit in his theological method. Theology, he said, has two foci: the "message" and the "situation."[27] Theology not only speaks about God; it speaks its message about God from and to its cultural situation. Therefore, it is important to recognize that there is no one final theology. Even if the message is addressed to all cultures, all theologies interpret that message within the context of particular believers in particular communities.

Every theology, then, is as much a reflection of its context as it is an embodiment of the gospel. We have not inherited from Scripture and tradition a

27. Paul Tillich, *Systematic Theology*, vol. 1 (Chicago: University of Chicago Press, 1951), pp. 3-6.

fixed deposit of beliefs and practices; we have inherited a story of developing and expanding faith. A mistake some students make is to think they are in search of a timeless, fixed set of true beliefs and practices that transcend every context. They think theology is the search for a changeless God, changeless doctrine, changeless morality, changeless forms of architecture and hymns. Now they are going to learn what these are! It takes time to recognize that all of these so-called fixed beliefs and practices are in fact contextual interpretations of the story and symbols of faith to answer the needs of particular people in particular times and places.

There have been, are, and will be *many* appropriate and plausible forms of Christian faith. All theology is relative in the sense that our questions and answers are shaped as much by our own historical and cultural context as by the gospel, which transcends cultures. This does not mean that ideas are simply projections of social interests, but it does mean that ideas are not independent of their social settings.

Paul had to preach a Jewish messiah to a gentile world; the apologists Justin and Origen had to explain the gospel in a culture of Greek language and learning; Augustine had to counter the loss of the meaning of history with the imminent collapse of the Roman Empire; Thomas Aquinas had to make a radical shift in his intellectual framework when Aristotle replaced Plato as the new philosophy of the educated; Luther had to reinterpret the gospel when the medieval Roman Catholic synthesis began to shatter; Friedrich Schleiermacher had to ask what faith is and what it can affirm when Enlightenment modernity challenged most traditional Christian assumptions; Karl Barth had to resist some of the horrible consequences of modernity and affirm that the gospel stood against all human wisdom and culture; Latin American, African-American, and feminist theologians have had to de-ideologize Christian theology with a "hermeneutic of suspicion" and offer a postmodern reconstruction of Christian faith. The thought of every theologian reflects at least as much personal context as it does the gospel. No theology fully transcends a context; all theology is contextual.

Perspective

Because of its contextual nature, theology is also *perspectival*. All theologians bring, first, a *worldview*, which determines how they interpret everything. Worldview provides the basic categories and principles by which to organize and interpret the world. It serves as a template or as a pair of glasses through which to decipher and construct the world. Worldview shapes how you think the world works and your opinions on what is possible and what is not, what the significant questions are, how to go about answering them, and how to judge the truth of an idea.

Worldview outlines your view of "the big picture." It provides the notions you take to be so obvious that you cannot even think without them. It provides the metaphors and images through which you picture the world. Worldview tells you whether the natural world you live in is or is not overlaid with a supranatural one; it tells you whether miracles can or cannot happen; it tells you how to explain what is not now clear; it tells you what claims to accept and not to accept. Some contemporary theologians argue that the Scriptures and the Christian story provide an alternative worldview to the worldview of our common culture. The Christian faith is a choice we make to replace the secular perspective that organizes what we know and how we are to act. Other theologians argue that our worldview comes to us simply by learning the language of our culture and acquiring the general knowledge of our culture. Consequently, theologians must use our culture's framework to interpret the symbols and practices of our faith. Your conclusion about this debate will shape how you interpret each doctrine.

Perspective also involves a second factor. Frameworks of thinking are never neutral; they are affected by the *social location* of the thinker. The time and place, and, more specifically, the race, gender, and social class of the thinker shape the fundamental meanings of language and the criteria of judgment. Social location forms what you think is important to think about, how you frame the questions, what answers you think are possible, and what conclusions seem plausible. Theology originates from and serves our interests, and those interests are conditioned by our race, gender, and class. There is always an ideological component in every theology.

Although ideas are not socially restricted, they are socially shaped. They can be used as rationalizations to mask the cultural, political, economic, racial, and gender interests of the persons using them. How you interpret Jesus' statement "The poor you always have with you" is likely to be different if you begin with a capitalist instead of a socialist theory of the means of production and distribution of goods and services. Even if ideas reflect reality, at least to the extent there is some reciprocity between the world and language, "the social construction of reality"[28] is abundantly clear from Marx through contemporary deconstructionism.

Most of us raised in the modern world have been imbued by means of

---

28. Peter Berger and Thomas Luckmann, *The Social Construction of Reality: A Treatise in the Sociology of Knowledge* (New York: Doubleday, 1966).

our grade-school education through our college degrees with the Enlightenment ideals of neutrality and objectivity in the search for truth. We do not readily acknowledge the role of worldview and social location in our theological reflection. But nothing is gained and much is lost in theology if we fail to recognize the role of perspective in thinking about faith. Although theology is more than ideology, we must ask, in our thinking about the meaning and truth of the Christian faith, whose interests are served, and how are they served, by understanding Christian doctrines in one way or another. It is not accidental that a white, middle-class evangelical is likely to designate John 3:16, interpreted as "having a born-again experience," as the center of the gospel, while a Latin American Roman Catholic living in a base community in Peru or an African-American liberation theologian living in Chicago is likely to designate Luke 4:18-19, interpreted as the "preferential option for the poor" for God's liberating justice, as the center of the gospel.

V. Modes of Thinking Theologically

There are many modes of theological reflection besides writing papers for class assignments or ordination requirements, or writing books about theology as I do. Theology has often taken the form of letters, frequently from prison, as in the case of St. Paul, Dietrich Bonhoeffer, and Martin Luther King Jr.[29] It has come in the form of autobiography, as in the case of St. Augustine and Will Campbell.[30] The commentaries of Luther, Calvin, and Walter Brueggemann, and the sermons of St. John Chrysostom, Origen, and John Wesley, are ways of thinking about faith. When a pastor writes a weekly column in a church newsletter explaining the liturgy of the worship service, or teaches a catechism class, or leads a study group in the church on baptism or on matters of life and death, or conducts a Lenten series using movies with christological themes, the pastor is thinking about faith with her or his congregation.

There is also a mode of thinking about faith in which "the Christian faith" becomes the explicit object of thought, and critical reflection about that faith is pursued systematically. The professional theologians of the

29. See Dietrich Bonhoeffer, *Letters and Papers from Prison* (New York: Macmillan, 1953); Martin Luther King Jr., "Letter from a Birmingham Jail," in *Religion for a New Generation,* ed. Jacob Needleman et al. (New York: Macmillan, 1973), pp. 238-47.

30. See Augustine, *Confessions,* in *Basic Writings of Saint Augustine,* vol. 1, ed. Whitney Oates (New York: Random House, 1948), pp. 3-358; Will Campbell, *Brother to a Dragonfly* (New York: Continuum, 1989).

church consist of a team of thinkers who engage self-consciously in reflection on the themes of the faith of the church. Basically there are three positions on this team, and each concentrates on a particular assignment for interpreting faith. There are scholars who concentrate on past forms of faith (historical and biblical theologians), on the future forms of faith (practical theologians), and on the present forms of faith (systematic theologians).

> "Thus, in the very act of defining theology, we find ourselves engaged in the process of theologizing. Quite simply, to *define* theology is to *do* theology."
>
> **STANLEY GRENZ AND JOHN FRANKE**

On the team (the guild) of theologians, those who think about the historical forms of faith are either *biblical theologians* or *historical theologians*. For them the question is what the Christian witness of faith in its Scriptures and its traditions was in the past and how the past and present interact.

The second group within the team are *practical theologians*. Sometimes they are called pastoral or applied theologians. Practical theologians focus on the interaction of belief and behavior in the present and future. They ask what the Christian witness of faith should now become for the church and for the world. Practical theology includes ministerial formation in the narrower sense around such matters as homiletics (preaching), liturgy (worship), education, and pastoral care. But pastoral formation also occurs within a larger context as shaping and reflecting on the practice of all Christians. Here faith is thought about in connection with ethics and with the behavioral and social sciences, most especially sociology and psychology. Practical theologians ask how fitting our beliefs and practices are in our context, and how faith and practice should be played out in the future. One of the most notable characteristics of theology in the last quarter century has been the blurring of the line between practical and systematic theology. The emphasis on the inseparability of belief and practice, and the use of the social sciences to interpret beliefs and practices, has reshaped the field of systematic theology.

This leads us to the third kind of team member, the *systematic theologians*. This is the hardest position on the team to define, because there are so many disagreements about the proper task and the proper tools for systematic theologians. In the broadest sense, systematic theology seeks to answer the question, What is the Christian witness of faith today? The systematic theologian offers an interpretation of the appropriateness and credibility of the Christian witness for our time. Her task is to understand the meaning and truth of the faith embodied in the Scriptures, creeds, theologies, spiritualities, and practices of the church for the church today. Systematic theologians who believe that theology should be confined within the borders of the church, and who focus on the received tradition of the church's creeds and confessions (dogmas), are called *dogmatic theologians*. This is not a pejorative term. Dogmatic theologians see the subject matter of theology as the creeds, and the criterion for the meaning and truth of faith as the church's witness itself. Karl Barth, the greatest modern dogmatic theologian, changed the title of his massive work from *Christian Theology* to *Church Dogmatics* in order to be clear that the church's witness did not depend in any way on any criteria of meaning and truth outside the community of faith and its canon, beliefs, and practices.

At the other end of the spectrum of systematic theologians are the *philosophical theologians,* represented by Paul Tillich, who interprets the Christian faith by correlating its message with the truths of general human experience derived from outside the church, usually mediated through philosophers and their metaphysical visions. Throughout most Christian history, from the early apologists to contemporary process theologians, philosophy has been the resource used by most theologians for critical thinking. Speculative philosophy, however, has fallen on hard times in the late modern period. It is criticized as simply another form of ideology ("a tool of white male oppression") or as an illusion ("there is no big picture"). Also, as the relationship between belief and practice has been emphasized by theologians in the last quarter century, the language of the social sciences has tended to replace the stranglehold philosophy had on theology throughout most of Western Christian history. It has become the language of theologians who are willing to use the wisdom of secular culture to help Christians understand their faith.

It might be apparent in this description of the modes of theology and some of the examples that there are competing types of systematic theology.[31] Many of them overlap in their agendas, emphases, and conclusions. There are liberal theologies that "ground" theology in human self-consciousness (Friedrich Schleiermacher) and self-understanding (Rudolf Bultmann). There are dialectical or neo-orthodox theologies that locate theology in the self-revelation of the wholly other God; they are usually christocentric (Karl Barth). There are also various postliberal theologies that affirm the autonomy of distinctive Christian language and emphasize the structure and authority of the Christian metastory (George Lindbeck and narrative theologians). Finally, there are forms of postmodern theology that approach theology "from the underside." These theologians are concerned primarily with the

---

31. See Joerg Rieger, *God and the Excluded: Visions and Blindspots in Contemporary Theology* (Minneapolis: Fortress, 2000).

significance of the gospel for liberation of the oppressed (Gustavo Gutierrez, Rosemary Radford Ruether, and Andrew Sung Park).

You might be overwhelmed by the many modes and types of theology, and by references to unfamiliar names from history and contemporary theology. My description of diversity within theology may remind you of the biblical story of Babel, where God confused the language of prideful people who were building in order to "make a name for ourselves" (Gen. 11:4). In conclusion, however, I want to emphasize that most theologians share more in common than might be apparent at first sight. They share a common canon, a common story, a common set of symbols, a common history (although much of it has been ignored or hidden). Above all, they share a common goal, namely, a faith seeking understanding. They seek to understand the Christian faith in order to keep it alive, in order to construct a world of understanding and action where God's promise of well-being is established "on earth as it is in heaven." Once your surprise about new names and words, about diversity, and about an uncertainty of some of the answers subsides, you will conclude, I hope, that you too want to become involved in this long, hard, productive, and joyful task of thinking about faith.

CHAPTER TWO

Resources for Thinking about Faith

I. The Question of Authority in Theology

When I was a graduate student I was taught that if I got my method right, I could count on secure conclusions. The debate was over which foundations established theological certainty. Theological liberals used philosophy, science, and human experience, as well as the Bible and tradition, to derive their conclusions. Theological conservatives appealed to the Bible alone as the source of guaranteed truths.

Theologians in the modern West, both liberals and conservatives, sought new grounds for belief because of "the collapse of the house of authority."[1] They watched the elaborate premodern synthesis of Scripture and tradition collapse before their eyes. The first cloud of smoke from the implosion appeared in the Protestant Reformation, when tradition was repudiated as corrupt and subordinated to *sola Scriptura* (Scripture alone). But as the modern critical spirit — summarized in the shibboleth "reason alone" — was applied to the Bible, Protestants found their sole authority engulfed by scientific assumptions and methods. Their structure of faith seemed to collapse into a pile of rubble. When the debris was cleared, faith seemed groundless. The theological task was to find new foundations on which to rebuild the faith of the church.

Initiated by Descartes's quest for certainty through reason, the Enlightenment was a positive response to this deeply felt crisis.[2] Tiring of the culture

---

1. Peter Hodgson and Robert King, *Christian Theology: An Introduction to Its Traditions and Tasks* (Philadelphia: Fortress, 1982), pp. 46-51.

2. Stephen Toulmin, *Cosmopolis: The Hidden Agenda of Modernity* (New York: Free Press, 1990), especially chapter 2.

wars and the military battles ravaging Europe, creative thinkers set out to find a way beyond these bitter, endless conflicts. Reason would overcome our liability to error and our petty disagreements. The modern preoccupation with methodology was born in these noble intentions, and it has been dominant among the elites of Europe and North America for the last two hundred years.

Preoccupation with the correct method is a hallmark of theology in the modern era. Like builders of buildings, theologians must have secure foundations in a set of unquestioned and unquestionable principles or facts that are universal and available to any reasonable person. Christians have no right to believe anything unless their beliefs are based on other prior certain beliefs.[3] The debate between conservatives and liberals was about what provides the substratum for all other beliefs. Is it reason and human experience (liberals), or an infallible Bible, a storehouse of divinely revealed facts and doctrines (conservatives)?

During the last three decades, however, theology has been sideswiped by postmodernism.[4] We live in a transition period between the modern and postmodern eras. Many postmoderns have provided scathing condemnations of the last two hundred years of Western Enlightenment. Modernity promised to liberate humanity from superstition and injustice; it offered elaborate designs for making reality fit reason. But these have functioned as tactics and covers for making exploitation and repression seem noble and for lending barbarism an aura of progress. Arrogance, delusions, imperialism, colonialism, racism, sexism, repression, holocaust, and genocide were hidden behind modernity's "objectivity" and "universality." Postmodern liberals and conservatives alike speak of "cultural-linguistic worlds," "the contingency of all judgments," and "social location." "Methodophiles" no longer debate *what* method is the means to theological certainty but *whether* there is any method by which we can make claims that are more than indicators of the needs and aspirations of me, my group, my race, and my social class.

Although the word "postmodern" may be new for some beginning students in theology, the condition is not a new one. Many students bring with them a strong sense of the relativity of cultures — even as they retain some form of foundationalism in their view of the authority of Scripture (conservatives) or religious experience (liberals). Some students, therefore, face a dilemma. They are foundationalists when they believe the Bible or experience is

---

3. Stanley Grenz and John Franke, *Beyond Foundationalism: Shaping Theology in a Postmodern Context* (Louisville: Westminster/John Knox Press, 2001), pp. 28-38.

4. For a brief description of this "sideswipe," see Lisa Sowle Cahill, "Mother Teresa: Postmodern Saint or Christian Classic?" *Criterion* 39, no. 3 (Autumn 2000): 18.

the grounds of certainty. But, simultaneously, they live in and affirm a pluralistic worldview that tells them there is no one truth that can be determined for all time and all people by settling on the right method. Consequently, a few students are tempted to retreat to some form of fideism ("I just believe it") or tribalism ("This is what *we* do, though *you* do something different").

> "Method? Hell, we gotta get something done around here!"
>
> **THOMAS EDISON**

Even though preoccupation with method is out of fashion in our postmodern context, we cannot conclude that questions about authority are inappropriate or unnecessary. People *within* communities can ask who or what they trust, and they can offer warrants for believing what they do. Furthermore, it is possible to offer reasons for belief *among* different communities as well. Even though authority is by nature debatable, and differences cannot be settled decisively, the methodological question persists as much in a postmodern era as it did in the modern era.

"Theological methodology" is the technical term for describing the authorities each of us accepts in thinking about faith. The methodological question concerns what sources we use and what criteria we employ for explicating the Christian faith. Theologians differ — in principle and in fact — about how they interpret and how they order the "formative factors"[5] of Scripture, tradition, reason, and experience in thinking about faith. My design here is to consider these as a dialectic of sources and norms for interpreting faith.

II. The Primacy of Scripture

Most beginning students in my classes think the answer to the methodological question is obvious and indisputable. The Bible is the sole source and norm for Christian thought and practice. They are right, of course, to the extent that almost all Christians agree that without Scripture, theology would be unthinkable. Theology must be done "in accordance with Scripture." Yet there is basic disagreement about how the Bible is authoritative in theology. The critical questions center, first, on the way theological assertions are related to and justified by the Bible as Scripture, and, second, on how the Bible relates to tradition, reason, and experience.

Some Protestant students assume that theology is little more than quot-

---

5. John Macquarrie, *Principles of Christian Theology,* second ed. (New York: Scribners, 1977), p. 5.

ing a Bible verse to prove that their practices and beliefs are correct (theology as "proof-texting"). If they are a bit more sophisticated, they recognize that theology is the harder work of interpreting biblical texts, stories, teachings, or themes for contemporary Christian life and thought (theology as hermeneutics). The view held prior to the Reformation was that Scripture contains revealed doctrine and the church as successor to the apostles interprets Scripture and adds to it through its tradition. But by the fourteenth century cracks in this synthesis began to appear. When Luther came on the scene in the early sixteenth century, a cleavage between Scripture and tradition became irreconcilable. He believed he disobeyed the church in the name of Scripture for the sake of the gospel. Rejecting the ideas that revelation was given to the church apart from Scripture and that the church is the determiner of the gospel, he offered *sola Scriptura* as the watchword and principle for Protestant theology. Scripture is the sole source of the gospel and the sole authority for the church and each Christian.

Sola Scriptura as a slogan, however, has generated a predicament for Protestant theology for two reasons. For one, theologians increasingly have applied the same scientific methods to biblical studies that they apply to other history and literature.[6] By explaining the events and beliefs of Scripture — the creation, the exodus, military defeats and victories, and ecstatic visions — in the same way scientists explain nature and historians explain the events and beliefs of the past, the Bible as the supernatural storehouse of revealed knowledge came under question. As the line from *Porgy and Bess* says, "It ain't necessarily so, it ain't necessarily so; the things that you're liable to read in the Bible, they ain't necessarily so."

Another reason is that "ideology critique" has had a deep impact on how we view Scripture. Awareness that every reader brings a specific set of questions, assumptions, and interests to every biblical text has convinced us of the limited perspective of every interpreter. As the various liberation theologians have shown, race, gender, class, and culture affect what texts I choose to interpret, how I interpret these texts, what I use as my criteria of truth, and how I use these texts in determining my practices and beliefs. Contemporary ideology critique has relativized our view of Scripture just as the historical-critical method earlier naturalized it.

In our transition from a modern to a postmodern context, there are three distinct approaches to the authority of Scripture that might appeal to the different students of theology: conservative, modern, and postmodern.

---

6. Ernst Troeltsch, "Historiography," in *Encyclopedia of Religion and Ethics*, ed. J. Hastings, vol. 6 (Edinburgh: T&T Clark, 1922), p. 720.

Conservative Views of the Authority of Scripture

Conservative theologians claim the Bible is the sole source and norm for theology because the Bible is the infallible or inerrant words of God. God's Word is not only contained *within* or *through* the words of the Bible or attested to *by* the Bible; the Bible *is* God's words by the inspiration of the Holy Spirit.

The biblical verse many conservatives appeal to as proof of the inerrancy of Scripture is 2 Timothy 3:16: "All scripture is given by inspiration of God, and is profitable for doctrine, for reproof, for correction, for instruction in righteousness" (KJV). The meaning of this verse, however, depends in part on how the Greek is translated. Is it best translated "All scripture is inspired by God and is useful" or "Every scripture inspired by God is also useful"? It is possible, of course, that the author meant something like the modern theory of plenary (complete) verbal inerrancy, since "the Scripture principle" did exist in first-century Judaism. Such a view, however, is clearly stated only in the first-century apocryphal book of 2 Esdras 14:37-48, especially verse 42: "Moreover, the Most High gave understanding to the five men, and by turns they wrote what was dictated, using characters that they did not know." Nothing in 2 Timothy indicates the writer presupposes this view. Although the author surely understood the Hebrew Scriptures used in the Jewish community (though not canonized until the Council of Jamnia in 90 CE) to be "useful" for faith and life, he could not be referring to our New Testament, since it did not yet exist as canon. Nevertheless, this text is interpreted by many conservative Protestants as proclaiming the Bible as the infallible words of God.[7]

7. There is, however, a spectrum of views among contemporary conservatives. A few teach an oracular view of Scripture, in which the truth comes from the mouth of God through the pen of the writer to the eye of the believer. The Scriptures are the oracles of God, received through a mechanical dictation as outlined in the 2 Esdras text. Not many reflective conservatives defend this view today, however. Most speak instead about the inerrancy of Scripture. Acknowledging the human factor in the writing process, they claim that the Holy Spirit superintends the author's words while allowing for human particularity. The Spirit, however, through inbreathing into the mind and heart of the writer, assures the deliverance of revealed propositional truths in everything of which the autographs speak, including historical and scientific as well as doctrinal and moral knowledge, reducing the human role to a minimum. A third view among conservatives focuses on the infallibility instead of the inerrancy of Scripture. Infallibilists see the words of Scripture as God's infallible rule for faith and life, as sufficient and secure "soteric knowledge" to provide salvation (it does not mislead), though not necessarily inerrant historical and scientific knowledge. What is common across this spectrum is that the Bible is viewed in a temporal vacuum so that the authority of Scripture resides outside the church or the interpreter in the book as itself the words, doctrines, or instructions from God. See Gabriel Fackre, "Evangelical Hermeneutics: Commonality and Diversity," *Interpretation*, April 1989, pp. 117-29.

Even though I will critique this view below, I think it is helpful to see how this approach to Scripture plays out in theology. Modern theologians who hold this view treat the Bible as a storehouse of "data" or "facts," which theologians simply organize into a coherent scheme of doctrine and practice. As Charles Hodge stated so clearly, theology "assumes that the Bible contains all the facts or truths which form the contents of theology, just as the facts of nature are the contents of science." Theology is simply the "exhibition of the facts of scripture in their proper order and relation."[8] The Bible is the source of objective information and principles theologians use. Their task is to order a somewhat disorganized set of propositional statements into a sort of concordance of truths.[9]

Although this view of the nature of scriptural authority claims to stand in sharp contrast to the modern view, I think it is important to see how thoroughly modern this concordance-of-truths approach to Scripture in fact is. Contemporary conservative views of Scripture are motivated by the modern quest for objective, absolute knowledge. If Scripture is not inerrant or infallible, it has no authority because it does not present us with absolute knowledge. This is one form of a thoroughly modern quest for absolute knowledge. What makes this form of modernity conservative instead of liberal is the belief that the only source of such certainty is the Bible.

But this approach to Scripture simply is not plausible for modern and postmodern Christians for a number of reasons: (1) Even if one grants the conservative claim that the Bible is inerrant or infallible, it is a useless claim (except, perhaps, as a shibboleth). Scripture has not only to be infallible in principle but unmistakably clear in fact if it is to provide us with absolute knowledge. But since many texts are unclear, contradictory, or morally outrageous, texts have to be interpreted. Someone has to interpret these texts as a theologian. (2) When interpreting the Bible and arranging it into a system of doctrine, we inescapably do this in the light of our denominational or theological heritage and in the light of our contemporary points of view and interests. (3) Theologically, however, the most serious problem with this view is a christological one. Ironically, many conservative views of Scripture flirt with heresy by denying the core of the Chalcedonian creed, which affirms that Jesus Christ was fully human and fully divine. To affirm the complete humanity of Jesus Christ but exempt the Bible that is his "cradle" (Luther) would be ironic at best.

8. Charles Hodge, *Systematic Theology*, vol. 1 (New York: Scribner and Armstrong, 1872), pp. 17, 19.
9. Grenz and Franke, *Beyond Foundationalism*, pp. 13-14.

Christ is the context for speaking about the authority of Scripture as the Word of God.[10] For this reason, we should not be threatened by the human character of the biblical writers, their limitations, contexts, ambiguity, and other fallibilities. Fully human texts that reflect human limitations and biases, embody human motives and limited visions, are as important in understanding the Bible as revelation as the claim that God speaks and acts through the story of Jesus. Refusal to see the human character of the text challenges the claim that God's Word is incarnate in human form: "If we are embarrassed by the humanity of the biblical writers," notes Daniel Migliore, "we are also probably embarrassed by the humanity of Jesus the Jew from Nazareth and by our own humanity."[11]

Liberal and Other Modern Views of Scripture

Using modern historical-critical methods, classical liberal theologians understand the authority of Scripture to be a written "witness to faith." Liberals abandon the claim that certain properties of the Bible (inerrancy, infallibility) make it authoritative. Authority of Scripture is located, rather, in the experience of the faith it prompts. Consequently, the Bible is (1) a record of the inner religious experience and moral insights of spiritually sensitive people expressed through myths and symbols (extreme liberalism); (2) a record of Israel's history and faith and of the teachings and faith of Jesus as these are reconstructed by modern historical methods (classical liberalism); (3) a witness of faith with power to elicit a decision to trust God when the reader hears God's Word confront her in the text (existentialist theology); or (4) a proclamation about Jesus as the Christ, who is the object of the church's faith and witness (kerygmatic theology).[12]

This fourth view, also called "neo-orthodox theology," offers a position

---

10. "All the genuine sacred books agree in this, that all of them preach Christ and deal with him. That is the true test, by which to judge all books, when we see whether they deal with Christ or not, since all the Scriptures show us Christ (Romans 3), and St. Paul will know nothing but Christ (1 Cor. 15). What does not teach Christ is not apostolic, even though St. Peter and Paul taught it; again, what preaches Christ would be apostolic even though Judas, Annas, Pilate, and Herod did it." Martin Luther, "Preface to Epistles of St. James and Jude," *Works.*

11. Daniel Migliore, *Faith Seeking Understanding: An Introduction to Christian Faith* (Grand Rapids: Eerdmans, 1991), p. 50.

12. David Kelsey, "Scripture, Doctrine of," in *Westminster Dictionary of Christian Theology,* ed. Alan Richardson and John Bowden (Philadelphia: Westminster, 1983), pp. 528-31; see also his *The Uses of Scripture in Recent Theology* (Philadelphia: Fortress, 1975).

between the conservative "objective" and the liberal "subjective" views of the Bible. It also mediates the transition between modern and postmodern accounts of Scripture. Its greatest representative is Karl Barth. According to this view, theology is biblical when its thinking and speaking correspond to the thinking and speaking of the biblical witness to the revelation of God in Jesus Christ.[13] As Barth put it,

> The Bible tells us not how we should talk about God but what he says to us; not how we find the way to him, but how he has sought and found the way to us; not the right relation in which we must place ourselves to him, but the covenant which he has made with all who are Abraham's spiritual children and which he has sealed once and for all in Jesus Christ. It is this which is within the Bible. The word of God is within the Bible.[14]

In short, the authority of Scripture lies in the Word heard in the words of Scripture. Christians do not believe in the Bible; they believe in the living God who creates a new relation through Christ as God's Word recorded in Scripture. Barth, consequently, speaks of the living Word revealed in Jesus Christ, the written Word in the Bible, and the proclaimed Word in preaching. The Word of God occurs "as an event, when and where the word of the Bible becomes God's Word, i.e., when and where the word of the Bible functions as the word of a witness."[15]

Postmodern Views of the Authority of Scripture

Barth's mediating position (which combines an objective address to us by God in Jesus Christ and a subjective hearing of this Word within the inner life of faith) has taken a new direction in the postmodern understanding of Scripture and its authority in the church. Postmodern views of the Bible begin with the text itself as we have it in front of us. Scripture is a grand metanarrative. Its authority resides in the capacity of its story, on the one hand, to provide an identity and a description of the object of faith, which is God as known in Israel and Jesus Christ, and, on the other hand, to give identity and shape to the church's worship, moral quandaries, affections, and be-

---

13. John Leith, "The Bible and Theology," *Interpretation* 30, no. 3 (July 1976): 230.

14. Karl Barth, *The Word of God and the Word of Man* (New York: Harper and Row, 1928), p. 43.

15. Karl Barth, *Church Dogmatics*, I/1 (New York: Scribners, 1936), p. 127.

liefs. The meaning and authority of the Bible lies in the text itself, not in some experiences or events that lie behind the text or some moment of existential decision that is created by hearing it. The Bible is normative because it is formative. It has the capacity to "author" the corporate identity of the community that lives out of its worldview.[16] Its authority is its power to disclose the reality of God by shaping a new human identity and transforming communal and individual life through its narrative world.[17]

In postmodern understandings of Scripture, the priority given to Scripture and to the contemporary world in reading Scripture is reversed. The Bible as text absorbs the contemporary world, not vice versa. The stories of Israel and Jesus Christ embedded in Scripture and lived out in the faithful community of believers create "the world" for Christians. There is no cultural world of language and knowledge to which the Bible must conform in order to be believed by the community. The Bible provides the interpretive framework for experience and knowledge. Unlike modern views of Scripture, where the context absorbs the text, the meaning of Scripture is what it says about God's identity and character in these narratives. Its overall story, characters, events, and language are irreducible and irreplaceable.[18] The church reads the text as canon, not as an expression of religious experience or of hearing the Word addressed to the inner life of the believer. Beginning with Hans Frei, postmodern theologians have read the Bible as "a realistic narrative," which makes sense of our lives by locating our stories within the larger story. We fit our lives into its world, understand ourselves as participants in its view of history and reality, make sense of our world in its context.

The Bible As Scripture and Canon

The Bible is the Scripture (from Latin, "writing") of the church. To call the Bible Scripture is to say it is not merely an anthology of inspirational literature. It is the indispensable center of the church's worship, behavior, and beliefs. The church judged these writings as canon to be an authentic and reliable witness to the original and definitive revelation of God in Christ. It

---

16. Delwin Brown, *Theological Crossfire: An Evangelical/Liberal Dialogue* (Grand Rapids: Zondervan, 1990), pp. 28, 56-57.

17. This way of organizing these positions is suggested by Kelsey, *The Uses of Scripture in Recent Theology*. Kelsey reviews eight meanings of the authority of Scripture in recent theology, which I have organized into these three clusters. See also Hodgson and King, *Christian Theology*, pp. 51-55.

18. Roger Olson, "Back to the Bible (Almost)," *Christianity Today,* May 20, 1996, p. 33.

continues to be the revelation of God for the church today through the power of the Holy Spirit. When we say that the canon is "closed," we are not saying that there are no other highly esteemed and helpful writings contemporary with the canonical books, nor are we saying that there are not subsequent writings that are inspired and useful for the interpretation and empowerment of the faith of the church. We mean, rather, that Jesus Christ as witnessed to in Scripture is the revelation of God in light of which contemporary and subsequent revelation and inspiration are judged.

Church and canon, then, exist in a dialectical relationship. The church decided the canon, and so the canon is fallible and in principle subject to revision. In one sense the idea of canon represents the authority of the church over the Bible. The church decided which books were to be counted as canon. At the same time, however, Scripture exercised authority over the church even before there was an Old and New Testament in the sense that the testimony of the prophets and apostles was authoritative in worship and witness long before it was put into writing. Canon was the acknowledgment by the church, through the power of the Holy Spirit, that "these scriptures were authoritative in its life and were in the church's judgment authentic, reliable, and ancient accounts of the original testimony to Jesus Christ by which the church came into being."[19] We can say the church created and creates the canon, and the canon created and creates the church.

By referring to the work of the Spirit in the creation of the church's book, we say that the Bible is inspired. Inspiration means that in one sense God is the "author" of Scripture. This does not mean that God is the writer of the books. Rather, it means that God is the author in the sense that the Word we read in Scripture originates with God. A dialectic exists between the initiative of God and the human authors of the manuscripts.[20] Furthermore, the same Spirit who inspired the witness to God's revelation in Christ in the words of Scripture also inspires the reader or hearer of the text today: "This power of bringing again or re-presenting the disclosure of the primordial revelation so that it speaks to us in our present experience is what is meant when we talk of the 'inspiration' of scripture," writes John Macquarrie.[21] Authority rests first

19. Leith, "The Bible and Theology," p. 235. Again, "the people of the church, gathered together under the guidance of the Holy Spirit, are confident that it will convey to us the gospel of Jesus Christ. . . . The Bible is authoritative because it is the indispensable source for the truth to which the Spirit continually witnesses." Ted Peters, *God — The World's Future: Systematic Theology for a New Era*, second ed. (Minneapolis: Fortress, 2000), p. 60.

20. Terence E. Fretheim and Karlfried Froehlich, *The Bible As Word of God: In a Postmodern Age* (Minneapolis: Fortress, 1998), p. 16.

21. Macquarrie, *Principles of Christian Theology*, p. 9.

and foremost in the claim about the work of God's Spirit in the authors. "The Larger Catechism" is clear about this: "But the Spirit of God, bearing witness by and with the Scriptures in the heart of man, is alone able fully to persuade us that they are the very word of God."[22] The work of the Spirit did not cease when the canon was closed. From that time on the Spirit who speaks about Jesus Christ in and through Scripture makes Jesus Christ the truth for us to-day. We read the text to listen to the voice of the Spirit who seeks to speak through the Scripture to the church today.[23]

Sola Scriptura, then, means that theology must be done in light of the canon. This does not mean that the Bible is the only authority for Christian theology, or that nothing else matters as long as we have the Bible. It means that the Bible is the primary authority that authors and authorizes the distinctively Christian understanding of God. *Sola Scriptura* means, as Robert Brown notes, that "if we wish to know Jesus Christ, if we wish to be confronted by him, judged by him, and re-created by him, then scripture is the place to which we must go, for scripture is the means through which we discover for ourselves who he is and what he does. Without scripture we cannot find him or be found by him."[24]

Nevertheless, no Christian has ever practiced *sola Scriptura* as the source and norm for his or her theology. In actual practice theological method is more complex. Most of us encounter conflicts between some biblical passages and our scientific understandings of nature and history. Furthermore, we face a dilemma about whether Scripture always speaks the truth about God when some of its texts seem to subvert justice, mercy, and love — in their patriarchal subordination of women and in their picture of God as an abuser and killer of children and destroyer of cities,[25] as one who demands child sacrifice, and as one who condemns nonbelievers to everlasting punishment. Use of the Bible as canon requires a hermeneutic (principles of interpretation) as

22. *The Constitution of the Presbyterian Church (U.S.A.), Part I, Book of Confessions* (Office of the General Assembly, 1996), p. 201.

23. Grenz and Franke, *Beyond Foundationalism,* pp. 64-65.

24. Robert Brown, "Tradition As a Protestant Problem," *Theology Today* 17 (1960): 442.

25. For an example of the necessity of a hermeneutic of interpretation, see how different biblical scholars interpret God's command to "Canaanite genocide" in the Scripture. Some argue that the Israelites misunderstood God's ultimate plan and desire, or that there is a difference between Old Testament and New Testament dispensations, or that before Christ there was a command for the elimination of evil with physical violence but since Christ the battle has been a spiritual battle, or that now is not the time for this Old Testament–style physical eradication of evil and that the time for that will come in the eschaton. See C. S. Cowles, Eugene Merrill, Daniel Gard, and Tremper Longman III, *Show No Mercy: Four Views on God and Canaanite Genocide* (Grand Rapids: Zondervan, 2003).

well as a theory about the nature of its authority. Scripture must be interpreted in terms of some organizing insights or principles that we bring to the text to guide our interpretation of its meaning and truth.[26]

III. Shaped by Tradition and Traditioning

Suspicion of tradition lies at the heart of modernity. Modernity is primarily a search for the grounds of knowledge and action on the basis of something other than the authority of tradition. Instead, it appeals to reason or experience.[27] The replacement of the authority of tradition with confidence in each person's autonomous capacity to reason is the definition of the "Enlightenment":

> Enlightenment is man's emergence from his self-imposed nonage. Nonage is the inability to use one's own understanding without another's guidance. This nonage is self-imposed if its cause lies not in lack of understanding but in indecision and lack of courage to use one's own mind without another's guidance. Dare to know! "Have the courage to use your own understanding" is therefore the motto of the enlightenment.[28]

Most Americans share this negative attitude toward tradition. In movies like *Pleasantville* and *Chocolat,* for instance, the directors contrast the colorless life of a community of tradition with the vitality of the curious, open, self-sufficient individual. Communities of tradition are sanctimonious, impose repressive morality, support patriarchal abuse, and squash the human appetites. In contrast stands the vibrant individual who is the force of good sense and kindness. Individuality, acceptance, and creativity counter conformity, inhibition, and oppression.

A rare contrasting affirmation of tradition is offered in *Fiddler on the Roof.* Although the subject of the play and movie is the challenge to the authority of tradition by change and diversity in the modern world, the movie

---

26. Migliore, *Faith Seeking Understanding,* pp. 49-55. As part of our "principles of interpretation," we include such factors as historical and literary criticism, ideology critique, nonbiblical knowledge about the world and human nature, primary biblical themes and principles, theocentric criteria (the triune God), and contextuality then and now.

27. Bernard Meland, "liberalism, theological," *Encyclopedia Britannica,* fourteenth ed., vol. 13, pp. 1020-22.

28. Immanuel Kant, "What Is Enlightenment?" in *The Enlightenment: A Brief History with Documents,* by Margaret Jacob (Boston: St. Martin's, 2001), p. 203.

still succeeds in conveying a strong positive sense of the role of tradition. "Tradition" serves to keep our balance or stability so we don't fall off the shaky roof and break our necks. It helps us to perceive who we are, to know what God wants us to do, and to show our devotion to God. It shapes all of life — what we eat, how we sleep, how we work, how we wear our clothes, what our roles are (papa and mama and sons and daughters), how to keep a proper home, how to raise a family, whom to marry, our role in the community (matchmaker, beggar, rabbi), and how to settle squabbles.

The Concept of Tradition

For most Christians tradition is the set of practices and beliefs we learned in our local church. It consists of little more than what a particular church taught us and our families for the last generation or two. If most Protestant Christians have a theory about the concept of tradition, it is likely to be a pejorative one. The history of the church, from the close of the New Testament period to the founding of one's denomination and the opening of one's local church, with the possible exception of a restoration of the gospel by the Protestant Reformers, is seen as a corruption of the gospel or a declension from true Christian faith as contained in the Scriptures. Being modern in their estimate of tradition, conservative Protestants retreated to an inerrant Bible that gave them the "clear and distinct ideas" moderns seek, while liberal Protestants sought to establish religious knowledge on the basis of the authority of the inner world through experience and reason.

Among many theologians, however, "tradition" is not a pejorative term. "Tradition" is used in a *narrow* sense to refer to the official teachings of the church that interpret Scripture or complement Scripture.[29] So conceived it refers essentially to the dogma (creeds) of the church, divinely revealed truth proclaimed as such by solemn church teaching, hence binding now and forever among the faithful.[30] It is what the church in its ecumenical councils has decreed to be official church teaching. Roman Catholics believe that authority in theology rests in Scripture and tradition together, one the written and the other the oral form of the gospel.[31] Protestants tend to speak of the authority of the early church, which they see as based on the primacy of Scrip-

29. Iain Maclean, "Tradition," *Eerdmans Dictionary of the Bible* (Grand Rapids: Eerdmans, 2000), p. 1326.

30. "Dogma," *New Catholic Encyclopedia* (New York: McGraw-Hill, 1967), vol. 4, p. 948.

31. Bernard Loshe, *A Short History of Christian Doctrine* (Philadelphia: Fortress, 1985), pp. 30-32.

ture but also including the early ecumenical councils and the theology of the major theologians in the early church.[32]

The concept of tradition, however, refers in a *broad* sense to the whole sweep of Christian history, what we can call "the Christian past," "the Christian heritage," "the Christian inheritance." It includes the stories all Christians tell about their origins and destinies, their beliefs and practices through which they understand and act in the world. In this broad sense tradition refers to "the deposit of faith" with which Christians live. This heritage includes such things as the Anglican *Book of Common Prayer,* the United Methodist *Hymnal,* and gospel songs; good and bad leaders; movements of faith and life, such as monasticism, pietism, revivalism, dispensationalism, and the social gospel; ethnic heritages, such as African-American Baptist, German Lutheran, and Irish Catholic denominations; hidden traditions not contained in textbooks but instead in the living memories of slaves, Native Americans, and Hispanic Christians; scholarly legacies, such as Platonism, Thomism, Personalism, liberalism, evangelicalism; and the living history of my local congregation. Our inheritance also includes the heretics or other marginal groups (peasants, women, the lower classes) who were oppressed or ignored by the elites who define the tradition and so are forced to create their own alternative tradition of memory. The authority of tradition, then, resides both in the authority of the "official" teachings of the church's councils and in the diverse tradition(s) of the church as a whole.

The Dynamic Nature of Tradition

The modern view of tradition is not only that it is the past, but that the past is fixed and changeless. Therefore, tradition is oppressive because it thwarts our creative movement toward the future. When you study history, however, you

---

32. Thomas Oden, *Agenda for Theology* (New York: Harper and Row, 1979), p. 34. Although some churches do not proclaim dogma as such, most Christians in the West use the Apostles' Creed in some fashion, along with some acknowledgment of the Nicene and Chalcedonian Creeds. Roman Catholics also have a "Catechism of the Catholic Church," which is somewhat short of dogma but nevertheless official church teaching, and some Protestant denominations have official books of creeds, such as the *Book of Concord* (Lutheran) and *Book of Confessions* (Presbyterian). Other Protestant churches have "Articles of Religion" (Anglican) or "Articles of Faith" (National Baptist and Church of the Nazarene) or a "Statement of Faith" (United Church of Christ), while United Methodists speak of "our doctrine," which consists of John Wesley's abbreviation of the Anglican Articles of Religion, the EUB Confession of Faith, Wesley's *Standard Sermons* and *Notes on the New Testament,* and the "General Rules."

learn that traditions have never remained static. They change and develop. In both the "Faith and Order" documents of the World Council of Churches and the Roman Catholic doctrine of the two forms of revelation, tradition is both "tradition" and "traditioning." Tradition includes the historical development of the faith of the church.[33] It is a living process of "traditioning," of subtracting and adding, of appropriating and reshaping of the past. As Jaroslav Pelikan once said, tradition is the living faith of those now dead; traditionalism is the dead faith of those still living.[34]

A postmodern view of tradition, therefore, understands it to be more than a static inheritance. The present is the moment in which the past is appropriated and reshaped according to new possibilities, needs, and decisions. The past lives only in the present; the present is a continuation of the past in new configurations. The present is an interactive negotiation between inheritance and imagination.[35] Traditions are continuous and creative simultaneously. They change over time, with the result that traditions exhibit great variety as well as apparent constancies. The "principal claim," writes Delwin Brown, "is that the past creatively appropriated, imaginatively reconstructed, is the material out of which the future is effectively made."[36]

> "The past is never dead; it's not even past."
>
> **WILLIAM FAULKNER**

Change, therefore, is inherent to tradition. Our bias against the past as hopelessly oppressive can be modified when we see that language and culture are a game that plays players even as the players play the game. Tradition, though powerful, also can be challenged by the creativity of the players. In this way tradition is subversive of itself. Theology is one of the ways the tradition plays the players and the players play the tradition through creative interaction. Antiquarian, nostalgic views of tradition as static are just as mistaken as are the radical, revolutionary views of tradition as inherently oppressive.

---

33. Grenz and Franke, *Beyond Foundationalism*, p. 118. "The Christian tradition is comprised of the historical attempts by the Christian community to explicate and translate faithfully the first-order language, symbols, and practices of the Christian faith, arising from the interaction among community, text, and culture, into the various social and cultural contexts in which that community has been situated."

34. Jaroslav Pelikan, *The Vindication of Tradition* (New Haven: Yale University Press, 1984), p. 65.

35. The following discussion is dependent on Delwin Brown, *Boundaries of Our Habitation: Tradition and Theological Construction* (Albany: State University of New York Press, 1994).

36. Brown, *Boundaries of Our Habitation*, p. 118.

The Authority of Tradition

The usual way Protestants ask about the authority of tradition is to ask how authoritative "extrabiblical" traditions are. In one sense, of course, Scripture is simply one part of tradition, the record of the earliest practices and beliefs of the church. As canon it is that part of tradition by which we measure the identity, practices, and beliefs of the other traditions. In fact, however, tradition functions as both source and norm for theology along with Scripture. Even if *sola Scriptura* is the formal norm for theology, the meaning of the Bible must be penetrated and understood — interpreted — if it is to be more than merely words on a page. Scripture is always interpreted within a tradition of interpretation. Even anti-tradition is a tradition of interpreting Scripture.

What holds Scripture and tradition together as a unity is not the infallibility of either, but the work of the Spirit within both. The work of the Spirit did not cease with the closing of the canon. Regardless of whether one adopts the one-source or two-source view of revelation, the authority of Scripture and tradition is ultimately an authority derived from the work of the Spirit in the creation and transmission of both. Neither Scripture nor tradition is inherently authoritative in the foundationalist sense of providing self-evident and infallible grounds for constructing and measuring theological assertions. The authority for both lies in the work of the Spirit of the triune God. Since the church has a canon, there is a sense in which Scripture is the "sole" or "primary" norm for theology. The church cannot exist without its Scripture. But the authority of Scripture and the traditions of interpretation and appropriation ultimately rest on the one Spirit who spoke and continues to speak to and in the church.

> "No dogma or article of the creed can be simply taken over untested by theology from ecclesiastical antiquity; each must be measured from the very beginning, by the Holy Scripture and the Word of God."
>
> **KARL BARTH**

Finally, then, the authority of tradition in theology must be considered both descriptively and normatively. I make this distinction because Protestants occasionally delude themselves into thinking that, because they employ phrases like *"sola Scriptura"* or "the primacy of Scripture," their theology is nothing more than exegesis of Scripture. Or they think they believe and practice only what Scripture plainly teaches, permits, or implies. But no Christian derives practices and beliefs only from Scripture. To be sure, many are clever enough to think they find everything they believe or practice in Scripture. But wise theologians recognize what they actually draw from their tradition as well as from Scripture. Beyond that, at certain points they use tradition normatively as the criterion to judge a theological claim. The question is not *whether* but *how* tradition is used as authority in relation to Scripture, reason, and experience.

Tradition functions as authority, then, at two levels. It functions *descriptively* as the source of what we actually believe and practice; beliefs and practices are inherited from a community as the content of our faith (the faith of the Christian church). But tradition also functions *formally* in theology. Tradition as a *norm* in theology not only means I believe and practice things I in fact inherited from my tradition; it means I believe and practice them *simply because they are the tradition*. When I say, for example, that I believe in the Trinity because that is how the Christian tradition identifies God, or that I practice two sacraments because they are the tradition of the Protestant church, I am saying that tradition is a *norm* as well as a source for my theology. When I say I think or do something not because it is from the Bible or a conclusion of my reason or confirmed by my experience but *because* it is the Christian tradition, I make tradition a formal norm in thinking about faith.

IV. Reasoning Faith

The role of reason in theology is controversial because "reason" is an undefined concept in theology. Most Christians would balk at the charge that their faith and theology are irrational. Yet many of the controversies in theology are based on disagreements about the proper meaning and role of reason. Theological arguments sometimes seem to get nowhere because the idea of reason is used with a range of meanings.

Uses of the Concept of Reason

1. *Clear and Consistent Thinking.* Every theologian employs reason in the sense that we attempt to be as clear and consistent in our thinking as we can be. We want our words to be clear instead of ambiguous or meaningless and our statements to be consistent instead of self-contradictory. To be sure, there are theologians who repudiate reason or set it over against faith, such as Tertullian, who says, "It is to be believed because it is absurd" and "It is certain because it is impossible,"[37] or Luther, who says, "Reason is the greatest

---

37. Tertullian, *De Carne Christi*, 5.

enemy that faith has: it never comes to the aid of spiritual things, but — more frequently than not — struggles against the divine Word, treating with contempt all that emanates from God."[38] But even Tertullian and Luther were not irrationalists. Instead, they repudiated certain uses and claims about reason. Even though our words and sentences often are emotive, rhetorical, symbolic, metaphorical, or analogical instead of direct and literal, we all affirm reason to the extent that we claim our words and statements are clear and consistent in contrast to being meaningless and self-contradictory.

2. *Comprehensive and Coherent Thinking.* Some of the great theologians are more "occasional" than "comprehensive" thinkers. Through timely tracts, sermons, or essays they responded to particular problems, such as christology, human freedom and grace, justification by grace through faith, and Christian perfection (Athanasius, Augustine, Luther, and Wesley). Some of the other great theologians, however, are systematic in the sense that they described the depth and breadth of the Christian faith as a comprehensive and coherent system of thought (Thomas, Calvin, Schleiermacher, Tillich, and Barth). To be rational means both that the claims of the church are coherent with each other (they explain how belief in an all-powerful and all-loving God is consistent with an eternal hell), and consistent with other things they believe about the world (they explain how a person can believe in the resurrection of Jesus when dead people do not walk around after they die).

3. *Rationalism.* While all theologians use reason in the first sense, and some in the second, a few identify reason with "rationalism." Reason is for them identified with logic. In the West, logic refers first to the law of noncontradiction — no one can do two contradictory things at the same time. God cannot make a stone so heavy God cannot lift it — this is a contradiction and so is meaningless. Logic also refers to syllogistic logic — if A is B and B is C, then A is C. Finally, logic refers to modal logic, the logic of necessity and contingency — we know some ideas are necessarily true simply by understanding the idea itself, such as the necessary existence of God as explained by Anselm and Charles Hartshorne. Theologians who employ reason as deductive logic are usually called "rationalists," and their theology is called "rationalism." Rationalists claim we can know some innate or necessary ideas and can deduct from these ideas, which we can know as true apart from experience. Although no theologian has ever deduced an interpretation of the Christian faith from innate ideas, some are "rationalists" in that they claim some things can be known about God by reason alone apart from any special revelation or experience. For example, from reason alone we can know the necessary existence of God: the concept of

---

38. Luther, *Table Talk*, 353.

God is the (necessary) implication of there being anything at all, or of the idea of perfection, or God is a requirement for concepts of motion or causation, design or morality (Aquinas, William Paley, and Immanuel Kant).

4. *Reason as Philosophy.* Prior to the twentieth century, most Western theologians depended on philosophy as the way to explain themselves. Philosophy usually meant metaphysics, a metanarrative about reality. The metaphysician constructed a scheme of interlocking ideas that integrated all the fragments of the world into an all-encompassing vision of the whole.[39] The task of the theologian was either to be a metaphysician and use his vision as a means to interpret doctrine, as in Paul Tillich's theology of correlation,[40] or to borrow the concepts and categories of a philosopher and interpret theological ideas within that language, as in John Cobb's Whiteheadian theology.[41] Many of the great Protestant theologians of the eighteenth through the twentieth centuries used idealism, existentialism, or process philosophy as the tool by which to interpret Christian doctrine. One of the major shifts in theology throughout the last century, however, beginning with Barth, was to repudiate the use of philosophy in theology.

5. *Reason as Science.* Even though speculative philosophy came under severe criticism from both philosophers and theologians throughout the twentieth century, reason as a term for the activities and products of human intelligence, especially the knowledge derived from the modern sciences, remains alive. For many theologians, reason refers to scientific knowledge. The theologian employs knowledge from the hard sciences and the social sciences to understand and interpret the faith and practice of the church. To correlate faith and reason is not to correlate faith with a system of philosophy. It is, rather, to interpret the function, context, and meaning of faith within our knowledge of the world and human nature garnered from physics, biology, psychology, and the social sciences. Evolutionary theory tells us something about creation and how the world came to be in its present form, while genetics, physiology, psychology, and social sciences help us understand how human beings came to be the way they are, what motivates and guides their behavior, and why they believe and act as they do.

---

39. "The aim of philosophy, abstractly formulated, is to understand how things in the broadest possible sense of the term hang together in the broadest possible sense of the term." Wilfred Sellers, *Science, Perception, and Reality,* quoted in Charles Wood, *Vision and Discernment* (Atlanta: Scholars Press, 1985), p. 21.

40. Paul Tillich, *Systematic Theology,* vol. 1 (Chicago: University of Chicago Press, 1951), pp. 59-66.

41. John Cobb, *A Christian Natural Theology: Based on the Thought of Alfred North Whitehead* (Philadelphia: Westminster, 1965).

6. *Reason as Worldview.* When theologians appeal to reason as science, however, they often refer to more than the specific information about the world and human life offered by the sciences. Reason refers to the modern worldview that undergirds the sciences, the *weltanschauungen* (picture of the world). This worldview began with the "this-worldly" focus of the Renaissance. It was shaped by the naturalistic assumptions of the Enlightenment, according to which the laws of cause and effect explain the origin and operation of everything without reference to any transcendental realm or causes beyond nature. The natural world is all there is. Nature is a creative and interpenetrating field of forces that are organically related wholes. Knowledge is empirical in that it depends on the tough-minded appeal to the stubborn facts of experience, to the empirical method of inquiry of the sciences, and to common human experience as the source and justification of all truth.[42] While doubt about claims for the adequacy or ultimacy of this worldview is characteristic of postmodern thinking, this understanding of reason remains "in the bones" of many theologians who accept the use of reason in theology.

7. *Reason as Linguistic Usage.* Most theologians do not understand reason to dictate that any idea which does not fit into the modern worldview is irrational or unusable. Philosophers of language have shown that the meaning of words and sentences depends on the context in which they are used. There are reasonable ways to use language besides stating facts or literally describing the world. Human beings employ many different "language games" (Ludwig Wittgenstein). They use language in aesthetic, moral, and religious contexts to narrate, motivate, express, and guide through paradox, symbol, metaphor, analogy, parable, myth, and narrative. These usages convey a kind of meaning that also informs us about the world. We are rational when we show how our words and sentences function in their proper contexts. Meaning and truth cannot be determined by imposing language from one context into another context to determine its only reasonable meaning.

8. *Reason as Reasoning.* Reason refers, finally, to our capacity for disciplined thinking. It refers to our capacity to be self-critical, to elucidate, sift, analyze, and expound, to bring into the light the reasons we do what we do and believe what we believe.[43] Because we can reason, we can ask questions,

---

42. Nancy Frankenberry, "Major Themes of Empirical Theology," in *Handbook of Empirical Theology*, ed. Randolf Crump Miller (Birmingham: Religious Education Press, 1992), pp. 39-42.

43. "Arguments need not be logical deductions but consist in the giving of reasons, of showing connections, of presenting juxtapositions, or criticizing mistakes. Human brains are hardwired for images connected with argument." Robert Neville, *The God Who Beckons: Theology in the Form of Sermons* (Nashville: Abingdon, 1999), p. 12.

submit our ideas to criticism, remove what is ill-founded or irreconcilable, and confirm what is well-founded and appropriate. Reason in this sense is our appeal to evidence and argument, somewhat the way a lawyer or a historian "builds a case." We reason more by saying, "Look at it this way; isn't it clearer and doesn't it make more sense if we say . . . ," or "If we interpret it this way instead of that, doesn't it fit better with what we have already said about . . . ?" Reasoning is not so much a knock-down proof of truth or error as it is an ability to make a case for one interpretation as better than another.

Criticism and Defense of the Authority of Reason in Theology

Not all theologians make reason an explicit norm for theology in any of these eight meanings. For some, reason is irrelevant to the theological way of thinking. For Pascal, "the heart has its reasons which reason knows nothing of."[44] This is, of course, an equivocal use of the term. Pascal then goes on to explain his claim: "We know the truth, not only by reason, but by the heart."[45]

Reason as a norm is rejected by Christians who locate the meaning and truth of faith solely in the authority of the Bible or the tradition of the church or the heart of the believer instead of the mind's reason. An even deeper criticism of the use of reason is offered in "apophatic theology," however. Apophatic theology claims God is so far beyond human perception, apprehension, and comprehension that nothing positive can be said about God from a human point of view. We can only say what God is not *(via negativa)*. More precisely, anything positive we can say about God can be only inferred from what it can be said that God is not. For example, God is not finite, temporal, or limited in knowledge and power; therefore, by implication, God is infinite, eternal, omniscient, and omnipotent. Reason, however, is not a way to know that God is, who God is, and what God is like. We may not want to say that theology is irrational, but we can say that theology is a-rational or nonrational in the sense that reason cannot say anything positive about the transcendent God.

> "The idea of demonstrating that this unknown something (the God) exists, could scarcely suggest itself to the Reason. For if the God does not exist it would of course be impossible to prove it; and if he does exist it would be folly to attempt it."
>
> **SØREN KIERKEGAARD**

44. Blaise Pascal, *Pensées*, number 277.
45. Pascal, *Pensées*, number 282.

There is another criticism of the use of reason in contemporary theology: Every appeal to reason is a rationalization or an ideology. Psychology has shown us how reason is used as a tool to rationalize what we are going to believe and do on some other grounds, such as past experience, fear, ego, self-justification, or whatever needs our beliefs satisfy. The social sciences have shown how knowledge, along with other social goods and services, is socially located, defined, and distributed according to the interests of those with the power to determine what is true and reasonable.[46] Reason is an ideology, a way of using our language to impose our power on other people by justifying the social agendas of our race, class, and gender.[47]

Nevertheless, we do not need to be thorough skeptics about our capacity to use reason for some other purpose than rationalization or ideology. To be sure, we must adopt a chastened postmodernist view of reason. Our language does not mirror the world in some objective way; our language constructs the world. Constructive views can replace rationalistic views of the world and knowledge. Through the reciprocity between the language of the knower and the environment of the knower, we know a world out there and some truth about it. Within a constructivist perspective, we can talk about knowledge and truth both of science and of faith.

In the next chapter I will examine how Christians claim to know what they know about God through their concepts of revelation and faith. Here I intend to affirm the role of reason in that knowledge. My critiques of reason do not ban it from theology. To be sure, reason does not originate or define the faith of the church. It is not a way of knowing prior to or independent of revelation and faith. It is, rather, "the faculty of reasoning"[48] about what we receive through revelation and faith. It is "a way of using the sources available to us"[49] in Scripture, tradition, and experience. It is a component of faith seeking understanding.

46. See Peter Berger and Thomas Luckmann, *The Social Construction of Reality: A Treatise in the Sociology of Knowledge* (New York: Doubleday, 1966).

47. Except, of course, the reasoning which produces our knowledge that all other reasoning is ideological in nature, a viewpoint which is not an ideology but is the truth.

48. John Wesley, "An Ernest Appeal to Men of Reason and Religion," in *John Wesley*, ed. Albert Outler (Oxford University Press, 1964), p. 394.

49. Maurice Wiles, *Archetypal Heresy: Arianism throughout the Centuries* (New York: Oxford University Press, 1996), p. 23.

V. Confirmed by Experience

The Concept of Experience in Theology

Experience is one of the most commonly appealed to yet disputable components of modern theology. Both liberals and evangelicals appeal to experience as a source and a norm for theology. Liberals usually point to a specific religious *dimension* or *quality* of general human experience. Religious experience consists of a pervasive sense of *duty* or ought (Kant), a feeling of *absolute dependence* as an accompaniment of every experience (Schleiermacher), a sense of the *holy* with its qualities of attraction and dread (Rudolf Otto), an inescapable *confidence* in the meaningfulness of life (Schubert Ogden), the feeling of *value* accompanying our bodily experience of the world (Henry Wieman), a dimension of *ultimacy* and sacredness within experience (Langdon Gilkey). All human beings perceive these qualities of experience regardless of culture and tradition. They are the base upon which the theologian can interpret the meaning and truth of Christian symbols.

Evangelicals, on the other hand, appeal to *a special experience* as the ground and authority of their faith. Theology is based on my immediate awareness of God as a loving and forgiving God, of Jesus as a loving companion. The person who has "been born again" or "been saved" knows God loves her through a direct awareness of Jesus that goes beyond "normal" knowledge of God gained through the "ordinances" of the church, such as reading Scripture, reciting creeds, or participating in the liturgy. The person who experiences God this way has a sudden, overwhelming, direct, personal experience of Jesus.

Before either the liberal or the conservative can appeal to experience as a *basis* for Christian beliefs, however, each has to answer some questions about whether experience can be an autonomous source for theology. Can experience be the raw material for theology independent of Scripture and tradition? One problem in claiming this is posed by "neurotheology," the theory that mystical experience, spiritual moments, or religious epiphanies are rooted in the alteration of specific brain circuits where the sense of self dissolves and the person has the feeling of being united with God.[50] There is, of course, no way

---

50. Andrew Newberg, Eugene d'Aquili, and Vince Rause, *Why God Won't Go Away: Brain Science and the Biology of Belief* (New York: Ballantine, 2001), especially chaps. 2, 3, and 6. "The evidence further compels us to believe that if God does indeed exist, the only place he can manifest his existence would be in the tangled neural pathways and physiological structures of the brain." Newberg et al., *Why God Won't Go Away*, p. 53. See also Sharon Begley, "Religion and the Brain," *Newsweek*, May 7, 2001, pp. 50-57; and William Braden, *The Private Sea: LSD and the Search for God* (New York: Bantam, 1967).

to determine whether our discovery that religious experience has a neural circuit means that the brain is causing those experiences or that it is perceiving a spiritual reality through the circuits of the brain. But there can be little doubt that religious experience is a body-brain event. If one concludes that this bodily event is a "doorway" or "window" to God instead of the "cause" of the experience itself, one can claim that only on the basis of something other than the experience itself. One is not stuck with either a supranaturalistic view (the experience is caused by a supernatural agent and is therefore true) or a naturalistic view (the experience is simply a bodily event and therefore delusional). "Neurotheology" plausibly can be seen either as the discovery that God is "nothing but" an event in the brain of the person having an experience of God, or as the discovery of the bodily pathway to God.

The second problem is whether there is even such a thing as "pure experience," experience apart from the interpretation of language — that is, apart from culture. No one denies, of course, that we have experiences, events in which we participate through bodily sensations and brain circuits. We feel cold, pain, heat, wetness, dryness; we feel the sense of self in the midst of our negotiation with our environment. But if these sensations have any meaning whatsoever, these bodily experiences have to be interpreted in our minds through language. Experience is not a thing we possess; we have bodily sensations that we interpret as certain kinds of experiences. For humans — and perhaps apes and sea mammals — experience involves sense experience *and* interpretation. And interpretation occurs in a linguistic, cultural context, as Gordon Kaufman notes:

> There is no such thing as a raw, pre-linguistic experience of "transcendence." . . . Each of these "experiences" is shaped, delimited and informed by the linguistic symbols which also name it. Without these symbols to guide our consciousness these "experiences" would not be available to us at all. . . . It would be truer to say that the language we speak provides a principal foundation for our religious experience.[51]

Everything we know, including what we know through experience, we know through our language and culture. Thus experience does not, and cannot, exist apart from a social context. If we are going to speak of experience as a source and norm for theology, we must include culture as a part of what we mean by experience. When we experience God, we know this only as an interpretation through the language we inherit from our culture.

51. Gordon Kaufman, *Essay on Theological Method* (Atlanta: Scholars Press, 1975), pp. 5-6.

Experience As Source and Norm for Theology

If we appeal to interpreted experience as a source and norm for theology, we must decide *what kind* of experience and *whose* we invoke. Do we select as the source and norm for our reflection a born-again experience, or the religion of the heart, or an experience of healing, or an encounter with God, or a mystical union with the divine, or the quality of ultimacy in everyday experience, or the experience of economic repression and liberation from it, or the generation of life, or any other number of "religious experiences"? Is the proper subject matter for theology my individual experience of one of these, or the experience of oppression and liberation of a group (female or male, black or white, Third World or middle class, North American or Asian, heterosexual or homosexual)? For example, some contemporary feminist theology appeals to "women's experience" as the proper subject matter of theological reflection instead of the traditional sources of theology.[52] A generalized appeal to "the authority of experience" is nearly meaningless until we are clear about whose and what experience is privileged.

The primary way experience operates in theology, I believe, is through an *appropriation* and *confirmation* of Scripture and tradition. My belief stands in some contrast to the liberal view that religious experience is a primary source and norm for theology independent of Scripture and tradition. I do not go as far as Gordon Kaufman and John Cobb go, however. Although they do not give contemporary experience the first word in theology (Scripture and tradition come to us from the past as given), it has the last word for them in the sense that our contemporary experience is the ultimate test of our symbols and doctrines, the final court of appeal for our conclusions: "Experience will sit in judgment on that tradition and history to see whether it can still make sense in our life," writes Kaufman.[53] Nevertheless, I do believe that where general and contemporary experience supplement, or even contradict, the experience of Scripture and tradition, general and contemporary experience are an important authority for thinking about faith. I also stand in some contrast

---

52. Rosemary Ruether's formal norm for theology in feminist theology is found in *Sexism and God-Talk: Toward a Feminist Theology* (Boston: Beacon, 1983). "The critical principle of feminist theology is the promotion of the full humanity of women. Whatever denies, diminishes, or distorts the full humanity of women is, therefore, appraised as not redemptive. Theologically speaking, whatever diminishes or denies the full humanity of women must be presumed not to reflect the divine or an authentic relation to the divine, or to reflect the authentic nature of things, or to be the message or work of an authentic redeemer or a community of redemption" (pp. 18-19).

53. Kaufman, *Essay on Theological Method*, p. 8.

to the more conservative position that experience is never a source and norm for theology. For conservatives the subject matter of theology is given to the theologian in the Scripture and tradition. Experience is simply the *medium* through which the truth is received in the contemporary situation. The task of the theologian is to interpret the message of Christian faith in the language of the age.[54]

I propose a more dialectical way of thinking about the authority of experience in theology. It is a source and a norm for theology, but it operates in concert with the authority of Scripture and tradition. If one understands the Christian faith in a postmodern way as a content that comes to us from the past as the symbols, rituals, and beliefs we have inherited, we can still hold the modern view of the importance of experience in theology. Unless our inheritance is *appropriated* and *confirmed* by the believer in such a way that her behavior and inner life are incorporated into, shaped by, and lived out in terms of the faith of the church, that faith is not true. Experience is not an autonomous source for theology; it is a medium through which we appropriate the faith of the church. In addition, experience is not an autonomous norm for theology; it is a criterion by which we confirm Scripture and tradition. Otherwise, there is no genuine faith.

Most Protestant theologians, except modernistic infallibilists, have held that the Bible is not and cannot be the Word of God apart from the witness of the Holy Spirit in the life of the believer. The Christian faith cannot be apprehended as true until the experience of the believer appropriates it as true. The confirmation of faith by the believer is one side of the dialectic through which we receive grace given to us as the Word of God in Scripture and tradition. "The heart," therefore, *is* a criterion for theology. The Christian faith can be known as true only as the passions and tempers of the believer are shaped by the Scripture and tradition through the inward witness of the Spirit. Theology is subject not only to the criteria of "orthodoxy" (following the right teachings of the church) and "orthopraxy" (following the right practices of aiding the needy, fighting oppression, and seeking justice), but also to the criterion of "orthopathy" (possessing the right "feelings" [Schleiermacher] or "affections" [Edwards] or "passions" [Wesley] that indicate authentic faith).[55] This is not simply a modern claim about the authority of experience. It stands at the center of evangelical Christianity, is embodied in Pietism and Methodism, and, along with the Calvinist emphasis on the testimony of the Holy Spirit, remains at the center of any version of Christian faith that claims the name "evangelical" and "Reformed."

---

54. Tillich, *Systematic Theology,* vol. 1.

55. Theodore Runyon, *The New Creation* (Nashville: Abingdon, 1998), chapter 5.

An Approach for Beginners:
The Dialectical Nature of the Sources and Norms

I designate the perspective on methodology described in this chapter, and, I hope, exhibited throughout the book, as dialectical rather than hermeneutical. In the hermeneutical model, the role of tradition, experience, and reason is limited strictly to the interpretation of Scripture. In the dialectical method I go beyond the admission that tradition, reason, and experience play a role in theology. Instead, I give them as well as Scripture some authority. Each of the four sources and norms not only does but *should* guide our thinking about faith. Each is subject to criticism, correction, and supplementation by the other three.[56]

To be sure, there is a sense in which Scripture is primary for the dialectical method. But *primacy* does not mean that the Bible is the *only* source and norm for theology. The primacy of Scripture means that Scripture is decisive. Primacy means that among all the sources and norms theologians appropriately use to think about faith, the criterion of all doctrine is the triune God who is revealed in the story of Israel's history and of Jesus as the Christ, the story narrated in the Scriptures and declared normatively in the apostolic witness of the church's canon. It means that the God the other sources testify to is interpreted as the triune God. Such a claim, however, does not mean no other sources and norms are appropriate for Christian thinking.

Method cannot be determined beforehand, but only in retrospect. Gradually, we become aware of how we actually have worked through our interpretation of faith. Once we are clear that the modern obsession with foundationalism is a will-o'-the-wisp, we can think about method through a reflective description of the resources and criteria we actually used instead of as some prior restraint on how we can and cannot think about faith. The question about method, however, cannot be answered indefinitely as a de-

---

56. Cobb, *Christian Natural Theology,* p. 162. So, for example, the theologian does not deal with the moral dilemmas posed in Scripture by setting the Bible over against our modern moral judgments, forcing us to choose one or the other (arguing that the Bible is inerrant and infallible in every idea it presents), or, as in the hermeneutical method, by trying to show that the Bible does not mean what it appears to mean but actually supports our modern moral sensibilities, or, even, by arguing that the primary testimony of Scripture counters its own teachings in some places. In the dialectical understanding of method, one concedes that the Scriptures are mixed and ambiguous in the picture of God they present and argues that theology is, in fact, a mutual conversation between Scripture, tradition, reason, and experience, and so each stands in a dialectical relation with the others. For an excellent discussion of the methodological issues as well as the moral issues posed by Scripture, see Terence Fretheim, *The Bible as Word of God in a Postmodern Age* (Minneapolis: Fortress, 1998), pp. 79-126.

scription of how we have proceeded. We must also ask about the *proper* criteria, especially when the hard issues are before us. "Methodology" becomes a distinctive theological problem when we have to adjudicate conflicting claims. After we describe what resources we *actually* used (Bible, tradition, philosophy, science, experience, church, culture, the religions), we must be prepared to answer the normative question about what criteria we *should* use and *how* we should use them to interpret faith.

As a beginning student in theology, therefore, you should not become preoccupied or stymied by having to decide on your methodology in advance. You should not feel that you cannot begin until you have elaborated and defended your method. Thinking about method in the way I suggest implies there is no one right preexisting method that will give you the right to proceed toward the right answers. This chapter, therefore, might just as well have been placed at the end of the book as near the beginning. I did not place it here to establish the grounds on which you are permitted to proceed; I placed it here to keep before us an awareness of the resources we actually use in our work.

This take on method stresses that no theologian begins as a blank slate. We already exist as believers in believing communities. We have inherited stories, rituals, symbols, interpretations, and beliefs before we ever begin to think theologically. Theology entails a dialectic between the resources we inherit and critical reflection on that faith. Joseph Sittler formulates it this way:

> My own disinclination to state a theological method is grounded in the strong conviction that one does not devise a method and then dig into the data; one lives with the data, lets their force, variety, and authenticity generate a sense of . . . "a way of knowing" appropriate to the nature of the data. . . . Every theologian, to be sure, has a theological method, but the clarity and permeative force of it is likely to be disclosed even to himself only in the course of his most mature work. When that method does become clear it will be seen to have been a function of a disposition toward the evaluation of data in their living historical force, and not an imposition of abstract norms for "truth" or "authenticity" arrived at early and exercised consistently.[57]

The issue of method will arise over and over throughout this book. I have already indicated that I understand there to be some truth on different sides of the disagreements. My strategy is to establish a conversation between them.

---

57. Joseph Sittler, *Essays on Nature and Grace* (Philadelphia: Fortress, 1972), pp. 20-21.

In theology, the option is not always, even usually, an either/or choice. There is frequently some truth on several sides. Here I have argued that conservatives are correct in their insistence that the church cannot exist without its canon; that the canon has a unique place (a primacy) in the thought of the church; that all theology must be consistent with its canon. I have argued that liberals are correct in that Scripture both is and should be understood within the context of tradition, reason, and experience; that the Bible is not self-interpreting but must be interpreted anew in each generation of Christians; that the Bible can be interpreted, even measured, by the context of the perceptions and concerns of a particular age. My way of correlating these truths is to describe what I mean by such theological concepts as Scripture and canon, the dynamic nature of tradition, the several uses of reason, and the confirmatory role of experience in theology. I remind you that these are preliminary considerations for you to rethink at the end when you examine how you actually used these sources both as resources and as norms in your interpretation of the faith of the Christian church.

CHAPTER THREE

Revelation and Faith

I. The Idea of Revelation in Recent Thought

In 1966 *Time* emblazoned across one of its covers in inch-and-a-half red letters against a black background the question, "Is God Dead?" The story described a cadre of theologians who claimed one could still be a Christian following "the death of God."[1] One response to their claim was this:

> However absurd talking about God might be, it could never be so obviously absurd as talking of Christian faith without God. . . . Faith in God of a certain kind is not merely an element in Christian faith along with several others; it simply *is* Christian faith, the heart of the matter itself.[2]

Christian faith is about knowing God and ourselves in relation to God.[3] Beyond knowing about the reality and character of God, faith knows who God is and who we are through God's self-disclosure to us through our encounter with the living God.

The primary theological answer to the question, "How do we know God?" is, "We know God through revelation and faith." The meaning of these

---

1. "Toward a Hidden God," *Time*, April 8, 1966, pp. 82-87.

2. Schubert Ogden, *The Reality of God and Other Essays* (New York: Harper and Row, 1966), p. 14.

3. "Nearly all the wisdom we possess, that is to say, true and sound wisdom, consists of two parts: the knowledge of God and of ourselves. But, while joined by many bonds, which one precedes and brings forth the other is not easy to discern." John Calvin, *Institutes of the Christian Religion*, 2 vols., ed. John T. McNeill, trans. Ford Lewis Battles (Philadelphia: Westminster, 1960), p. 35 (1.1.1).

two terms, however, is unclear. Do they mean we know God through a *direct* encounter with God (an immediate mystical union or communion) or through an *indirect* encounter with God (mediated to us through the events and persons of history interpreted in Scripture)? For many Christians knowing God is a simple and self-evident matter. They know God personally because they know God "in my heart" through a born-again experience or a direct conversation with God. While I maintain that personal knowledge of God through faith is essential to the Christian life, I also claim that the way Christians know the reality, character, and presence of God involves more than the immediate knowledge of God. The God the Christian knows is mediated to us through the history of Israel and the story of Jesus embodied in the Scripture and interpreted by the church.

"Revelation" is the English translation of the Greek word *apokalypsis*. The word signifies an "uncovering" or "unveiling" of what was concealed or unknown. In Scripture God is revealed in nature (Ps. 19:1-4; 29:3-11) as well as in direct visions (Exod. 33:17-23; Num. 24:2-9; Isa. 6), auditions (1 Sam. 3:2-14; Isa. 22:14), dreams (Gen. 28:10-17; 1 Sam. 28:6), and theophanies (Exod. 3). Nevertheless, Scripture understands revelation primarily to be God's *indirect self-disclosure* through the "acts of God" which are discerned within the events of Israel's history and the story of Jesus' life, death, and resurrection. The key self-disclosure of God in the Old Testament is through the "saving deeds" of God which rescued the slaves from the pits of Egypt (Exod. 15:1-21) and gave the Law to the people through Moses on Sinai (Exod. 19–20). "The secret things belong to the LORD our God, but the revealed things belong to us and to our children forever, to observe all the words of this law" (Deut. 29:29). In the New Testament God's self-disclosure is known by the people who see and hear God's Word in the ministry of Jesus (Mark 4:11). The gospel reveals God through the story of Jesus as the Christ who imparts God's saving power to the person of faith (John 3:16-17; Rom. 1:16-17, 1 Peter 1:17-21). •

The key to the meaning of revelation is the *divine initiative.* The first movement is made by God to us. Revelation includes two poles: (1) the *process* of God coming to us through the history of Israel and the life, death, and resurrection of Jesus — God acting, and (2) the *knowledge* about God's character, purposes, and economy which we learn through this story — the results of God acting. Both poles indicate that God comes to us; we do not discover God. And they indicate that knowledge of God is mediated through the people and events in Scripture; we don't know God primarily through our direct experience of God. As Barth taught us, Jesus Christ is the primary revelatory *symbol* of the Christian faith, the Bible is the primary revelatory *document*, and the church is the primary *bearer* of that revelation. *Revelation,* then, is the technical term used by theologians to affirm that our knowledge of God depends on God's self-disclosing initiative in moving toward us through the history of Israel and the story of Jesus and his significance.

Revelation, therefore, is the key concept in answering the question about how Christians know God. Through Israel's history and the story of Jesus we are given the knowledge of God that we would not have simply on our own. Something new and decisive is given to us. Even if something about God is apparent in general human experience, the gift-like nature of knowledge of God as the ultimate mystery who is with us must be stressed. Although we must grasp revelation through faith for it to be revelation,[4] just as a gift must be both given and received to be a gift, we, nevertheless, would have no knowledge of God if God had not made Godself known to us first. "We love him, because he first loved us" (1 John 4:19 KJV).

> "The Spirit cannot give a new revelation, but through the preaching of his witnesses he will cause everything that Jesus said and did to be revealed in a new light. . . . Revelation is not a closed doctrinal system, nor is it a completed history, but through the Spirit it must constantly be made a new reality, a new event."
>
> **HANS KÜNG**

Revelation, therefore, is not first of all a theory about the foundations of knowledge on which all the other Christian doctrines can be justified. Rather, revelation is the first word we use to talk about God which is appropriate to who God is, namely, a gracious mystery who comes to us beyond our grasp as a gift. The idea of revelation is *the first affirmation of grace* we encounter in the faith of the church. Its primal meaning is to affirm the prevenience or priority of God in God's relation with us. It is the first assertion of the recurring claim that grace is the primary word to say about God's work for our salvation. This understanding of the idea of revelation in recent thought implies that there are four things revelation is not.

1. Revelation as the self-disclosure of God through the biblical narrative does not mean there was no revelation prior to or subsequent to the history of Israel and the story of Jesus as the Christ. The idea of God did not begin with the Jewish-Christian heritage. Ideas of ultimate mystery, holiness, and divinity exist before and outside the Jewish-Christian legacy. Furthermore, for Christians knowledge of the God they worship already existed for the Hebrews in Old Testament times; Jesus did not reveal God's existence either for

---

4. Paul Tillich, *Biblical Religion and the Search for Ultimate Reality* (Chicago: University of Chicago Press, 1955).

Jews or Christians for the first time. As Ted Peters writes, "[T]he gospel of Jesus Christ assumed knowledge of God and then goes on to define a new understanding of God."[5] Finally, revelation continued to occur both outside and inside the church, both in the sense that God may be known under other names in the non-Christian religions (Allah), and in the sense that the Spirit continues to lead the church into new understandings and new dimensions of the gospel as time goes on.

2. Revelation does not mean that knowledge of God exists apart from faith. Faith is necessary for there to be revelation. Revelation requires both an objective pole (the initial work of God) and a subjective pole (our subsequent response in belief, trust, and loyalty). This, therefore, is another of the many pairs of dialectical concepts important to theology. The gospel of Jesus cannot be revelation unless the Spirit leads the church to confess that Jesus is decisive for our knowledge of God and unless the church continues to make that confession of faith through the power of the Spirit today. Christian revelation, therefore, cannot be revelation apart from faith in the saving power of the gospel. In the actual life of faith, where we find ourselves already in the midst of a community of living faith, the claim for the priority of revelation is a logical one and does not describe the actual life of our encounter with God through belief, trust, and loyalty.[6]

3. Revelation does not refer primarily to an interior and private experience of God or to a direct, unmediated, mystical union with God. It also does not refer primarily to an inner ecstatic state where an individual hears voices, sees visions, or has dreams in which God appears to the individual. The only way to interpret such an experience as a revelation of God is to have in hand a concept of God derived from the faith of the church in order to interpret it as knowledge of God instead of indigestion or auto-suggestion. If I do not have the filter of Scripture and tradition as the language for interpreting private, subjective experiences, I do not have any basis to call such experiences knowledge of God. If we know God as Christians we know God by seeing, perceiving, and interpreting our experiences through the history of Israel and the story of Jesus.

4. Although revelation is connected with Scripture and tradition, revelation cannot be identified with the words of the Bible or doctrines. Scripture and tradition are products of a historical context. If the words of Scripture are taken simply as the revealed words of God, then everything Scripture teaches, such as patriarchy and holy wars, is sanctioned by God. Scripture and doctrine

---

5. Ted Peters, *God — The World's Future*, second ed. (Minneapolis: Fortress, 2000), p. 68.
6. Ted Peters, *God — The World's Future*, pp. 67-71.

are revelation because they witness to the God revealed to us in the gospel of Jesus Christ, not because they convey propositions dictated by God to biblical writers or Christian teachers. The Bible as revelation, then, is tied to the "canon within the canon," specifically, the gospel through which all stories and symbols and teachings of Scripture must be interpreted. In place of a notion of revelation as propositional statements, then, I want to emphasize revelation as our encounter with God through the story of Jesus. The Bible and doctrine are revelation when they are the context of our encounter with God.

II. General Revelation

This concept of revelation as God's gracious move toward us in self-disclosure, however, leaves some questions unanswered. Is God revealed to all people through our common experience of nature, or does God come to us only through our particular group of people, events, symbols, and traditions? This fundamental question in theology typically is discussed through the concepts of "general revelation" and "special revelation." "General revelation" refers to the claim that there is a natural knowledge of God inherent in human experience. Simply as humans, we have a hint, an awareness, an intuition, an innate idea of God grounded in our experience of the world. By thinking critically about our experience as humans, we can at least know *that* God exists, even know God personally through our experience of the world. Knowledge of God based on common experience and reason (theologians call it "natural theology") is available to all human beings and should be convincing to all sensitive and reflective people regardless of whether they are part of a religious tradition or not. At least some knowledge about God does not depend on a special revelation by God.

> "The Scriptures function as a servant of their Lord. We are meant not to rest in them but to move through them and beyond them to the One they serve."
>
> **ARTHUR McGILL**

The idea of general revelation is affirmed in the Scriptures. Creation itself reveals something of the invisible or hidden creator.

The heavens are telling the glory of God;
    and the firmament proclaims his handiwork.
Day to day pours forth speech,
    and night to night declares knowledge.

There is no speech, nor are there words;
    their voice is not heard;
yet their voice goes out through all the earth
    and their words to the end of the world.

(Ps 19:1-4; see also Pss. 8, 104, and 139)

The Wisdom literature — Proverbs, Job, and Ecclesiastes — testifies to the God known in human experience across religions and cultures. In the New Testament, Paul claims that "Ever since the creation of the world his eternal power and divine nature, invisible though they are, have been understood and seen through the things he has made" (Rom. 1:20), and he addresses the Athenians in front of the Areopagus in the name of "an unknown god" whom we as "God's offspring" share in common as the one in whom "we live and move and have our being" (Acts 17:22-31).

The primary grounds for the concept of general revelation is the belief that God the Creator leaves "footprints" or "fingerprints" in nature itself or in some dimension of common human experience as evidence. Beginning with the creation story in Genesis, one can interpret the Bible to teach that all that happens subsequently throughout human experience and history depends on the God who is already known to be the creator of all things visible and invisible. God is present in sunsets and flowers and the beauty of the DNA molecule. God can be known by anyone or everyone through meditation and the inner spiritual life, in times of inward ecstasy and wonder, and in moments of personal integration within the self.

The primary human experience appealed to by theologians who advocate a concept of general revelation is the overwhelming sense of mystery in human experience. All human beings have an innate consciousness of God as the transcendent ground of the world through their awareness of its sheer givenness and the possibility of it not existing at all. Paul Tillich called this "metaphysical shock,"[7] the shock of possible nonbeing that is evident in the question, "Why is there something; why not nothing?" The question itself points to our intuitive awareness that the world is a mystery, that it is more than we can see and touch. The cosmos is grounded in a transcendent yet present reality which is its "ground of being" or "power of being."[8] This intuition has led to the "question of God," which, in turn, has led theologians to

---

7. Paul Tillich, *Systematic Theology,* vol. 1 (Chicago: University of Chicago Press, 1951), p. 163.

8. "When confronted with the brute thereness of things, and the accompanying awareness of possible nonbeing, we suddenly sense that what is is not just what is. Is there something more?" Peters, *God — The World's Future,* p. 88.

ask where in human experience one might look for positive evidences of the reality which is hinted at in our intuition of "the mystery of existing and not existing."[9] The quest for an answer to this question has led some theologians to pursue a "natural theology," including the so-called "proofs for the existence of God." At all times and places, so the thinking goes, humans are confronted with the fingerprints of God left on certain features of nature, history, experience, and reason, which are proofs or evidences of a supreme reality that is the cause, foundation, or ground of the world. Christians and non-Christians alike have reason to speak of God because of certain features of our common experience. Among others, four have been particularly persuasive for people in the Western tradition of philosophical theology and philosophy of religion: the order of the world, moral experience, religious experience, and reason itself.

1. Most humans have a sense of wonder and awe for the grandeur, beauty, intricacy, and order of nature. We say, "I see God in the beauty of the sunset," or "I see God in the order of the natural world," or "The world as a whole of which I am but a part must have a transcendent designer." How can we look at the wonders of nature — the galaxies, the mountain ranges, the human body and mind — and doubt that there is a God? When philosophers have reflected on the beauty and order of nature, many have concluded that such a world is not self-explanatory. All penultimate explanations for the beauty and order of the world depend upon the necessity of a transcendent first cause or a designer.

Thomas Aquinas began his proofs for the existence of God with a focus on such basic characteristics of the world as change, cause and effect, contingent beings (not necessary), degrees of value, and purpose. He argued that the world could not exhibit these features unless there was an ultimate reality behind them, a Prime Mover, a First Cause, a Necessary Being, an Absolute Value, and a Divine Designer.[10] In order to account for the existence of contingent beings, for example, we must acknowledge the reality of a nonobservable being who is utterly different from contingent beings and is their ultimate ground and source.

Other philosophers, such as William Paley, appeal to the apparent design of the world. When we look at the world, both the parts and as a whole, it appears to be one grand machine. Paley used the analogy of a watch, which is so complex and purposive that it cannot be explained by chance; similarly, the world is so intricate and purposive that it requires an intelligent mind

---

9. Bernard Meland, *Fallible Forms and Symbols* (Minneapolis: Fortress, 1976), chaps. 4-5.
10. Thomas Aquinas, *Summa Theologica,* part I, question 2, article 3.

who is its Designer.[11] Although arguments for the existence of God which appeal to nature are liable to criticisms as proofs, they nevertheless confirm the degree to which the idea of God is raised by the finite structure of the world.[12]

2. Others are impressed by the significance of our moral experience. Through our conscience, our sense of ought, duty, and right, we know God as the supreme lawgiver. Our ethical experience, especially our sense of inalienable obligation to our fellow human beings, and indeed, to the whole creation, presupposes the reality of God as the source and ground of this obligation. This argument is in one sense a logical one, an inference from objective moral law to a lawgiver, from objective moral value or values in general to a transcendent ground of values, from the fact of conscience to God whose voice is heard through conscience. Anyone seriously committed to respecting moral values as legitimate claims on one's life implicitly believes in a transcendent source of these values, which we call God.[13]

3. For still others, our religious experience points to the reality of God. Religious experience may be a moment of direct awareness of divine presence through a mystical experience, or it may be a dimension of all our everyday experience, such as our quest for truth or value, or our feeling of absolute dependence upon the "whence" of our existence. In one of these ways we know the reality of God. Two examples will illustrate the breadth of a religious dimension of ordinary experience which points to our experience of God.

First, Langdon Gilkey points to our (oblique) awareness of and openness to a dimension of ultimacy or unconditionedness in various dimensions of our common human experience. These include contingency (our joy of being alive and our anxiety about death), relativity (the interacting nexus of relative causes), temporality (the world of becoming, of transitoriness), and autonomy (our capacity to know, create, and decide). Each reveals ultimacy in a negative way ("the negative terrors of the Void without the sacred") and in a positive way ("the positive creativity of the given on which values and the capacities of our finite being and powers rest").[14]

Second, many Catholic theologians since the 1950s, such as Karl Rahner, have argued using a method called "transcendental analysis" that general knowledge of God is available because human beings are inherently open to

---

11. William Paley, *Natural Theology: Or Evidences of the Existence and Attributes of the Deity Collected from the Appearances of Nature* (1802).

12. Tillich, *Systematic Theology,* vol. 1, pp. 208-10.

13. Immanuel Kant, *Critique of Practical Reason,* book II, chapter 2.

14. Langdon Gilkey, *Naming the Whirlwind: The Renewal of God-Language* (Indianapolis: Bobbs-Merrill, 1969), p. 311. See also part 2, chapters 3-4.

"the presence of absolute mystery."[15] In such experiences as asking questions, loving, and hoping, humans are open to the infinite, and in this infinite thirst for truth are satisfied only by infinite truth, or God: in loving we move toward the infinite and are satisfied only by the infinite love that can satisfy our thirst for love; in hoping we express an infinite capacity for life, which can be satisfied only by the source of life, God. We are structured toward the infinite and can be satisfied only by the infinite God.

4. A few have argued that every rational human being knows that God necessarily exists. According to Anselm, when we recognize that "God" is a unique idea, we know God necessarily exists. Anselm defines God as "that than which nothing greater can be conceived." He then notes that the *idea* of something is always inferior to the *reality* of it; therefore a being that exists in reality as well as in thought would be greater than a being existing only in thought. Therefore, if God is "that than which nothing greater can be conceived," then God must exist. Anselm offers other support for God's existence as well, including the reflection that all perfections belong to God; existence is a perfection; therefore, necessary existence belongs to God.[16]

III. Special Revelation

A number of arguments have been made as to why general revelation is an inadequate means for Christians to know God and why special revelation is required:

1. None of the arguments for our knowledge of God based on general human experience or reason is compelling. Each one is in the end a "probability" or "most likely" argument, not a coercive one. Furthermore, each one has been shown to have decisive flaws, especially through the devastating critiques of Hume and Kant. Although revelation cannot exist apart from the human reception of it within our capabilities, and although some features of nature, history, and experience are notable enough to provide hints, possibilities, or even probabilities of God as an ultimate reality, these experiences and features of the world are so ambiguous that their significance is unavailable to us apart from some sort of "positive" or "specific" framework or lens to re-

---

15. Karl Rahner, *Foundations of Christian Faith* (New York: Seabury, 1978), pp. 44-89.

16. See Anselm, *Proslogion*, chapters 2-4. For critiques of his arguments from a philosopher's point of view, see John Hick, *Philosophy of Religion*, second ed. (Englewood Cliffs, N.J.: Prentice-Hall, 1973), chapter 2; Rem B. Edwards, *Reason and Religion* (New York: Harcourt Brace Jovanovich, 1972), chapters 9-12; Malcolm Diamond, *Contemporary Philosophy and Religious Thought* (New York: McGraw-Hill, 1974), part 4.

ceive and interpret these as implying God. While faith can be supported by features of common experience, experience can be convincing only within a particular frame of interpretation, only after we have already learned about God and have committed ourselves to search for God, only after our hearts already have been moved toward God. Although general revelation points to the possibility of our knowing God, we cannot know that our sense of mystery, wonder, order, ultimacy, or ought points to God until we have some way to interpret our sense of mystery as God.

2. General revelation suggests an idea of God as "the divine," "a divine being," "divinity," "ultimacy," or "the transcendent." But such ideas are not equivalent to the Christian concept of God. General revelation suggests the location of the idea of God within our sense of mystery, but it does not identify "the divine" as the God of Christian faith, the God of Israel and of Jesus Christ. Although any idea of special revelation depends upon our capacity as human beings to perceive and construct ultimate meanings, any concept of God growing out of our intuitions of transcendence depends on the context within which we interpret "the ultimate" as God.

3. In addition, the concept of God derived from general revelation is soteriologically inadequate. That is, it is insufficient for our "knowing God" as the source and goal of our salvation. Saving knowledge of God is, as Calvin wrote, "that by which we not only conceive that there is a God but also grasp what befits us and is proper to his glory, in fine, what is to our advantage to know of him. Indeed, we shall not say that, properly speaking, God is known where there is no religion or piety." But because of "the ruin of mankind" (original and actual sin), "no one now experiences God either as Father or as Author of salvation, or favorable in any way."[17] We may still possess a kind of secular faith in God rooted in an intuition of ultimate mystery, or in a Maker who nourishes us and blesses us. But saving knowledge of God is unavailable in general revelation apart from the gospel as special revelation.

These appraisals lead to the conclusion that the old distinction between general and special revelation cannot be sustained. As there is never any common human experience apart from historical context, so there is never any general revelation of mystery as God apart from special revelation as the way to interpret it.[18]

The old distinction depended on a notion of experience and reason which

17. Calvin, *Institutes*, vol. 1, pp. 39, 40 (1.2.1).

18. One of America's foremost philosophers, George Santayana, says, "The attempt to speak without speaking any particular language is not more hopeless than the attempt to have a religion that shall be no religion in particular." Quoted in Edwards, *Reason and Religion*, p. 5.

assumed human beings are independent of a social context. To be sure, there is no revelation apart from the capacity of the human mind to perceive the world as mystery. And we must say that all knowledge is revealed in the sense that what is known is determined by something that is already there waiting to be known. "The fact is that no true knowledge, no act of perceiving or of thinking, can be explained by beginning from the human end," writes John Baillie.[19] The mind must attend what is presented to it. So there is a passive as well as an active element in all knowledge. The mind is active in attending, selecting, and interpreting what is "out there," however. There is no revelation of mystery apart from its interpretation as mystery through the language, narrative, and concepts of human beings in particular cultures. There is no universal awareness or concept of God apart from a cultural context of such awareness. Even knowledge about what transcends particular cultures depends on the categories provided by the linguistic frameworks of culture.

There is, then, no general revelation apart from culture. Even if there are qualities or dimensions of experience that all humans experience, such as the joy of birth, the threat of death, and so forth, the meaning of these can be interpreted only through the language of particular symbol systems. Even the idea of general revelation depends on the language and symbols of a particular religion which interprets these experiences as religious, as transcendent, as knowledge about God, as saving knowledge of God.

There is, therefore, a dialectic between the ideas of general and special revelation. The specific religions could not exist apart from certain dimensions, qualities, and perceptions of the mind and spirit which human beings share simply as human beings. But none of these can have religious meaning apart from the concrete languages, rituals, and symbols of the various religions. Although the Christian revelation is rooted in and addresses our common humanity as creatures created in the image of God and creatures who are sinful through our free choices, the language of creation, creatures, image of God, freedom, fall, and sin is a distinctly Christian way to interpret the humanity we share as human. The difference between the religions is not that some depend on revelation and others do not, but that the content of what is given, how it is given, and how it is interpreted differs.[20]

In summary, then, there are two reasons the idea of general revelation cannot exist apart from special revelation, one an anthropological reason, the other a theological reason. First, we are historical creatures. We are immersed

---

19. John Baillie, *The Idea of Revelation in Recent Thought* (New York: Columbia University Press, 1956), p. 22.

20. Baillie, *The Idea of Revelation*, p. 45.

in history, so knowledge of anything, including God, is shaped by our specific place in history. The idea of revelation requires our recognition that the spatio-temporal point of view of the observer is a part of any knowledge which transcends our context. The Bible is historically and culturally conditioned; common ideas and universal experiences are always culturally shaped. Although it is "not apparent that one who knows his concepts are not universal must also doubt they are concepts of the universal,"[21] the general revelation of a transcendent God can be known only within concrete communities of believers.

Second, the Christian idea of revelation ties our knowledge of God to history. Revelation refers to a particular kind of history, not simply to a succession of events seen by an uninterested spectator from the outside, but to our inner history, our history as selves interpreted within the light of Jesus and his significance for us.[22] When we speak of revelation we mean, writes H. Richard Niebuhr, "that something has happened to us in our history which conditions all our thinking and that through this happening we are enabled to apprehend what we are, what we are suffering and doing and what our potentialities are."[23] Revelation means God discloses Godself to us through the Old Testament prophets as the Lord of history and through the New Testament as our savior.

For Christians revelation refers to God's coming to us through the people and events of Israel's heritage and through Jesus Christ. God is the God of Israel's history; God is Wisdom and Word incarnate in Christ; God is the abiding Spirit. God's self-revelation to Christians is christomorphic (Christ-shaped). Jesus, the one in our inner history who makes all the other events of history and nature intelligible, is God's self-revelation to us. Had the prophets and apostles not interpreted the events of the Bible as God's self-revelation, we would not find God in them. And yet we cannot know of God's self-revelation to the prophets and apostles unless we now see God revealed to us in them through the power of the Spirit.[24] Thus, I conclude with another one of the dialectics of theology: revelation to be revelation must be given to us; revelation to be revelation must be received and perceived as revelation. Revelation is like the denouement or decisive moment in a drama, like the point at the top of a high mountain from which all the surrounding territory can be seen and organized. Through these biblical events God is revealed to us in the

21. H. Richard Niebuhr, *The Meaning of Revelation* (New York: Macmillan, 1960), p. 18.
22. Niebuhr, *The Meaning of Revelation*, pp. 59-73.
23. Niebuhr, *The Meaning of Revelation*, p. 138.
24. Baillie, *The Idea of Revelation*, p. 105.

present. The Bible and the doctrines of the church are revelation only in the sense that they are the sources and accounts of the primary meaning of revelation, the triune God who is with us in Christ through the power of the Spirit.

IV. Elemental Faith and Saving Faith

Although revelation as self-disclosure is necessary for knowing God, revelation cannot occur until it is received and interpreted as such through faith. Neo-orthodox theologians wanted to make a distinction between revelation and religion, but, as Tillich reminds us, "they forget that revelation must be received and that the name for that reception is 'religion.' . . . He who gives an account of divine revelation simultaneously gives an account of his own religion."[25] Faith, therefore, is the anthropological counterpart to God's movement toward us. It is the epistemological correlate of revelation. There is no revelation apart from faith.

But what is this faith that is the dialectical counterpart of revelation? Does faith mean "I simply believe what I have no grounds to believe" (fideism), or "I affirm the creeds of the church" (creedalism), or "I experience God in my heart" (religious experience), or "I know God is real because everyone has a sense of mystery and awe" (common experience)?

Throughout the first two-thirds of the twentieth century, many Protestant theologians were overwhelmed by their discovery of how distorted religious feelings, commitments, and practices could become. Under the leadership of Karl Barth, these theologians made a sharp disjunction between the Word of God and human religiosity. Faith depends on the objective content of God's gracious revelation to us in Jesus Christ and in Scripture. Faith is a consequence of God's Word addressed to us as the kerygma, the message about Christ.[26] An account of faith is, first and foremost, an account of God's movement toward us. Only secondarily is it an account of the believer's response to God.

In a controversy with one of his close allies, Emil Brunner, Barth came to the point of denying there is even a "point of contact" between the divine and the human words. God addresses God's Word to us anew and from afar, a Word so dissimilar to our words ("Nein!") that we can "hear" God's Word of

---

25. Tillich, *Biblical Religion and the Search*, pp. 3-4.

26. John Webster, "faith," *Blackwell Encyclopedia of Modern Religious Thought*, ed. Alister McGrath (Oxford: Blackwell, 1993), pp. 208-10.

hope to us ("Yes!") only through God's gift of Jesus Christ as the incarnate Word and God's gift of faith to hear him as God's Word. These dual gifts have no connection with our innate human religious sensitivities and practices.[27] Faith is possible only because of revelation. Grimly, the twenty-first century has begun as another reminder of how corrupt and demonic human religion can become, "ours" as well as "theirs."[28] Nevertheless, little is gained in understanding the dialectic between God's Word and our faith by separating them, making "revelation" the good category and "religion" the bad category. The treasure of God's Word is given to us through the "earthen vessel" of religion in all its brokenness and ambiguity.

Whatever knowledge revelation provides, it is enmeshed within the fallibility and the vitality of human religiousness. I must, of course, insist from the beginning that without the logically prior graciousness of God, faith would have neither a basis nor an object. On the other hand, in our actual experience, without the active faith of the believer, there would be no revelation in the first place.[29] Although revelation is received as a gift — we are empowered by the Spirit to accept it as a call from God to us — that gift cannot be a gift until it is received through the response of faith by which it is apprehended as revelation. Faith is received through the power of grace working within the possibilities, sensibilities, and ambiguities of our experience.

This dialectic between divine grace and human possibilities, therefore, leads me to give an account of faith as a common human gift, as intrinsic to human reality.[30] The saving faith that receives Jesus Christ as God's Word to us is a species of the genus faith which belongs to us simply as human beings. There is a kind of elemental or secular faith in human existence. Although Christian faith as saving faith belongs to Christians, faith as such belongs to all people simply as human beings who cannot live without faith as a dimension of experience. Humans cannot exist apart from faith. If we can, then revelation can mean nothing to us because the faith that saves us can only be something foreign to us, some imposition from outside us which has no connection with our real character, needs, and possibilities as human beings.

I think there are two levels of this elemental faith by which human beings live. First, faith is an implicit awareness of God that exists in many, if not most, human beings. This form of faith I have discussed above as our com-

---

27. Karl Barth, "No! Answer to Emil Brunner," in *Natural Theology,* by Emil Brunner and Karl Barth (London: Centenary, 1946).

28. Andrew Sullivan, "This *Is* a Religious War," *New York Times Magazine,* October 7, 2001, pp. 44-48.

29. Ted Peters, *God — The World's Future,* pp. 69-71.

30. Webster, "faith," *Blackwell Encyclopedia.*

mon experience of God. Second, faith is a dimension of the human existence as such. There can be no human life without the presence of faith. The opposite of faith is not doubt but nihilism — the loss of order, meaning, and purpose in life.[31] But most human beings cannot and do not live their lives in such a condition, at least not for very long. While we cannot prove a world beyond our sense experience and minds, we cannot seriously doubt it either. Doubt is purely theoretical. We know it, but we can know it only by faith.

The scientist cannot operate apart from faith — faith in the dependability of nature, the orderliness and intelligibility of the universe, the unity of nature and the harmony of its laws.[32] Social life is impossible apart from faith. We cannot exist without an elemental trust in each other. If you doubt this, consider what one terrorist attack can do to undermine our confidence in the social order. And we act as if this social order is to some degree moral. We assume and affirm that there are things we ought to do and things we ought not to do.[33] Although we may not agree on which things are which, we act with moral demands that are binding. These beliefs point to the fact that we cannot exist as humans apart from faith. They are justified not because they are demonstrable but because we cannot live without them. They constitute a primordial faith.[34]

When we juxtapose generic faith with general revelation, we can say that most humans share a "creation faith." The content of the faith of secular people and the religions differs, but we all exist within the reality of faith. Christian faith is not something foreign to our existence simply as human beings. Christian faith is set within the faith capacity of human beings. Christians have a "point of contact" with others who simply as human beings are open to transcendence and structure. What is distinctive about Christian faith is the particular form and content it gives to generic faith (it is a claim about our knowledge of God in Jesus Christ), and the means by which we know the God who is revealed in Christ (it is redemption as saving faith in Christ).

In order to understand the depth of Christian faith as saving faith, we can examine more carefully the English word "faith." This word has several distinctive meanings as ways we participate in revelation,[35] meanings deriving

---

31. B. A. Gerrish, *Saving and Secular Faith: An Invitation to Systematic Theology* (Minneapolis: Fortress, 1999), p. 19.

32. Charles A. Coulson, "The Similarity of Science and Religion," in *Science and Religion: New Perspectives on the Dialogue*, ed. Ian Barbour (New York: Harper and Row, 1968), pp. 57-77.

33. Roger Rosenblatt, "The Age of Irony Comes to an End," *Time*, September 24, 2001, p. 79.

34. Gerrish, *Saving and Secular Faith*, p. 40.

35. Baillie, *The Idea of Revelation*, p. 85. See also Theodore Jennings, *Loyalty to God: The Apostles' Creed in Life and Liturgy* (Nashville: Abingdon, 1992).

from the fact that the primary New Testament word for faith (*pistis, pisteuo,* etc.) has three discrete but related meanings.[36]

1. Faith in the New Testament means *belief,* specifically, belief in God's Word in Scripture. To have faith is to assent or to give credence; it is to believe. Faith refers to our acceptance of the message of the gospel (Rom. 10:9), the kerygma; it is the saving acceptance of Christ's works as proclaimed in the gospel. Believers believe in God and in the life, death, and resurrection of Christ as this is known through the Scriptures and the preaching of the church. Faith means "belief in and acceptance of His revelation as true . . . an act of the intellect assenting to revealed truth."[37]

For Thomas Aquinas, the primary teacher of Roman Catholic theology, emphasis falls on belief as intellectual assent. He says, "Faith signifies the assent of the intellect to that which is believed . . . first, through being moved to assent by its very object . . . secondly . . . through an act of choice, whereby it turns voluntarily to one side rather than to the other."[38] Faith is not sheer fideism, however. It is assent inspired by the love of God, a theme which brings Thomas closer to the Reformers' emphasis.[39] The predominant Roman Catholic statement about the nature of faith, however, was issued by Vatican I in its efforts to correct the Reformers' distorted interpretation of faith as primarily trust in God's mercy and forgiveness. According to Vatican I, faith is a "supernatural virtue" by which "we believe that what He has revealed is true . . . because of the authority of God revealing it."[40]

A contemporary Catholic theology of faith teaches that "faith in general is to be described as a firm persuasion whereby a person assents to truths that are not seen and cannot be proved but are taken on trust in the reliability of another";[41] moreover, this persuasion contains two elements, one intellectual (firm persuasion) and the other affective (commitment to the truthfulness and trustworthiness of a witness). This first dimension of faith thus entails the belief that certain doctrines are true, and the intellectual as-

---

36. Rudolf Bultmann, "The *pistis* Group in the New Testament," in *Theological Dictionary of the New Testament,* ed. Gerhard Friedrich, trans. and ed. Geoffrey Bromily, vol. 6 (Grand Rapids: Eerdmans), pp. 203-28.

37. C. H. Pickar, "Faith, in the Bible," *New Catholic Encyclopedia,* vol. 5 (New York: McGraw-Hill, 1967), pp. 792-93.

38. Thomas Aquinas, *Summa Theologica,* II, II, question 1, article 4, in *The Basic Writings of Saint Thomas Aquinas,* vol. 2, ed. Anton Pegis (New York: Random House, 1945), p. 1060.

39. Gerrish, *Saving and Secular Faith,* pp. 6-8.

40. A. R. Jonsen, "Faith, Patristic Tradition and Teaching of the Church," *New Catholic Encyclopedia,* vol. 5, p. 797.

41. T. Urdanoz, "Faith, Theology of Faith," *New Catholic Encyclopedia,* vol. 5, p. 798.

sent to these things which are known. Faith, then, presupposes some knowledge about the God in whom we believe and the story of Jesus and its meaning for us.

2. Faith in the New Testament also means *trust* or reliance, as in Mark 5:36, Acts 3:16 and 14:9, and Hebrews 11. Faith is not only belief *about* God; it is belief *in* God. The use of the preposition "in" implies trust and confidence beyond mere intellectual belief. Faith trusts in the goodness of God like a child, faith relies on the favor of God, faith deposits our confidence in God. Faith believes in the significance of Christ for the believer, but it also trusts and depends on him as the saving person. This is the characteristic emphasis in the Protestant understanding of faith. Luther does not deny there is an element of belief in faith, but he reverses the priorities between belief about and belief in. The objective content of faith is not so much a set of propositions to which we give assent as it is our trust in the gospel story itself as God's love and forgiveness of us. "Faith is the yes of the heart . . . a confidence on which one stakes one's life," said Luther.[42] Likewise, for Calvin, although knowledge about God is a part of faith, "It is plain, then, that we do not yet have a full definition of faith, inasmuch as merely to know something of God's will is not to be accounted faith." Faith is "a firm and certain knowledge of God's benevolence toward us, founded upon the truth of the freely given promise in Christ, both revealed to our minds and sealed upon our hearts through the Holy Spirit."[43]

Although belief is part of faith, Calvin and others argued that faith "is more of the heart than of the brain, and more of the disposition than of the understanding."[44] For Calvin, faith as knowledge is closer to what we call personal knowledge than to factual knowledge, a "recognition" of the goodwill or benevolence of God directed toward us in Christ.[45] This dimension of faith has also been placed at the forefront of the Christian life by pietists, such as John Wesley and Friedrich Schleiermacher. For Wesley faith is a disposition which God brings about in our heart, "not only a divine evidence or conviction that 'God was in Christ reconciling the world unto himself,' but a sure trust and confidence that Christ died for my sins, that he loved *me,* and gave himself for *me.*"[46] For Schleiermacher Christian faith is the feeling of absolute dependence formed by the experience of redemption in Jesus

---

42. Martin Luther, Sermon for the Sunday after the Feast of Circumcision, January 4, 1540, Wiemar Edition, vol. 49, p. 9.

43. Calvin, *Institutes,* vol. 1, pp. 550, 551 (3.2.7).

44. Calvin, *Institutes,* vol. 1, p. 552 (3.2.8).

45. Gerrish, *Saving and Secular Faith,* pp. 12-13.

46. John Wesley, "Justification by Faith," *John Wesley's Sermons: An Anthology,* ed. Albert Outler and Richard Heitzenrater (Nashville: Abingdon, 1991), p. 118.

what is saving faith?

Christic.[47] This dimension of faith has also been emphasized by modern existentialists, such as Søren Kierkegaard ("the leap of faith"), Rudolf Bultmann ("openness to the future"), and Paul Tillich ("ultimate concern").

Saving faith, then, includes the communion between the person of faith and Jesus Christ himself. Faith is a kind of spirituality in which the presence of the true God is known and experienced in the midst of all kinds of experiences. N. T. Wright puts it well: "I cannot . . . imagine a Christianity in which the would-be Christian has no sense, and never has had any sense, of the presence and love of God, or the reality of prayer, of their everyday, this-worldly life being somehow addressed, interpenetrated, confronted, embraced by a personal being understood as the God we know through Jesus."[48] It includes our response to the power of the Spirit who ties us to Jesus.

> "Thou movest us to delight in praising Thee; for Thou has formed us for Thyself, and our hearts are restless till they find rest in Thee. Lord, teach me to know and understand which of all these should be first, to call on Thee, or to praise Thee; and likewise to know Thee, or to call upon Thee."
>
> SAINT AUGUSTINE

3. Faith in the New Testament also means *loyalty* (faithfulness or fidelity) to Jesus. To have faith is to commit oneself in allegiance as a faithful witness (Rev. 2:10, 13); it is to obey Jesus; it is to be loyal in life and death to the God whom we meet in Jesus Christ. Faith as faithfulness is analogous to the kind of loyalty we express outside the church, such as in the Pledge of Allegiance to the flag or in the marriage vows.[49] The Pledge is our affirmation of loyalty to the flag, that is, to the nation for which it stands. We pledge our commitment to it as an embodiment of liberty and justice for all, a pledge to which we may prove to be faithful or treasonous. Likewise, in the wedding vow we pledge our faithfulness to the other person, our exclusive loyalty to that person, renouncing all competing loyalties. "In both cases," explains Theodore Jennings, "what we claim is not belief in certain propositions about the object of our loyalty but that we will be faithful to this object of our loyalty, whether nation or person."[50] In the case of our faith in God, faith is our loyalty to the

47. F. D. E. Schleiermacher, *The Christian Faith,* vol. 1 (New York: Harper Torchbooks, 1963).

48. N. T. Wright, "The Truth of the Gospel and Christian Living," in *The Meaning of Jesus: Two Visions,* by Marcus Borg and N. T. Wright (San Francisco: HarperSanFrancisco, 1998), pp. 208-9.

49. Jennings, *Loyalty to God,* pp. 13-15.

50. Jennings, *Loyalty to God,* p. 14.

God who is known in the biblical story, especially in the life and destiny of Jesus who is the Christ, rather than to any other lesser god (i.e., to Caesar in any of his many guises).

Assent (believing that), trust (believing in), and loyalty to (faithfulness), though distinguishable, cannot be separated. Roman Catholics and Protestants increasingly are coming closer together in this understanding of faith. The danger of the Roman Catholic emphasis on belief is intellectualism. The danger of the Protestant emphasis on trust is subjectivism, which may lead not to God but to feeling itself as the object of faith. Whichever is given priority or primacy, however, these emphases belong together. We cannot embrace saving faith without affirming certain claims; we cannot trust God without believing something about God — for example, that God is, that God has come to us in a saving way in Jesus Christ, that Christ indeed can and does save us. "It's impossible to please God apart from faith. And why? Because anyone who wants to approach God must believe both that he exists *and* that he cares enough to respond to those who seek him" (Heb. 11:6, *The Message*). Even if faith is primarily trust and confidence, beliefs are the way by which our recognition of God's graciousness to us is interpreted and nourished. Even though we may not be self-conscious about those beliefs, we are believing something. Faith as belief, trust, and loyalty converge as saving faith when we become conscious enough about our faith to say, "I believe," meaning "I believe most deeply that . . . I base my deepest confidence in . . . I am loyal to the convictions that. . . ."

Saving faith, however, does not mean two things it is frequently assumed to mean. First of all, it does not mean that there is no doubt amidst faith. Faith does not mean that I believe odd propositions which I simply repeat and swallow without any questions or thought. Indeed, the kind of faith I have been describing here entails a degree of impudence. Faith in God not only permits but requires questioning. Genuine saving faith is an "audacious faith"; it is "a dialectic of trust and chutzpa." Moses haggles with God (Num. 11:10-15); Jeremiah complains against God (Jer. 20:7-12); Job grills God throughout the entire book that bears his name; one third of the Psalms are laments. Tillich goes so far as to include existential doubt within the act of faith itself.

> Existential doubt and faith are poles of the same reality, the state of ultimate concern. . . . The doubt which is implicit in every act of faith is neither the methodological nor the skeptical doubt. It is the doubt that accompanies every risk . . . the doubt of him who is ultimately concerned about a concrete content. One could call it existential doubt. At the same

time, the doubt which is implicit in faith accepts this insecurity and takes it into itself as an act of courage. Faith includes courage. Therefore, it can include the doubt about itself.[51]

Faith that includes doubt is apparent among the letters and diaries of Mother Teresa, which indicate that she lived a lifetime of spiritual struggle, including years of loneliness, helplessness, and abandonment, and that she was tempted to abandon her work caring for the poor and dying.[52] The experience of darkness within the life of faith can be found in the work of Julian of Norwich, Luther, Wesley, and Bonhoeffer as well.

Second, Christian faith does not imply there is no saving faith in the other religions. To have saving faith in the God of Jesus Christ in the three senses described here does not imply that God is not free to speak wherever and however God chooses to bring well-being to the creation. Here I simply note that claims about saving faith in Jesus Christ do not require the claim that saving faith cannot be and is not known outside the church. I will explore that question later.

V. The Faith of the Church

Saving faith is our response in belief, trust, and loyalty to God in Christ as proclaimed in the faith of the Christian church. Saving faith includes belief as well as trust and commitment. Recognizing how anathema this claim is to some modern Christians, I nevertheless want to claim that one cannot be a Christian without being part of — or at least drawing directly upon the resources of — a living community which possess a story and set of practices, symbols, and beliefs which constitute "the Christian faith." There is no private Christian faith apart from the language, narratives, and behaviors of the church or the Christian tradition. I do not mean by this a particular denomination. Rather, I refer to the community which loves and serves God by taking on the stories and practices of those who believe, trust, and are loyal to Jesus Christ.

Faith as the faith of the church takes many forms. Paul, in perhaps the earliest "statement of faith," says, "I handed on to you as of first importance what I in turn had received," and then proceeds to summarize the gospel, concluding that "Whether then it was I or they, so we proclaim and so you have

---

51. Paul Tillich, *The Dynamics of Faith* (New York: Harper Torchbooks, 1957), pp. 20-22.

52. Laurinda Keys, "Writings Express Mother Teresa's Doubts," *Dayton Daily News,* September 15, 2001, p. 6A.

come to believe" (1 Cor. 15:3, 11). Elsewhere he refers to the message of the church as "the faith he once tried to destroy" (Gal. 1:23). Acts 6:7 and Ephesians 4:5 refer to faith as the church's teaching, as do 1 Timothy 1:2 and 2:7; Titus 1:1, 4; 2 Peter 1:1; and Jude 1:20. Saving faith is dependent on our reception and response in belief, trust, and loyalty to God's gracious revelation in Jesus Christ as that is received, formed, and proclaimed by the church. Faith in this sense, then, refers as much to the object of faith, the content of faith, "the deposit of faith" *(fides quae),* as to the apprehension of and response to Christ by the faithful believer *(fides qua).*

There are many forms of this faith which make up the content of the church's proclamation. Some of them are nonverbal forms, some are strictly verbal forms, most are a combination of verbal and nonverbal forms. Nonverbal forms of faith include dance, genuflecting before an altar, rising for the reading of the gospel, moving to the table to receive the bread and wine, raising one's arms with palms turned up while singing a praise song. Moving through the stations of the cross, gazing at stained glass windows in a church building, "going forward" in an evangelistic meeting to make "a decision for Christ" are also nonverbal but ritualized forms of faith, as is standing in awe under the overarching vault of a medieval cathedral. The Christian faith combines behaviors and words in the cadences of a sermon of an African-American preacher or of Handel's *Messiah,* in singing a praise song or a hymn like "Love Divine, All Loves Excelling," in standing to recite the Apostles' Creed following the sermon. These are "forms of faith" through which we participate in the faith of the church.

For human beings, language has a fundamental role in making us human. We are constituted as "human" by our language.[53] Indeed, one way to describe the Christian faith is to call it "a language," meaning it is one way to construct the world through words. Although nonlinguistic forms of faith are essential to this faith of the church, Christian faith also consists of symbols metaphors, narratives, propositions, teachings, and creeds. The basic symbols which convey our primary meanings to us include not only symbols, such as the cross and water, but also metaphors, such as the Word of God, the Kingdom of God, and the Lamb of God. The faith also encompasses myths, prayers, poetry, rhetoric (preaching), and moral directives (morality), as well as hymns and histories, the biographies of heroines and heroes of the church, and the various forms of worship and polity.[54]

---

53. Gordon Kaufman, *Systematic Theology: A Historicist Perspective* (New York: Scribners, 1968), p. 4.

54. Gerrish, *Saving and Secular Faith,* p. 84.

One form of the faith of the church is its theology. The theological content of faith is located, primarily, in the great theological symbols of the church, such as the Trinity, creation, providence, sin, grace, reconciliation, justification, sanctification, and eschatology. Though rooted in the language of Scripture, these theological symbols are formulated in the confessions of faith of the church. By "confessions," I refer to such documents as the dogmas and creeds of the ecumenical church (Apostles', Nicene) and the formal confessions of faith of many denominations: the Book of Concord (Lutheran), the Book of Confessions (Presbyterian), Articles of Religion (Episcopalian), Articles of Faith (Church of the Nazarene, National Baptist Convention), Statement of Faith (United Church of Christ), and Articles of Religion, Confession of Faith, and General Rules (United Methodist).

In some Protestant churches, however, this "content" of the church's faith is not acknowledged in official formulas. Indeed, some church members do not know or even deny that they subscribe to a "confession" of faith. Faith is individual and personal: they will not be confined by any creed or normed by any dogma which will stifle the vitality of their living faith. Nevertheless, all Christians are part of a church which has some functional equivalent of a confession of faith. They repeat it when the sacraments are celebrated; they hear it recited again and again as doctrinal information and formation through the preaching and teaching of the pastor; they sing their confessions of faith as hymns every Sunday (which frequently include the language and formulas of the ecumenical creeds of the church). Even "we have no creed but Christ" is a creed.

> "The biblical story came to me first as prayer in worship, and nobody spent any time insisting on its factuality, its inerrancy, or its literal truth."
>
> **JOHN DOMINIC CROSSAN**

Although some Protestant churches formally reject the authority of the creeds, or more typically simply ignore them because their church is not a "formal" or a "catholic" or a "liturgical" church, the reality is that the members of almost all Protestant churches learn and affirm the content of the ecumenical creeds of the church — through their spiritual formation retreats, teaching seminars, or Emmaus Walks, but especially through their preaching, liturgy, and hymnody. Although hymns serve many functions in the life of the church, one of their functions, especially in the case of those hymns written by the Protestant Reformation (those by Luther, Isaac Watts, and Charles Wesley, for example), is to help us learn and recite the content of the creeds and doctrines of the church Sunday after Sunday by singing them to memorable verses and tunes. "For the most part, Watts' hymns are rhymed theology, and the theology is derived from John Calvin. . . . Charles Wesley's hymns are a textbook of Methodist theology."[55] Increasingly, this claim can be made of Roman Catholic worship. It is also true of some of the songs sung in contemporary worship among the megachurches.

Faith as the confessions of the church, then, can be defined in both a very broad and a very narrow sense. Conceived in the larger sense, the confessions of faith of the church are the recitals of the story of the gospel, that is, those great narrative events connected with Israel, with the life, death, and resurrection of Jesus, and with what happened to the community of his disciples. The church's creed, in this sense, is its repetition and affirmation of the apostolic witness to Jesus Christ as Savior and Lord. The church's primary confession of faith is its recital of the mystery of salvation in and through Christ, its affirmation of God's redemptive love in human life by the activity of the Holy Spirit. In this way the community through adoration, proclamation, and service is conformed to Christ and his present and future reign.

The Christian confessions refer in the narrower sense to the community's formal "confessions of faith." Faith in this form lies at the heart of Scripture. Central to the Old Testament is the primary creed of the Hebrew faith in the form of a narrative summary:

> you shall make this response before the LORD your God: "A wandering Aramean was my ancestor; he went down into Egypt and lived there as an alien, few in number, and there he became a great nation, mighty and populous. When the Egyptians treated us harshly and afflicted us, by imposing hard labor on us, we cried to the LORD, the God of our ancestors; the LORD heard our voice and saw our affliction, our toil, and our oppression. The LORD brought us out of Egypt with a mighty hand and an outstretched arm, with a terrifying display of power, and with signs and wonders; and he brought us into this place and gave us this land, a land flowing with milk and honey." (Deut. 26:5-9)

In the New Testament kerygmatic faith frequently takes creedal form, sometimes in very short form, such as "Jesus is the Messiah" (cf. Mark 8:29) and "Jesus is Lord" (Rom. 10:9), sometimes in diadic or triadic formulas, such as those in 1 Corinthians 8:6, Matthew 28:19, and 2 Corinthians 13:13, and sometimes in longer summaries, such as 1 Corinthians 15:3-7 and Philippians 2:6-

---

55. Albert Bailey, *The Gospel in Hymns: Backgrounds and Interpretations* (New York: Scribners, 1950); cf. S. Paul Schilling, *The Faith We Sing: How the Message of Hymns Can Enhance Christian Belief* (Philadelphia: Westminster, 1983).

11. These confessions of faith state the basic affirmations of the church's beliefs in brief, direct, and summary propositions.

Nevertheless, creeds and confessions of faith are problematic for some modern Christians. They object both to the content of the creeds and to a role for creeds in the Christian life. Creeds compete with the unique authority of Scripture. Adherence to creeds violates the freedom of conscience of the individual Christian. Creeds close the mind of the believer to the communication of new truth through the Holy Spirit. They will not repeat something in a creed or confession of faith which they do not believe, such as the virgin birth, bodily ascension, or the return of Jesus. Any effort on the part of the church to state its faith — a confession of faith as orthodoxy (right teaching) — is authoritarian. Creeds are instruments of intolerance and are filled with obsolete ideas. They make faith formal instead of spiritual. Creeds substitute orthodoxy for the true faith embodied in orthopraxis (right practice) and orthopathy (right sentiments).

There is something to say on behalf of our modern suspicion of the creeds. The most important caution is that creeds do not constitute the being of the church. The church is constituted by belief in, trust in, and loyalty to Jesus Christ as God with us. Nevertheless, creeds serve the well-being of the church in a variety of ways:[56]

1. Creeds are one among the many instruments of socialization of faith. Because faith in its three forms — belief, trust, and loyalty — must be acquired, one of the ways it is acquired is through learning to speak, act, think, and feel as the community of faith does. Through constant recollection and repetition, the creeds help to construct and preserve identity, to form the believer as part of the Christian community. Justifying that faith, by explaining what we do and do not mean by our symbols and doctrines, reforming that faith by purging it of its ideological elements and repudiating them, interpreting that faith in the language and thought forms of our time, correlating that faith with our other beliefs — in short, engaging in theology — is a next step in our inhabiting and living out "the deposit of faith" we receive through tradition as an inheritance from our community. But we think reflectively about what we have received as our common heritage.

2. Just as there are common practices in which most Christians engage — hearing and reading Scripture, praying, preaching, sacraments, singing, acts of love and mercy — so there are common beliefs which underlie these practices. These are affirmed by most Christians. Unlike the distinctive doctrines and idiosyncratic opinions of denominations and individual Christians, the

---

56. Gerrish, *Saving and Secular Faith*, p. 66.

ecumenical creeds provide a near consensus of the ecumenical church about our common beliefs.

3. Confessions of faith are one form of our pledge of allegiance and loyalty to Jesus Christ and to his community, the church. They are ways we personally and as the church declare our reliance on the good news of the gospel. F. D. Maurice puts it well:

> The view which the Liturgy takes of the Creeds is sufficiently evident from the mode of their introduction into it. They are made parts of our worship; acts of allegiance, declarations by the whole congregation of the Name into which each one has been baptized; preparations for prayer; steps to communion. The notion of them as mere collections of dogmas is never once insinuated, is refuted by the whole order of the services.[57]

It is worth noting that the only creeds that have been able to sustain nearly universal support among Christians are creeds which for the most part are recitations of primary events of the gospel. They are reminders of the events in the history of Israel and Jesus by which our salvation is secured.

---

57. F. D. Maurice, *The Kingdom of Christ*, third ed. (1883), 367, quoted in Baillie, *The Idea of Revelation*, p. 104.

CHAPTER FOUR

Faith in God

I. Awareness of God

"God" is the subject and the object of theology. God is both a proper name (the subject whom we worship) and a noun (the object of our thinking). God is at once a wholly transcendent reality, infinitely beyond our comprehension, and the most intimate reality in our lives, closer than our own hands and feet. One quandary a new theologian faces in thinking about God is whether to begin with our common awareness of mystery, and give distinctive Christian content and shape to that experience, or to begin with the triune God, speaking only of the Lord of creation who has come to us distinctively in Jesus Christ and continues to work through the power of the Spirit.

Mystery and Transcendence

While the *content* and *shape* of the Christian idea of God depend on the Bible, liturgies, creeds, and doctrines of the church, the *concept* of God is rooted in a nearly universal sense that reality is more than we perceive through our five senses. As we discussed in the last chapter, every concept of God, including the Christian one, originates in our awareness of mystery. We are awed by the sheer givenness of the world and of ourselves. Even as children we ask, "Why is there something rather than nothing?" "Why do I exist?" Negatively, we know the possibility of nonbeing; positively, we are aware of the brute "thereness" of things.[1]

---

1. See Paul Tillich, *Systematic Theology*, vol. 1 (Chicago: University of Chicago Press, 1951),

Our intuition of mystery includes both an experiential and a conceptual dimension.[2] Simply as humans we are aware of something we know not what — the Beyond, the More, Being-Itself, Ultimacy, Creativity — some "dimension of depth." Conceptually, mystery refers to something we cannot get our minds around, cannot manage to grasp. Mystery is not the same as a puzzle whose pieces we have to fit together, nor is it the same as a problem we face as a difficulty to overcome. Both of these are solvable. In face of mystery we face utter bafflement.[3] Our response is not as much a matter of knowledge as it is of acknowledgment. We encounter this dimension of reality as an experience of the utterly incomprehensible, the sheer awesomeness of existence. Paul appealed to this pervasive experience when he introduced his God by arguing,

> he allotted the times of their existence and the boundaries of the places where they would live, so that they would search for God and perhaps grope for him and find him — though indeed he is not far from each one of us. For "In him we live and move and have our being"; as even some of your own poets have said, "For we too are his offspring." (Acts 17:26-28)

Our experience of mystery prompts us to speak of the transcendence of God. Transcendence is the theological word for the "otherness" of God. God is the source or origin of the world, not simply one more being in the world. God is beyond the world. No one has ever seen God; no one can imagine the ultimate reality. As the Westminster Confession of Faith states,

> There is but one only living and true God, who is infinite in being and perfection, a most pure spirit, invisible, without body, parts, or passions, immutable, immense, eternal, incomprehensible, almighty, most wise, most holy, most free, most absolute, working all things according to the counsel of his own immutable and most righteous will, for his own glory.[4]

---

pp. 187-99; and Bernard Meland, *Fallible Forms and Symbols: Discourses on Method in a Theology of Culture* (Philadelphia: Fortress, 1976), chapters 4-5.

2. Gordon Kaufman, *In Face of Mystery: A Constructive Theology* (Cambridge: Harvard University Press, 1993), p. 60.

3. Kaufman, *In Face of Mystery,* pp. 60-61.

4. "The Westminster Confession of Faith," *The Constitution of the Presbyterian Church (USA), Part I, Book of Confessions* (Louisville: Office of the General Assembly, 1996), p. 128 (number 6.011).

Nearness and Immanence & transcendence

The danger in overemphasizing God as "wholly-other" is that God becomes utterly unknowable. And whatever is unknowable is unknown. Theologians who fixate on the otherness of God threaten to make it impossible to affirm the other side of our common experience of the divine mystery, the nearness of God. God is present in the creation and dwells in the hearts of the creatures. "I dwell in the high and holy place, and also with those who are contrite and humble in spirit, to revive the spirit of the humble, and to revive the heart of the contrite," we read in Isaiah (57:15). God cares, reprimands, tries one thing after another, is involved in the troubles of creatures, redeems the creatures, and brings the whole creation to its ultimate purpose. The Westminster Confession also affirms this side of the dialectic in the same article of the creed: "Most loving, gracious, merciful, long-suffering, abundant in goodness and truth, forgiving iniquity, transgression, and sin; the rewarder of them that diligently seek him; and withal most just and terrible in judgments; hating all sin, and who will by no means clear the guilty."[5]

The danger in overemphasizing the nearness of God is that God will seem not to exist independent of human creatures. Therefore, Christians introduce a dialectic into their concept of God. God is utterly unlike the ordinary things with which we are familiar, yet God is concerned about and involved with the world. Our basic theological claim is that God is both transcendent *and* immanent. God is absolute *and* related, impersonal *and* personal, eternal *and* temporal, changeless *and* changing, self-sufficient *and* dependent. Any effort to construct a Christian idea of God from the mystery which surrounds our existing and not-existing entails this dialectic of transcendence and immanence. "The central problem for a doctrine of God is how to unite intelligibly the absoluteness of God as the unconditioned source of our total being with the dynamic relatedness and the reciprocal activity of God as the ground, guide, dialogical partner, and redeemer of our freedom," writes Langdon Gilkey.[6] Our task is to explain how these poles can be joined without contradiction. Classical theism, recent developments in theism, and the doctrine of the Trinity all seek to affirm this dialectical relationship in our concept of God.

---

5. "Westminster Confession of Faith," p. 128 (number 6.011).

6. Langdon Gilkey, "God," in *Christian Theology: An Introduction to Its Traditions and Tasks,* ed. Peter C. Hodgson and Robert H. King (Philadelphia: Fortress, 1982), p. 82.

Language about God

I want to be clear that I am talking about our *concept* of God. In thinking about God we must distinguish between the "reality" of God (the mystery to which the term God refers) and the "concept" of God (the idea we create in our religious practices and thought). Our concept points to something metaphysically *real*, a cosmic agent, agency, or activity that creates us and moves us toward fulfillment. The idea of God implies that our being conscious, purposive, loving, and free is undergirded by the very nature of things.[7] But we cannot deny that the *concept* of God is a human construct.

The first thing to emphasize in constructing our concept of God is the limits to all God-language. The transcendence of God emphasizes that we do not and cannot know the Godhead or God because as finite creatures we are incapable of any direct knowledge of the ultimate mystery. Since finite minds cannot comprehend the infinite, we are incapable of describing God directly. There is a sense in which all theology is *apophatic* (*apophasis* in Greek means "denial"). We can speak of God only *via negitiva* (by way of negation), saying what God is not. God is not complex (so is one), does not change (so is immutable), is not finite (so is infinite), and is not limited by time (so is eternal), or by space (so is omnipresent), or in power (so is omnipotent), or in knowledge (so is omniscient).

In the end, however, *via negativa* prohibits all talk about God. "Pure denials tell us nothing about what God *is*," writes Gordon Kaufman. "Indeed, they cannot even distinguish him from nothingness, of which everything positive can also be denied."[8] Furthermore, the mystery referred to in Scripture and in Trinitarian doctrine is not mystery per se, but rather is the mystery of the presence of the God of Israel and the God of our Lord, Jesus Christ. We can conclude along with Clark Williamson that apophatic theology is "a high price to pay for our talk of God, if our language is to be appropriate to the gospel of God's love graciously offered to each and all in Jesus Christ and God's command that justice be done to each and all."[9]

The task of theology, then, is not to produce an infallible concept of God. It is to construct a concept that is adequate to the testimony about the living God who comes to us in gracious love and mercy in the history of Israel and

7. Gordon Kaufman, *The Theological Imagination: Constructing the Concept of God* (Philadelphia: Westminster, 1981), pp. 46-51.

8. Gordon Kaufman, *Systematic Theology: A Historicist Perspective* (New York: Scribners, 1968), p. 121.

9. Clark Williamson, *Way of Blessing, Way of Life: A Christian Theology* (St. Louis: Chalice, 1999), p. 102.

metaphors

the gospel of Christ. The alternative, *cataphatic* theology, moves toward positive language by talking about God as immanent in the world, whether by using the most general concepts available (such as Being, Life, Creativity, the Source of Human Good), or by using the biblical story of Israel and Jesus (with its metaphors of Creator, Lord, Father, Wisdom, Word, and Spirit), or by using the Trinitarian language of baptism, Eucharist, liturgies, and creeds. An adequate doctrine of God, therefore, stands somewhere between complete skepticism (the apophatic insistence that God is not, in reality, any of these things) and blasphemy (the effort to overcome ultimate mystery with claims that we can know directly and literally who God is). All our language about God is limited because we are finite, limited, and sinful. Our idea of God can easily become an ideology. For example, God can become a male, or white, or on our side in a holy war on terror.

The solution to this danger is to be clear about the character of all our language about God. We possess no direct, literal, univocal language about God. Scripture offers a revealed name ("I am"), and some philosophical theologians suggest that God can be literally designated. For example, for St. Thomas God is *"Purus actus"* (pure actuality), for Tillich God is "Being itself," for others God is simply "the Godhead." But such terms are so abstract that they are not very useful for a doctrine of God. Even if one accepts one of these terms as literal language about God, I must emphasize that *all* our other language is symbolic. Our language resides somewhere along a continuum between univocal or literal reference, on the one end (which threatens to end in idolatry), to equivocal or apophatic, on the other (with the threat of being empty of any meaning). We must say that all of our talk about God is symbolic, metaphorical, or analogical, each of these terms emphasizing that our language to some degree does *and* does not properly speak of God.

Christians name God as "I am," "Yahweh," and "Trinity." We describe God as spirit, living, personal, good, loving, sovereign, free, holy, and just. We affirm that God acts, loves, judges, and delivers. But how can these words apply to God when God is infinite and all our language is derived from the finite world? They can when we acknowledge that these words are symbolic (image, parable, metaphor, story, analogy).[10] As spirit God is living, most apparent

10. Some theories of symbols understand symbols to be sacramental in the sense that they "figure" or "re-present" or "participate in" the world of ultimate reality or being itself. The larger meaning of symbol, however, and the one used here, is that symbols serve as images and metaphors, words which spot a thread of similarity between two dissimilar objects, events, or whatever, one of which is better known than the other, and use the better known one as a way of speaking about the lesser known one. Metaphor says, "it is and it is not." Almost all of our language about God is symbolic, or metaphorical, in this sense. It may be through images such as

when in the Scripture God decides, plans, acts, alters, withdraws, draws near, and repents. Many Christians, therefore, speak about God as "a person." But this language can be dangerous to use, especially when we describe this "person" as a Father.[11] If God is "a person," even a "world-transcending super person," God is still one more "thing" in the world. If the noun "person" or the

---

that of God as our rock; or it may be through "analogies of being" (we can say God is wise because there is a similarity as well as a dissimilarity between divine wisdom and human wisdom since human wisdom "participates in" divine wisdom on the basis of the relation between the creator and creatures); or it may be through the "analogy of faith" (in which our language can and does refer to God because God from time to time causes our words to conform to the divine being, through the whole understanding of the Christian gospel [Barth] or through the notion that God "accommodates" our finitude and sin by speaking in familiar signs and images [Calvin]; but however the case may be, all language about God describes God as the ultimate reality which in some ways is similar to our experienced and constructed reality of the world and in others ways is not like our experience and words at all. For highly influential accounts of theological language as metaphor, see several works by Sallie McFague: *Speaking in Parables: A Study in Metaphor and Theology* (Philadelphia: Fortress, 1975); *Metaphorical Theology: Models of God in Religious Language* (Philadelphia: Fortress, 1982); *Models of God: Theology for an Ecological, Nuclear Age* (Philadelphia: Fortress, 1987); and *The Body of God: An Ecological Theology* (Minneapolis: Fortress, 1993).

11. The question of the nature of our language about God, and the importance of being clear about how the language applies, is obvious in calling God "Father," in the Scripture, in the doctrines of the Trinity, and in the liturgical life of the church, most especially in prayer. Since there is a close connection between our language about God and the exercise of power in the church, by describing God as "Father," and by referring to God in our doctrine and in our prayers primarily if not exclusively as "he," we learn that like God who is a male, males name and control the world in their image also. Exclusive language about God as "Father" and "he" not only reflects the history of patriarchy but continues to justify male domination in the church and in society. If God is the ultimate reality, and if the ultimate reality is "he" instead of "she," and "father" instead of "mother," then there is something at the very heart of reality which makes the male preferable to the female. Exclusively male language about God implies this conclusion, sometimes in subtle and sometimes in not so subtle ways. Although no language about God is free of ambiguity, the predominant language about God as "Father" and "he" has been disastrous for women. One strategy for remedy is to be clear about what the metaphor does and does not mean. It does not mean God is a male. "Father" refers, rather, to the God who covenants with Israel and to the God whom Jesus loved, obeyed, and prayed to as his heavenly parent. Above all the metaphor refers to the nearness and intimacy of God. "God the father" is not a doctrine (even by implication) about the gender of God. It is a form of address to God (Abba), used by Jesus and derivatively shared by his followers (in the Lord's Prayer). It connotes intimacy with and trust in the one who loves us and who is faithful and merciful to us like a parent (features more commonly associated with motherhood!). God the Father in the Scripture is not primarily the patriarch of male domination but is the source and origin of the clan or the family inheritance, the one who protects and provides, the one to whom obedience and honor is due. (See Marianne Meye Thompson, *The Promise of the Father: Jesus and God in the New Testament* [Louisville: Westminster/John Knox, 2000].)

adjective "personal" apply to God, we must be clear that there are ways in which the noun and the adjective do apply, and there are ways in which they do not apply.[12]

God is living as opposed to dying, yes; God is living in the sense that God is an agency to whom the above verbs apply, yes. But "living" is a biological term that applies properly to the vegetable and animal world, a very limited range of cosmic reality. Therefore the term does not apply directly to God, who is the transcendent source and ground of all living things. All of our God-talk is symbolic.

II. God in the Bible

While our concept of God is rooted in our human awareness of mystery, transcendence, and presence, this holy mystery is identified by Christians as Yahweh and the Father of our Lord Jesus Christ. Prior to any doctrine of God, God is presented, identified, and described in the Bible. Christians cannot think about God apart from the story of Israel and of Jesus. This does not mean that thinking about God is restricted to the biblical narrative and images. The doctrine of the Trinity, classical theism, openness theism, and pan-

---

12. Attempts to avoid all anthropomorphisms will not work, for all language, even the language about a "world transcending" personal being, agency, or power, takes its bearings from the finite world of human experience and is constructed by human thinking. Furthermore, the christological language about God in the Trinity ties the meaning of God to a human person, and therefore, the Christian conviction about the nearness of God through covenant, mercy, and love, and ultimately in Jesus Christ, requires that Christians use personal language to talk about God. Nevertheless, we do better by speaking of God as "personal" instead of as "a person," indicating that although Christians do not think that God is simply one more being, or a unique cosmic creature in the universe, God is not impersonal. God is not "a person" and is not "personal" in the sense that God is *more than* a person or personal. But God is not impersonal either, an "it," for only a "thou" is capable of the relationships of love and mercy and kindness we discover about the God of Israel and incarnate in Jesus Christ. Therefore, personal language about God is necessary. On the analogy of faith, as in Barth, God is the full meaning of the word "person," God alone is the truly "personal one," God is the one who freely decides to love and redeem all of the creation through the incarnation in Jesus Christ. A similar concept of "person" is proposed in panentheistic concepts of God, such as Charles Hartshorne's, in which God is the universal and all-inclusive person, the eminent person, the one individual who is perfectly related to all individuals, the one in whom personhood is made possible, we being the imperfect and dependent occasion of "a person" because we can relate only fallibly and to a few of the creatures while God relates perfectly to all. God is not a human person, not a supernatural person, but the all-embracing cosmic person through whom all personhood is possible and has its meaning and fulfillment.

entheism all move beyond the language of the Bible. But the primary source and norm for our thinking about God is the Bible.

Scripture, however, does not reward us with a doctrine of God. It tells us a story of the history of Israel and the life of Jesus and the church in which God is the central character. "It is remarkable that the Old Testament does not accent thought or concept or idea, but characteristically *speech*. God is the one about whom Israel speaks," writes Walter Brueggemann.[13] Biblical talk about God, the subject of hundreds of verbs, is the language of testimony rather than theology or ontology. What most of us refer to as "the biblical God" is in fact a theological-philosophical construction retrojected back into the Bible through the glasses of the doctrine of "classical theism."

The task of the theologian who intends to be biblical, then, is to describe what the Bible says about God and to use that testimony as the norm to construct a Christian doctrine of God.[14] The Bible itself, however, simply affirms God and then testifies to the identity and character of God by using names ("I am," "Yahweh," "Lord," "God," and "Father"), images (judge, king, warrior, artist, healer, gardener, mother, and shepherd), and accounts of events in Israel's and the church's history. The Bible describes God primarily by describing God's activity. God is the central agent in a long, complex, ambiguous, but hopeful story which begins with creation and ends with a new heaven and a new earth.

God speaks, is spoken to, and is spoken about in Scripture. God's capacity both for sovereignty and for solidarity with creatures is disclosed through a series of verbs as the one who creates (Isa. 42:5), makes promises (Gen. 22:16-18; Deut. 6:23), delivers (Exod. 6:6), commands (Exod. 34:11), leads (Deut. 8:2-3), brings good news to the poor and needy (Luke 4:18-19), and suffers on behalf of all humanity (Phil. 2:6-11). In both testaments God is an agent of unlimited sovereignty and risky solidarity with the enslaved and op-

---

13. Walter Brueggemann, *Theology of the Old Testament: Testimony, Dispute, Advocacy* (Minneapolis: Fortress, 1997), p. 117.

14. My discussion here draws heavily on the work of Terence Fretheim, "God," *Eerdmans Dictionary of the Bible* (Grand Rapids: Eerdmans, 2000), pp. 510-14, his *The Suffering of God: An Old Testament Perspective* (Philadelphia: Fortress, 1984), especially chapters 3-5, and his (with Karlfried Froehlich) *The Bible As Word of God: In a Postmodern Age* (Minneapolis: Fortress, 1998), part 2. I also use the work of Brueggemann, *Theology of the Old Testament*, especially parts 1 and 2, and his *Old Testament Theology: Essays in Structure, Theme, and Text* (Minneapolis: Fortress, 1992), especially chapters 1 and 2; and I draw on Thomas R. W. Longstaff, "God," in *Harper Collins Bible Dictionary* (San Francisco: HarperSanFrancisco, 1996), pp. 381-82; and Richard Rice, "Biblical Support for a New Perspective," in *The Openness of God: A Biblical Challenge to the Traditional Understanding of God,* ed. Clark Pinnock et al. (Downers Grove, Ill.: InterVarsity, 1994), pp. 11-58.

pressed in Egypt and the poor and marginalized in Palestine. The first and primary biblical word about God, then, is that God is "merciful and gracious, slow to anger and abounding in steadfast love" (Ps. 103:8); God's steadfast love "shall not depart from you" (Isa. 54:10) and "endures forever" (Ps. 136:1-3; Jer. 33:11). "Whoever does not love does not know God, for God is love" (1 John 4:8). Indeed, the claim "God is love" is about as close as the Bible comes to defining God.

If we try to define the biblical God in theological terms, we can say that God is unique and incomparable. God is a living and eternal agent, whose existence is assumed to be without beginning or end and who is not dependent on anyone or anything for existence. God is one, not composed of various divinities or beings, and so is united as one self. God is holy and other, but God is also present and active in the world, a part of the map of reality and related to all that is not God. Thus God is a social reality, functioning within a community in a relationship of mutuality, richness, and complexity with the creatures. God chooses to be dependent on the creatures for the decisions of history and the continuing care of the world. God enters into relationship with the creation, so creatures make a difference to God. God is lovingly present, never actually absent though that may be perceived to be the case. God has a range of intense feelings, including joy, delight, grief, anger, and regret. God's actions are intentional acts of the will serving God's purposes for the world. God makes decisions (Gen. 18:23-32; Exod. 32:14), and repents or changes God's mind (Gen. 6:6-7; 1 Sam. 15:35; Jer. 18:7-11; Hos. 11:8-9). God dwells with Israel and the church, acting in Israel's history, especially through the exodus, monarchy, exile,

> "It is not enough to say that you believe in God. What is important finally is the kind of God in whom you believe. Metaphors matter. The images you use to speak of God will not only shape how you think about God, but will also shape your life."
>
> **TERENCE FRETHEIM**

and restoration, and in the church through Jesus Christ and Pentecost. But God's work is not limited to Israel and the church. God is universally active in the whole world.

Nevertheless, it is impossible to formulate a thoroughly coherent account of God in Scripture given the diverse narratives, verbs, and adjectives used to describe to God. As anyone who has worked her way through "Disciple Bible Study" or similar in-depth Bible study knows, very early in the story there is contradictory testimony about God. God is sometimes an actor whose character is ambiguous, described in ways that fly in the face of the primary witness to God's faithful mercy and lovingkindness. Sometimes hidden and inscrutable, God is at other times unreliable, negative, abusive, and extraordinarily destructive. There are "texts of terror" in the biblical testimony, such as the *cherem* or "ban" passages in Joshua 6–7, where "The city and all that is in it shall be devoted to the LORD for destruction" (6:17). God "blot[s] out" (Gen. 6:7); God seems willing to abuse children by commanding Abraham to "Take your son, your only son Isaac, whom you love . . . and offer him there as a burnt offering" (Gen. 22:2); God "kills and makes alive, wounds and heals" (cf. Deut. 32:39); God "[makes] my lifetime as nothing in your sight" (cf. Ps. 39:5), "put[s] me in the depths of the Pit" (Ps. 88:6); God's "dread assaults destroy me" (Ps. 88:16); God is a leader of bloody battles who consigns millions of nonbelievers to eternal punishment (Rev. 19–20).

What shall we to do with the texts that describe God as sometimes for and sometimes against us?[15] Some have argued that such "texts of terror" are marginal to the whole biblical witness and therefore negligible — a dismissal rather difficult to promote in a day when Jewish, Christian, and Islamic fundamentalists use such texts to justify a holy war. Others interpret such texts as the misguided efforts of some culturally bound groups within Israel or the church to understand God's will (*cherem* is a term used in the Moabite Stone and so comes from Israel's surrounding culture, not God). Still others let these texts stand beside the dominant texts as unresolved tensions in the biblical testimony. Such texts witness to something about God that the biblical writers experienced and did not deny, namely, that God's mercy and lovingkindness is, indeed, also, at times, arbitrary, harsh, and destructive.

Many interpreters, however, believe such texts describe characteristics of God which fit properly within the context of God's whole covenant with Israel and the church. There is no conflict, they say, if these texts of terror are seen as witness to complementary sides of the righteousness of the God who makes a covenant with Israel and the church. God's wrath is not an expression of self-indulgent self-assertion but the complementary side of God's righteous resolve in mercy to prevent humanity's slide into chaos and amorality. They are corresponding sides of the love of God who out of covenant faithfulness acts in these ways to sustain a moral universe.[16] Divine mercy and wrath require each other. Love (mercy) and harshness (vengeance, retribution, arbitrariness, unpredictability) are compatible.

---

15. Brueggemann, *Theology of the Old Testament*, p. 282.

16. Paul Hanson, "A New Challenge to Biblical Theology," *Journal of the American Academy of Religion* 67, no. 1 (1999): 454-59; "Can We Find God without History?" *Bible Review* 15, no. 6 (December 1999): 44.

But I believe we cannot resolve these tensions simply by saying that believers must live with a dark, arbitrary, or destructive side of God, or that these characteristics are complementary and therefore coherent under the concept of God's covenant. Not every biblical statement about God speaks the truth about God. We do not have to assume that every writer of every text got everything right. The writers' own finitude, prejudices, and sinfulness also are apparent in the text. Controversy within and among texts is evidence enough that questions and challenges are raised in the Bible itself about who God really is and what God is really like. Difficult as it is to do, some decision must be made about the differences between the textual God and the actual God, between the character of God represented in each text and the God who transcends it.

How, then, can we decide who is the God of Scripture amidst a diverse witness? I believe, on the one hand, we cannot identify (equate) the actual God and the textual God, and, on the other hand, we can identify (distinguish) the actual God only in the light of biblical texts. I make this distinction on the basis of the entire canonical depiction of God in which differing interpretations of God are presented, in which certain dominant themes run throughout the text, and in which the text itself makes generalizations about God through its confessional forms (Exod. 34:6-7 and Matt. 28:19-20). We finally have to decipher the deep underlying assumptions and primary claims about God that pervade the Scripture and bring coherence to biblical talk about God. Interpretation of each story or image, in the end, must be guided by the ruling metaphors and generalizations which describe the God who acts in Israel and the church. The God of the exodus, exile, and Jesus Christ is the norm for deciding who is the biblical God.

Such a judgment depends, in effect, on a canon within the canon. This norm is required because, finally, we must make a choice between different characterizations of God that are equally biblical but irreducibly different. Believers cannot honor equally everything the Bible says about God. A Christian doctrine of God is not simply a repetition of everything the Bible says. It is the construction of a concept which is derived from Scripture as it is guided by Scripture's basic themes and generalizations.[17] A Christian doctrine of God has always been more than simply a reiteration of Scripture. It entails constructive work in which the primary biblical witness is extended and elaborated into a coherent, plausible, and compelling picture of God. "The gos-

---

17. "While the Bible is indispensable in the search to understand God more fully, it is not finally sufficient, as Trinitarian formulations show." Fretheim and Froehlich, *The Bible As Word of God*, p. 106.

pel," Old and New, sets the parameters within which diverse biblical views must be interpreted and used in constructing a doctrine of God. The gospel is represented primarily in the Old Testament by the creedal summaries of Israel's faith, in the New Testament by God who is incarnate in Jesus and known to us through the power of the Spirit.[18] Within a biblical context, then, there are three concepts of God which claim to define who is the Christian God: classical theism, dialectical theism, and Trinitarianism. I argue that these three concepts of God are authentic candidates for an interpretation of the biblical concept of God and a Christian doctrine of God.

III. The Theistic Concept of God

Christian belief is monotheistic (belief in one God), in contrast to polytheistic (belief in many gods), henotheistic (belief in many gods but loyalty to one), pantheistic (belief that God is the world), and deistic (belief that God created the world, set it in motion, and is now uninvolved with the world). God is a unitary actuality who is supremely worthy of our worship — that is the center of Christian belief. Theism, the classical Christian *doctrine* of God, is an uneasy marriage between biblical henotheism (loyalty to Yahweh, the tribal God of Israel) and monotheism (worship of the one universal God, who is the ultimate ground of all the creation).[19] On the one hand, the early church reaffirmed the idea of God it inherited from Judaism, the concept of Yahweh as the God of all creation, who was reconceived in the light of the new creation in Jesus as the Christ and in the light of the work of the Holy Spirit in the creation of the church, a conviction which led to the concept of God as Trinity. In their everyday practices — their prayers, liturgies, and personal testimonies — Christians used predominantly biblical language to speak about God. They described God as personal, sovereign, judging, merciful, forgiving, and loving. On the other hand, as the church moved from Judaism into the Greco-Roman world of the first and second centuries, the theologians of the church moved away from the biblical account of God

18. Fretheim and Froehlich, *The Bible As Word of God;* see also Fretheim's *The Suffering of God,* pp. 24-28.

19. For discussions of the history of Christian theism, see Langdon Gilkey, "God," in *Christian Theology,* ed. Hodgson and King, pp. 2-87; S. G. F. Brandon, "God, Idea of, Prehistory to Middle Ages," *Dictionary of the History of Ideas,* vol. 2, ed. Philip Winer (New York: Charles Scribner's Sons, 1973), pp. 331-46; James Collins, "God, Idea of, 1400-1800," *Dictionary of the History of Ideas,* vol. 2, pp. 346-54; John Sanders, "Historical Considerations," in *The Openness of God,* ed. Pinnock, pp. 59-100.

to the philosophical language of Greek philosophy to develop their concept of God. As a result of this uneasy marriage, the transcendent side of our transcendence-immanence dialectic came to dominate.

There are several reasons for the development of the classical theistic concept of God. First, as the church moved into the Greek-speaking world, it needed to distinguish its idea of God from the pagan deities. Second, the church had to show that it worshiped the one universal God, not merely a tribal deity. Third, the church moved into a culture in which the historical view of God presented in the Bible was a problem. In the Hellenistic world, time and so history was not interpreted in a friendly manner. Time was a threat to human existence; it meant change, and change meant death. The goal of Greek philosophy was to discover a reality which escaped the ravages of time and death.[20] Christians soon adopted this Hellenistic mind-set as the framework in which to develop their concept of God as the answer to the ravages of time and change. By the end of the first century theologians had appropriated philosophical ideas from middle Platonism and Stoicism, primarily the language of Being, essence, and substance, as the means to designate the one God which was beyond the destruction of time and history. The language of Being led to the classical concept of God as an eternal essence or substance beyond the temporal world.[21] *Very Good.*

Since the end of the first century, then, the Christian God has been an uneasy marriage between biblical and theistic concepts. The church's liturgies and prayers have been shaped predominantly by biblical images and Trinitarian language, but its doctrine of God has been determined by philosophical assumptions and words which are not easily compatible with the church's worship. To speak in a broad generalization, the theologians of the early church (Ignatius, Justin, Athenagoras, Irenaeus, Origen, and Augustine) used the language of neo-Platonism — the language of Being — to develop a concept of God by which to explain and defend their biblical and devotional language, while the medieval theologians (St. Thomas Aquinas) substituted the Aristotelian language of Substance to develop a concept of God as the unmoved mover who was beyond time and change.

At the core of theism resides our basic intuition of irrevocable mystery, of awe, of holiness (*mysterium tremendum* and *mysterium fascinans),* of absolute dependence, of unconditioned worth. Any concept of God as the supreme re-

---

20. Willem Zurdeeg, *Man Before Chaos* (Nashville: Abingdon, 1968).

21. In this chapter I use the word "monotheism" to refer to the universal Christian concept that there is one God, and the word "theism" to refer to the specific Christian concept of God informed and shaped by the classical world of Greek language and philosophy.

ality with which we have to deal reflects this sense of ultimacy. Classical theists, however, extend these sensibilities to imply a concept of God who is timeless and unrelated to the world in any essential way. Such a concept is not derived from Scripture or the doctrine of the Trinity; it is deduced from the assumptions of Greek philosophy. Eternity means timelessness and changelessness, and as a result theists infer that God is not temporal in any sense and so cannot change in any sense. Time and change are less than real — the really real is beyond time. Time is finite, and so is dependent on and ultimately overcome by that which is changeless and nontemporal, namely, eternal and timeless Being (God). God is not related in any essential way to time and space, to other creatures, indeed, to anything less real than the eternal realm of the Godhead. If God were related to the world, God would not be a real God wholly independent of the world. Insofar as God is related to the world, God is not related in any essential way, for to be essentially related would make God in some sense dependent on the world for the full reality of God's love, knowledge, and power. God, therefore, is omniscient and omnipotent; God is passionless *(apatheia)*. As such God is related by a free decision, and the relations only go one way, from God to the world and not from the world to God. God loves the world, but it is pure agape love, a passionless and self-contained love, not a reciprocal love of real mutual relationship and interdependence.

The formal theistic definition says that God is "a person without a body (i.e., a spirit), present everywhere, the creator and sustainer of the universe, a free agent, able to do everything (i.e., omnipotent), knowing all things, perfectly good, a source of moral obligation, immutable, eternal, a necessary being, holy, and worthy of worship."[22] God is infinite or unlimited. God's infinity includes God's aseity (God is self-existent), and so God is not dependent for existence or character on anything other than Godself. Furthermore, God is eternal, which means not only without beginning or end but wholly independent of time. God exists in ontological independence as the creator of the world *ex nihilo* (out of nothing). Nevertheless, God is also affirmed, simultaneously, to be personal, loving, good, and holy.[23] Thus, the Westminster Confession of Faith says, first, "There is but one only living and true God, who is infinite in being and perfection, a most pure spirit, invisible, without body, parts, or passions, immutable, immense, eternal, incomprehensible, almighty, most wise, most holy, most free, most absolute, working all things according to the counsel of his own immutable and most righteous will, for his own

22. Richard Swinburne, *The Coherence of Theism* (Oxford: Clarendon, 1877), p. 2.

23. John Hick, *Philosophy of Religion,* second ed. (Englewood Cliffs, N.J.: Prentice-Hall, 1973), chapter 1.

glory." Then the article continues in the same paragraph following a semi-colon, "most loving, gracious, merciful, long-suffering, abundant in goodness and truth, forgiving iniquity, transgression, and sin; the rewarder of them that diligently seek him; and withal most just and terrible in his judgments; hating all sin, and who will by no means clear the guilty."[24]

Central to the theistic idea is the assumption that anything less than perfection is inappropriate to the concept of God. Who would disagree? The theistic idea of perfection, however, is defined by the assumptions of Greek philosophy, not by biblical language or by other possible meanings of perfection. Theists' claims about God's ultimacy are defined by the Greek notion of complete and static perfection; this is what the Bible and theology must mean by the perfection of God because this is what perfection means. Perfection cannot include internal relationships, time, change, or increase. For theists perfection means to be in need of nothing, to depend on nothing or no one, in short, to be wholly self-sufficient. Dependence and change are impossible for a perfect reality. Not only is change imperfect, but time itself is the threat of nonbeing. Becoming represents weakness and corruptibility, which stand over against eternity and being, which are stable and reliable because they represent absolute perfection. God, then, is the Being which transcends time, change, history, flesh, and matter.

The key figure in the biblical-classical synthesis was Philo, who described God as eternal or timeless, not subject to temporal decay or the ravages of time. He inferred from his concept of perfection the omnipotence (omni-causality), omniscience (complete knowledge of past, present, and future), omnipresence, simplicity, incorporeality, self-sufficiency, immutability (acts, but cannot be acted upon), and impassibility (is not susceptible to passions or emotions) of God. Augustine simply assumed these characteristics, and assumed that immutability and impassibility meant that neither God's knowledge nor God's will ever changes. All of this, of course, stands in direct contrast to most of the biblical language about God, in which God is responsive to the creation, loves and gets angry, and even repents (changes course). Theists usually resolve this *tension by claiming there are two levels of scriptural teaching: some parts of Scripture teach us the direct truth about God, such as divine immutability (Num. 23:19; 1 Sam. 15:29), whereas most of the language about God in Scripture is anthropomorphic, which means that it is language through which God accommodates the simple-minded and less sophisticated reader of Scripture.

Although few Protestant theologians in the last 250 years have been strict

---

24. "Westminster Confession of Faith," p. 128 (number 6.011).

classical theists,[25] many of classical theism's features remain central to the thinking of many theologians and are assumed by most laypersons in their reading of Scripture and in their prayer and worship. Any questions about the theistic definition of God are taken to be a denial of God or blasphemy.

I must admit to a dilemma here. Any effort to define theism too narrowly is misleading. Classical theism does not adequately represent the complex and subtle thought of most theologians, and few of the great theologians have restricted their thinking about God to only this concept. Indeed, most theologians spend much of their time elaborating what God as personal, loving, good, and just means. Nevertheless, many theologians and laypersons still assume the theistic concept of God as their beginning point, and these assumptions shape their discussion about how the loving and personal God is related to and acts in the world. For most beginning students, some form of theism is the "embedded theology" which underlies their inherited beliefs and personal piety. Their understanding of how God relates to the world, the attributes of God, and how the will of God relates to suffering are all deeply shaped by theistic assumptions. As I will show below, the liability of classical theism is the way in which the biblical characteristics of God are interpreted by nonbiblical and inappropriate philosophical assumptions. Given the language of Scripture, worship, and piety, it is important to contrast classical theism with other kinds of theism which are closer to the biblical language about God, namely, panentheism, free-will or open theism (Section IV), and Trinitarianism (Section V).

IV. Dialectical Theism[26]

Since the Enlightenment the idea of God we have inherited from ancient, medieval, and Reformation theologians has struggled against serious objections.

25. Langdon Gilkey, "God, Idea of, Since 1800," *Dictionary of the History of Ideas,* pp. 354-66.

26. Although many, if not most, theologians are engaged implicitly, at least, with rethinking classical theism, this task has become the explicit agenda of two contemporary types of theology, namely, "free-will theism" (also called "the open view of God" or "open theism") and "panentheism" (or "neo-classical theism" or "process theology"). Each advocates to one degree or another a reconception of the divine perfections (transcendence, omnipotence, immutability, impassibility, eternity, and omniscience). I do not want to leave the impression that these are idiosyncratic revisions, however, for I could show, if I had more space, how the majority of theologians today concur to one degree or another with these revisionary theists. Indeed, revisions of theism have been one of the most important developments in theology in the last nearly half century. Among many examples, see Daniel Migliore, *Faith Seeking Understanding: An Introduction to Christian Faith* (Grand Rapids: Eerdmans, 1991); Michael Jinkins, *Invitation*

Those who have studied philosophy of religion in college will have encountered many of these protests as variations of the towering question of whether classical theism is compatible with human freedom. There are, also, serious theological questions to ask, such as whether classical theism is compatible with the Trinity (there can be no relations either within the Godhead or between God and the world if God is simple, changeless, and impassible) and with the incarnation (Jesus can suffer death only in his human nature). Classical theism also poses liturgical problems, such as how intercessory prayer and other forms of worship and service could make any difference to an impassible and immutable deity. In the light of such problems, I believe we must rethink the Christian version of monotheism so that our concept of God is more in line with the God witnessed to in Scripture and presupposed in our worship of the One who is identified as triune.

As was apparent in my discussion of the biblical God, the Bible does not witness to a God who is eternal, infinite, immutable, and impassible in the classical sense.[27] Classical theism, to be sure, does appropriately emphasize the transcendence of the God who is immanent in lovingkindness in the messiness of history. And there is much in the traditional concept which is important for us to affirm: God is the source and ground of our lives and the life of the world (the Creator), God is the dependable power at work directing history (the Lord), God is an abiding and stable agency impervious to the whims of history (God is sovereign), and God establishes moral structure and seeks justice (God is just).[28] But the *full* reality of God, the one who covenants with the creation and brings the creation to fulfillment, is not eternal, immutable, impassible in the classical sense. The primary sources of our doctrine of God — the Bible, worship, the creeds, the sacraments, and prayer — witness to a God who is quite different than the immutable and impassible God of classical theism. We speak of a God who is personal and purposive, open and

---

to Theology (Downers Grove, Ill.: InterVarsity, 2001); Clark M. Williamson, *Way of Blessing, Way of Life* (St. Louis: Chalice, 1999); Bradley C. Hanson, *Introduction to Christian Theology* (Minneapolis: Fortress, 1997); Langdon Gilkey, *Message and Existence: An Introduction to Christian Theology* (New York: Seabury, 1979); Kaufman, *Systematic Theology;* Ted Peters, *God — The World's Future,* second ed. (Minneapolis: Fortress, 2000); Alister McGrath, *Christian Theology: An Introduction* (Oxford: Blackwell, 1994); John Macquarrie, *Principles of Christian Theology* (New York: Scribner, 1966); Douglas Hall, *Thinking the Faith: Christian Theology in a North American Context* (Minneapolis: Augsburg, 1989).

27. "Indeed, I think the God of most biblical texts is not impassible or immutable or atemporal or omnipotent or omniscient, at least in any conventional understanding of those terms." Fretheim and Froehlich, *The Bible As Word of God,* p. 112.

28. Delwin Brown, *Theological Crossfire: An Evangelical/Liberal Dialogue* (Grand Rapids: Zondervan, 1990), pp. 83-84.

sensitive to the world, whose love is dependable and present regardless of the uncertainties of the future.[29] We worship God and live our lives as if what we do is important to God. God hears our prayers and responds to our suffering and joys. The God of the Bible and worship does not lack relationships. Rather, this God is the one who is perfectly related to all.

During the last few decades, many theologians have begun to rethink the otherness of God within the landscape of God's nearness to us.[30] Theists of every sort, of course, affirm that God is both transcendent and immanent. Classical theists stress the transcendence of God, and interpret immanence within the horizon of absolute transcendence. God is "high and lofty" (Isa. 6:1), self-sufficient, ontologically "other" than the creation, eternal, omniscient, and omnipotent. Nevertheless, classical theists also say God is immanent, "with us," close to us, present in the world, and involved with creatures. The transcendent God is committed to us and wills the well-being of the whole creation. The significance of rethinking the classical concept of God in light of Scripture and worship and through the revisions of free-will theism and panentheism is apparent when we consider "the divine perfections" (qualities, characteristics, or attributes of God).

What I am calling dialectical theism is embodied in two major schools of theology today. One is called "free-will theism," the other "panentheism."[31] They share much in common. Both affirm that God is "that than which nothing greater can be conceived," that God is a personal, purposive being, that God is relational within Godself (Trinity) and with the world, that because of human freedom the ideas of divine determination and complete knowledge

29. Brown, *Theological Crossfire*, pp. 85-86.

30. See, for example, Pinnock et al., eds., *The Openness of God;* Clark Pinnock, *Most Moved Mover: A Theology of God's Openness* (Grand Rapids: Baker, 2001); Clark Pinnock and Robert C. Brow, *Unbounded Love: A Good News Theology for the 21st Century* (Downers Grove, Ill.: Intervarsity, 1994); David Basinger, *The Case for Freewill Theism* (Downers Grove, Ill.: InterVarsity, 1996); Gregory A. Boyd, *God at War: The Bible and Spiritual Conflict* (Downers Grove, Ill.: InterVarsity, 1997); John Sanders, *The God Who Risks: A Theology of Providence* (Downers Grove, Ill.: InterVarsity, 1998); John Cobb Jr. and Clark Pinnock, *Searching for an Adequate God: A Dialogue between Process and Free Will Theists* (Grand Rapids: Eerdmans, 2000); Ronald Nash, ed., *Process Theology* (Grand Rapids: Baker, 1987). For a rejection of free-will theism by evangelicals, see Douglas Huffman and Eric Johnson, eds., *God Under Fire: Modern Scholarship Reinvents God* (Grand Rapids: Zondervan, 2002).

31. There is a raging debate among evangelical theologians today about open or free-will theism. Many believe our concept of God must be derived from Scripture alone, and that the classical theists' interpretation of the God of Scripture is normative. Open or free-will theists, on the other hand, argue that the proper interpretation of Scripture does not support many features of classical theism. The content of their evangelical interpretation of the biblical God is much closer to process theology or panentheism.

of the future are mistaken, that impassibility and immutability are inappropriate because God is love, that God is genuinely affected by a give and take with the world, and that God's primary mode of operation is persuasive love rather than coercive control. There is a growing consensus among some evangelical theologians, all process theologians, and many who stand somewhere near these two schools, that God's character must be reconceived in the way dialectical theism does it. There are a number of points on which a majority of these theologians agree:

1. Most revisionists remain theistic in their concept of God as *creator*. All power belongs essentially to God. God *could* create a world in which all things are determined by God, but out of love God chooses to create some creatures with the derived and relative freedom to decide. Therefore, God created the future as open, not closed and predetermined. To be sure, a theistic version of freedom is not new. It was taught by the medieval theologian William of Ockham, who distinguished between the absolute power of God *(potentia absoluta)*, which is the power God possessed before making the commitment to create time and creatures, and the ordained power of God *(potentia ordinata)*, which refers to the established order now in which the divine power is restricted by God's own decision so that God now works through the secondary causes of the created order.[32] As absolute power, God committed to the self-limitation of absolute power for the sake of a loving relationship with creatures.[33] Therefore, the transcendent God is now the living, related God involved in history (more like a dynamic event than an absolute substance). God even "emptied himself" (Phil. 2:6-7) by becoming incarnate, setting aside the absolute attributes and identifying with us in Christ. This means God assumes risk and vulnerability in choosing to create a world of free creatures in which loving relationships can flourish.

2. Because of their emphasis on the reality of freedom, dialectical theists reinterpret all of the other attributes of God. *Omnipotence* does not mean omnicausality. Since God wills the existence of creatures possessing the relative power of self-determination, God accepts limitations on the divine power.

---

32. McGrath, *Christian Theology,* pp. 224-25.

33. Free-will or open theism attempts to avoid the dilemma of classical theism and still retain the idea of omnipotence by arguing that after giving freedom to creatures, the omnipotent God in principle cannot unilaterally intervene in those creatures' freedom, because the "principle of irrevocability" which God established as a "covenant of noncoercion" sets "metaphysical constraints that God cannot avoid when he decides to limit himself by giving nondivine creatures free will. . . . God is not free to 'unlimit himself' any time he chooses." Gregory A. Boyd, *Satan and the Problem of Evil: Constructing a Trinitarian Warfare Theology* (Downers Grove, Ill.: InterVarsity, 2001), pp. 184-85, 212.

The issue is not whether God is sovereign but whether God exercises sovereign power through domination or through nurturing and empowering free creatures. In dialectical theism God is not omnipotent in the sense of determining all things ("nothing happens that is not the will of God") or in the sense that nothing can go contrary to the will of God (the puppeteer), but in the sense that "the sovereign love of God has no equals."[34] God is fully able to deal with any situation that arises even after allowing it vulnerability. Although everything is dependent on God, not everything is determined by God. God has made room for the exercise of free creaturely power. In Scripture, divine power is more the power to deliver from captivity, to raise Jesus from the dead, to transform the present eon into the kingdom of God, to accomplish the final redemption, than it is to determine all things.[35] God is the superior power in that God depends on nothing in order to be and is free. But this does not mean that God determines all things.

> "The God who is the object of evangelical theology is just as lowly as he is exalted. He is exalted precisely in his lowliness."
>
> KARL BARTH

3. God is *immutable* in a certain sense. God is immutable in essence (God could not begin to be God and cease to be God at some point in time) and in character (God everlastingly is love and is trustworthy). In other respects, however, God changes. Because of God's intrinsic relationships (both inter-Trinitarian and between God and the world), God is mutable in the sense that God's experience and knowledge of the world change as creatures make decisions and the world changes. Furthermore, God's action in the world changes as God responds to the creatures' decisions and actions in order to serve the well-being of the world. Immutability refers to God's steadfastness in character and purpose; it does not refer to God's changelessness.[36]

4. God is *impassible* in the sense that God's experiences and feelings do not change God's nature and character. The life of God is not controlled by the sorts of passions that rule and destroy alienated human life.[37] But God *is* passible in the sense that God's experience of the world depends on what happens in the world. What happens in the world affects the passions of God. A love that does not suffer with the suffering of the beloved is not love at all. The pathos of God is most evident in the divine compassion portrayed to-

---

34. Migliore, *Faith Seeking Understanding*, p. 73.
35. Peters, *God — The World's Future*, pp. 97-98.
36. Migliore, *Faith Seeking Understanding*, p. 73.
37. Migliore, *Faith Seeking Understanding*, p. 73.

gether in the prophetic tradition in the Old Testament and the incarnation in the New Testament. The Hebrew word for compassion has the same root word as that for womb *(rhm)*. God has a womb-like love for us, the way a mother loves her child in her womb and suffers in labor to birth the new creation (Isa. 42:14). God is affected by what happens in the world and reacts accordingly. Instead of being the "unmoved mover," God is "the most moved mover,"[38] the infinite one who is the true person because of the capacity to relate infallibly in love to all creatures. Events and human actions arouse God to joy and sorrow, pleasure and wrath. "God is concerned about the world and shares its fate," writes Abraham Heschel. "Indeed, this is the essence of God's moral nature: His willingness to be intimately involved in the history of man."[39]

5. God is *eternal.* But the eternity of God does not mean that God is exempt from time, untouched by time. God is not eternal in the sense that God is timeless. Rather, God is eternal in the sense that God is everlasting, "perduring through time," faithful over time.[40] God's faithfulness endures forever (Isa. 40:8); God makes promises and keeps them; God remains steadfast. It is impossible to think of timelessness as a state of being with no succession of events. Such an eternal state would constitute eternal death,[41] and certainly is contrary to the biblical portrayal of God's involvement in history. Eternity, rather, affirms the everlastingness of the related God. Time cannot destroy God or God's faithfulness to the creation. Though not temporal as creatures are temporal — namely, coming into being and ceasing to be — and though certainly not subject to the ravages of time, God nevertheless is temporal in the sense that God is with us in time, a fact most apparent for Christians in God's incarnation in Jesus Christ.

6. God also is *omniscient,* but not in the sense that God has exhaustive foreknowledge of future events. Such an idea implies that the future is not open but is fixed (in eternity where there is no tense). Nothing could be decided in the future. Rather, God is omniscient in the sense of knowing infallibly everything that can be known: the past as it actually was, the present as it is, and the future as the range of possibilities which constitute the open future. The future is partly settled and partly unsettled, partly determined and partly undetermined, and therefore partly known and partly unknown. This is true even for God because the future is not yet actual.

38. Pinnock, *The Most Moved Mover.*

39. Abraham Heschel, *The Prophets* (New York: Harper and Row, 1969), p. 224.

40. Peters, *God — The World's Future,* pp. 94-95, 113.

41. Peters, *God — The World's Future,* p. 95.

The methodological issues discussed in the previous three chapters, and many of the resulting questions to be discussed in the following chapters, come to focus in the question of whether, why, and how to rethink God outside the classical theistic framework. Although these issues are in the foreground (or background) of every theological topic, and the decision you make will shape what you say about every topic, I hope it is apparent that, regardless of whether you are conservative or liberal in your method (and who fits which label!), it is necessary to reconstruct a doctrine of God in light of Scripture and experience. The triune identity of God makes this agenda of reconstruction even more compelling.

V. The Triune God

The primary thing Christians say about God is that God is revealed in the Scripture as the triune God, as God the Father, God the Son, and God the Holy Spirit. As one of the two successors of Israel following the destruction of the Second Temple — Judaism and Christianity — Christians redefine God as the triune God. This identification of God is not only offensive to Jews and Muslims, for whom the Trinity is tritheism and therefore blasphemy; it is a problem for many Christians as well, for whom the Trinity is at best a nonsensical mathematical puzzle of how three can equal one and vice versa, and at worst a male hierarchy that serves as justification for male domination.[42]

> "Overall, there is a suspicion that the [Trinity] is a bore, a matter of mathematical conundrums and illogical attempts to square the circle."
>
> **COLIN GUNTON**

Christians initially learn their concept of God from their liturgies, which affirm God as triune: from baptism ("I baptize you in the name of the Father, and of the Son, and of the Holy Spirit), from the Eucharist, from hymns ("Holy, Holy, Holy! . . . God in three Persons, blessed Trinity!"), from the *Gloria Patri* ("Glory be to the Father, and to the Son, and to the Holy Ghost"), from the Apostles' Creed, and from benedictions. Trinitarian language identifies God and regulates our talk about God. To be sure, the doctrine of the Trinity does not appear explicitly in Scripture; it is an implication of the biblical testimony. As Catherine Mowry LaCugna puts it, "The doctrine of the trinity is the summary statement of faith in the

---

42. "If God is male, then the male is God." Mary Daly, *Beyond God the Father: Toward a Philosophy of Women's Liberation* (Boston: Beacon, 1973), p. 19.

God of Jesus Christ."[43] I believe both the importance and the meaning of the triune God can best be understood when we grasp that the doctrine makes three different affirmations about God; these are described here in ascending order of abstraction.

1. The Trinity is *a summary of the biblical concept of God*. When Christians affirm the Trinity, they are affirming the biblical story about God. Each time they speak of the triunity of God, they recite and affirm their belief in, trust of, and loyalty to the God of the Scriptures who creates the world, calls the patriarchs and matriarchs, covenants with Israel, delivers the oppressed, judges the unrighteous, restores the exiled, suffers on the cross, raises Jesus from the dead, calls and empowers the church, and fulfills the creation. The Trinity is a summary of the Bible's testimony to God's love in the covenant with Israel and the incarnation in Jesus Christ.[44]

This summary is most apparent where the use of the Trinitarian formula is most used, namely, in the sacraments. In the prayer of thanksgiving over the water in the sacrament of baptism, the story of salvation is reviewed from the waters of chaos when nothing existed through being raised with Christ in the final victory. In the Eucharist the formula shapes the Great Thanksgiving where again the story from creation through the heavenly banquet is recited. Although the Trinity is not biblical in the sense of the Bible teaching what the creeds teach, the triunity of God is rooted in Scripture in the sense that the Scriptures witness to the living God of Scripture.

We must be utterly clear: Scripture witnesses to one God. Nowhere is the unity of God questioned, but rather it is assumed and affirmed (Mark 12:29; 1 Cor. 8:4-6; Eph. 4:4-6). The Old Testament God is one, as is most clearly stated in Deuteronomy 6:4 — the Apostles' Creed of ancient Israel. But the seeds of a Trinitarian interpretation of the one sovereign God are there, a proto-Trinitarianism, from which the Nicene doctrine is a natural development.[45] God is a complex, organic, or differentiated unity, a living unity more on the analogy of the human self than the numeral one. God in the Old Testament exhibits various attributes or powers (spirit, word, wisdom), sometimes semi-personalized or hypostatized powers. These point to differentiations within the Godhead, similar to the way the New Testament understands God as Father, Son, and Holy Spirit. One might even discern a "triadic structure"

43. Catherine Mowry LaCugna, *God for Us: The Trinity and Christian Life* (San Francisco: HarperSanFrancisco, 1991), p. 21.

44. Migliore, *Faith Seeking Understanding*, p. 59.

45. For a summary of the biblical grounds for the doctrine of the Trinity, see Owen Thomas, *Introduction to Theology*, revised ed. (Wilton, Conn.: Morehouse-Barlow, 1983), pp. 59-60.

or "Trinitarian pattern"[46] in the living God who exhibits distinct centered personal ways of acting and being.

2. The Trinity is *the claim that God is for us.*[47] It is the church's attempt to interpret its experience of God in the light of the gospel.[48] The Trinity is a confession of faith grounded in the experience of salvation, a summary of the ways we know the saving work of God. It speaks of God for us in the good news of Christ. Although the church believed in one God ("Hear, O Israel: The LORD our God is one LORD," Deut. 6:4 RSV), the church experienced the one God in different ways. As Jews they knew God as one, who is also triune in the sense that God is spirit, word, and wisdom. As disciples of Jesus they knew God as manifest in the life, ministry, death, and resurrection of Jesus through the power of the Spirit. As apostles they knew the gift of the Holy Spirit as the empowerment of the church and its mission, which was the mission of Jesus.

The doctrine of the Trinity is the result of reflection on this testimony to the experience of redemption. Following the resurrection of Jesus and the establishment and empowerment of the church at Pentecost, the church found it necessary to talk about the work of Jesus Christ and the power of the Holy Spirit whenever it talked about God's saving work. God was experienced not only as the creator of the world but also as the redeemer from sin and the sustainer of the church through the power of the Spirit. The Trinity is a summary of this experience of the work of God, a *witness* to the work of God as creating, redeeming, and sustaining the world.

The Trinity, then, describes three modes of our experience of God's activity. The *economic doctrine of the Trinity,* or the "Trinity of manifestation," however, is not merely a statement about our experience. It is a claim about the "economy" of God (how God works in the world). It summarizes how God works for our salvation, the ways God acts as creator, redeemer, and sanctifier in the work of creating, redeeming, and sanctifying the world. The Trinity speaks of God's work over us, with us, in us (Hendry); revealer, revelation, revealedness (Barth); creative power, saving love, and ecstatic transformation (Tillich); primordial nature, consequent nature, and intersubjective nature (process theology); presence, wisdom, and power of God (Suchocki).

3. The triunity of God is the claim that *God is not less than what God does.* On the basis of what God does, we can say who God is. The *immanent, essen-*

46. Migliore, *Faith Seeking Understanding,* pp. 60-61, and Shirley Guthrie, *Christian Doctrine: Teaching of the Christian Church* (Atlanta: John Knox, 1968), pp. 92ff.

47. Marjorie Suchocki, *God, Christ, Church: A Practical Guide to Process Theology,* new revised ed. (New York: Crossroad, 1989), chapter 18.

48. Migliore, *Faith Seeking Understanding,* p. 59.

tialist, or *ontological* doctrine of the Trinity is not a snapshot picture of the Godhead or a literal description of God. It is, rather, the claim that *the Trinitarian pattern of salvation reflects the eternal being of God.* According to "Rahner's rule," "the economic trinity is the immanent trinity, and vise versa."[49] God is the everlasting intercommunion between the persons of the Godhead. And God's relationship to the world is internal to the divine life, since the everlasting life of God is personal life in relationship.[50]

Because the incarnation is decisive for the Christian understanding of God, then, a dialectic must characterize every form of theism. God is not a static monad in an eternal realm, related externally to the world only through a free act. "God is the supremely complex one."[51] There is infinite complexity and dynamism within the being and unity of God. The Trinitarian understanding of God, then, is that God's incarnation redefines divinity to include humanity, the humanity of Jesus. Catherine Mowry LaCugna explains the concept this way:

> The point of trinitarian theology is to convey that it is the essence or heart of God to be in relationship to other persons [within the Godhead and between God and the world]; that there is no room for division or inequality or hierarchy in God; that the personal reality of God is the highest possible expression of love and freedom; that the mystery of the divine life is characterized by self-giving and self-receiving; that divine life is dynamic and fecund, not static or barren.[52] *OMG... this was Jesus christ*

God was defined as triune by the Council of Nicea in 325. A two-century debate finally came to a head in the controversy between Arius (250-336), a popular preacher in charge of one of the main churches in Alexandria, and his bishop, Athanasius (296-377). Arius argued that the Son must be subordinate to the Father (not of the same divine essence but the firstborn of all creatures), since the full divinity of God could not be directly involved in the world without being corrupted by finitude, whereas Athanasius argued that the Father and Son must be equally divine because the Son could not mediate salvation to us if he is not fully divine.

49. Karl Rahner, *The Trinity* (New York: Herder and Herder, 1979), pp. 21-22.

50. Migliore, *Faith Seeking Understanding,* p. 67.

51. Suchocki, *God, Christ, Church,* p. 229; see also Thomas, *Introduction to Theology,* chapter 4.

52. Catherine Mowry LaCugna, "God in Communion with Us," in *Freeing Theology: The Essentials of Theology in Feminist Perspective,* ed. Catherine Mowry LaCugna (San Francisco: HarperSanFrancisco, 1993), p. 106.

self - giving
↕
self - receiving

The 250 bishops at Nicea eventually sided with Athanasius. They dispelled any hint of subordinationism, affirming that the Word or Son was eternally begotten (born from) the same substance as the Father, not a creature created out of nothing ("begotten, not made"). The Son comes out of the Father's substance as a child comes out of its parents' substance. If the Son had been created and not (eternally) begotten, the Son would have been on the wrong side of the time/eternity divide, and, therefore, could not save us. Furthermore, the Son was declared to be "of the same substance" *(homoousios)* with the Father, not "of similar substance" *(homoiousios)*. Finally, the Word *became* flesh; it did not pretend to be flesh; it did not seem to be flesh; it did not enter into a human being. It became flesh. The bishops agreed with Athanasius that "if the works of the Logos Godhead had not been done by means of the body, humanity would not have been divinized. Furthermore, if the properties of the flesh had not been reckoned to the Logos, humanity would not have been completely liberated from them."[53] What was at stake in a very complex argument — along with conflicting personalities and power politics — was soteriology.

While Nicea affirmed the relation between the Father and the Son as one of substance, it never defined what that "substance" is.[54] In ordinary language, *ousia* and *hypostasis* were both translated as "substance," as, indeed, Nicea had done. But the Cappadocian Fathers introduced a subtle distinction which can be grasped by way of an analogy:

> Consider three people: Peter, Mary, and John. Each of them is a particular individual (a *hypostasis*), but the three of them are all human beings; they

53. Robert Gregg and Dennis Groh, *Early Arianism — A View of Salvation* (Philadelphia: Fortress, 1981), p. 77.

54. Whatever "Godness" is, both the Father and the Son (and the Spirit) as equal "participants" in the Godhead share in it equally and fully. What was needed was a doctrine explaining how God could be one and yet consist of two or three separate entities. The task of saving the creed from being a mere empty formula fell to three Cappadocians from northern Turkey: Basil, Gregory of Nyssa, and Gregory of Nazianzus. The Cappadocians saved *homoousios* theology by making a *terminological* distinction; they clarified the key words. Athanasius used "essence" *(ousia)* and "being" *(hypostasis)* interchangeably. Their secret was to distinguish clearly between essence and being. While the Father and the Son (and the Spirit) were "of the same substance" or essence *(homoousia)*, there were three beings *(hypostases)* between them. "The Father, the Son, and the Holy Spirit are three separate beings, each with its own individual characteristics — they are three hypostases. But they are one and the same in essence — they are *homoousios*" (Gregg and Groh, *Early Arianism*, p. 64). Whereas for Athanasius there is one God whose mystery lies in the threeness of the Trinity, for the Cappadocians there are three persons whose mystery lies in their unity (Peters, *God — The World's Future*, p. 107). The unity and the tripartite division of the Godhead were now explained.

share the same essence or substance *(ousia)* of humanity. If you point to Peter and ask, "What is that?" there are two appropriate answers to the question simultaneously: "That is Peter" (a particular individual or *hypostasis*) and "That is a human being" (a substance or *ousia*). Similarly, Christ is "the Son" *(hypostasis)* and "God" *(ousia)* — a different hypostasis than the Father, but, nevertheless, "of the same substance" *(homoousios)*, as the Nicene Creed has said.[55]

All of this debate about the meaning of "person" (a distinguishable identity but not a separate personality or being or god) and about the unity and distinctions within the Godhead may appear to be at best hair-splitting and at worst idle speculation. But I emphasize again, they believed soteriology was at stake, the work of the Father and the Son and the Holy Spirit for our salvation.

Because God is incomprehensible mystery, it is proper at times to speak of God in nonpersonal or suprapersonal terms, such as the biblical phrase "I am who I am," Thomas's pure actuality, Tillich's ground of being, Ruether's primal matrix, Neville's indeterminate source of the determinate, or Rahner's holy mystery. Nevertheless, because God is triune and related to the creation in love, it is also necessary to use personal language, including metaphors such as "father" and "king." When we recognize how repressive the nearly exclusive masculine language about God in Scripture and tradition is, however, we must ask — and answer — how normative male language about God is for Christians. This problem is especially problematic in the dogmatic language of God as "Father" and "Son." To what extent does this language contribute to patriarchal repression inside and outside the church? How normative is language about God the Father and Son for sacraments, hymns, prayer, and, specifically, how normative is the language of Father and Son in the doctrine of the Trinity for Christian theology?

There are several ways to deal with the problem of patriarchy in Trinitarian theology.[56] My solution is to propose that once we recognize that the idea

55. William Placher, *A History of Christian Doctrine: An Introduction* (Philadelphia: Westminster, 1983), p. 78.

56. Some theologians argue that the language of Father, Son, and Holy Spirit is the revealed name of God, and so is exclusive and normative and is not revisable. (See, for example, Alvin F. Kimel Jr., ed., *This Is My Name Forever: The Trinity and Gender Language for God* [Downers Grove, Ill.: InterVarsity, 2001]; and Robert Jensen, *The Triune Identity* [Philadelphia: Fortress, 1982].) If we reject this understanding of the doctrine, we might take the apophatic route, emphasizing that God is incomprehensible and unnameable, and so an infinite variety of metaphors for God beyond God the Father is appropriate; no metaphor is normative. Such an approach emphasizes that *no* metaphor can be taken literally or exclusively but each points to a

of the Trinity is rooted in the history of salvation, that is, that it summarizes God's coming to us in Jesus Christ through the power of the Spirit, we must emphasize that the doctrine is tied first and foremost to the economy of God, not to a literal description of the Godhead — God is not a cosmic male. Therefore, there are different ways of describing salvation and different ways of naming the "persons" of the divine economy.[57]

By emphasizing this point, I propose to open the way for liturgical and theological terms for the "persons" (modes of divine being) of the Trinity that are not exclusively male. Owen Thomas is correct to say that "No particular words are essential to the doctrine of the trinity nor to any other doctrine."[58] Decisions about the words used in prayers, hymns, liturgies, and confessions of faith can be affected by traditional, ecumenical, aesthetic, psychological, and political considerations alongside theological ones. There is no theological requirement that language for God can only be Trinitarian or that the Trinitarian formulation of the economy of salvation and the divine identity can be formulated only in male language. Father, Son, and Holy Spirit are the historical terms of the creed. They are historically particular and relative ways of speaking about God. "The problem," sums up Marjorie Suchocki, "is not in the initial revelation of God through use of the words Father, Son, and Spirit, but in the fact that the historical relativity of the words is lost to view."[59]

What is crucial is that God comes to us in Christ through the power of the Spirit. Economic language alone (creator, redeemer, sanctifier) is not fully adequate, for the first, second, and third "persons" refer to eternal and inter-communicating modes of the divine being (the doctrine of *perichoresis*) as well as to our experience of the divine activity. Therefore, the language of the Trinity cannot be completely replaced by economic language. But Christians

---

dimension of our experience of God. Therefore, we must always use Father-language in a way which makes it clear that there are ways in which God is and is not like a father, or that the image of Father is not a theological dogma about God's maleness but a form of address to God expressing confidence and trust, or that Father in the New Testament refers primarily to the Father who is the source and origin of clan or family inheritance, the one who protects and provides, the one to whom obedience and honor is due; it is not a dogma about the gender of God (see Thompson, *The Promise of the Father*). Furthermore, we can draw on biblical feminine imagery for God. We might suggest that the Holy Spirit introduces a feminine dimension into the divine life, modifying or negating the patriarchal framework of the formula. Many seminarians today resolve the problem by substituting Creator, Redeemer, and Sustainer for Father, Son, and Holy Spirit, eliminating any gender implications for God.

57. LaCugna, "God in Communion with Us," p. 108.

58. Thomas, *Introduction to Theology*, p. 72.

59. Suchocki, *God, Christ, Church*, p. 234.

can use complementary language: "The language of Father, Son, and Holy Spirit must not be absolutized in theology and the liturgy of the church," writes Daniel Migliore.[60] William Placher's suggestion is thus worth considering: we can speak of God as "Father, Son and Holy Spirit, one God, mother of us all."[61]

My interpretation of the Trinity makes it a practical doctrine with radical consequences for Christian life.[62] Since the subject matter of the Trinity is the shared life of God and creatures, what is said about God in terms of the divine economy and the divine identity has consequences for our lives together. The Trinity gives us a framework for thinking about human personhood, the relationship between us and other creatures, and the relationship between God and ourselves.

To affirm the triune God is to enter into the life of God's love and communion with other persons. "The truth about both God and ourselves is that we were meant to exist as persons in communion, in a common household, living as persons from and for others, not persons in isolation with withdrawal or self-centeredness," writes LaCugna.[63] Existence, divine and human, is a mystery of commingling persons within a common life. To live is to live within the life of God, where life is governed for the sake of communion. It is a reshaping of our attachments, family, worship, anxieties, and ways of relating to each other according to the life of God in Jesus Christ and his coming reign.

In the move from theistic monotheism to Trinitarian theism, where persons and activity takes precedence over substances, where communion is emphasized, where power belongs not to one person alone (to the Father or to males) at the exclusion or subordination of other persons (the Son or persons at the margins) but is shared equally, the implications for our life together are transformative. Belief in the Trinity leads to "trinitarian politics,"[64] where God's rule, as in the Godhead, is a shared rule of equal persons in communion. If the triune concept of God shapes Christian practice, then shared power, equality, mutuality, and fellowship determine our religious, social, political, and economic life with God, the world, the church, each other, and within ourselves as we become "transcripts of the Trinity."[65]

---

60. Migliore, *Faith Seeking Understanding*, pp. 66-67.

61. William Placher, *Narratives of a Vulnerable God* (Louisville: Westminster/John Knox, 1994), p. 61.

62. See LaCugna, *God for Us*, chapter 10.

63. LaCugna, *God for Us*, p. 383.

64. LaCugna, *God for Us*, pp. 91ff.

65. The phrase is from John Wesley, *Bicentennial Works* 7:88.

CHAPTER FIVE

Faith and the Natural World

I. Scripture and Creation

The Bible and the Apostles' Creed begin with the affirmation of God the Creator: "In the beginning when God created the heavens and the earth" (Gen. 1:1), and "I believe in God the Father Almighty, Maker of heaven and earth" (Article One). Today some Christians are uncomfortable affirming this belief. Because they accept the assumptions, methods, and conclusions of modern science, they think they must make an either/or choice and so abandon the faith claim. At the other extreme, a significant minority defiantly and militantly defend "creation science" against modern science in another either/or decision.

The history of the conflict between theology and science is a long and nasty one, beginning in the seventeenth century with the appearance of Galileo's *Dialogues* (1632) and his subsequent heresy trial, reappearing in the nineteenth century with the publication of Darwin's *Origin of Species* (1858), and culminating in the Scopes "monkey trial" in Dayton, Tennessee (1925), and the "creationism trial" in Little Rock, Arkansas (1981), in the twentieth century. My thesis throughout this chapter is that both the "abdicators" and the "resisters" are mistaken in their response to the creation/science debate, in part because they over-read what modern science says about the origins and nature of the natural world, but, more important, because they misunderstand what it means to affirm that God is "creator of heaven and earth."

The affirmation that God is creator is central to biblical faith. Beginning with Genesis 1:1–2:25, the belief that God is the creator appears in numerous places in the Old Testament, including in the Proverbs (8:22-31), in many of the Psalms (8, 19, 33, 104), in Job (38:12–41:34), in Second Isaiah (40-55), and in Ezekiel (47:1-12). The New Testament reaffirms this belief (Matt. 19:4; Mark 10:6; 13:19; John 1; Rom. 1:20; 8:18-30; 1 Tim. 4:4; 1 Peter 4:19; 2 Peter 3:4-6; Rev. 4:11; 10:6; 22:1-5). Although the biblical view is shaped by ancient Near Eastern cosmologies (elements of the Babylonian *Enuma elish* and the Ugaritic Baal epic remain in the struggle against chaos in Job 26:12, Psalm 74:13-14, and Isaiah 27:1 and 51:9b-10), creation, according to the priestly writer in Genesis 1, occurs peacefully and systematically through the sovereign word of God. Furthermore, it proceeds in an evolutionary manner, moving from lower to higher, more complex forms of life, culminating in the appearance of humankind.[1]

One can read the Bible and the creeds in such a way as to assume creation is the first and foremost Christian doctrine from which all subsequent theological doctrines flow. Israel's and the church's faith in God the creator did not begin with the concept of God the creator of the universe, however. Israel's faith moves *from* redemption (exodus and exile) *to* creation. *After* God was known as redeemer and covenant maker, *then* the sovereign God who redeemed and made the covenant was affirmed as the universal Lord of history and nature. Creation thinking moves from the creation of Israel (Deut. 26:5-9) toward the creation of the cosmos. The redeeming God is the ultimate source and ruler of the world. Belief in God the creator is a logical implication (or presupposition) of faith in the God who is Israel's Lord. Working backward, the Bible teaches that the God who has the power to establish a covenant community, and to bring about the new creation in Jesus Christ, is the God who created and continues to create from beginning to end. The God who established the covenant with Moses and the New Creation is the ultimate ground and source of the world. The one who saves is the one who creates.[2]

As Israel understood her election within a cosmic context and purpose, creation is added as chapter one to her story of redemption. "Thus says the LORD, your Redeemer, who formed you in the womb: I am the LORD, who made all things, who alone stretched out the heavens, who by myself spread out the earth" (Isa. 44:24). This one is the ground and source of all that is. Genesis 1:1 expresses more the (theo)logical priority of the beginning point of Israel's faith than the historical priority of a creation cosmology as the context for subsequent redemption theology.

For Christians, then, the Bible can be read backward. We can begin with

---

1. William Brown, "Creation," *Eerdmans Dictionary of the Bible* (Grand Rapids: Eerdmans, 2000), pp. 293-94.

2. Ted Peters, *God — The World's Future: Systematic Theology for a New Era*, second ed. (Minneapolis: Fortress, 2000), pp. 133-35.

Moses, the exile, and Christ, and read from there to belief in God the creator. Another way to say this is that creation can be interpreted from the point of view of christology rather than cosmology. God is not known as creator first through cosmological speculation about the universe but through God's election of Abraham, Moses, and Jesus Christ. Belief in creation is an implication of the God known in the covenant and the incarnation. Although the doctrine of creation may have cosmological or philosophical presuppositions or implications, and is logically prior, the claim is not rooted in philosophy, cosmology, or science.

When the question of ultimate origins is raised, no theologian can know the time of origins, nor can a scientist know there was no such time. When a scientist says the world simply is (positivism), how can he know that is all there is to say? When a theologian says the world began in a certain way at a certain time, how can she know such a thing? No one was a spectator at the beginning of the universe, and no one can ever be outside it to know its origins. The affirmation of a creator is not the conclusion of a speculative argument or of a scientific confirmation but is a presupposition and statement of faith about the ultimacy of the God known in Israel's history and in Jesus Christ. As the author of Second Isaiah, Jesus, the writers of the Gospels, and the visionary of the Apocalypse knew, God the Almighty Creator refers not to a mythological time of origins which recedes ineluctably into the past but to the Lord of the impending future, to the one who is creating the new creation while overthrowing the forces of domination that destroy history and nature.[3] Since the creation is the work of the triune God, it must be set in the context of the whole activity of God. In creation all three persons are at work simultaneously, including the Holy Spirit (Gen. 1:2) and the Word (John 1:1).[4] The concept of creator of heaven and earth directs our attention and commitment not toward a primordial past but toward an ultimate future which has been inaugurated in the life, death, and destiny of Jesus Christ.

To the extent that this theological claim has philosophical and cosmological implications, Christians can develop an understanding of the relation between our faith and modern science. Is belief in God the creator compatible with modern science? Can the Christian believe in modern physics (Big Bang theory) and in modern biology (evolutionary development), on the one hand, and in God the creator of heaven and earth at the same time? The an-

---

3. Theodore Jennings, *Loyalty to God: The Apostles' Creed in Life and Liturgy* (Nashville: Abingdon, 1992), p. 42.

4. Daniel Migliore, *Faith Seeking Understanding: An Introduction to Christian Theology* (Grand Rapids: Eerdmans, 1991), p. 91.

swer to this question continues to be revisited every generation in modern theology, most notably today in the debate in the churches over "creationism" or "creation science." To answer this question, though, we cannot be too cavalier, simply asserting "yes" or "no." Christians must be prepared to answer why they think theology and science are or are not compatible.

My agenda is to set science and theology in conversation with each other. Conversation, however, does not mean there can be no disagreement about how things happen.[5] For example, if a scientist claims that God is not an agent or agency who needs to be taken into account as a certain kind of cause in any explanation of the world, a theologian can reply by arguing there is no situation in which God is not operative as a causal agent or agency. If a scientist claims it is not necessary to invoke God in order to account for the evolution of novel forms of life, a theologian can show how God is the source of novelty in the world. It is important to point out, however, that these are issues over worldview, not issues over scientific method and conclusions. My conversation with physics and biology is not based on an effort to use science to prove the existence of God; rather, it is intended to show that the God in whom Christians believe on other grounds is consistent with and complementary to the scientific theories of the origins and development of the natural world.

I do not have the space here to trace in detail the various forms of the relation between science and theology today, such as (1) conflict, in which scientific materialism and biblical literalism make rival objective statements about the history of nature; (2) independence, in which science and theology ask different questions using different language within separate domains; (3) dialogue, in which both science and theology explore many similarities between their presuppositions, methods, and concepts; and (4) integration, in which scientific theories strongly influence the interpretation and reformulation of certain doctrines (a theology of nature).[6] I reject the first strategy on the grounds that reality, though complex, is one, therefore, science and religion should at least complement each other if not be brought into synthesis. Furthermore, the change in the twentieth-century view of nature from a materialistic, deterministic machine to something more like a dynamic, creative organism in which rigid law is replaced by statistical probability and mechanism is replaced by an organism involving novelty and dynamism makes the notions of faith and science more compatible.

5. Clark Williamson, *Way of Blessing, Way of Life: A Christian Theology* (St. Louis: Chalice, 1999), p. 135.

6. Ian Barbour, *When Science Meets Religion: Enemies, Strangers, or Partners?* (San Francisco: HarperSanFrancisco, 2000).

Though different languages, theology and science are not mutually exclusive. They need not be at war, unless Scripture is an infallible science text or physics and biology are coupled with an explicit atheism.[7] There is nothing inconsistent in affirming both the speculative cosmology of the Big Bang theory in physics and creation *ex nihilo* in theology, or holding both to evolutionary biology and to faith in God the creator of all things. Christians have learned from scientific cosmology and evolutionary theory that creation is dynamic and open rather than static and closed, that creation consists of change, novelty, and an element of indeterminacy. Both can be held in good faith by persons of faith. I will develop my conversation between theology and science, then, by explaining what Christians mean by their claim that God is maker of heaven and earth and by showing how this claim is and is not compatible with certain views of science. I will do this, in Section II, by exploring the relation of faith and physics, focusing specifically on two different meanings of the concept of *creatio ex nihilo* (creation out of nothing), and, in Section III, by focusing on the relation of creation and evolution, extending this discussion into Section IV on *creatio continua* (continuing creation or providence), concluding, finally (Section V), with a discussion of what all of this implies about miracle and prayer.

> **"Science without religion is lame; religion without science is blind."**
>
> **ALBERT EINSTEIN**

II. Creation and the Question of Origins: *Creatio ex Nihilo*

There are two different ways to translate and interpret Genesis 1:1 and 1:1-4. The KJV translates Genesis 1:1 as, "In the beginning God created the heaven and the earth"; the NRSV renders it, "In the beginning when God created the heavens and the earth. . . ." A footnote in the NRSV, however, indicates that the Hebrew *bara'* (to create) can also be translated, "When God began to create the heavens and the earth," implying a much longer view of creation than is implied in the earlier English translations of the text. The verse also can be translated, "At the beginning of creation, the earth was formless and void." The text is not clear whether there was some pre-existing matter ("formless void") prior to God's speaking, or whether matter is the result of God's originating act. There is no way to determine what philosophical or cosmological view of origins is advanced by the priestly writer. How one translates and in-

---

7. Migliore, *Faith Seeking Understanding*, pp. 95-96.

terprets these texts depends on theological assumptions about what it means to say that God is "creator of heaven and earth." The text does not clearly teach *ex nihilo;* neither is there sufficient grounds on which to deny it. Both are speculative views which can be settled only on grounds other than exegesis of the texts.

The Greek language is of some help in clarifying the issue. "Nothing" can mean *me on,* which refers to "nothingness" as a kind of primordial stuff out of which the world is creatively fashioned (there are not yet any "things"), which implies a "second principle in addition to God."[8] In *creatio ex nihilo,* however, the *nihil* out of which God creates is *ouk on* (nothing), which implies that God is the sole source of all that exists, the original Other on which everything depends for existence, including a primeval stuff or "formless void." Since Genesis does not clearly teach *ouk on,* one might read the story as presupposing a pre-existing formless "stuff" already there, over which the Spirit hovers and "breathes," thereby creating a world. "No-thing" was at the beginning of our cosmic epoch; God created some "thing" out of this "no-thing-ness"; God provided the order to form a universe of interconnected causes and effects. In this framework, God and "a world" (some cosmic epoch) are eternal. Our world of finite time and space is one of the epochs in God's eternal creativity.

The major advocates of this view of creation today are the "naturalistic theists." For the naturalistic theists, creation is not identified with a "time of origins" but rather with the process of creativity as such. In such a framework, God is identified as "serendipitous creativity"[9] or "the source of human good"[10] or "the sensitive nature within nature"[11] which brings novelty and order to any world whatsoever. God is not thought of as a supernatural person or agent who creates from nothing everything that is. Naturalistic concepts of God replace the notion of God the Creator with the notion of an agency of creativity, so that God is the cosmic serendipitous creativity which manifests itself throughout the cosmos in a series of trajectories of creativity, including not only nature but the biohistorical beings we call hu-

8. Paul Tillich, *Systematic Theology,* vol. 1 (Chicago: University of Chicago Press, 1951), pp. 188, 253-54.

9. Gordon Kaufman, *In Face of Mystery: A Constructive Theology* (Cambridge: Harvard University Press, 1993), chapters 19-20.

10. Henry Nelson Wieman, *Religious Experience and the Scientific Method* (New York: Macmillan, 1926), p. 9, and *The Source of Human Good* (Carbondale, Ill.: Southern Illinois University Press, 1946), chapter 3.

11. Bernard Meland, *Seeds of Redemption* (New York: Macmillan, 1947), pp. 57, 60; *Faith and Culture* (New York: Oxford University Press, 1953), pp. 105-6; *The Realities of Faith: The Revolution in Cultural Forms* (New York: Oxford University Press, 1962), p. 184.

man.[12] In process forms of naturalistic theism, God is the cosmic person (among other persons) who creates the world by presenting "initial aims" for every event which occurs in the ongoing process of becoming. There is no world or "event" at all without the creator God who calls each moment into being. But there also is no creation apart from the response of creatures to the creative lure of God toward increasing complexity and harmony. Although naturalistic theisms succeed in moving us beyond the outmoded and dangerous concept of God as a supernatural cosmic puppeteer who unilaterally creates and controls the world from beyond, like Christof in *The Truman Show,* most naturalistic theists have a difficult time thinking of God as a divine agent in a way that reflects the biblical view of God as the creator upon whom the world depends for its very existence.

Creatio ex nihilo (nihil in the sense of *ouk on*) is an important concept for our understanding of creation. The doctrine of creation is not concerned with how the world came to be as it is. It is concerned with the ultimate question of why there is something and not nothing, why there is a space-time energy system in the first place. The idea of creation addresses this "limit question." Science, on the other hand, is not concerned with what preceded the space-time continuum (it has no methodology by which to answer such a speculative question), but with how this system works and how this cosmic epoch came to be as it is. Thus, "creation" is a *religious* affirmation about the world, not a scientific or philosophical concept. At one level, of course, the doctrine excludes certain philosophical ideas as incompatible with faith in the monotheistic God. For example, it rejects dualism, the idea of two eternal, equal, and self-sufficient ultimate realities, Spirit and matter, eternal principles of good and of evil. It also rejects monism or pantheism, the idea that the world originates out of God and is therefore inherently divine or even identical with God. The world is not God but is a creation of God. To understand *creatio ex nihilo,* there are a number of points we must consider.

1. *Creatio ex nihilo* is primarily a *religious* claim about the world. To say "I believe in God . . . Maker of heaven and earth" is to profess the *radical dependence* of the world on God, not only for its future, present, and past, but for its origination. God is the sole source of all things and is the one through whom all things came to be. Prior to finite beings is a transcendent ground of being and becoming; there is no world without this transcendent ground.[13] Tillich

---

12. Gordon Kaufman, *God-Mystery-Diversity: Christian Theology in a Pluralistic World* (Minneapolis: Fortress, 1996), pp. 101-9.

13. Langdon Gilkey, *Reaping the Whirlwind: A Christian Interpretation of History* (New York: Seabury, 1976), p. 129.

writes that "Creatureliness implies nonbeing, but creatureliness is more than nonbeing. It carries in itself the power of being, and this power of being is its participation in being-itself, in the creative ground of being."[14] *Creatio ex nihilo* affirms that creation is a gift of grace, an act God was not compelled to do by something or someone outside God, though it is necessary in the sense that it flows from the triune God's social and relational nature as pure unbounded love.

God is the source and ground of the world in its entirety, the cause of all things necessary for there to be any world at all, including metaphysical principles, such as creativity and pure potentiality.[15] "Put bluntly," writes Robert Neville, "curiosity about why there is a world can be answered only by reference to an act or acts that make there be a world, with whatever character it has. An appeal to first principles or to the nature of basic things is unhelpful if the question is why or how there are principles and beings at all."[16] The world as a whole as well as all creatures are finite and contingent, a fact permanently and existentially apparent to us in our own temporality ("time like an everflowing stream"). We infer that the world is a creation from our firsthand experience of our own creaturely dependence on God. We affirm the first article of the creed if in our anxiety about our experience of our temporality and contingency we live in absolute dependence on and ultimate confidence in the God of covenant and incarnation. Creation affirms God as the source, ground, security, meaning, and destiny of any world whatsoever, however our world came to be in the form in which we now find it, which it is the task of science to discover and describe.[17]

2. To call the world "God's creation" is also to make a *moral* claim about the world. In Genesis 1, the descriptions of the successive "days" of creation of light, the seas, vegetation, the seasons, and living creatures conclude with the refrain, "and God saw that it was good." The world is essentially good because it is God's world, because it is a gift of the primordial love and goodness of God. This intuition is expressed in the popular bumper sticker, "God don't make no junk." The world, the result of the loving will of God, is a reliable or-

---

14. Tillich, *Systematic Theology,* vol. 1, p. 253.

15. Williamson, *Way of Blessing, Way of Life,* pp. 106-7. See also Peters, *God — The World's Future,* and two works by Robert Neville: *A Theology Primer* (Albany: State University of New York Press, 1991), and "The Depths of God," *Journal of the American Academy of Religion* 66, no. 1 (1988): 1-24.

16. Robert Neville, *Religion in Late Modernity* (Albany: State University of New York Press, 2002), p. 23.

17. Langdon Gilkey, *Maker of Heaven and Earth: A Study of the Christian Doctrine of Creation* (New York: Doubleday, 1959), chapters 2-4.

der and harmony; it reflects the glory of God; it is to be rejoiced in by all crea-tures.[18] This created order can be known, understood, and explained within the limits of finite reason and understanding, including both the arts and the sciences. Furthermore, human existence has meaning and is not the result simply of a meaningless accident.[19] Although it is not good in the sense of be-ing perfect or complete, or in the sense that there is no evil and sin in the world (which means evil and sin are in some sense contingent, even though God created a world in which sin, suffering, and evil were inevitable), it is good in the sense that it is not essentially or necessarily evil. The world is cre-ated, valued, dynamic, purposeful, redeemable, and redeemed by God who in love and grace risks the growth of creaturely goodness and wills the well-being of all creatures.[20] The claim that creation is good, therefore, commits us in some ultimate sense to this world.

3. *Creatio ex nihilo* has some *cosmological* implications. While the idea that our universe has a finite beginning within God's own time and space is rooted in our sense of the absolute dependence of the finite on the infinite, by using the language of "time" and "space" and "beginning," theological doc-trine and speculative cosmology share an overlapping boundary. In terms of cosmology, *creatio ex nihilo* affirms a creation without antecedents in "God's Supertime before (and after) our time, the time of our 15 billion year old uni-verse."[21] Contemporary cosmology, which grows out of contemporary phys-ics and, specifically, the Big Bang theory, can help theologians interpret what they mean by the "beginning" of creation. We can say, from a speculative point of view, that a universe caused by God alone is as conceivable as a uni-verse produced out of an antecedent universe. The only way a scientist can know the answer to that particular kind of origins is to turn her methodolog-ical naturalism into an ontological naturalism, which is knowable only if one becomes a philosopher. Positively, the meaning of "in the beginning" can be informed by contemporary cosmology through its Big Bang theory of the or-igins of the universe.

Big Bang astrophysics hypothesizes that our space-time system can be traced back to a chaotic Big Bang originating about fifteen billion years ago. Physicists have discovered that the universe has not always been around but suddenly exploded into being billions of years ago in a flash of light and energy.

18. Owen Thomas, *Introduction to Theology,* revised ed. (Wilton, Conn.: Morehouse-Barlow, 1983), p. 104.

19. Thomas, *Introduction to Theology,* p. 104.

20. Williamson, *Way of Blessing, Way of Life,* p. 140.

21. Rem Edwards, "How Process Theology Can Affirm Creation Ex Nihilo," *Process Studies* 29, no. 1 (2000): 85.

All events in our space-time system are causally connected with other events within the system traceable back to the Big Bang. All the material in all the galaxies was originally concentrated at a single point of incalculable density and heat when in less than a second a single bit of reality began to expand at lightning speed. The entire cosmos consists of fragments still flying through space, of which the planet earth is an example. "For all practical purposes, we can say time began when the big bang first began its bang," explains Ted Peters.[22] Both scientific cosmology in its reconstruction of cosmic history beginning immediately after the Big Bang and theology in its claim that time is finite and has a first moment share the idea that the universe had a beginning.[23]

Although astrophysicists are at the fringes of philosophical speculation if they say anything more about the Big Bang, it is significant that scientific knowledge about origins, represented in the Big Bang theory, is *consistent with* (it does not prove) the religious affirmation about origins in the idea of an infinite and transcendent space-time, an infinite divine creativity, and a universe or universes created "out of nothing." Theists can interpret the Big Bang as compatible with the divine inauguration of the world. The scientific idea of the sudden appearance of a world bears some resemblance to the religious idea of *ex nihilo*. Indeed, a theistic interpretation can be an intellectually as well as spiritually satisfying interpretation of what would otherwise be simply an unintelligible good fortune.[24] Within such a view God's time is a time before and after our time of a fifteen-billion-year universe, and God's space is beyond the space of our cosmic epoch. God's everlasting creativity in God's superspacetime is not tied to one single temporal strand of one spatially finite universe.

I am not proposing a new natural theology, which presumes to prove the reality of God the creator *ex nihilo*. If theological and scientific thinking are kept strictly apart rather than coherently related, however, there are destructive consequences to each, especially in the temptation of each to overreach their respective boundaries. Contemporary physics can help us interpret how creation "in the beginning" might be understood by the believer. Nevertheless, even if the Big Bang theory triumphs in contemporary science, that still would not answer whether or not the cosmos is absolutely dependent on God as its source and goal. To affirm that God is creator of heaven and earth is to affirm an unqualified "yes" answer to that question. But that "yes" is a reli-

---

22. Peters, *God — The World's Future*, p. 139.

23. Barbour, *When Science Meets Religion*, pp. 40-41.

24. John Polkinghorne, *Belief in God in an Age of Science* (New Haven: Yale University Press, 1998), pp. 10-11.

gious belief about the source, character, and destiny of the world, not an alternative theory of physical origins. Belief in creation is not tied to any cosmological theory; it is grounded in our faith. Nevertheless, there is no necessary or inevitable conflict between accepting (provisionally) a particular scientific cosmology about what "beginnings" might look like from a speculative point of view, and affirming in faith "that all things come from God, are dependent on God, and are therefore good, potential of creative meaning and hope."[25]

III. Six Days or Forever? Creation and Evolution

For many people creation and evolution are combatants on a battleground in which these two incompatible concepts are at war with each other and a winner must be declared. According to scientists such as Richard Dawkins and Daniel Dennett, science is the only authentic form of explanation, and science has proved there is no purpose to the universe. The world is the product of a mindless, aimless evolutionary process. Mutations and natural selection are responsible for evolution, and these are the result of the physical determinism of the past and of random, chance mutations latent in the lifeless matter from our cosmic beginnings. Evolution is nothing more than the reshuffling of the inert matter that has always been there. There is no genuine novelty, aim, or purpose in nature. The problem with this view of nature and evolution is that no scientist as scientist can know the truth about such a claim apart from assuming a metaphysical materialism. Since science is not philosophy but is a methodology for discovering how the world works and how it came to be as it is, the scientist can know that the world is groundless and purposeless only on the basis of this philosophical commitment that is no less arbitrary than any other commitment.

> "Creation myths — including even the Big Bang — share an essential problem: they never really explain how we get from nothing to something."
>
> **WENDY DONIGER**

The other side of the conflict, which includes a few scientists who claim to speak as scientists, advocates an anti-evolutionary interpretation of the idea of creation. The position is called "creation science," and its main repre-

---

25. Langdon Gilkey, *Creationism on Trial: Evolution and God at Little Rock* (Minneapolis: Winston, 1985), p. 230.

sentatives come from the Creation-Science Research Center in San Diego. What is novel about creation science, in contrast to earlier forms of anti-evolutionary thinking, is that it claims to be science. According to creation scientists, there are two (and only two) scientific theories about how the world came to be, and creation science is the correct one. It stands in sharp contrast to evolutionary theory, which claims both the "fact" of evolutionary change over an enormous time span and the "explanation" of this change by way of natural selection. Creation scientists claim to establish on scientific grounds the sudden creation of all things out of nothing, the fact that all permanent species go back to the beginning (with change only within species), a separate creation of humans and apes, an explanation of geological formations by way of a catastrophic flood, and the recent creation of all things, ten thousand to twenty thousand years ago instead of fifteen billion years ago. Since science is nothing more than the "facts" or "data" it explains by giving possible, coherent, and plausible explanations of "evidence," they claim their interpretation of the facts is as plausible as evolutionary explanations. The main problem with creation scientists, however, is that they fail to understand that science is not merely a collection of facts but is its theories — its canons — for explaining facts.[26] Evolutionary theory is the core of modern biology.

Evolutionary science, however, is not atheistic. It does not and cannot know that there is or is not a God, a "time" of origins, or purpose to the world. It simply assumes something is already going on; there can be no scientific theory about the origins of everything or anything or why there is something and not nothing. Science is a methodology for answering specific kinds of questions about the world. It cannot on principle recognize a supranatural explanation which is beyond its assumptions about givenness and natural explanation. It is by definition a "secular" discipline, dealing with secondary or natural causes. It is more "methodological non-theism"[27] than it is atheism, for it simply leaves philosophical and theological matters to other ways of knowing. When science is identified with atheism, it has become an alternative theology. So, ironically, it is creation science which expands the claims of science beyond its methodological assumptions, theories, and strategies (its "canons") into theology, thereby attempting to force a choice between creation and evolution. Ironically, it is duped into playing the same game the metaphysical materialists play from the scientific side. Science is transformed by each into a forum for debate between competing philosophies and theologies.

26. Gilkey, *Creationism on Trial*, pp. 39, 96-97, 111-17.
27. Gilkey, *Creationism on Trial*, p. 115.

When, however, we recognize that science and religion are two different approaches to two different kinds of questions, two different realms of understanding the cosmos, nature, history, human nature, and ourselves, we do not face a choice between creation (God as the ground, source, and direction of the world) and evolution (the gradual appearance of new species as a result of random mutations and natural selection). Each differs in what it is about.

Creation affirms that any world whatsoever depends for its ground, origins, and purpose on the creative God, while evolution describes how this particular world emerged and is emerging over enormous time and space according to a combination of randomness, chance, natural selection, and the reliable natural laws which create enough order within which novelty can emerge. Within this "domain" thinking, God acts through the laws of evolutionary development to create the kind of world God intends. God's purposes are achieved throughout time and space through the interplay of randomness, chance, natural selection, order, novelty, and emergence to create a world of meaning and purpose. God is the primary cause of the world; evolution describes the secondary causes through which God works — cooperatively, patiently, faithfully, responsively, and creatively — to accomplish the divine purposes. William Stoeger puts it this way: "If we put this in an evolutionary context . . . we can conceive of God's continuing creative action as being realized through the natural unfolding of nature's potentialities and the continuing emergence of novelty, of self-organization, of life, of mind and spirit."[28] My primary way of resolving the so-called conflict between creation and evolution, therefore, is to see them as complementary domains.

As with physics, so with biology, however: evolutionary thinking can enhance our theology of creation through dialogue and integration. Though I do not endorse a new natural theology or a synthesis of creation and evolu-

> "Creation science represents a direct repudiation of perhaps the most general and pervasive theorem basic to all the physical and biological sciences. This is the concept of a universe in process, changing over vast stretches of time, interrelated and interacting in all of its aspects, out of whose developing interrelations novel forms of existence arise and come to be."
>
> **LANGDON GILKEY**

28. William Stoeger, "Describing God's Action in the World in Light of Scientific Knowledge," in *Chaos and Complexity: Scientific Perspectives on Divine Action,* ed. Robert Russell, Nancey Murphy, and Arthur Peacocke (Berkeley: Center for Theology and the Natural Sciences, 1995), p. 249, quoted in Barbour, *When Science Meets Religion,* p. 102.

tion, there are ways evolutionary theory can help believers understand what it means to say God is creator of heaven and earth. We can interpret God as creator in such a way that the ground and purpose of creation and evolution interact.

God did not create the world once upon a time as the sole cause of a predetermined universe but creates the world over a long span of time through the processes of change and development. As the loving and (self)limited source of a world of becoming with freedom and novelty, God works in cooperation with the creatures, laws, and randomness of nature to create a purposeful world. Instead of thinking of the creator as the ultimate reality from the past or the ultimate reality in a timeless eternity (a metaphysics of being), God can be thought of from the future (a metaphysics of becoming), the God of lure and promise from Abraham through the eschaton. When this shift is made, a determined cosmos or a timeless eternity gives way to creation from the future in which God works through the processes of evolution to create, redeem, and fulfill the world. God creates in cooperation with the creatures through the freedom, randomness, and laws of the natural world.[29]

God as creator can provide for believers an intellectually satisfying understanding of what would otherwise be simply the unintelligible good fortune of blind chance within a materialistic framework. John Polkinghorne suggests that instead of thinking about God as the designer of the predetermined cosmos, we should "shift from design through making to design built into the rational potentiality of the universe." God endowed matter with an "anthropic principle," meaning "that this universe which contains ourselves must be compatible with our having appeared within its history."[30] Because of a purposeful God, higher levels of order can emerge through self-organizing systems, fulfilling their potential for the richness which is latent in the world. We might even say that creation is designed for evolution.

Arthur Peacocke argues that the evolutionary concept of random genetic changes through variation introduced by chance which are passed on genetically can be enriched by the idea of God as the purposeful creator of the world if we think of two kinds of causation, namely, bottom-up and top-down.[31] Bottom-up causation says the behavior of the parts accounts for the

---

29. Barbour, *When Science Meets Religion*, p. 113.

30. Polkinghorne, *Belief in God*, p. 6.

31. Arthur Peacocke, *Theology for a Scientific Age: Being and Becoming — Natural and Divine* (Minneapolis: Fortress, 1993), chapter 9, and *Creation and the World of Science* (Oxford: Clarendon, 1979), pp. 131-38; see also John Polkinghorne, *The Faith of a Physicist: Reflections of a Bottom-Up Thinker* (Minneapolis: Fortress, 1994), p. 77.

behavior of the whole, while top-down causation says the system as a whole influences the behavior of the parts, much as the mind influences the body through the transmission of information. God is thus the unifying influence on the world, analogous to the way our minds influence our bodies. God is like the choreographer of a dance or composer of an unfinished symphony, using law and chance to fulfill the potentialities that have been given to the world.

In short, God creates through the evolutionary process. In process theology, God is the source of emergent novelty in the world. God creates by presenting each moment of the world's becoming with the best possibility among the rich range of real possibilities, and lures the creation to greater forms of complexity and harmony through co-creation. God the creator is thought of not so much as the push from the past as the pull from the future. As John Haught writes, "The novel informational possibilities that evolution has available arise from the always dawning future. It is the arrival of the future, and not the grinding onward of an algorithmic past, that accounts for the novelty in evolution."[32] The explanation of why the world has the features it has and why they are mingled in the way they are for the evolution of life is God the creator who is the source not only of the being and becoming of the world but also of the emergent novelty within nature. Again, Haught's comments are helpful: "And just as the arrival of God does not enter the human sphere by crude extrinsic forcefulness but by participating in it and energizing it from within, we may assume that it does not enter coercively into the prehuman levels of cosmic and biological evolution either."[33] Clearly, creation entails providence as well.

IV. Continuing Creation and
Divine Providence: *Creatio Continua*

The Bible affirms that the Creator faithfully upholds and preserves the creation throughout all time. "When you send forth your Spirit, [all things] are created; and you renew the face of the ground" (Ps. 104:30). Indeed, most Old Testament references to creation emphasize more God's power to sustain the creation than God's power to create out of nothing.[34] Psalms 33:6-7, 74:12-17,

---

32. John Haught, *God After Darwin: A Theology of Evolution* (Boulder, Colo.: Westview, 2000), p. 87.

33. Haught, *God After Darwin*, p. 99.

34. Jon Levinson, *Creation and the Persistence of Evil: The Jewish Drama of Divine Omnipotence* (New York: Harper and Row, 1988).

and 104:9, as well as Isaiah 27 and 51:9-11, assume creation is God's mastery over chaos and capacity to hold the chaos at bay in order to protect the community within a benevolent and life-sustaining order. Although the forces of chaos were not annihilated in primordial times and the creation remains fragile (Ps. 104 and Job 30 and 40), God's power sustains the world with enough structure to accomplish God's purposes within a dynamic and threatening world of becoming. Creation is as much a future as a past act of God (Isa. 40–55; Ezek. 40–48; Rev. 21). If so, the idea of providence is an essential part of a Christian doctrine of creation. Calvin says, "to make God a momentary Creator, who once for all finished his work, would be cold and barren, and we must differ from profane men especially in that we see the presence of divine power shining as much in the continuing state of the universe as in its inception."[35] Without creation as divine providence, God is extraneous to what is going on in the world today. Creation is the whole dynamic process of becoming from the first split second of the universe obscured in mystery through the emergence of humans and whatever follows us in the history of cosmic time and space. God's work as creator includes the sweep of cosmic history as a single creative work.[36]

In much of the tradition providence means everything that happens is willed and caused by God from the foundation of the world. Nature and history are merely the stage for the execution of the eternal plan. Theologians had difficulty affirming ultimate confidence in God's sustaining and fulfilling power without claiming God is the ultimate determiner of everything that happens. Pure chance or strict determinism were their options. Calvin says,

> Suppose a man falls among thieves, or wild beasts; is shipwrecked at sea by a sudden gale; is killed by a falling house or tree. Suppose another man wandering through the desert finds help in his straits; having been tossed

35. John Calvin, *Institutes of the Christian Religion*, 2 vols., ed. John T. McNeill, trans. Ford Lewis Battles (Philadelphia: Westminster, 1960), p. 197 (1.16.1).

36. Within the dominant tradition the "continuing state of the universe" has been interpreted in such a way as to deny any genuine novelty within a world of becoming. As the Heidelberg Catechism says, "Q. 27. What do you understand by the providence of God? A. The almighty and ever-present power of God whereby he still upholds, as it were by his own hand, heaven and earth together with all creatures, and rules in such a way that leaves and grass, rain and drought, fruitful and unfruitful years, food and drink, health and sickness, riches and poverty, and everything else, come to us not by chance but by his fatherly hand." "The Heidelberg Catechism," Question 27, *The Constitution of the Presbyterian Church (USA), Part I, Book of Confessions* (Louisville: Office of the General Assembly, 1996), p. 33.

by the waves, reaches harbor; miraculously escapes death by a finger's breadth. Carnal reason ascribes all such happenings, whether prosperous or adverse, to fortune. But anyone who has been taught by Christ's lips that all the hairs of his head are numbered will look farther afield for a cause, and will consider that all events are governed by God's secret plan. And concerning inanimate objects we ought to hold that, although each one has by nature been endowed with its own property, yet it does not exercise its own power except in so far as it is directed by God's ever-present hand. These are, thus, nothing but instruments to which God continually imparts as much effectiveness as he wills, and according to his own purpose bends and turns them to either one action or another. . . . Yet from it I infer that no wind ever arises or increases except by God's express command. . . . what for us seems a contingency, faith recognizes to have been a secret impulse from God.[37]

Natural causes and human decisions are "instruments" of the divine determination. Nothing happens that is not willed by God.[38]

The traditional understanding of providence is incompatible with a world of genuine freedom.[39] But in the worldview of modern cosmology and evolution, where mechanism has been replaced by an open future, where creativity, contingency, spontaneity, and freedom are characteristics of the world of becoming, we must distinguish providence from philosophical fate and theological determinism. In an open world, God as creator grounds the world

37. Calvin, *Institutes of the Christian Religion*, pp. 198-99, 206, 210 (1.16.2).

38. No theologian in the tradition admitted to being a fatalist. If one did, sin and redemption would be meaningless concepts. Instead, such theologians tried to hold freedom and divine determination together by arguing that God works *through*, not against, human willing. Even though God is the *ultimate* cause of what we will and do, we nevertheless actually will what we will, and therefore, we do it "freely," even though that willing and doing is the "instrument" for the accomplishment of God's changeless will. Freedom meant simply the absence of external coercion. Choices proceed from the person who chooses, regardless of the divine cause of our choices. Gilkey, *Reaping the Whirlwind*; Kenneth Cauthen, *Systematic Theology: A Modern Protestant Approach* (Lewiston, N.Y.: Edwin Mellen, 1986), pp. 132-38. The benefit of this strategy was that it allows us act as if we are free while we know that the world is determined by God's changeless will. God is in control of the world from the great movements of nature and history to the tiniest details of everyday life.

39. A concept of "genuine" freedom in a theological framework can be thought of as dependent on an ontological principle independent of God (as in process theology), or divine self-limitation (as in open theism), or the presence of chance and novelty in a created world of possibilities (as in modern evolutionary thinking), each presupposing a world of dynamic becoming and interconnectedness instead of a world of eternal being consisting of eternally fixed substances, species, possibilities, and decrees.

of emerging complexity in possibilities, and causes the world by drawing events into greater complexity and value. In a dynamic world, God is not so much the creator from the past as the creative power from the future, the lure or persuasion of inner direction present in every situation.[40] Providence includes the real (if relative) autonomy of nature and humanity. Providence operates within an open creation and includes a dynamic dimension within God. Contingency, chance, randomness, temporality, potentiality, and relationality are affirmed within both the world and God, either symbolically (Tillich) or ontologically (process theism). The idea of sovereignty affirms the unconquerable power of creative divine love, through lure, persuasion, and empowerment, working with free and creative covenant partners to create a flourishing world of well-being.

This shift from theological determinism to the divine creativity which works for the actualization of structure and complexity through time, freedom, and novelty, makes a dynamic idea of creation compelling. Such an idea, however, is rooted not only in contemporary science and cosmology. It is rooted in creation as the activity of the triune God. Creation involves simultaneously and interdependently God the Son and God the Holy Spirit as well God the Father. Any limitation of the creation to an act once upon a time in the past in which the First Person of the Trinity predetermined the world is a denial of the triune identity and work of God. The God who is in covenant with the creation in Jesus Christ through the power of the Spirit is not only the ultimate ground and source of the world, but is active in nature and history through incarnation and empowerment to bring all things to their well-being. Within this context, we can distinguish three modes of divine creativity: originating (Section II above), sustaining, and directing.[41]

Sustaining the Creation: The Principle of Continuation

God is not an absentee landlord overlooking the world from a distance, but is the faithful caregiver of the world, upholding, blessing, and guiding the creation (Ps. 104:27-30; Matt. 5:45; 6:26-30; 10:30). The world does not run on its own once it has been established. God is immanent as one who protects the world against the threat of destruction or nonbeing. Because God's creative power is continuous, we can trust the structures of the world to continue.

---

40. Peter Hodgson, "Providence," in *A New Handbook of Christian Theology*, ed. Donald Musser and Joseph Price (Nashville: Abingdon, 1992), pp. 395-96.

41. Tillich, *Systematic Theology*, vol. 1, pp. 253-70.

Even if we destroy the earth, we cannot destroy God's power to create another world (or other worlds) of being and becoming. As the power of being and becoming, God carries forward the decisions of the past into the present as part of what God and we have to work with in creating the present and the future. "The first principle of providence is the conquest of the passingness of time and the continual creation and recreation of each creature through the creative power of God," writes Langdon Gilkey.[42] God's providence is not an occasional interference in the otherwise routine affairs of the world that runs on its own. God is the power upon which the world depends in every moment for its being and becoming.[43]

Directing the Creation: The Principle of Possibilities

The world, also, depends upon God for its direction forward into an open future. As a reality which is not God, creation has its own independence; its own purpose to actualize its potentialities, which are inherent in a world of becoming; its own power to produce something new. God is the ground of the telos or inner aim of creatures to actualize their potential. Unlike ideas of providence in which God causes our motivations, ideas, and decisions, either directly or indirectly and hiddenly, God is the ground of real possibilities within the world and the goal toward which they move. "Even the most creative, autonomous action requires a universal, systematic order of possibilities that spans past, present and future and so can relate real possibility as possibility creatively to what has been," writes Gilkey.[44] Providence is the work of God through the structures of the world directing everything toward its flourishing so that it will glorify God. Providence works in and with, not against, the free activity of women and men and the novelty latent in the evolutionary processes of the natural world.

How does this providence work? Much traditional theology held human freedom and divine determination together by making a distinction between primary and secondary causality.[45] While God is the first and primary cause of all things from timeless eternity, and therefore the ultimate determiner of all things, God works *through* (not with) the immediate or secondary causes of events in the natural world, including the fact that we will and decide what

42. Gilkey, *Reaping the Whirlwind*, p. 250.

43. William Placher, "The Acts of God: What Do We Mean by Revelation?" *Christian Century*, March 20-27, 1996, pp. 339, 341.

44. Gilkey, *Reaping the Whirlwind*, p. 251.

45. Thomas Aquinas, *Summa Theologica*, 1a, q. 105, a. 5.

we do, in order to effect the perfect and changeless will of God, appealing to miracle within the realm of secondary causes if necessary to effect the divine will. This view of providence focused on God's unfolding decrees from all eternity. Within the view of providence I am describing, however, divine power and human freedom are not mutually exclusive. God takes a personal interest in the affairs of people and works in interaction *with* the creation.

In this view of providence, God works by means of what process theologians call the "initial aim" of every event, or what John Polkinghorne calls "information input," to respond to (relatively) free creatures and draw and guide them forward toward fulfillment of the possibilities God has built into the open and somewhat unpredictable creation.[46] God works to persuade, lure, and empower life toward fulfillment, to build direction toward complexity and harmony into the evolution of the universe, to realize the divine purpose of justice and shalom within the larger sweep of history. God works in and with the powers of the world to pull the world toward the fulfillment of the purposes of God revealed in the work of Christ.

When one thinks of providence from Trinitarian and christological grounds instead of from an abstract idea of timeless eternity, it is thought of more as God's faithfulness to the creation elected in Jesus Christ to be God's covenant partner, guiding the creation to its goal through the Word and Spirit instead of through unilateral and coercive power.[47] Like any artist or parent, God has preconceptions and designs, but God does not impose these on the creation. According to the Bible, God will wait, respond, and take up into the divine plan our decisions and actions, working with them to serve the Creator's ultimate good.[48] God is not the cosmic puppeteer, tyrant, controller, or determiner of all things, but rather is the creative, redemptive, and fulfilling power of love exemplified in the life, death, and resurrection of Jesus. God's script is not the prewritten script of a play for which the world is a stage, but rather is an ongoing story with God's goal in mind, a goal not defined within a prewritten script but rather defined by creation, redemption, and fulfillment according to the norm of Jesus Christ.

Such a view of providence has very practical consequences for the practice of the believer. If the triune God is related to the world as creator in the way described here, then the world matters to God. Both the world and *all* of its creatures are of intrinsic value in themselves because they matter to God

46. John Polkinghorne, *Serious Talk: Science and Religion in Dialogue* (Valley Forge, Pa.: Trinity Press International, 1995), pp. 84-86.

47. Migliore, *Faith Seeking Understanding*, pp. 114-19.

48. Douglas Hall, *Thinking the Faith: Christian Theology in a North American Context* (Minneapolis: Augsburg, 1989), p. 91.

and are interconnected with each other as covenantal partners through the providence of God. God's covenant extends not only to Israel, or to the church, or to humanity, but to nature as well. The value of creatures and of nature itself is not defined by their usefulness to humans. They are not to be dominated, controlled, or exploited for economic gain or for personal or cultural satisfaction. Each is intrinsically valuable. Furthermore, as covenant partners, each part of the creation is interdependent with the other and so has its appropriate place within the divine purpose of enriching the creation through the unity of all creatures.

An ecological ethic is an implication of faith in God the Creator. An ethic based on providence recognizes and welcomes the many levels of nature as part of God's realm. It affirms and sustains other forms of life as valuable whether or not they are useful to our economic, military, and cultural value. Such an ethic is based on our hope for the final unity of all creatures within the promised reign of God's shalom.[49] The practice of a theology of creation affirms human stewardship instead of ownership of creation, affirms the co-partnership with the other creatures for co-habitation of the earth, and affirms our commitment to inhabit a sustainable earth within the creative power of God who grounds, sustains, directs, and ultimately fulfills the creation.

V. Miracle and Prayer

In addition to the "general providence" by which God sustains and directs the natural world, does God intervene through a "special providence" to override the order of nature? The Bible is replete with extraordinary events which manifest God's providential rule. Many of these are recounted in the Exodus and covenant stories, which depict God as destroying the enemy and delivering the people of Israel, and in the Elijah and Elisha stories, in which God's power to provide food, bring back to life, control drought and rain, and heal the sick is recounted. In the Gospels, Jesus is presented as a miracle-worker. His works, such as healing the sick and casting out demons, are "signs and wonders" of the coming reign of God. Miracles as a gift of the Holy Spirit accompany the preaching of the gospel in Acts and Paul's writings.

For many Christians belief in miracles is a litmus test of true faith. For some modern Christians, however, the idea of miracles is an embarrassment and unnecessary to faith. Miracles do not happen, some Christians argue, be-

49. Bradley Hanson, *Introduction to Christian Theology* (Minneapolis: Fortress, 1997), pp. 77-80.

cause God does not work in ways that contradict the laws of cause and effect; God works *through* natural laws described by science. If something unusual or "unnatural" happens, we simply do not yet know how to explain it according to the laws of nature. If supernatural events seem to happen, they can be explained naturally; if they cannot be explained now, they will be able to be in the future when we have a unified theory of nature. Even if nature is more dynamic and open than metaphysical materialism permits, contemporary science has not abandoned its assumption that we do not require the idea of miracle to explain what happens. In addition, believers face the moral problem of divine love and justice if God works through miracles. If God intervenes supernaturally, why do miracles occur so rarely and with such arbitrariness? Why does God intervene for some and not others? Why does God not feed a mass of starving children with bread and fish amidst a famine? Does faith in God's providence include belief in miracles?

The preliminary question is what you understand the idea of miracle to mean in the first place. The word "miracle" does not have a clear and fixed meaning. The concept may point simply to any event that has some religious significance, that is, any event that excites wonder, awe, or reverence, any event that is a sign of God's providential work as creator. The birth of a baby is a miracle when it is an event through which the presence and power of God are perceived. For most persons of faith, however, the word "miracle" is reserved for an event that cannot be explained according to our scientific understanding of the world through physics, biology, medicine, or psychology. Miracles are examples of God's power to suspend human freedom and natural law and to operate outside both by doing something contrary to natural law through an extraordinary, supernatural act.

This idea of miracle, however, seems difficult to defend in light of the ontological or self-limitation of God discussed in the previous chapter. For this reason many theologians, like C. S. Lewis, have tried to defend miracles as supernatural events within a free and natural world by insisting we not begin with a view of the world which simply defines a miracle as an illusion or a mistake. Lewis argues that to believe in miracles we must begin with a view of nature itself as the realm of God's activity. From Noah's time to ours, God's power turns water into wine, feeds us, and heals us. Miracles simply do locally and uniquely (special providence) what God is already doing universally (general providence). All who drink and eat and are healed do so through the power of God, a routine providence which we usually do not see. In a miracle God does instantaneously what God usually does through the natural process; God short-circuits the natural process. Miracles work within the space-time world but in a different mode to do quickly and as a special case what

God does universally (provide birth, drink, food, and health) or will do universally (resurrection).[50] Miracles are a retelling in small letters of the same story written across the whole world in large letters, namely, that God is in control of the world.

There is, however, a third understanding of miracle which stands between miracle as "religious language" and miracle as "supernatural intervention." Instead of thinking of miracles as God's overriding of the laws of nature, we can think of them as God's working within the natural laws of nature to bring about *novel* events, and therefore *extraordinary* events, which exhibit divine creativity without contradicting the laws of nature. This is the concept of miracle which is most compatible with the view outlined above of nature as open and creative and providence as "initial aims" and "divine input." This concept of miracle both accepts the orderliness of nature and scientific explanation and witnesses to the unpredictable power of God to work an unexpected and novel configuration of events within our everyday life. God stands in free and purposive relation to the created order and is not locked into the finite realm of nature and history without the power to do something new. Furthermore, I do not want to assert that God does not and cannot ever act in ways that transcend the principles of any particular metaphysical system or the laws of nature as currently understood by philosophy and science. Ours is not the only mode of being and becoming into which God is locked.

> "The miracle is the only thing that happens,
> but to you it will not be apparent,
> Until all events have been studied and
> nothing happens that you cannot explain."
>
> W. H. AUDEN

But the understanding of nature as deeper and wider than our typical worldview does not require a concept of miracle as a supernatural intervention into an otherwise wholly fixed nature. Only when nature is seen as generally independent of the creative and providential work of God must miracles be seen as a divine intervention or violation of the laws of nature. Miracles occur within nature where God is at work as providential guide within the natural occurrences of nature. God's sustaining and directing providence creates novel events out of the possibilities God has structured into the world as creator. In a miracle, God acts in a special way, but not in such a way as to contradict nature. Miracles refer to those events in which God's work (not only in our perception) creates something genuinely unex-

50. C. S. Lewis, *Miracles* (New York: Ballantine, 1970), chapter 14.

pected and unpredictable, sometimes even something new. God's presence, power, and activity are everywhere and always, and yet, in some events, this presence and power and activity get focused.[51] The presence and power of God are so apparent to the believer, whether the event can or cannot be explained by contemporary science, that it is an "act of God" or a miracle to those who believe in God's providence. Miracle is not a contradiction of natural law; miracle is the providential work of God for something new within the natural processes. The word "miracle" is used to note and to emphasize the novelty of some events in the creative work of God, as God works in ways that cannot be described through the language we use everyday to describe divine providence.

> "[Tinker and Calvin Creek are] the mystery of the continuous creation and all that providence implies: the uncertainty of vision, the horror of the fixed, the dissolution of the present, the intricacy of beauty, the pressure of fecundity, the elusiveness of the free, and the flawed nature of perfection."
>
> **ANNIE DILLARD**

The work of the Spirit, who is "the Lord and giver of life," sometimes takes dramatic form. Certain events come as such a surprise, as so unpredictable, as so genuinely new in the light of what we know about the past and expected about the present, that we call them miracles. Who, at the time, could have predicted Vatican II, or the fall of communism through the self-destruction of the Soviet Empire, or the passing of apartheid in South Africa without mass slaughter? A healing may be called a miracle because it was so unpredictable or unexplainable that we must emphasize the providential creativity of God within the natural event. Even though these all happened through natural causes, they were the result of the Spirit who was working in such an extraordinary and surprising way that we describe these novel and shattering events as miracles.[52]

---

51. John Macquarrie, *Principles of Christian Theology*, second ed. (New York: Scribners, 1977), p. 252.

52. John Polkinghorne suggests that the miracle of novelty can be thought of as consistent with scientific understanding if we consider such a notion as "regimes" in physics, which are sets of circumstances in which substances behave in certain ways (for example, the three states of water). Our knowledge of regimes, however, is limited, so that God can act within the laws of nature but in a physical "regime" unknown to us. (See Hanson, *Introduction to Christian Theology*, pp. 96-97.) The world is more complex and mysterious than we normally think. Any paradigm of nature is susceptible to critique when it does not take account of the unpredictable and the novel events within an open world created from the future as much as the past. "If there is

One of the most pressing ways the question of miracle is posed for many Christians is the role of intercessory and petitionary prayer. The fundamental problem is that petitionary prayers are an embarrassment within a classical theistic view of God. "If God orders and controls all things in accordance with his eternal purpose, what difference can our prayers make?" asks Lewis Ford.[53] Why and how could we petition God to change what in God's infinite knowledge, wisdom, will, and power God has determined to do or to permit? Walter Wink understands the implications: "Before that unchangeable God, whose whole will was fixed from all eternity, intercession is ridiculous. There is no place for intercession with a God whose will is incapable of change."[54]

This does not mean that prayer is insignificant for classical theists. But prayers, even petitionary prayers, are for resignation and thanksgiving. The father of modern liberal theology, Friedrich Schleiermacher, in a great sermon on prayer from a theistic perspective, instructs us to lay before God our wishes about the important concerns in our lives, although we are by no means to feel that what we ask will take place because of our prayers. "Whatever your heart may long for, sooner will heaven and earth pass away than the slightest tittle be changed of what has been decreed in the counsels of the Most High."[55] We may lay before God in prayer our desires, but we must remember that we are laying it before the Unchangeable, in whose mind no new thought or purpose has arisen since the day when God created the world.

What does prayer mean within this theistic concept of God? Schleiermacher writes that

> It should make us cease from our eager longing for the possessions of some earthly good, or the averting of some dreaded evil; it should bring us courage to want, or to suffer, if God has so appointed it; it should lift us up out

---

substantial evidence that reality is not or has not always been the way post-Enlightenment scientific analysis suggests, then the evidence should be allowed to stand. The world of the Spirit may be often an unrecognized or poorly understood part of nature." Mark Allen Powell, *Jesus As a Figure in History: How Modern Historians View the Man from Galilee* (Louisville: Westminster/John Knox, 1998), pp. 179-81.

53. Lewis Ford, "Our Prayers As God's Passions," in *Religious Experience and Process Theology: The Pastoral Implications of a Major Modern Movement,* ed. Harry James Cargas and Bernard Lee (New York: Paulist, 1976), p. 429. See also Robert M. Cooper, "God As Poet and Man As Praying: An Essay in the Thought of Alfred North Whitehead," *Personalist* 49 (1968): 474-88; also reprinted in *Religious Experience and Process Theology.*

54. Walter Wink, *Engaging the Powers: Discernment and Resistance in a World of Domination* (Minneapolis: Fortress, 1992), p. 301.

55. Friedrich Schleiermacher, *Selected Sermons of Schleiermacher* (New York: Funk and Wagnalls, nd), p. 43.

of the helplessness into which we are brought by fear and passion . . . that so we may be able in all circumstances to conduct ourselves as it becomes those who remember that they are living and acting under the eye and the protection of the Most High.[56]

Prayer is the means by which we bring our will into accord with the changeless will of God. It is the means by which we face the dreaded evil in our lives and in our world with courage, calmness, and submission. The function of prayer, including our prayers of petition and intercession, is submission to and thanksgiving for the eternal will of God. The effect of these prayers on us is to bring us gratitude, courage, and submission to the purposes of the absolute God. Schleiermacher concludes his comments on prayers of petition and intercession with the advice, "Then entreat, until true prayer makes you forget entreaty."[57]

My own day-to-day experience as a professor of theology is that most students are offended, even horrified, when they see the assumptions and implications of their theism laid out with this kind of utter clarity and consistency. But this is, indeed, what many Christians assume providence and prayer to be. And this kind of theology and piety is pragmatically true for many Christians. Prayer as thanksgiving and submission to the unchangeable will of the absolute God is precisely what makes it possible for them to survive, and to survive with courage and stamina, the suffering and evil of their everyday lives, whether it be a protracted illness, the death of their child, the violence of abuse, terrorist attacks, or a genocidal century. There are good grounds in Scripture, tradition, experience, and reason for understanding prayer in the midst of suffering to be primarily thanksgiving and submission to the will of an omnibenevolent and omnipotent God. As Kierkegaard said, "Prayer does not change God but it changes the one who offers it."[58]

But there is an alternative to this theistic notion of God: the notion that our prayers of petition and intercession make a difference. As I outlined in the previous chapter, the God of the Bible is the compassionate and responsive God. God responds to the prayers — the supplications, the demands, the ordering, the haggling, the cage-rattling — of God's people. God's will can be altered because it is affected by the prayers of the people. The Bible assumes that God repents, that is, regrets, is sorry, grieves, has compassion, retracts,

---

56. Schleiermacher, *Selected Sermons,* p. 44.

57. Schleiermacher, *Selected Sermons,* p. 50.

58. Quoted by Joseph T. Nolan, "Can Prayer Make God Change His Mind?" *US Catholic,* January 1978, p. 9.

changes course, and relents as a result of prayers. If we see God related to the world — whether as the Hebrew Bible's God of mercy and lovingkindness, or as the New Testament's triune God who suffers and redeems through the cross and resurrection of Jesus Christ, or as the neoclassical theistic God who is eternally and internally related to the world — the conclusion is that the world, its pain and suffering, and our prayers of petition and intercession make a difference to God. Within that framework there are three things to say about the power of intercessory and petitionary prayer.[59]

1. Intercessory prayer is praying *receptively* in the midst of the world's needs. God is the primary pray-er. It is God rather than ourselves who initiates intercessory prayer. Paul says, "Likewise the Spirit helps us in our weakness; for we do not know how to pray as we ought, but that very Spirit intercedes with sighs too deep for words. And God, who searches the heart, knows what is the mind of the Spirit, because the Spirit intercedes for the saints according to the will of God" (Rom. 8:26-27). God is always praying in us and prays first. "When we turn to pray," writes Walter Wink, "it is already the second step of prayer. We join with God in a prayer already going on in us and in the world."[60]

2. Our prayers of intercession *affect the life of God*. If the Holy Spirit prays in us even before we pray, and if God is as intimately related to the anguish of the world as contemporary Trinitarian, open, and process theologies claim, then there is a sense in which the passions of our prayers of intercession can be considered also the passions of God. "Prayers, as the feelings of creatures addressed to God, form the passions of God," writes Lewis Ford.[61] When we receive the promptings of the Spirit, and our response is our passionate prayers of petition and intercession, God takes in our passions in all their depth and fullness. What we offer back to God in our own cry becomes a part of what God has to work with in creating and redeeming the world. God feels our need and our petition even more deeply than we feel it ourselves. The God of some philosophers may be dispassionate, but not the God of Abraham and Sarah, not the God of Jesus Christ, not the God who prays in and through us even before we pray ourselves. From the inside God feels what we feel, what we need, and what is possible.[62] "When we pray," writes Polking-

---

59. This discussion has been informed by Marjorie Suchocki, *In God's Presence: Theological Reflections on Prayer* (St. Louis: Chalice, 1996); by John Cobb, *Praying for Jennifer: An Exploration of Intercessory Prayer in Story Form* (Nashville: Upper Room, 1985); and by Wink, *Engaging the Powers,* chapter 16.

60. Wink, *Engaging the Powers,* p. 304.

61. Ford, "Our Prayers As God's Passions," p. 433.

62. Marjorie Suchocki, "Prayer in Process Perspective," Videocassette, Center for Process Studies, 1325 N. College, Claremont, CA, 1986.

Oh My God!

horne, "we are offering our room for maneuver to be taken by God and used by him together with his room for maneuver, to the greatest possible effect."[63]

3. Prayer not only matters to God; *intercessory prayer changes the world* by adding something new to the full reality of the world. Prayer is one way we can have an effect on the events of the world, indeed, sometimes it is the only way. If our lives are the outcome of our creaturely decisions made in response to the initiating will of God, then what we pray makes a difference to the world. "Because prayer is added to the world," explains Marjorie Suchocki, "the reality of what-can-be changes. . . . As we pray, we change the world by changing ourselves in our deepest orientation. And with that change, we alter the total situation with which God works. Prayer releases the power of God to lead the world toward the reign of God."[64]

No doubt our intercessions change us as we open ourselves to new possibilities we had not yet even imagined. But if we take the biblical understanding of God seriously, intercession is more than moments of the self with the self, or moments of our bonding with each other. Again, Suchocki's thoughts are insightful: "Redemptive possibilities that might have been irrelevant, and therefore inaccessible to the world without prayer, can be released by the power of prayer."[65] Our prayers of intercession give God something more to work with that is not already there in the world without our praying. Prayer is one of our most powerful resources in fighting the evil of our world, transforming ill will into goodwill, healing the broken and abused, saving and supporting whatever good is possible amidst all of the demonic powers of our world. This is why Christians must "pray without ceasing."

Providence, miracle, and prayer, however, do not define the whole of God's activity. Though God is the ground of possibilities and the providential power to actualize these possibilities and to create something new from the future, God is not the only power within the creation. The power of the past, the limited range of real possibilities, and the decisions of creatures also contribute to the creation of the present. Given the waywardness of our freedom, the depth of the power of sin and evil in the world, and the fact that the world does not progress toward its well-being on the basis of providence alone, however, providence must be supplemented by the grace of redemption through the incarnation, atonement, and hope for the fulfillment of God's purposes if the scope of God's activity and the whole gospel is to be received.[66]

63. Polkinghorne, *Serious Talk,* pp. 87-88.

64. Suchocki, *God, Christ, Church: A Practical Guide to Process Theology,* new revised ed. (New York: Crossroad, 1989), pp. 220-21.

65. Suchocki, *God, Christ, Church,* pp. 220-21.

66. Gilkey, *Reaping the Whirlwind,* pp. 266, 270.

CHAPTER SIX

The Threat to Faith

I. How Long, O Lord? Suffering and Evil

No human experience challenges our faith in a sovereign and benevolent God more deeply than the suffering caused by the violence of individuals, communities, and nature.[1] Although most of us have a strong sense of the goodness and well-being of our lives, our experience of pain, suffering, conflict, war, disease, plague, famine, hardship, hatred, cruelty, terror, destruction, and utter madness are just as real. Our most immediate encounter with evil is the suffering of the innocent. If suffering is unjustified, that is most obvious in the suffering of children. As Ivan says to Alyosha in Dostoevsky's *The Brothers Karamazov*,

> For the hundredth time I repeat, there are many questions that could be asked, but I ask you only one — about the children — because I believe it conveys fully and clearly what I am trying to tell you. Listen, even if we assume that every person must suffer because his suffering is necessary to pay for eternal harmony, still do tell me, for God's sake, where the children come in?[2]

The twentieth century was so dominated by wars that it has been called "the century of violence." The genocide of the Holocaust is a primary symbol

---

1. For an extended treatment of the problems of suffering and evil as a theological problem, see my *The Transforming God: An Interpretation of Suffering and Evil* (Louisville: Westminster/John Knox, 1997).

2. Fyodor Dostoevsky, *The Brothers Karamazov* (New York: Bantam, 1970), p. 294.

of the century. Soon after mid-century one historian estimated the number of "man-made deaths" at not less than 80 and probably not more than 150 million.[3] Robert McNamara, Secretary of Defense under President Lyndon Johnson, set the figure at 160 million throughout the twentieth century.[4] Sexism, racism, and genocide threaten not only our well-being but perhaps even our survival, as warfare is an unpredictable and unrelenting threat. Radical evil, the abusive violence of sheer destruction — through a terminal illness or a premature death, or through dehumanization of one group by another — remains the most deep-seated challenge to a trust in and loyalty to God that modern intellectual skepticism cannot touch.

Although all human beings try to fit grief and wickedness into their understanding of the world, monotheists have a distinctive problem. If you are an atheist, you might explain suffering as the consequence of random mutations which occur within the evolutionary process. Genes are as baneful as they are beneficial; they leave us with a large number of genetic maladjustments which bring new forms of suffering, as well as with deep psychological drives and insecurities which lead inevitably to suffering. Natural selection, for example, cannot prevent the estimated four thousand genetic defects in the human genome or weed them out once they have occurred.[5] Or you might say we must simply accept the fact that suffering is an irrational but inescapable element of human existence which we must respond to with defiance.[6] For monotheists, however, unrelieved suffering seems to contradict the notion of an all-powerful and all-loving God.

Classical theism affirms simultaneously that God is omnipotent and omnibenevolent and that evil is real. If you deny any one of these three ideas, the problem can be resolved. Affirming these three ideas concurrently, however, creates a conceptual problem. Most classical forms of theism include transcendence, eternity, simplicity, infinity, immutability, holiness, omniscience, omnibenevolence, and omnipotence as God's attributes. The key concepts for understanding evil within a theistic framework are the latter two.

The conceptual problem in theology is called theodicy. Can I hold together without contradiction the ideas that God is omnibenevolent, that God is omnipotent, and that evil is real? Technically formulated, the problem of

---

3. Gil Eliot, *Twentieth Century Book of the Dead* (New York: Charles Scribner's Sons, 1972), chapter 1. Elise Boulding set the number at 108 million in *Cultures of Peace: The Hidden Side of History* (Syracuse, N.Y.: Syracuse University Press, 2000), p. 233.

4. Robert McNamara, interview, "Good Morning America," ABC, November 24, 1995.

5. Timothy Anders, *The Evolution of Evil: An Inquiry into the Ultimate Origins of Human Suffering* (Chicago: Open Court, 1994), p. 52.

6. Albert Camus, *The Myth of Sisyphus and Other Essays* (New York: Vintage, 1955).

theodicy is thus: If God is omnipotent, God could prevent all evil. If God is all-loving, God would want to prevent all evil. But there is evil in the world. Therefore, we must question whether an omnipotent, perfectly good God exists. More broadly conceived, however, the problem is how to understand our experience of suffering and evil within the framework of what we believe God to be like. William Blake formulated the broad question in his poem "The Tyger": "When the stars threw down their spears/And water'd heaven with their tears,/Did he smile his work to see?/Did he who made the Lamb make thee?" How can this deepest challenge to our faith in a loving and all-powerful God be resolved, conceptually and religiously?

Omnipotence, in the theistic tradition, means "omnicausality." God is the originative or ultimate cause of everything in the world. According to a modification of this idea, called the "free will defense," God is the only power there is but provisionally has delegated finite power to the self-regulating processes of nature and to morally free agents; still, God retains "veto power" or "overriding power." Moreover, in the midst of natural law and human freedom, God works as the hidden but ultimate agent in determining whatever happens. All things, down to the most detailed event in the world, are caused or determined by God's eternal decree, divine plan, or ultimate will. As Calvin put it, "Therefore the Christian heart, since it has been thoroughly persuaded that all things happen by God's plan, and that nothing takes place by chance, will ever look to him as the principal cause of things, yet will give attention to the secondary causes in their proper place."[7] Following Augustine, Calvin meant that "the will of God is the necessity of things," and therefore all events "are governed by God's secret plan in such a way that nothing happens except what is knowingly and willingly decreed by [God]," so that God "directs everything by his incomprehensible wisdom and disposes it to his end."[8]

This idea has been formulated as doctrine in the Westminster Confession of Faith: "God from all eternity did by the most wise and holy counsel of his own will, freely and unchangeably ordain whatever comes to pass."[9] Although many Christians are horrified when they see the concept of omnipotence spelled out with such clarity and remorseless logic, they have, nevertheless, internalized this doctrine at the core of their piety. The questions, "Why did God kill my baby?" or "Why did God take my baby?" or "Why did God permit my baby to die?" all presume that God willed and is the ultimate cause of my

7. John Calvin, *Institutes of the Christian Religion*, 2 vols., ed. John T. McNeill, trans. Ford Lewis Battles (Philadelphia: Westminster, 1960), vol. 1, p. 218 (1.17.6)

8. Calvin, *Institutes*, vol. 1, pp. 198ff. (1.16.2, 3, 4).

9. The Westminster Confession of Faith, *Book of Confessions* (Louisville: Office of the General Assembly, Presbyterian Church [USA], 1991), p. 8 (number 6.014).

daughter's death. Many Christians affirm that God wills everything that happens, down to the last detail, the bad as well as the good. Attempting to soften the bite of the claim, they say, "Nothing happens that is not the will of God," or, "Everything that happens is part of God's plan for my life." There are no accidents, nothing random in the world, no chances in life, no good luck or bad luck. All events, even the most minute details, are God's doing. God works through my genetic inheritance, my family experiences, my freedom and decisions to complete God's "blueprint worldview"[10] in which everything fits into the secret plan which God decreed for me when I was conceived in order to display divine sovereignty. There is a divine reason for everything that happens in the world.

Classical theism, then, resolves the threat to faith by ultimately denying the reality of evil. Stated more positively, no matter how bad something may seem to be, it is really a disguised good. Theists claims that once we believe that all things have their necessary place within the love and purposes of God, we know there is nothing the world would genuinely have been better off without. On the surface this seems like an absurd claim. Who, possibly, could deny that we undergo radical suffering and that the experience seems to be evil. So I must be clear that theism denies the reality of evil in a very special way. No theist denies that suffering is existentially real and therefore appears to be evil. Our view that suffering is evil is based on our limited and finite perception, however, our inability to see the world from God's perspective. If we saw the world as God sees it, we would know that each thing that happens in the world has its appropriate, even necessary, place in God's perfectly good plan for the world. Evil is simply our limited perspective on an actual good and so is not "ontologically" real. As Augustine

> "And to Thee is there nothing at all evil, and not only to Thee, but to Thy whole creation."
>
> **SAINT AUGUSTINE**

says in his *Confessions,* "To thee is there nothing at all evil."[11] God wills everything that happens; nothing happens that is not the will of God.

Many Christians have compelling reasons to advocate this kind of theodicy. To claim to know that the world would have been better off without some events seems like arrogance, or even blasphemy, to many Christians. What makes God God are all the omnis. Any concept of God which does not

---

10. Gregory Boyd, *Satan and the Problem of Evil: Constructing a Trinitarian Warfare Theodicy* (Downers Grove, Ill.: InterVarsity, 2001), p. 13.

11. Augustine, *Confessions* 7.13, in *Basic Writings of Saint Augustine,* vol. 1, ed. Whitney Oates (New York: Random House, 1948).

include the classical idea of omnipotence is a denial of divinity. In addition, many Christians adopt a theistic theodicy because they see it as the only guarantee against the threat to the meaning of their lives and of the whole creation. Theism is the only adequate source of comfort, security, and meaning for millions of Christians. To believe that God caused or willed or permitted the death of my child or the genocides of the twentieth century or the terrorist attack on the Twin Towers is their only assurance that a child's death, or genocides, or the collapse of the towers is not ultimately meaningless. Even though I may not know why God caused or permitted these events to happen, I know *that* God did and therefore that they are part of the plan of the one who is all-powerful and all-loving. Such a belief reassures many Christians that their world is finally safe, secure, coherent, and meaningful, because all that happens is part of the plan of God.

> **"I don't ask [the death of my son] to make sense. I believe in the will of God."**
>
> **REV. SHAW MOORE,**
> *FOOTLOOSE: THE MUSICAL*

Nevertheless, I reject a theistic theodicy. The claim that radical evil is not genuinely evil seems to be not only counter to all human experience but an outrage, even a blasphemy, against humanity and in the end against a loving God. It is, finally, a defense of the horrors of nature and history which turns God into a demon.

I do not dismiss such ideas as conceptually impossible. The problem, however, is that theists must be willing to follow out to the implications of their claim. As Rabbi Brad Hirschfield said following the terrorist attacks,

> You want plan? Then tell me about plan. But if you're going to tell me about how the plan saved you, you'd better also be able to explain how the plan killed them. . . . The test of that has to do with going and saying it to the person who just buried someone and look in their eyes and tell them, "God's plan was to blow your loved one apart." Look at them and tell them that God's plan was that their children should go to bed every night for the rest of their lives without a parent. If you can say that, well, at least you're honest. I don't worship the same God.[12]

Another question is whether omnipotence is the highest conceivable form of power. Every form of theism holds that God is the highest power. But

12. Rabbi Brad Hirschfield, "Faith and Doubt at Ground Zero," "Frontline," PBS, September 4, 2002, http://www.pbs.org/wgbh/pages/frontline/shows/faith/questions/god.html.

it is not obvious that the creator of the world and the sovereign Lord of the creation requires the power to decide and to determine any or every detail of what happens in the world. Is it sheer power, the capacity to control everything unilaterally, which is awesome and worshipful, or is it our confidence in the faithful and trustworthy mercy and lovingkindness of the biblical God and compassionate power of the cross and resurrection of the triune God who is the object of our devotion and loyalty and service?

II. We Deserve What We Get: A Theistic Explanation of Suffering and Evil

In spite of claims that the ways of God are beyond our comprehension, theology brims with speculation about the reasons God causes or permits the kind of world we experience. Amidst their march toward their ultimate conclusion that evil is not real, theologians have offered a number of penultimate explanations for the presence, depth, and extent of human suffering. The fountainhead of most Western theodicies is Augustine, the fifth-century North African theologian and premier Western theologian. John Hick detects four major themes scattered through Augustine's writings.[13]

First, evil is not a substance, a thing, but rather is a "privation of the good." In order to uphold God's absolute power and goodness, Augustine rejects any notion that evil has any status apart from God. Evil is simply the corruption or malfunctioning of something that is intrinsically good. For example, disease is simply the loss of normal bodily functioning. In this sense evil is not real. It is not a positive constituent of the universe; it is the loss of the natural form and functioning of anything. One reason evil is only apparent, then, is that it is not something independent of God but, rather, is simply a declension from the inherent goodness of all beings.

Augustine's second theme answers the question of how, then, there is sin and suffering in the world. He maintains that the inherently good creation went wrong because of the misuse of freedom. All evil, both natural and moral, is directly or indirectly attributable to the wrong choices of free creatures and the penalty for those wrong choices made by the angels, Adam and Eve, and finally every human. Death and suffering entered the world as God's punishment for this free but bad choice. Although most Augustinian theolo-

---

13. A brief but rather comprehensive summary of Augustine's theodicy can be found in his *Enchiridion*, but his treatment throughout his writings has been summarized by John Hick, *Evil and the God of Love*, revised ed. (New York: Harper and Row, 1978), chapters 3-4.

gians, then, have claimed that the origin of suffering, and evil, resides in the mystery of freedom, there is another sense in which the origin is part of the eternal plan of God. The free choices of angelic and human beings occur within the purpose of God. In *The City of God* Augustine writes,

> But because God foresaw all things, and was therefore not ignorant that man also would fall, we ought to consider this holy city in connection with what God foresaw and ordained, and not according to our own ideas, which do not embrace God's ordination. For man, by his sin, could not disturb the divine counsel, nor compel God to change what He had decreed; for God's foreknowledge had anticipated both — that is to say, both how evil the man whom He had created good should become, and what good He Himself should even thus derive from him.[14]

Although creatures freely chose to rebel against God, that rebellion occurred within God's overall plan for the creation. Ultimately sin and suffering were foreknown and foreordained by God from all eternity.

Third, Augustine goes a step farther to explain why God made such imperfect creatures as angels and human beings who could and would sin: he adopted a principle of plenitude, namely, the belief that in the mind of God a universe containing every possible variety of creatures, events, and qualities, from the highest to the lowest, is a richer and therefore a better universe than would be one consisting only of the highest possible kinds of created beings. This idea is deep within the modern consciousness as well. For example, both romanticism and pluralism affirm variety, diversity, complexity, difference, and richness to be intrinsically more valuable than similarity and uniformity.

To this, then, Augustine adds, fourth, an aesthetic element to his argument. Seen from the infinite point of view of the Creator, each element of the creation is good because it has its necessary place in the overall beauty, the aesthetic harmony, of all things. If we saw the world as God sees it, we would see that and how every element of the creation, including every moment of suffering, is a necessary element in God's perfect creation. "Nothing happens that is not the will of God" because everything, including the most horrendous evils, contributes to the divine mosaic of creation. The world as God's work must contain animal and human suffering, and even hell, in order that God's creation may be aesthetically balanced.

This Augustinian framework provides the context within which to explain what is in God's mind in causing or permitting so much pain, suffering,

---

14. Augustine, *City of God* 14.11, in *Basic Writings of Saint Augustine*, p. 255.

sin, and evil. Why did God take my daughter? Why did God permit the Holocaust? Why did God allow many people to escape the collapsing Twin Towers on September 11, 2001, but not protect the approximately twenty-eight hundred who perished in the collapse and the related attacks? The primary theistic explanation is that because human beings misused their freedom, God punishes these free creatures by introducing death and suffering into the world. "We deserve what we get!" No one is an innocent victim of unjust suffering; we suffer because of God's judgment on our sinfulness and guilt, first, that of Adam and Eve, and subsequently our own sin and guilt. "If we want to magnify the 'fairness' issue and demand our rights," notes Joel Freeman, "we'd better be thankful that He doesn't take us up on our requests. Let's face it — we all deserve hell and damnation. There's not an obedient bone or tissue in our bodies. Our hearts are deceitful and desperately wicked."[15] In Christiaan Beker's less vengeful language, this explanation assures us that divine punishment is part of a rational view of the world "which moves away from punishment and suffering as irrational fate or as demonic possession toward a standard of equitable justice and order."[16]

A second explanation of suffering within a theistic framework is that suffering is necessary to shape, refine, and test our virtues, strengthen our characters, and develop us into mature, loving, complete persons. Suffering is necessary for personhood. Suffering purges us of our impatience, selfishness, superficiality, and egotism. It teaches us the virtues of strength and endurance. It makes us into majestic creatures who can love and even exhibit sacrificial love for the sake of others. The best advocate for this kind of theodicy is John Hick's "Irenaean" alternative to an "Augustinian" theodicy.[17] It is not the case that humanity was created perfect and then fell; rather, it was created with the purpose of "soul-making." God created an environment in which creatures could be brought freely to a conscious, spiritual relationship with God. This God-appointed environment, therefore, must include not only freedom but finitude, death, temptation, sin, and evil, which is a state of "epistemic distance" from God which can develop into a full God-consciousness over a long period of time. What justifies suffering and evil is not that God wills them as part of the overall plan, but that sin and evil are part of the only kind of environment which can bring creatures freely, either in this world or the next, into the full image and likeness of God.

15. Joel Freeman, *God Is Not Fair: Coming to Terms with Life's Raw Deals* (San Bernardino, Calif.: Here's Life Publications, 1978), p. 58.

16. Christiaan Beker, *Suffering and Hope: The Biblical Vision and the Human Predicament* (Grand Rapids: Eerdmans, 1987), pp. 45, 48.

17. Hick, *Evil and the God of Love*.

This prepares us for the third primary explanation within a theistic framework: eschatology. The depth of suffering and evil are justified because "all's well that ends well." All suffering and evil will be made right, in that we will be shown in the next life why it was necessary in this life, or will be rewarded for enduring in the midst of despair, or will be compensated for our losses, or will be fulfilled through the completion of our partial, truncated, or frustrated goals in this world. God's justice will be apparent to the faithful after death, suffering, and evil are defeated. Loss, apparent absurdity, hopelessness, and the terror of death will be reversed and made good in the next life. God will complete God's purpose of relationship with all creatures following death.

With a theistic framework, however, even if none of these theistic explanations is convincing, there is one final assurance: All is finally consumed in mystery. *That* God causes or permits every suffering for a good reason is certain. God's reasons may not be apparent, or even available, to the minds of creatures. But we know that hidden in the divine will, foreknowledge, wisdom, and power is a good, indeed, perfect, reason for everything that happens. If an innocent child dies, or if an ethnic group is exterminated in a genocide, we know *that* this had its place in the divine plan or the divine providential rule. The tapestry may look frayed or ugly to us, either in spots or as a whole, but we know that it is good, even though its meaning is lost in the ultimate mystery of the ways of God.

There are two very good reasons many Christians affirm a theistic theodicy. First, it is for many the answer to the ultimate threat to faith in God, the threat that all, or even a part of life, is meaningless. A theistic explanation is the only way they can establish meaning and security in the face of the ultimate threat that the love and power of God are overcome by the power of hatred and destruction. Furthermore, even for those of us who cannot accept these explanations as adequate, we must acknowledge that there is some truth in all of them. Any theological understanding of suffering and evil in a created world must include some notion of creatural freedom. And much if not most of the suffering in our world is related in one way or another to sin and its consequences. We do not encounter radical evil in which some degree of human transgression, complicity, pride, sloth, perversity, or passivity is not involved.

The basic problem with a theistic theodicy, however, is that the theistic God is not the God of the Bible and is not the triune God. I will elaborate this claim in Sections IV and V below (and have already in my discussion of free-will and process theisms in Chapter Four). Furthermore, although suffering and sin are deeply intertwined in human experience, it is incredible that anyone could believe that there is even an approximate balance between the depth of sin and the depth of suffering of most people. There is frequently little correspondence between the seriousness of sins and the depth and degree of suffering endured by many individuals and groups. Even if punishment, provisional or eternal, is justified, punishment neither makes good nor justifies the disproportion between sin and its consequences in this life. Finally, although moral and spiritual pedagogy are essential to the development of genuine character and loving relationships, "soul-making" can also result in bizarre and distorted character, and even crush people, as often as it produces mature character. When so many people end up with callous, perverted, and even demonic character as a result of the character-building experiences they undergo, we must ask what kind of God would establish an education curriculum which produces as much evil as good, or whose syllabus destroys as much character as it builds.

The decisive problems for a theistic theodicy, however, are even deeper. I find any theodicy which ends up denying the reality of evil to be intolerable at the end of the twentieth and the beginning of the twenty-first centuries. Obviously we are not God and cannot see everything (anything) from God's point of view. But, if "everything is beautiful in its own way," if at least some of the events we call evil are not genuine evil, then God is indifferent to our experience of suffering. When we come to that conclusion, we have abandoned the core of the biblical idea of God. In the end the reality of suffering and evil makes a theistic theodicy implausible. But this conclusion does not call us to abandon belief in the goodness and power of God. Rather, it calls for an understanding of God shaped more by the Bible and the triune identity. I will offer such a reconstruction after an excursus into the role of the Devil, the demons, and the demonic within an interpretation of suffering and evil as the deepest challenge to faith in a loving and powerful God.

III. The Devil, the Demons, and the Demonic

Although certain biblical passages claim that God is the creator of evil as well as good ("I form light and create darkness, I make weal and create woe, I the LORD do all these things" [Isa. 45:7]), many Christians recoil at the assertion that God is the cause of evil; if God is the ultimate cause of evil as well as good, then humans finally cannot be held responsible for sin and evil. Nevertheless, because of the depth, enormity, and intractability of wickedness, evil seems to demand an explanation beyond mere human willing, to require some kind of superhuman source, such as angelism, demons, or an evil god. Since an ultimate dualism (a counter-God who is evil or an eternal principle of evil which stands over against the good God) is unacceptable to monotheism, the Christian tradition has typically located the ultimate source of the origin of sin, suffering, and evil in the concept of the Devil.

After teaching a course in theodicy for many years, ignoring any discussion of Satan or the Devil, I decided to include an excursus on the Evil One because so many students insisted on talking about the Devil as the one responsible for the origin of sin and evil and the cause of so much of the suffering and evil in the world today. Consequently, I address the question of whether some concept of the Devil is necessary for a Christian understanding of suffering and evil. Although I do not believe it is necessary to include any concept of the Devil as "a being" in a theology of suffering and evil, I do believe that wickedness is too vast to credit to human beings alone. We must take account of a "reality," "depth," and "structure" to evil that emanates not from humanity alone but from something beyond human will, a "power" which is not divine but is transcendent, superhuman, opposed to God and to humans, and seeks our destruction, damnation, illness, and death.[18]

The name "the Devil" derives from the Old English *doefel*, Latin *diabolis*, Greek *diabolos*, and Hebrew *satan* (adversary, opponent, one who obstructs).[19] Christians have referred to him as Satan, Lucifer, Beelzebub, Belial, and other names. Satan plays a very minor role in the Old Testament, however.[20] There are only three clear references to "the satan" or "satan" in the Old Testament (Job 1 and 2; Ps. 109:6 KJV; Zech. 3:1-2;), and perhaps a fourth (1 Chron. 21:1), all from post-exilic materials (538 BC or later). In the passages from Psalms and Zechariah "the satan" is a member of God's court and serves as an accuser. In Job he is even part of the heavenly court, an observer and tester on behalf of God; in 1 Chronicles he seems to serve as an instigator.[21]

---

18. Walter Wink, *Naming the Powers: The Language of Power in the New Testament* (Philadelphia: Fortress, 1984), p. 23.

19. For a larger discussion of much of what follows in this section, see the entries on "Devil" and "Satan" and "Demonology" in *Westminster Dictionary of Christian Theology*, ed. Alan Richardson and John Bowden (Philadelphia: Westminster, 1983).

20. Some of the creation stories view creation in the context of God's conflict with chaotic and hostile waters which surround the creation (Job 38:6-11; Ps. 77:16; Ps. 104:7, 9), with cosmic monsters, such as Leviathan and Rahab (Ps. 74:12-17; Job 41), and with other gods (1 Kings 22:20; Job 1:6; Ps. 82:1, 6-7). Jon Levinson, *Creation and the Persistence of Evil: The Jewish Drama of Divine Omnipotence* (San Francisco: Harper and Row, 1988), p. 12.

21. In each of these references "the satan" is conceived as an adversary (as in a lawsuit), but is never evil, demonic, or fallen, an enemy of Yahweh or a leader of demonic forces. He is employed by God as a faithful, if overzealous, servant of God, integrated into the godhead in a nondualistic fashion, as provocateur or prosecutor entrusted with quality control.

By New Testament times his character has degenerated to the point where he becomes the lord and leader of evil spirits who oppose God and oppress humans.[22] Paul speaks of the "principalities and powers" of the world and of this age (Eph. 3:10 and 6:12 RSV; cf. Eph. 2:1-2 RSV). In the book of Revelation Satan is not only the accuser (Rev. 12:10) but a being engaged in a cosmic battle with God at Armageddon. Thus, the New Testament contains what Gregory Boyd calls a "warfare worldview," in which God is in ultimate control of the world but is not in control of the behavior of angels and humans. Rather, God is engaged in warfare with Satan and other free evil agents because their purposes work against God's purposes.[23]

The church fathers offered further definition: Satan was created by God with a good nature; he was an angel who fell of his own free will, convincing many angels to join him; he was cast out of heaven with his followers down to the lower air, earth, and underworld; he tempted humanity to the original sin; he rules the world under God's permission, testing and punishing humanity. Although his power was broken by Christ, God allows him limited scope till the end of the world, when he will be defeated forever.[24] Indeed, the belief in an objective personal Devil and his minions was all but universal among theologians as well as lay Christians until the age of the Enlightenment. By the late seventeenth century belief in the Devil was in rapid decline, fueled by reaction against the witchcraft crazes and undergirded by thinkers who emphasized human freedom, moral responsibility, and the natural causes of suffering and evil. The Devil became something that many educated people could not believe in, and so was lost as a meaningful explanation of the origin and depth of evil.

---

22. There had emerged among some Jews the idea of a kingdom of Satan (Mark 3:23-26), which was the cause of sickness, calamities of nature, and human sin. In the Synoptic Gospels, Satan is not only the tempter of Jesus in the wilderness but is the prince of this world who has the power to thwart Jesus' mission. He became known as the devil (Matt. 4:1), the tempter (Matt. 4:3), ruler of the demons (Luke 11:15), the ruler of this world (John 12:31), and the evil one (Matt. 6:13b).

23. Gregory Boyd, *Satan and the Problem of Evil*, chapter 1.

24. While the desert fathers felt his presence everywhere, medieval theologians struggled with the idea of the freedom of humans and angels within the predestinating power of God. Homilies and folklore popularized both the power and ubiquity of the Devil as the chief of all evil power and his demon subordinates among the fallen angels. From the fourteenth to the seventeenth century belief in Satan's power and his hordes of demons increased to the level of mania in the witchcraft craze. Luther and Calvin fixed the idea of the Devil in Protestantism as much as it already existed in Catholicism. The ideas about Satan and the Devil most common in popular piety, however — such as the idea that Satan was an angel put out of heaven because of his rebellion against God and his desire to assume the prerogatives of divinity — owe much to Milton's *Paradise Lost* (1667).

Today, however, the disappearance of Satan into Enlightenment disbelief is anachronistic. How can anyone who lived through much of the twentieth century and faces an abyss of evil at the beginning of the twenty-first century be content with "the death of Satan"? "A gulf has opened up in our culture between the visibility of evil and the intellectual resources available for coping with it," argues Andrew Delbanco.[25] I admit for any number of reasons to standing in the modern tradition which questions the existence of "the Devil" as a personal being. Belief in the Devil as a personal being is part of a mythological worldview of a three-story universe. Furthermore, the concept leads almost inevitably to some form of dualism, which is a direct challenge to monotheistic faith. In addition, such a belief denies human responsibility for sin, violence, and suffering by shifting it onto a cosmic scapegoat. Finally, even in cases of radical evil, such as sadism and terror, or demon possession (*The Exorcist, Rosemary's Baby, Silence of the Lambs, Hannibal*), I am not convinced we need the concept of the Devil as a personal cosmic being to account for the depth and radical character of such evil.

And yet, the most successful accomplishment of the "principalities and powers" of evil may be to have convinced modern people that they do not exist. But their retreat into nonexistence or the human imagination is no longer acceptable today. The transformation of our outrage about the depth of violence and suffering into a postmodern sense of irony *(Pulp Fiction)* is inadequate in an era of the radical evils of genocide and terrorism. We need a language to talk about the depth of evil we now feel but have no language to talk about. "To pretend that an event like that which took place on September 11, 2001, can be explained with the ordinary language of politics or psychology seems to me quite inadequate to what happened," says Delbanco.[26] The Devil is alive as a symbolic way of representing the existence of the superhuman structures and power of evil loose in the world today. There is much to say for affirming the reality of the Devil in this sense. His symbolic persona points to the reality and depth of evil in our experience. In light of our acknowledgment that the destructive impulses of humanity are intractable, "the Devil" remains powerful as symbolic language for describing it.

Although I deny that radical evil can be personified as a metaphysical person or being such as "the Devil," I affirm the reality of "the demonic" as a suprapersonal force or power which is necessary to account for the depth of

---

25. Andrew Delbanco, *The Death of Satan: How Americans Have Lost the Sense of Evil* (New York: Farrar, Straus and Giroux), pp. 3, 9.

26. Andrew Delbanco, http://www.pbs.org/wgbh/pages/frontline/shows/faith/questions/evil.html.

suffering and evil. We can affirm the reality of the demonic as modes of experience, as structures of power, as patterns of action which are powerful in history with describable (objective) effects. The New Testament is filled with language about various kinds of power which cannot be simply reduced to categories of sociology, depth psychology, or general systems theories as "nothing but" institutional and cultural arrangements and effects. Radical evil has *a spiritual dimension* to it which transcends reductionistic explanations. Walter Wink suggests that these spiritual powers ("the principalities and powers") not be viewed as separate nonmaterial, invisible, heavenly or ethereal entities but as "the inner aspect of material or tangible manifestations of power,"[27] the inner or spiritual essence or structures of institutions, nation states, and social systems. The demonic exists in the forms of "institutional violence" we all inhabit and that inhabit us, the "patterns of culture," the "habits of the heart," the political and economic structures which transcend individual choices and practices, which limit, repress, dehumanize, and destroy individuals, communities, nations, human history, and the creation itself; these include gender subordination, racial exclusion, and economic exploitation. Demons are "the name given to that real but invisible spirit of destructiveness and fragmentation that rends persons, communities, and nations," writes Wink.[28] Elsewhere Wink maintains that "Satan is the peculiar constellation of alienation, greed, inhumanity, oppression, entropy that characterizes a specific period of history as a consequence of human decisions to tolerate and even further such a state of affairs."[29]

Purely psychological and sociological language is inadequate to express or to account for this depth of evil and violence. Professor of psychiatry and religion Ann Ulanov explains this well:

From the psychological side, there are a whole lot of theories that say destructiveness comes from privation or deprivation. It isn't something in itself; it's from bad parenting or low self-esteem. What religion . . . offers to that psychology is a recognition that evil is a force . . . a horrific force . . . a mysterious force. . . . it's like an undertow of the ocean. . . . There's something that you contact that's much bigger than what you did to me or what I'm going to do to you. And you get caught in that; you're in something that's outside yourself. The personal explanation is not enough. . . . It's a

---

27. Wink, *Naming the Powers,* p. 104.
28. Wink, *Naming the Powers,* p. 107.
29. Walter Wink, *Unmasking the Powers: The Invisible Forces That Determine Human Existence* (Philadelphia: Fortress, 1986), p. 25.

power that catches you, and you are not enough by yourself to defeat it. It's universal.[30]

One might even think of it in Wink's terms as "a layer of sludge beneath the murky waters that can be characterized only as a hellish hatred of the light," or as "the sedimentation of thousands of years of human choices for evil."[31]

Recognizing demonic power does not require belief in devils as supernatural beings flying about the world at the command of an archfiend, whose name is Satan. I doubt if Satan is "a person" or "a being." But we can believe in Satan or the Devil as a symbolic personification of these powers of radical destruction, bondage, and dehumanization that transcend human freedom and choice. These powers do not possess bodies of any kind; they are not metaphysical beings; they exist and reside as spiritual powers of destruction within persons, institutions, nations, and movements. Although they are not personal beings, they are real as structures of power, as dimensions of power which charm us, misconstrue our perception, demand more and more loyalty, undergird the inertia of systems of control, and erupt from beyond ourselves.[32] They point to, even disclose, depths or dimensions of the world that lead to utter annihilation.

The Devil and the demons represent the "structures within being" which are a "peculiar energy of destruction." They are transhuman powers or dynamics which intrude upon the human scene bringing destruction.[33] Although I am in the strict sense agnostic about whether these powers are superpersonal beings, I believe the demonic is a reality — psychological, sociological, historical, perhaps even cosmic powers — to which the reality of *grace* as the power of good not our own is the only adequate answer. The demonic powers have such an ontological depth to them that there can be no power to resist and respond apart from the power of grace, which comes to us as a gift from God.

---

30. Ann Ulanov, http://www.pbs.org/wgbh/pages/frontline/shows/faith/questions/evil.html.

31. Walter Wink, *Engaging the Powers: Discernment and Resistance in a World of Domination* (Minneapolis: Fortress, 1992), p. 69.

32. Daniel Day Williams, *The Demonic and the Divine* (Minneapolis: Fortress, 1990), pp. 6-14.

33. "Demons are not specific things at all. . . . They represent, rather, that peculiar energy of destruction. . . . Its essence is to twist and break apart the forms of other things, to stunt human growth, to disrupt the social order, to misshape animals and trees, to obstruct the fruitfulness of the earth. The demonic is only known by virtue of the destruction that it causes." Arthur McGill, *Suffering: A Test of Theological Method* (Philadelphia: Westminster, 1968), p. 48.

IV. Why Doesn't God Do Something?
Creation, Tragic Structure, and the Will of God

The mystery of suffering and wickedness, driven deeper by the reality of the demonic, remains the most serious challenge to faith in God. Is God in any way responsible for evil, and, as important, how does God respond to the suffering of the world? When we begin with a biblical concept of God, summarized and formulated by the doctrine of the Trinity, interpreted philosophically and theologically by free-will theism and process theism, we come to a different understanding of God's power and will, and of the origins, nature, and solution to the problem of suffering and evil, than when we begin with classical theism.[34] How might we understand the brokenness of the world within the context of creation as an ongoing process rather than the mere unfolding of a fixed blueprint?

If we interpret creation as the emergence of an ordered, open, and changing world within the divine creativity, notions of limited power, natural order, tragedy, and chance will affect our interpretation of sin and suffering. Creation *ex nihilo* means everything is dependent on the power of God for its existence. But that does not imply that God's power is the absolute control of all events. Regardless of whether God is inherently limited (process theism) or self-limited (free-will theism), God's power as creator is more God's formation of "a world that was without form and void." God's Spirit brings something out of nothing by speaking (Genesis 1), luring (theistic evolution), coaxing the order of nature out of the formless void. Such an idea of creation implies three affirmations about the creation which modify much of the understanding of evil within a theistic perspective.

First, creation as the formation of a structured world as a single bit of reality began expanding at lightning speed implies an orderliness to the world that we cannot ignore in understanding why and how so much suffering and evil occur in a world created by God. Although the orderliness of the world does not mean determinism, God nevertheless creates a universe of cause and effect, a world we can describe as a world of natural law. Sophisticated interpreters today know that natural laws are not things out there we can find if we look hard enough; they are not edicts of unfolding fate. Natural laws are statistical probabilities about how the world will work in the future given our past experience and our ability to predict how the world will operate under certain conditions. Within the perspective of evolutionary theism, the laws of

---

34. Sections IV and V of this chapter are adapted from chapters 6-8 of my *The Transforming God*.

cause and effect are part of a world guided by providence. If this is so, then the scientific accounts of pain and suffering are important to a Christian understanding of why people suffer in a world created by God. There are scientific explanations why bodily pain, mental anguish, and social oppressions occur. Suffering and evil cannot be wholly explained as the result of sin, guilt, and punishment (of the Devil or the angels or Adam and Eve or my parents or myself). I will discuss this in greater detail in Chapter Seven, where the role of sin in turning these natural sources of pain and suffering into radical evil will be uncovered.

Here my concern is the role of the structures of creation in suffering and evil. The body experiences pain because pain receptors are stimulated by some anomaly inside the body or some violence from outside the body. The tissues of the body get too hard or too soft because of genetic coding, diet, or stress, and so close off the blood supply or explode, causing strokes or heart attacks; the immune system of the body is weakened by defective genes, diet, stress, or environment and so succumbs to bacteria and viruses, or causes cells to reproduce at an uncontrollable pace. We can give similar accounts of many of the agonizing features of our daily experience of suffering through our psychological, sociological, and political explanations of our behavior and its consequences. Scientific accounts of our suffering are significant components of a theological understanding of suffering in a world created by God. This is potentially dangerous if misapplied, for it can become a counsel of resignation to the victim of suffering: "Well, that's just the way things are, so accept it and be happy." But employed within a larger perspective as one part of an interpretation of creation, we can use this insight to reassure ourselves that God did not trigger the malignancy in my mother's body, force your child to take drugs, or exile a group into slavery to punish them for their sins or teach them a lesson. God created a world in which the natural processes of cause and effect lead, under certain circumstances, to cancer, addiction, and oppression until the processes of healing, reconciliation, and liberation modify or transform them into a new creation.

Second, because the world is a world of becoming within and through which providence works, the creation is also a process of change, novelty, and development, a world with some degree of freedom instead of cosmic fate, scientific determinism, or fixed divine blueprint. Freedom is not an exception to the world of cause and effect; it is the element of novelty and unpredictability in the cosmos, and at the human level, the element of choice and decision within the ordered world. Creation and providence understood in this way establish an environment in which suffering, in some ways and to some degree, is inevitable or at least unavoidable. As the writer of Ecclesiastes says,

154

> Again I saw that under the sun the race is not to the swift, nor the battle to the strong, nor bread to the wise, nor riches to the intelligent, nor favor to the skillful; but time and chance happen to them all. For no one can anticipate the time of disaster. Like fish taken in a cruel net, and like birds caught in a snare, so mortals are snared at a time of calamity, when it suddenly falls upon them. (Eccles. 9:11-12)

Freedom, in some minimal sense, is not unique to the human species. It characterizes all creatures and things, almost negligible in some (stones), apparent only over vast eons of time in others (cells), and strikingly apparent in yet others (human beings). Freedom is evident in some degree of novelty throughout all of the creation.

Freedom, then, means there is an element of randomness to the world, and that some of what happens to us may be as much "misfortune" as it is the "injustice" of nature, neighbor, or the plan of God. Although we have a penchant to seek a scapegoat, human or divine, for each disaster that befalls us, it is difficult sometimes to sort out injustice from misfortune. Errors, dead ends, and false trails occur in an evolutionary process that includes randomness, chance, and novelty, because the processes of nature that God has created have an element of creativity and novelty. Some of what happens in God's creation happens as accident because of the unpredictable intersection of novelty and randomness within the natural and human worlds. Misfortune, chance, or bad luck intertwine with sin and injustice in accounting for why some bad things happen to us. Many of the events in our lives consist of a complex interweaving of original sin, actual sin, the demonic, injustice, randomness, and bad luck, the occurrence of events which could have been avoided only in a world where everything was determined by God. Although this argument about chance is unacceptable to some theists, I find many Christians, when faced with the implications of theism, believe in some degree of freedom in contrast to divine determinism.

This is not to say that God is not the creator and sustainer of this kind of world, that God does not have a purpose and a will in creating and directing this kind of world, that God is not the divine power which sustains this kind of world, that miracles do not occur, that individual and corporate responsibility are not appropriate, or that predictions and plans are useless. Rather, it means that some of what happens to us is the concurrence of two independent causal chains of events, not the will of God from all eternity. If someone sets a bomb to explode an airplane I am riding in midair, the plane will crash and I likely will die. Perhaps someone even planted the bomb to blow up the plane in order to kill the person seated next to me. But that does not mean that someone, human or divine, placed me on the plane in order to kill me. I was on the plane because my decision to travel swiftly to a specific destination caused me to board that plane at that time. I was there by accident or chance (though not without causes), not by divine decree.

Third, although theism has not been friendly to the concept of tragedy, because suffering has been tied primarily to the consequences of sin, I also believe some notion of tragedy is fitting when one interprets creation and providence within an evolutionary perspective. When Jesus was born, his birth was good news to Mary. But his birth was also bad news to all of the other mothers in and around Bethlehem for it meant the death of their newborn male babies. Was the death of their babies the punishment for someone's sin? Or was the "slaughter of the innocents" (cf. Matt. 2:16) the result of a flawed world in which light is often accompanied by darkness, in which great good is accompanied by the massive and undeserved suffering of innocent victims?

> "I learned that I do not have the right stuff for such hard-boiled theology. I am no more able to believe that God micro-manages the death of little children than I am able to believe that God was macro-managing Hitler's Holocaust. With one morning's wrenching intuition, I knew that my portrait of God would have to be repainted."
>
> **LEWIS SMEDES**

Tragedy as well as sin should play a role in our interpretation of suffering. Some suffering, especially radical suffering, is lived under the shadow of the "tragic structure" of the world, what Andrew Park calls *han*, the suffering of the sinned-against who are the victims, not the perpetrators, of sin.[35] The pole of choice and the pole of finitude together account for the kind of suffering that is "radical evil," such as death camps and child abuse, which no explanation can justify. We live under conditions over which we have little freedom or control and which can destroy us. Relationships can be conflicted, and sometimes necessarily so, as in the relationship between predator and prey. There is often an inevitable conflict between two goods, two rights, and good and right. "Tragedy is the price paid for existence," writes Wendy Farley.[36] These conflicts go beyond sickness, old age, death, or misuse of freedom to a conflict in the very way the world is structured.

---

35. Andrew Park, *The Wounded Heart of God: The Asian Concept of Han and the Christian Doctrine of Sin* (Nashville: Abingdon, 1993).

36. Wendy Farley, *Tragic Vision and Divine Compassion: A Contemporary Theodicy* (Louisville: Westminster/John Knox, 1990), p. 64.

Divine power, then, is a limited power, whether ontologically or by self-limitation. God does not create and control the world by fiat but by shaping a world with divine purposes and possibilities as these emerge over the long process of becoming through God's call and promise. God's purposes are to create and redeem the world by calling it to fulfill God's future evident in Jesus Christ. To affirm the will of God in the midst of evil, therefore, is not to say that God wills everything that happens, but that God has a will within everything that happens. No moment, no occurrence, no creature, no person could come to be or continue to be without the providential power of God and the will of God for the best possibility for every event. This is not the best of all possible worlds because God has willed it to be this way. Rather, God wills the best possible for this world.[37] While God does not will everything that happens, because creatures decide what to do with God's aim for every event, God has a will in every occurrence. God wills the best possibility for every moment given the real possibilities within the context of what has happened and what can happen.

When Christians interpret the suffering of the world in the light of God's power and will, the fundamental question is how that power and will are conceived. I propose that divine power and will are defined by the Trinity, not by theism. This means that God's power is a creating, sustaining, suffering, and transforming power, not the unilateral power of omnipotence.

> "For me, there was no mystery about where God was and what he was up to on the morning of September 11, 2001. He was right there doing what he always does in the presence of evil that is willed by men; he was fighting it, resisting it, battling it, trying his best to keep it from happening."
>
> **LEWIS SMEDES**

V. God with Us: God and Human Suffering

The challenge to theism in the late modern world has positive significance for the Christian faith. The dispute has cleared the way for the recovery of the biblical God. "Perhaps the end of theism has to begin to dawn in order to disclose the existential relevance of a doctrine of the Trinity which must be grounded and explicated anew," notes Eberhard Jüngel.[38] When God is iden-

---

37. Marjorie Suchocki, *The End of Evil: Process Eschatology in Historical Context* (Albany: State University of New York Press, 1988), p. 119.

38. Eberhard Jüngel, *God As the Mystery of the World: On the Foundations of the Theology of*

tified through the history of Israel and the story of Jesus in the power of the Spirit, that is, as the triune God, elaborated philosophically and theologically by free-will theism and panentheism, our concepts of what God wills and how God works with violence and grief can be rethought. Instead of seeking to explain wickedness as part of the decrees, blueprint, foreknowledge, foreordination, or will of God, we should ask, rather, how suffering and evil are understood by the biblical concept of God's presence and activity within the history of Israel and the story of Jesus.

The key to that reconception is a recovery of a Trinitarian understanding of how God is related to the world, and how the power of God is reconceived in that framework. Suffering, sin, and evil are no longer located in God's will, but are understood as arising within a finite, open, developmental, and future-oriented creation. They are dealt with by the power of God's love revealed in the cross and resurrection of Jesus Christ. God's answer to the problem of woundedness and wickedness is not to show us now or in the eschaton how they fit into God's design or mosaic, but to show us how God overcomes the brokenness and maliciousness of the creation now and in the eschaton through the redemptive power of the cross and resurrection. Divine power is rethought as the suffering and transforming power of Jesus' cross and resurrection, not as the omnipotent power of the timeless will of God. Incarnation, instead of immutability, defines God's will and way. God is the suffering and transforming God.

The twin concepts of the suffering and transforming God are the core of any distinctively Christian answer to the problems of suffering and evil. The notion of a suffering God is a repugnant idea to Christians who share the classical concept of God's nature and power. Logically, how can an immutable being undergo the change and jeopardy of finitude? Religiously, how can a mutable deity be God? It is ludicrous, isn't it, to think of the infinite God being liable to the conditions of the finite world? Many theists, like the ancient Stoics, believe that since no one can be greater than God, no one or nothing could have any effect upon the eternal God, and therefore God must be incapable of undergoing the liabilities of the finite world. This assumption plays itself out in the theistic doctrine of the *apatheia* of God, the doctrine that denies that God the Father or the divine nature of Jesus suffered in the death of Jesus on the cross. Many Christians believe that if God is subject to the same anguish we suffer, then God cannot redeem our suffering. Unless someone is wholly beyond the travail of this world, there is no answer to the

---

the Crucified One in the Dispute between Theism and Atheism (Grand Rapids: Eerdmans, 1983), p. 371.

problem of brokenness and suffering. So God must be thought of as immutable and impassible.

I will go to the heart of the matter in a distinctly Christian understanding of suffering and evil: the triune God (and the God of free-will theism and panentheism) is the suffering and transforming God. Although the Trinity can be interpreted within a classical theistic framework, implying such ideas as immutability, omnipotence, and apatheia, the concept of the power of God is consistently redescribed by the Gospel narratives and by Trinitarian doctrine when the life, crucifixion, and resurrection of Jesus Christ are decisive for our concept of God. The triune God is the related God, whose identity consists both of a mutual relationship and interdependence within the Godhead and of a freely chosen relationship and interconnectedness with the creation.

Seen and understood through Jesus Christ, God's power is not immutable, raw omnipotence, but is the power of suffering, liberating, reconciling, and transforming love. When divine power is defined by the triune identity, and specifically by the incarnation, instead of by philosophical theism, then the death and resurrection of Jesus say something about the being, nature, and power of God.[39] The Trinity is not only a description of the biblical story and our experience of the economy of salvation; it says something about who God is in Godself. The suffering of the Son says not only something about Jesus and the function of Jesus for us; it also says something about the eternal relationship between the First and Second Persons, which is not a static but a living relationship within God. The cross and resurrection are not simply the focus of soteriology (God for us). They are the basis for our theology (the being of God). "I think that the unity of the dialectical history of Father and Son and Spirit in the cross on Golgotha, full of tension as it is, can be described so to speak retrospectively as 'God,'" writes Jürgen Moltmann.[40]

The God of Scripture and the creeds is absorbed in and with our suffering in ways that are far more thorough and consequential for our thinking about God and human suffering than most classical concepts of God have acknowledged. In Trinitarian imagery, the anguish of the Father, the agonizing and endurance of the Son, and the groaning and travail of the Spirit are as essential to what the Christian means by God as is the transcendence of the Godhead and the reliability of God as creator *ex nihilo*.

The theistic problem of how to reconcile the omnipotent power of the absolute and unrelated God to the suffering of the world diminishes when the

---

39. Jürgen Moltmann, *The Crucified God: The Cross of Christ As the Foundation and Criticism of Christian Theology* (New York: Harper and Row, 1974), pp. 243-45.

40. Moltmann, *The Crucified God*, p. 247.

story of Jesus is taken to be decisive for our understanding of the power of God. Christians who take their Scripture and creeds as normative have in hand a concept of God which should never have got them involved in the conceptual problems of theism to begin with. The typical Christian answer to the challenge to faith has been based on a false assumption about divine immutability (the idea that there is one individual who stands outside our suffering, is unthreatened by it, and can rescue us from the outside) and on a false assumption about divine omnipotence (the idea that God does or could from the outside unilaterally use omnipotent power to eliminate suffering, but usually does not because of some higher purpose). However, "Not by might, nor by power, but by my spirit, say the LORD of hosts" (Zech. 4:6). A biblical concept of God requires a revision of our natural assumption that real power is brute force, the ability to control and coerce, the capacity to impose unilaterally one's will on someone who is less powerful. When God is defined by God's relationships of mutual love and interdependence, by the power to identify with, to suffer, to persuade, to transform, to re-create, our understanding of sovereign power changes.

God looks on our suffering not from the outside but from within, from the brow and hands of Jesus hanging on the cross. God is "on the gallows" (Elie Wiesel), "the fellow sufferer who understands" (Alfred North Whitehead), "on the cross" (Martin Luther). What God reveals in Christ by undergoing our pain and anguish is not the cause, or the purpose, or the ultimate meaning of the mystery of suffering. God's answer is to enter the travail of human life. Through identification God exhibits the power to conquer pain, suffering, travail, radical evil, and death from within. What God shows in the compassion of the incarnation is the power to accept, undergo, and endure suffering. God keeps company with those who suffer, feels what it is like to have a child who suffers, and takes that suffering into the depths of the divine life. Unlike dualistic theodicies, which picture God as a commander in chief threatened by an evil empire, the incarnate God does not set up a Star Wars shield around vulnerable skies to zap the threatening evil satellites hovering overhead with laser beams. And unlike the God of monistic theodicies, God is not a positive-thinking huckster who diverts our attention away from the grit of life or anesthetizes us to suffering by having us imagine that in God's grand scheme of things evil is not real. Instead, God "emptied himself, taking the form of a slave, being born in human likeness. And being found in human form, he humbled himself and became obedient to the point of death — even death on a cross" (Phil. 2:7-8).

I want, however, to be as clear here as I can be. For Christian faith, the cross and the resurrection are two interconnected moments intrinsic to the divine life. The power to identify with us in the suffering of the cross and the power of the resurrection to transform death, sin, violence, suffering, and injustice into a new creation are the two sides of the power of the triune God.

Christian talk about the divine compassion, the vulnerable God, the suffering God, even "the death of God" (Luther), is one side of God's sovereign triumph over the power of evil. The other side of God's sovereignty is the power of resurrection to re-create life. The Christian answer to suffering and evil is not merely that God looks on with sympathy, empathetic but defeated by radical evil. The word that turns the cross into promise and assurance instead of defeat, the word

> "Let us take Auschwitz not simply as a paradigm for genuine evil but also as a paradigm for the way the world as a whole and in general is. . . . But when we look at the world with expectations established by Auschwitz, we will also find much to astonish us. There are many patterns of human relations in which people seem genuinely concerned for the good of others in community. . . . Must there not be something at work other than narrow and brutal self-interest and absolutization of one's own group? Can we not call that God?"
>
> **JOHN COBB**

that affirms meaning and even glory in the midst of suffering, is the resurrection as transformation, as re-creation, as "the new creation." The cross and resurrection, therefore, do not dispense with, or even diminish, the idea of divine power, even sovereign power. Rather, they radically transform our Caesar-like notion of what sovereign power means. The victory of the cross and resurrection is not the victory over sin, death, the demonic, suffering, and radical evil from the outside which eliminates the forces of suffering and sin through their unilateral destruction. It is a victory which draws the suffering of the world into the very heart of God, which knows real pain and loss, and which transforms death in all its dimensions into the new life of resurrection, into God's kingdom.

Ultimately we will either be transfixed by evil, resigning to it as fate or as the hidden will of God, or we will be transformed by grace into the "new creation." The Christian answer to the mystery of suffering and evil is Christmas, where God's power hits us with all the force of a hint; the answer is Good Friday, where God's power of identification undergoes and endures the pain of death to its end; the answer is Easter, where broken life is transformed through the power of the resurrection into the new creation; the answer is the kingdom of God, where the reign of God brings the purposes and promises of God to their fulfillment.

One of the reasons suffering is such a deep challenge to faith in God is that our concept of God's power has been defined by a false notion of power, the notion that divine power is omnipotent power in the classical meaning of the term. We have been led to believe that God could unilaterally prevent or abolish all the ills of the creation if God wanted to, that God manipulates the script of our lives. Since God doesn't, we simmer in our juices of despair about why the omnipotent God does not do that for us, and conclude that God is not perfectly good, or that God's purposes are beyond our imagination, or, in utter despair, that God does not have sovereign or even sufficient power.

But the sovereign power of the triune God is not unilateral power. Sovereign power, the power that is ultimately more effective than unilateral power, is the power of the resurrection. There is no more omnipotent, sovereign, triumphant power than the power of the Creator God to bring "the new creation" out of the open, free, and risky creation. We do not need omnipotent power to answer the deepest challenge to the meaning of our lives, unless what we worship is not the God of the triune identity but rather the God of absolute, unilateral power, which according to the book of Revelation is the false God of Caesar rather than the ultimate power of the Lamb. The ground of our confidence is the promise God made evident and confirmed by the resurrection of Jesus from the dead. "The transformation of Jesus that occurred in resurrection is no absolute and new beginning. Rather, the transformation is fashioned through the experience of crucifixion. . . . The resurrection power of God does not annihilate the past, it transforms the past."[41]

By holding the power of the cross and the power of the resurrection together dialectically as the kind of power revealed by the sovereign God in the history of Israel and the story of Jesus, Christian faith represents a new understanding of the power of God in the midst of suffering that leads to despair. Will this kind of answer satisfy all Christians? I doubt it. Many Christians think of God as a cosmic Caesar who causes or permits everything that happens for some purpose, and who could eliminate their suffering by decree, and so they burrow deeper and deeper into self-pity and anger, and finally into despair, over their deepest question of why God caused or did not prevent the evil that has caused their heartache. The Trinitarian God, however, is not a gentile lord or a cosmic Caesar. God is the God of Jesus Christ, the cross, and resurrection, the God whose power is the power of love and whose might is the power to transform death in its many forms into rebirth, the old creation into

---

41. Marjorie Suchocki, *God, Christ, Church: A Practical Guide to Process Theology*, new revised ed. (New York: Crossroad, 1989), p. 114.

"the new creation," the sin, suffering, and death of the old heaven and earth into "a new heaven and earth." Although there are supplementary and complementary truths to be learned by Christians from other theodicies, including classical theism, the center of the Christian response to the deepest challenge to faith is the triune God. When the depth of our suffering is located within the life of God and within the power of God to transform suffering and evil through the power of the resurrection, we have found the central Christian reassurance to the deepest challenge to our faith in God.

CHAPTER SEVEN

The Lack of Faith

I. The Image of God

Are Helen and Matt in *Dead Man Walking*, Willy in *Death of a Salesman*, Ralph, Piggy, Simon, Roger, and Jack in *Lord of the Flies*, Salieri in *Amadeus*, Bess in *Breaking the Waves*, Judah in *Crimes and Misdemeanors*, and Sophie in *Sophie's Choice* inherently good, loving human beings, or inherently bad, driven by dark inner impulses toward conflict and destruction? The most difficult task in developing a theology of human nature is to maintain a dialectic between an optimistic and a pessimistic view of human nature. Tempted to jettison a dialectical view, some Christians want to emphasize our "original righteousness," our innate goodness, while others want to emphasize our "original sin," an inner core that drives us toward ruin. A Christian anthropology, however, requires a dialectic in which "the image of God" and "the fall" offer a realistic interpretation of this creature who is made "a little lower than God, and crowned . . . with glory and honor" (Ps. 8:5). The human story is a drama consisting of three acts: we are created in the image of God from the dust of the earth; we are alienated from God, nature, each other, and ourselves; and we are redeemed by Christ who restores the image of God.

A Christian understanding of humanity has its underpinnings in the Old Testament account of creation. Yahweh forms 'adam (humankind) from the 'adamah (earth, matter, dust, ground). Genesis contains two stories of human origins, the priestly account in Genesis 1:26-31 and the Yahwist account in 2:4b-24. I note three things about these texts. First, there is a strong affinity between these accounts of human origins and the emphasis in biology, genetics, and chemistry on *homo sapiens* as a product of the earth. "Then God said, 'Let us make humankind ['adam] in our image, according to our likeness. . . .

So God created humankind in his image, in the image of God he created them; male and female he created them" (1:26-27), and "then the LORD God formed man ['adam] from the dust of the ground ['adamah], and breathed into his nostrils the breath of life; and the man became a living being" (2:7). The idea that 'adam is made from 'adamah affirms that all creatures are products of the earth. We are interconnected in our basic structure.

Second, 'adam is not a proper name but is a collective noun meaning "humankind." Therefore, all humanity is made in the image of God. Humankind exists as two creatures, but no gender subordination is permitted by these texts.[1] "In both creation stories mutuality is the key to their relation," writes Elizabeth Johnson.[2] God blesses both sexes and both are given dominion over the earth. The capacity to be a bearer of God's image is a gift that is not restricted to a particular sex.[3] Male and female are thus created together to be the image of God, to be representatives of God.

Third, this creature is a complex creature, consisting of body, soul (*nephesh* or *psychē*, which means life or animating vitality), and spirit (*ruach* or *pneuma,* which means our spiritual capacities to relate to God). We are not essentially a spirit or a soul or a mind which happens to be trapped in a physical body until we shed it at death. We are animated bodies with spiritual capacities. The human creature, therefore, is distinguished from other creatures because it was endowed at a certain stage of its emergence with the divine image. This image does not deny our animal origins. What Christians deny is the adequacy of a reductive understanding of this creature (we are "nothing but" our chemistry, biology, genes, and drives). This earthling is "a little lower than God." "The human relationship to God is not something that was added to human existence; they are created in such a way that their very existence is intended to be their relationship to God," explains Klaus Westermann.[4] As creatures, therefore, we are essentially good. Whatever our problem is, it is not our finitude, limitations, sexuality, drives, or desire for survival, comfort, and pleasure.

The assumption in traditional Western theology was that Adam and Eve were the first two parents of the human race. They were humanity in its ideal perfection, a perfection that existed at the beginning of the race. There was

---

1. The best discussion of these texts can be found in Phyllis Trible, *God and the Rhetoric of Sexuality* (Philadelphia: Fortress, 1978), chapter 1, esp. pp. 12-21.

2. Elizabeth A. Johnson, *She Who Is: The Mystery of God in Feminist Theological Discourse* (New York: Crossroad, 1992), p. 71.

3. Johnson, *She Who Is,* p. 75.

4. Klaus Westermann, *Genesis 1–11,* quoted in John Leith, *Basic Christian Doctrine* (Louisville: Westminster/John Knox, 1993), p. 100.

no death, evil, suffering, or sin; humanity was perfect, complete, and ful-filled. The pair existed in paradise in the condition of "original righteous-ness." The high point of this interpretation of human origins and nature was Augustine, for whom Adam and Eve existed in a state of justification, illumi-nation, beatitude, and immortality. They were immune to physical ills and had supreme intellectual gifts. They were able to avoid sin and to be pre-served in their righteousness.[5]

Long before Augustine provided this dominant Latin church's interpreta-tion of the image of God, however, the Greek church adopted an alternative view, formulated by Irenaeus, bishop of Lyons (France), who lived from 130-202 CE.[6] Assuming a more evolutionary view of humanity, Irenaeus made a distinc-tion in Genesis 1:26 between the image and the likeness of God. Instead of ori-enting our thinking about human nature toward the past, and to restoration, he oriented human being toward the future, and so to the hope of completion. The Garden of Eden was thus not a paradise but was more like a kindergar-ten. Being creatures, Adam and Eve were not yet perfected. They were distant from God in their knowledge of God. They were intellectually, morally, and spiritually children, existing in an "epistemic distance" from God. Only by a long process of responding to the Spirit could they advance toward a mature relationship (likeness) to God. Because of their weakness and inexperience, this process was interrupted, almost from the start, as they fell prey to Satan's wiles and disobeyed God.[7]

Adam and Eve were not perfect, according to Irenaeus; they were perfect-ible, capable of being actualized only in their historical careers.[8] In our mod-

> "God has given us not so much the colors of a picture as the colors of a palette."
>
> G. K. CHESTERTON

---

5. Before the fall, Adam and Eve were not able not to die *(non posse non mori)* because they were created *ex nihilo* and so could fall back into nothingness, nor were they not able not to sin *(non posse non pecarre)* because they were free. They were able not to sin *(posse non pecarre)*, however, and able not to die *(posse non mori)*, because they knew nothing of concupiscence, since the body served the soul and reason reigned, as divine assistance was within reach and they were able but not compelled to serve the good. They existed in an original perfection.

6. For Irenaeus's views on Adam and Eve, see his *Against Heresies*, especially chapters 3-5. For secondary discussions see J. N. D. Kelly, *Early Christian Doctrines* (New York: Harper and Row, 1960), pp. 170-72, and John Hick, *Evil and the God of Love*, revised ed. (New York: Harper and Row, 1978), pp. 211-15.

7. Kelly, *Early Christian Doctrines*, p. 171.

8. Robert R. Williams, "Sin and Evil," in *Christian Theology: An Introduction to Its Tradi-tions and Tasks*, ed. Peter Hodgson and Robert King (Philadelphia: Fortress, 1982), pp. 191-92.

ern framework, we could say that Irenaeus transmuted the first human pair into symbols of the first million years of our transition from humanoid to human being.[9] He does this by distinguishing between the image of God, the spiritual capacities with which we are formed, such as reason, free decision, and capacity for fellowship, which make it possible for us to move toward spiritual relationships, and the likeness of God, which is the goal of our spiritual development, actualized as we are transformed by God's Spirit. Our perfection is not an original perfected perfection mysteriously lost, but a potential or perfecting perfection of mature relationships toward which we are nurtured by the Spirit of God.

In modern Christian thought, a decisive issue for an interpretation of the image of God is whether that image is an original endowment we lost, or a potentiality which we are called to complete through the providential Spirit of God. If it is the latter, we can say that like all creatures, we emerged from simpler, less complex forms. By the creative power and purposes of God, our possibilities for complexity increased and our capacity to be "like God" emerged from inorganic to organic to living to consciousness of our spiritual possibilities. When we became self-conscious we gained a degree of freedom from our past and from our bodily determinations, a degree of autonomy, self-transcendence, and awareness of both our finitude and our infinity. We became explicitly aware of our dependence on God, of our distance from knowing God in full spiritual communion, of our potential for faith, hope, and love of God. We became the image of God. As John Macquarrie notes, "We must think of the Imago Dei more in terms of a potentiality for being that is given to man with his very being than in terms of a fixed 'endowment' or 'nature.'"[10] It means primarily that our relationship with God is essential to our human nature.

Whether the image is interpreted as an original perfection or our capacity to be perfected through the power of the Spirit, there have been many interpretations of what that original or potential endowment is.[11] The notion most

9. Marjorie Suchocki, *The Fall to Violence: Original Sin in Relational Theology* (New York: Continuum, 1994), pp. 87-99.

10. John Macquarrie, *Principles of Christian Theology,* second ed. (New York: Scribners, 1977), p. 231.

11. Some have interpreted our uniqueness as human beings to mean that there is a physical likeness between the human creature and God, that God actually looks like us, which leads to an unacceptable anthropomorphism. In contrast, the tradition has interpreted the image to mean that "the many pre-eminent gifts with which the human mind is endowed proclaim that something divine has been engraved upon it." John Calvin, *Institutes of the Christian Religion,* 2 vols., ed. John T. McNeill, trans. Ford Lewis Battles (Philadelphia: Westminster, 1960), vol. 1, pp. 184-85 (1.15.2). But the question of just what these gifts are — just what God-given unique endowment

in line with the perspective of this book is to interpret the image of God as our capacity for relationships. We are created for a life of covenant with each other, nature, and God. Human beings are created to reflect the triune structure of God's own interrelationality and God's relation to us, with us, and for us. The image of God is our capacity for relational existence, our divine draw toward the future to be what we were created to be.[12] To claim that we are created in the image of God is to claim that God has made us sufficiently like Godself for communion between God and other creatures to be possible.[13]

The question of our humanity, therefore, is not only how we are to understand ourselves, but how we are to understand the other, including the neighbors and strangers on the planet whom God has given us to love and whose well-being we are to promote and protect.[14] So the image of God means there is an unconditional worth, an intrinsic equality, dignity, and freedom owed every human being through our love and justice, solidarity and compassion. To be human is to be free to be creative, to revolt against everything that is opposed to our humanity, "to be identified with the victims of humiliation and to participate in the liberation of all who have been denied dignity."[15]

The Christian view of humanity as the image of God, then, is not a theory about a perfect male and female pair of Urparents at the beginning of history.

---

or capacity makes humans "a little lower than God" — has prompted many speculations. Interpretations have ranged from our cranial capacity or our tool-making capacity to, especially in the West, our power of the mind to reason, which reflects the divine logos, or, in the East, our state of blessedness. Further proposals include our (1) dominion over the earth and its creatures (the human is a viceroy to till the earth and give it meaning); (2) our self-transcending and self-determining freedom, which includes the power of the self to objectify itself and transcend itself, especially its instincts and impulses; (3) our power of memory, including our cultural achievements of the past, and of anticipation; (4) our symbolizing power of language in the form of conceptual thought and analysis; (5) our morality; (6) our immortality; (7) our historicity, which includes our capacity to transcend our past and our capacity to create our future and to transcend our culture; (8) our creativity, or our created co-creative powers we share with God.

12. See Daniel Migliore, *Faith Seeking Understanding: An Introduction to Christian Theology* (Grand Rapids: Eerdmans, 1991), pp. 120-23; Ted Peters, *God — The World's Future: Systematic Theology for a New Era*, second ed. (Minneapolis: Fortress, 2000), pp. 147-51, 155; Leith, *Basic Christian Doctrine*, pp. 99-104; Clark Williamson, *Way of Blessing, Way of Life: A Christian Theology* (St. Louis: Chalice, 1999), pp. 158-60; Macquarrie, *Principles of Christian Theology*; David Kelsey in *Christian Theology*, ed. Hodgson and King, pp. 156-64; Robert Neville, *A Theology Primer* (Albany: State University of New York Press, 1991), p. 52.

13. Goeffrey Wainwright, *Doxology: The Praise of God in Worship, Doctrine, and Life: A Systematic Theology* (New York: Oxford University Press, 1980), pp. 16-17, 23.

14. Williamson, *Way of Blessing, Way of Life*, p. 158.

15. James Cone, *A Black Theology of Liberation*, second ed. (Maryknoll, N.Y.: Orbis, 1986), pp. 93, 101.

Rather, the image of God is embodied in an actual human life, Jesus as the Christ. "He is the image of the invisible God, the firstborn of all creation" (Col. 1:15); "He is the reflection of God's glory and the exact imprint of God's very being" (Heb. 1:3). Where do we see the image of God? The image of God is not the old Adam but the true Adam, Jesus Christ. We discover in Jesus a human being who was fully human in the way God intended humanity to be. The Logos, the Word of God, incarnate, is the true image of God. Christ makes us the image because as the incarnation of God "from above" he bestows dignity on every human being, and as the image of God "from below" he bestows the image as true humanity in us through our discipleship to him.[16]

What is decisive about him as the image of God is the way he lived as a human being in complete reliance on God and in trustful openness and obedience to God's power and God's future. He lived completely for his fellow human beings and in complete identity with them in relationship and community.[17] He is humanity as it is meant to be, as it has been received from the hand of God. "Jesus Christ is the secret truth about our essential nature, about what life was meant to be and about ourselves as we shall be in God's future. Our essence is to become what he was and is," writes Ted Peters. Christ as the "new Adam" calls us to the future of what we will yet be. "Who we were, are, and will be has been precapitulated at Easter."[18] Christ has already established what it is that will define who we as human beings will be. We can conclude along with Peters that "Becoming human, in the last analysis, then, is not a restoration to a prefallen state of grace that humans once possessed but lost. It is not a return to the old creation. It is rather a future arrived for the first time. It is a participation in the new creation."[19] We become the image of God when we are "in Christ," who is the true image of God (1 Cor. 15:45-49; 2 Cor. 4:4).

II. Sin and Original Sin

To talk about the image of God as a future reality, however, is to emphasize the gulf that exists between what we are now and what we can and will be. Our present reality falls short of our possibilities and promises. There is, indeed, a pervasive and deep fault in the creature God created to reflect the di-

16. Elizabeth Johnson, *Consider Jesus: Waves of Renewal in Christology* (New York: Crossroad, 1995), chapter 5, esp. pp. 71-72, 77-78.

17. Shirley Guthrie, *Christian Doctrine: Teachings of the Christian Church* (Atlanta: John Knox, 1968), pp. 192-93, 234.

18. Peters, *God — The World's Future*, pp. 152, 153.

19. Peters, *God — The World's Future*, p. 156.

vine image. Deep in our experience we know that we are not what we can be and ought to be, that we are alienated from God, nature, each other, and ourselves, that we do not love God and our neighbors as we were created to love them, that we do what we hate and do not do what we want to do (Rom. 7:15). We experience ourselves as sinners. Although some Christians emphasize sin so much that they lose sight of humans as the image of God, we pay too high a price to avoid the language of sin. "Sin" is the word that forces us to encounter the depth of brokenness in the world and our own capacity for violence and evil. "If there is no evil — if those 'mistakes' we make occur *solely* because of flawed toilet training or repressive social forces — then we trick ourselves into imagining that we can overcome future 'errors' through education or better socialization," writes Beverly Gaventa.[20] Theology needs the language of sin if we are to understand the depth of the problem to which the grace of redemption is the only adequate answer.

"Sin" is the term we use to point to the broken relationship between humanity and God. The Bible details endlessly the ways this relationship is broken, the consequences of this break, and the ways this relationship can be restored. Sin is both a moral concept (*ht'*, to miss a goal or way) and a religious concept (*'wn*, guilt or iniquity; *ps'*, transgression or willful crime; and *hamartia*, or falling short, error, deficiency, fault, transgression, rebellion, and revolt). It points to our failure to move toward our intended destiny, and the conflict, injustice, estrangement, and suffering that result from those choices. In Scripture by far the dominant idea is that sin is a violation of the will of God (Isa. 59:12-13; Rom. 1:18-32). It is a revolt, a rebellion, a willful disobedience proceeding from an evil heart, an inner corruption and perverse intention which results in acts of disobedience. It is faithlessness, disloyalty, idolatry, and lack of trust in God; it is injustice, exploitation, neglect, cruelty, and oppression of others. "To be a sinner," says Kenneth Cauthen, "is to live in a wrong relationship with God and others rooted in a deliberate refusal to honor and obey the Creator and to live in harmony with one's fellows."[21]

> "If sinful humanity ever hopes to save itself from the sin of pride, it *must* stop believing its own propaganda. We who write the press releases about our own goodness cannot be trusted to tell the truth."
>
> **MARSHALL GREGORY**

---

20. Beverly Gaventa, *First and Second Thessalonians, Interpretation: A Bible Commentary for Teaching and Preaching* (Louisville: John Knox, 1998), p. 120.

21. Kenneth Cauthen, *Systematic Theology: A Modern Protestant Approach* (Lewiston, N.Y.: Edwin Mellen, 1986), p. 185.

The Bible offers almost no theories about the origin of sin. It does suggest the marriages of the sons of God to the daughters of humans (Gen. 6:1-8), the fall of Adam and Eve (Gen. 3), and the evil imagination or impulse or inclination against following the Torah (Gen. 6:5), all of which suggest how sin began but say nothing of the cause of all subsequent sin. The Old Testament, especially the Law and Prophets, simply describes what sin is and how it works out. It is disobedience of the divine command which results in punishment. In the New Testament sin is simply acknowledged as an actuality and even radicalized through the superhuman alien powers who have invaded the creation and taken it over. But these are never developed into extended explanations of the origin of sin and the cause of all subsequent sin. Paul does appropriate the Adam story as a type/anti-type contrasting Christ and Adam (Rom. 5:12-21), arguing that just as redemption originates in and through Christ, so sin originates in and through Adam and spreads to all humanity as seen in the universality of death and the conflict between the flesh and the spirit.[22] Basically, however, the Bible assumes that the world is universally sinful, that sin is humanity's rebellion or revolt against God, and that salvation results from God's gift of Torah or the gospel addressed to sinners through the story of Jesus — his life, death, and resurrection.

Although Augustine did not invent the concept of sin, he did provide the West with its classic formulation of sin as a theological doctrine. His interpretation has so dominated the Western church that most Christians have assumed that his interpretation of the origins and nature of sin is the biblical view. Indeed, his interpretation has nearly achieved the status of dogma in the West. As noted above, he assumed that Adam and Eve were the first two historical human beings living in Paradise. They were endowed with an original righteousness which made them perfect human beings who were able not to sin, and they lived for a time in a state of sinlessness. Their bodies served their souls; reason reigned; they were able but not compelled to love God and to follow God's command not to eat any fruit from the tree of the knowledge of good and evil. When the Tempter arrived, however, they freely chose to eat the forbidden fruit, disobeying the divine command. They voluntarily defected from their perfection. Why, or even how, a perfect creature could choose freely to disobey is a logical question which can only be answered by appealing to the "mystery of finite freedom," since a creature who was perfect not only could but would freely choose always to obey in the light of his or her original righteousness. But the inexplicable fact is that they disobeyed, and in their disobedience they fell from their original righteousness into sin.

---

22. Williams, "Sin and Evil," in *Christian Theology,* ed. Hodgson and King, pp. 170-72.

As the result of the fall Adam and Eve not only sinned but became sinners. They changed their original perfect human nature into a fallen human nature. The image of God was vitiated; it became defective. Adam and Eve were now not able not to sin *(non posse non peccare)*. They became sinners, disobedient creatures who were guilty of sin and who were punished by being driven from Paradise and made subject to the suffering of the pains of childbirth and manual labor and other consequences of sin, including death. Furthermore, they not only became sinners, but they begat sinners. What the parent was, the offspring became, so that all subsequent humanity has become a "mass of perdition" liable to punishment for the guilt of the original sin of Adam and Eve. Augustine explained that their corrupt nature was transmitted to their descendants in three forms: a disease which distorts the good, a power which incites to sin, and a guilt liable to judgment. Sin is propagated not by imitation but by generation. All of us are now born with a corrupted, distorted human nature; we are born not only with a condition inclined to sin but with the inherited guilt of Adam and Eve. For all men were thus essentially in the loins of Adam when he was condemned, and therefore he was not condemned without them, so that even the newborn inherits the guilt of Adam and Eve and is liable to condemnation, although each person also freely decides to recapitulate the sin of disobedience and thereby confirms the sin and guilt of Adam and Eve in his or her own life.

Although the reason for the fall is located in the mystery of human freedom (and ultimately in the wisdom of the divine plan), the phenomenology of the fall is clear to Augustine. Though perfect, Adam was still capable of choosing the lesser instead of the greater good. Instead of turning his vision, love, and loyalty to God in faith, he turned toward himself and put himself before God, thereby denying his dependence on God for his perfection. Adam's sin was an act of *unfaith.* He turned away from God and toward a finite good. Specifically, Adam turned in *pride* toward himself. He became *incurvatus se,* incurved back in upon himself, instead of bending toward God as the object of his trust. The source of his sin is his pride, the absolutization of the self. The result of his pride is the bondage of the self to a finite good. In contrast to optimistic views of human nature, in which sin is accidental or contingent in the sense that it can be avoided, or to pessimistic views of human nature, in which sin is identified with creaturehood as such, Augustine offers an interpretation of sin in which sin is not essential to our nature but is a contradiction of our essential nature. Sin is a "second nature," a corrupt nature we inherit from our first parents, a fault or blemish which plunges us into disorder, a condition which biases us toward evil, drives us toward an inordinate desire for mutable goods. All human beings are born in sin, inherit the guilt of original sin, and recapitulate the original sin in their actual sins.

Although Augustine provided one of the most profound interpretations of the human predicament that every human being faces in the inner depths of her soul, an interpretation as compelling today as it was in the fifth century, there are, nevertheless, features of Augustine's anthropology that are highly problematic. First, Augustine's exegesis of Genesis 2–3 as actual history is no longer credible, even though such an idea is still affirmed by many Christians. There is not the slightest evidence from evolutionary biology, physical or cultural anthropology, or geology and archaeology of a historical period in which two perfect human beings lived in a Paradise in the Tigris-Euphrates river valley. There is no evidence anywhere of a time of perfection in the beginning, whenever and whatever one thinks "in the beginning" means. The ideas of creation and providence outlined in Chapter Five make the idea of perfection at the beginning impossible (and unimportant) to believe. Although it is not likely that we will ever know precisely how human life appeared on this planet, what we think we know contradicts the story of the Garden of Eden understood as "once upon a time" in history.

> "We belong to a long line of hate."
>
> **SAM CAYHALL, GENE HACKMAN'S CHARACTER IN *THE CHAMBER***

Second, although Augustine wants to protect God from responsibility in any sense for sin and to place responsibility wholly on human beings through their free decision, sin is already present in the biblical story in the form of a serpent roaming Paradise. The serpent and his unfaith are present alongside Adam's and Eve's faith. They did not originate something not already there counter to the will of God. Alienation and evil are already present in or with the creation in the form of the serpent before Adam and Eve introduce them as something new into the creation.

Third, the notion of an inherited guilt is intellectually and morally noxious, since it is difficult to imagine how guilt, a moral and a religious category, can be genetically inherited in the way we inherit eye color and bone structure. We also cannot accept the claim that everyone can be held morally responsible and damnable for the sin of Adam and Eve, even though some Christians immediately baptize newborns on the grounds that unless the guilt of original sin is washed away by the waters of baptism, the infant is liable to punishment. Augustine's interpretation ultimately makes responsibility for sin (though not our actual sins) impossible to sustain by locating it with the first two human beings. Many modern theologians concur with my conclusions, at least as far back as John Wesley, who conceded that we inherit the guilt of original sin, and that our corruption leads inevitably to actual sin, but doubted whether God would condemn anyone on the basis of original sin only.[23] He omitted from his revision (Article 7) of Article IX of the Anglican "Articles of Religion" the phrase "in every person born into this world, [original sin] deserveth God's wrath and damnation." Interestingly, this revision of the Augustinian tradition can be seen as recently as the LaHaye-Jenkins *Left Behind* series of books on the apocalypse, which reassures us time and time again that no one under the age of twelve is left behind following the Rapture.[24]

III. Becoming Children of God: Developments within the Classical Tradition

Many of these liabilities are reduced, however, when we interpret the Genesis story as a myth expressing the basis, depth, and breadth of our experience of alienation from God. The story of Adam and Eve is not a historical account of the origin of sin but a narrative description of the spiritual roots of our estrangement from God. Adam and Eve are Everyman and Everywoman. They symbolize the source of sin deep within the human spirit, the personal center of each of us. They expose how deep-seated (original) the estrangement of each self from God and from each other is. "I" and "we" are not what we were created to be, either as we were before a fall from perfection, or as we were created to become in the future. Original sin is not the first sin or the beginning of sin. "Original" refers to the foundation and depth of sin at the center of the human spirit. Adam and Eve describe in story form what theologians describe in more abstract form, namely, the inmost and universal substructures and underpinnings of sin within each human self. They are so deep and so wide that they go to the very origin of the self as a spiritual reality.

This understanding of sin characterizes most modern theologians who subscribe to my criticisms of the Augustinian view, including the most notable re-interpreter of the Augustinian view, Reinhold Niebuhr.[25] Niebuhr understands the story of Adam and Eve to be myth, not history. He accepts the conclusions of modern science about the beginning of the human species and

23. John Wesley, letter to John Mason, November 21, 1756, in *Works of John Wesley*, 8 vols. (London: Epworth Press, 1931), vol. 6, pp. 239-40.

24. Tim LaHaye and Jerry Jenkins, *Left Behind: A Novel of the Earth's Last Days* (Wheaton: Tyndale House, 1995), pp. 37, 46, 48, 62, 92, 93, 106, 119, 193, 211, 214, 235, 255.

25. The full statement of Niebuhr's theological anthropology is *The Nature and Destiny of Man* (New York: Scribners, 1941), vol. 1 *(Human Nature)* and vol. 2 *(Human Destiny)*. The key to his understanding of sin is vol. 1, chapter 7, "Man As Sinner," pp. 169-207.

distinguishes between pre-scientific and permanent myths. The story of Adam and Eve is a permanent myth, a symbolic representation of the human condition, the story of Everyman's and Everywoman's spiritual condition. The situation in the Garden represents in narrative form the deepest structures of the human self before God. We both are created in the image of God and are sinners. The concept of sin, Niebuhr writes, "affirms that the evil in man is a consequence of his inevitable though not necessary unwillingness to acknowledge his dependence, to accept his finiteness and to admit his insecurity, an unwillingness which involves him in the vicious circle of accentuating the insecurity from which he seeks escape."[26] As finite creatures we are weak, dependent, involved in the necessities and contingencies of the natural world, filled with drives and desires, liable to death as a part of nature. What is distinctive about us is that we are also spirit. We exist at "the juncture of nature and spirit." We have a capacity for free decision and for self-knowledge, through memory, introspection, and anticipation of the future.

This is a precarious place for this creature to live. As both bound and free, as limited and limitless, we are anxious. This situation, however, is itself not sin, since "it is not his finiteness, dependence and weakness but his anxiety about it which tempts him to sin."[27] Within this situation of anxiety we can either live in faith, that is, trust in God for the security and fulfillment of our future, or we can live in lack of faith (unfaith), that is, rebel against God either by denying our contingency and turning to ourselves in pride and self-love or by escaping our freedom by turning to sensuality. "When anxiety has conceived it brings forth pride and sensuality," Niebuhr maintains.[28] The doctrine of original sin is the claim that although it is not *necessary* it is *inevitable* that all human beings turn to finite goods rather than to God in their anxiety. The original or foundational sin, therefore, is *pride*, as we freely decide to turn to ourselves instead of God as the ground and object of our confidence. We become so incurved back in upon ourselves that we will do anything we think is necessary to establish our security. We trust our own power, our knowledge, our virtue, our self-discovery to save us. This pride expresses itself in the selfishness of individual pride and in the injustices of collective pride. The idolatry of self-love takes either the form of making the self god, or the alternative idolatry which seeks to escape from freedom by serving some other god, such as extravagant living, sexual obsession, or some other form of escape from responsibility. Apart from the power of grace, every individual in

---

26. Niebuhr, *Nature and Destiny of Man,* vol. 1, p. 150.
27. Niebuhr, *Nature and Destiny of Man,* vol. 1, p. 168.
28. Niebuhr, *Nature and Destiny of Man,* vol. 1, p. 186.

her situation of anxiety turns inevitably in pride to herself as the ground of her security. We are bound by pride to the consequences of personal exploitation through selfishness and social exploitation through injustice.

This is, I think, a compelling reinterpretation of the Augustinian understanding of the depth of the human problem and its consequences.[29] Niebuhr locates sin in the depths of the self. Sin is inevitable though we are responsible in our freedom. It arises out of the pretensions of the spirit instead of the lusts of the flesh. Like Augustine, Niebuhr sees sin as rebellion against God, though Augustine roots the origins of this rebellion in prehistory in the fall of the angels and the first human pair, while Niebuhr roots the origins of sin at the center of each human self. This is, in my opinion, a vast improvement of the Augustinian interpretation. Nevertheless, Niebuhr's re-interpretation of the Augustinian framework is not without its problems.

It has become more apparent in recent years the extent to which any Augustinian interpretation of original sin has been worse news for women than for men. The reason is that it tends to make male experience normative for an interpretation of sin, and that this interpretation has been used as a tool to ignore or subordinate women's experience of sin. This may seem like an unfounded claim: although both Augustine and Niebuhr identify sin with pride in its many forms, few Christians want to claim that sin is only a male problem or that women do not participate in the human experience of ego, pride, guilt, and injustice. But many feminists have argued that women's sin is not the same as men's. Instead of ego and pride, women's sins "are better suggested by such items as triviality, distractibility, and diffuseness; lack of an organizing center or focus; dependence on others for one's own self-definition; tolerance at the expense of standards of excellence; inability to respect the boundaries of privacy; sentimentality; gossipy sociability; and mistrust of reason — in short, underdevelopment or negation of the self."[30] Pride pre-

---

29. Many other variations of this kind of Kierkegaardian-existentialist interpretation have flourished. One of the most notable is that of Paul Tillich, who understands the fall as a universal symbol of our transition from essence to existence. Our existence is not a matter of essential necessity but is a fact. Since we exist in finite freedom, we can actualize that freedom. In actualizing it, we estrange ourselves from the ground of our being (God). This is the inevitable, necessary consequence of actualizing our freedom. Psychologically this is the transition from the dreaming innocence of childhood to our self-constitution, the original fact of our existence. So creation and fall are identical in the sense that actualized creation from potentiality and estranged existence are identical. This leap from essence to existence is the original fact, though, not a structural necessity. Original sin is this tragic universality of existence.

30. Valerie Saiving, "The Human Situation: A Feminine View," in *Womanspirit Rising: A Feminist Reader in Religion,* ed. Carol P. Christ and Judith Plaskow (San Francisco: Harper and Row, 1979), p. 37. (Originally published in the *Journal of Religion,* April 1960).

supposes enough sense of self and power to rebel against God and impose oneself on others. If through millennia of subordination women have been denied the sense of self which leads to pride and exploitation, then the identification of sin with pride is shaped by the male experience of the self, of the rebellious self before the sovereign Father.

The lack of self which is imposed by the roles assigned to women may itself be the cause of the anxiety which is the context of sin. Indeed, perhaps it is anxiety that produces the lack of being a true self, instead of the lack of a sense of true self that produces anxiety.[31] The internalization of inferiority and blame may be the form of sin as lack of faith in God which many women experience, not the sin of pride and will to power. Sin can be the lack of pride, the loss or diminishment of the self, as much as idolatrous false pride. Put in the Augustinian framework, if sin is the lack of faith in God, then sin can take the form of the lack of self or the loss of self, which reflects the lack

> "Sin is one of the most misunderstood words in the Christian vocabulary . . . the manifestations of sin are infinite, and therefore . . . the disciple community cannot presume to know a priori precisely what must be said and done. Sin as pride is vastly different from sin manifested as sloth; and how varied are the faces of both pride and sloth!"
>
> **DOUGLAS HALL**

of faith in God, as much as the overreaching, prideful trust in the self in rebellion against God. To identify sin with pride is to identify the lack of faith in God with only one form of the lack of faith — a stereotypically male form. To do so is to exclude other forms of unfaith. John Buchanan puts it this way:

> Sin may involve pride, the tendency in every one of us to think more highly of ourselves than we ought, but sin also involves the refusal to be fully human, to be the responsible moral agents God created us to be. The human predicament is not simply that we are vain, selfish and egocentric, that we want to be gods and are altogether too full of ourselves, but that we don't live fully enough or aim high enough, that we refuse to acknowledge our potential and our responsibility to be God's co-workers in creation.[32]

Furthermore, creation and fall must be connected more closely than the Augustinian tradition has permitted. Although sin is rooted in the self and its free decisions (no Christian theologian wants to deny that sin exists apart

31. Suchocki, *Fall to Violence*, p. 83.
32. John Buchanan, "Who Cares?" *Christian Century*, January 11, 2003, p. 3.

177

from freedom and decision), the Augustinian tradition does not acknowledge the degree to which our natural environment and our evolutionary background are implicated in the meaning of human sinfulness. Western theologians have restricted sin to the realm of human freedom alone in order to separate sin from creation as such, a connection they assume would impugn the absolute goodness of God's creation. But a breach is already present in the story of Adam and Eve long before they choose to disobey God. The reality of brokenness was already evident in the creation prior to the fall in the form of the serpent. Brokenness did not originate with and is not restricted to an unexplainable decision on the part of human beings. There was a flaw in the creation to which they yielded.

There is, therefore, a sense in which sin is inescapable. There is tragic inevitability as well as free decision involved in sin. We need the Irenaean tradition, which acknowledges the role of the natural world in our nature and destiny, to complement the Augustinian preoccupation with freedom and decision. Evil cannot be reduced to sin and its consequence; sin cannot be located solely in human freedom. Finitude and freedom exist in more of a dialectic than the tradition has acknowledged. Although sin does not coincide with our finitude, it is made possible by our finitude as much as by our freedom. If one begins with a dynamic instead of a static concept of perfection, the goodness of the creation does not exclude a tragic element for which humans are not wholly responsible. Evil is rooted in our finitude, ignorance, weakness, and disease as well as in our free decisions. Sin is the form of evil in which our freedom and decisions turn the limitations of our finitude — our chemistry, our genes, our aggression and violence, which we inherit as part of nature — into destruction. Much of our inheritance from nature distracts us and turns us away from God. There is a natural "epistemic distance" between God and the creature. John Leith offers this analogy: "The first sin, therefore, would be comparable to the fall a child suffers as the child learns how to skate. In order to learn to skate one must try, and in these initial efforts there will be many falls; but through the falls one comes to the maturity of a competent skater."[33]

Sin, therefore, is rooted in our evolutionary biology as well as our freedom. Our innate aggressiveness is not the consequence of an ancient fall from perfection but is part of our created nature as the image of God. Contrary to Augustine and Niebuhr, anxiety is rooted in our biology as well as in our self-transcendence and freedom. To be sure, sin is not some biochemical compound passed on in our genes; sin centers in our self and not in our physical bodies. "Yet we are by nature an aggressive species," notes Marjorie Suchocki.

33. Leith, *Basic Christian Doctrine*, p. 108.

"Our capacity for violence is our birthmark as a species through our instinct for survival. Tragically, all life is parasitic upon other forms of life. Survival necessarily entails violence." God calls us to transcend violence, however. It is when violence and aggression are unnecessary and unavoidable that they become sin. "Without the ability to transcend our violent tendency, there may be evil, but it is not yet sin. . . . To the extent that we do not avoid unnecessary violence, we live in sin."[34]

If we appropriate themes from both the Augustinian and the Irenaean traditions, we can say this about the Christian understanding of sin: Sin refers to more than our behaviors or tempers that violate moral or religious laws (sins). Sin refers to a *condition* or *state, namely, our lack* of faith, our alienation from God because of our refusal to trust the Creator and to love the neighbor. The opposite of sin is not virtue but faith. Sin is the theological term which acknowledges the tension between our essence (our capacity to exist before God in faith) and our existence (our fractured trust in God and love of our neighbors and ourselves).[35] No one single root metaphor is adequate to describe and account for this condition. Sin, a Hydra-headed monster, grows two heads for every one severed.[36] Our lack of faith can be manifest in a prideful, titanic, self-centered idolatry, an insurrection against God and every covenant partner through domination. And it can be manifest in a self-hatred in which we negate ourselves and allow other creatures to take the place of God in a banal, self-disparaging apathy or resignation from existence.[37] We can think of ourselves in self-centered ways, and destroy our well-being and the well-being of the creation through avarice, envy, lust, and anger. And we can refuse to think of ourselves highly enough as loved by God, and so live lives of sloth, passivity, lethargy, triviality, and fear.[38]

The notion of original sin underscores the reality that sin is not merely a particular act, and not merely an individual's decision, but that we are part of "a massive disorientation and perversion of human society as a whole," that we are part of a "kingdom of sin."[39] The sins of society and the sins of parents precede and corrupt every child. From generation to generation this condi-

---

34. Suchocki, *Fall to Violence*, pp. 94-95.

35. Paul Tillich, *Systematic Theology*, vol. 2 (Chicago: University of Chicago Press, 1957), pp. 31-36.

36. Mary Potter Engel, "Evil, Sin, and Violation of the Vulnerable," in *Lift Every Voice: Constructing Christian Theologies from the Underside*, ed. Susan Thistlethwaite and Mary Potter Engel (San Francisco: HarperSanFrancisco, 1990), p. 164.

37. Migliore, *Faith Seeking Understanding*, pp. 130-31.

38. Williamson, *Way of Blessing, Way of Life*, pp. 161-62.

39. Macquarrie, *Principles of Christian Theology*, p. 262.

tion is passed on in the ways that one human life penetrates another human life, before birth, at birth, in the family, in groups, in society, in culture, in the memories of the race. All human beings are born into a fallen world, and until we are open to the grace of God, we are sinners, not because we inherit guilt from Adam and Eve but because we pick up this condition with remarkable quickness and efficiency. We do not start out innocent and then fall into sin. We are born into the reality of sin, a tragic condition of the creative process for which we are not guilty but in which we nevertheless participate. Sin is "a layer of sludge beneath the murky waters" that hate the light and truth, "the sedimentation of thousands of years of human choices for evil," according to Walter Wink.[40] If we speak of total depravity, we do not mean that everyone is totally evil or that no one is capable of any good. We mean, rather, that sin insinuates itself into every crevice and corner of life and every act, the good ones as well as the bad ones.

The inevitability and universality of sin do not exonerate us from personal responsibility, however. Although sin is a universal condition, it is also a self-chosen act. We are without excuse. Therefore, one of the problems in theology is how to reconcile the ubiquity and inescapability of sin with each person's responsibility for it. The fact is that we each decide against the covenant of creation and against our own potential to be more than we are. Original sin and individual responsibility are dialectical concepts in understanding sin. Over and over in earlier chapters I have affirmed the reality of human freedom. The question of freedom arises again here. Is humanity genuinely free given the Christian concept of sin? If sin is as deep, structural, and inevitable as I have said, and if salvation is wholly dependent on the freedom, grace, mercy, and power of God, as I will say again, how can we be said to be free?

There is a strong impulse in Christian theology to claim that we are not as free as we think we are. This claim goes back to St. Paul's "problem of the divided self": "For I know that nothing good dwells within me, that is, in my flesh. I can will what is right, but I cannot do it. For I do not do the good I want, but the evil I do not want is what I do" (Rom. 7:18-19). Paul's dilemma received its classical interpretation in Augustine's account of the fall and of original sin.

Augustine tried to resolve this conundrum in his controversy with Pelagius in the early fifth century. For Pelagius, we still possess a completely free will and so are responsible for our own sin. If sin proceeds from necessity, it is not sin; if it proceeds from choice, it can be avoided. Sin is a free, conscious

---

40. Walter Wink, *Engaging the Powers: Discernment and Resistance in a World of Domination* (Minneapolis: Fortress, 1992), p. 69.

choice that breaks a commandment known to the perpetrator.[41] Augustine, too, affirmed the natural freedom of the will. We do not do things out of any necessity but as a matter of free choice. He argued, though, that the will was weakened and incapacitated through sin. He uses the analogy of a pair of scales with two pans, one representing good, the other evil.[42] If the pans are properly balanced, the arguments in favor of doing good or evil can be weighed and the proper conclusion drawn. For Pelagius the pair of balanced pans is in perfect equilibrium and not subject to any bias. But for Augustine the pans are not balanced. One pan is so weighed down with sin that every decision is inevitably biased toward an evil decision. Although the scales still work, and the will still makes decisions, the will is skewed toward evil. Thus the free will still exists in sinners but in a state corrupted by sin.

The Protestant Reformers, notably Luther in his concept of "the bondage of the will" and Calvin in his idea of "total depravity," went farther than Augustine to argue that we are no longer free at all. The will is in total bondage to sin. Calvin taught that sin had so corrupted the will that all that remained was a horrible deformity so that the mind was capable only of being an idol factory. Luther argued that the image of God is lost in all but name. The will is enslaved to sin. We are not free to turn away from sin because the consequence of our depravity is "the bondage of the will." Although Calvin and Luther did not teach a metaphysical determinism, they did teach that there is no human capacity apart from the grace of divine election to know God and do good.

An alternative exists, however, between notions of sin and grace which imply predestination, and the fifth-century Pelagian and modern notions that we are free and able to choose God on our own. Wesley taught that although humanity after the fall is not able to choose God because of the power of sin, God through Christ restored enough freedom to all humanity in its natural but fallen state through prevenient grace that there is a synergy between the grace of God and the free decision of the repentant sinner. Unlike Pelagius, who believed in a "natural freedom," Wesley taught that we are so enclosed by sin that only God can break through the barrier to liberate us. Although we cannot decide to turn to God on our own power, the freedom of every human being even in a sinful state is empowered enough by the prevenient grace of God through the power of the Spirit that we can choose to respond to God's call. Grace is effective in all humanity as a prevenient gift.

41. Cauthen, *Systematic Theology: A Modern Approach*, p. 188.
42. Alister McGrath, *Christian Theology: An Introduction* (Oxford: Blackwell, 1994), pp. 372-73.

In agreement with Calvin and Luther, Wesley believed that there is no longer a natural free will. But unlike the Reformers, for Wesley grace does not imply predestination. Prevenient grace empowers each person to choose whether or not her spirit will respond to the divine Spirit. Even sinners are free agents through the prevenient grace of God.

IV. Beyond the Tradition: Shame and *Han*

One problem with the traditional Western interpretation of sin is that it locates the problem of sin so thoroughly in the pride of the individual and the consequences of that pride for the sinner (guilt, judgment, condemnation) that the dimensions of sin that are connected to our social relationships are ignored or made merely the consequences of sin that is, again, seen primarily as a problem of the individual at the depth of the self. The problem of sin is the predicament of the individual sinner (a condition) and the consequences of his or her sins (behaviors) together. This truncation of the problem is being addressed by theologians who have introduced insights from feminist experience, insights about shame, and insights about *han* into a fuller understanding of sin. When we introduce notions of our social connectedness into our understanding of sin, we see that sin entails more than simply the pride of the isolated individual who subsequently wreaks social havoc. Sin also entails the experience of shame and *han* — there are social dimensions to sin itself. When speaking of sin within the context of the *perpetrators* of sin, individual sin and accountability are stressed; when speaking of sin within the context of the *victims* of sin, concepts such as vulnerability, shame, and *han* must be added for a fuller understanding of sin.

To be sure, sin refers to the free acts of responsible individuals who create and reinforce the structures of oppression as a result of their anxiety and pride. But sin even in this sense depends upon and reinforces the systemic structures of oppression that are larger than individuals. Sin depends upon the social, political, and economic arrangements that distort our perceptions and restrain our ability to such an extent that we find it difficult if not impossible to choose the good. Here the insights of the feminist critique, discussed above, are essential to an adequate understanding of the depth of sin. The feminist critique is not that the tradition is wrong, but that it is inadequate to understanding the situation of sin. The tradition provides an inadequate analysis of the situation of sin in which the victims of pride and power find themselves. Though many neo-Augustinians, including Niebuhr, thought of humans in society, they still understood them as essentially individuals who are caught up in social relationships. What is essential, according to such an understanding, is the self and God, and how the self comes to be a self, so that social relationships are subsequent relationships. Sin is essentially a description of the relationship between the individual and God, and then it is the consequence of the disruption of that relationship in our interrelationships.

But, as I noted above, sin as the condition of alienation and estrangement is a Hydra monster. It is not simply the problem of the false pride of the autonomous individual, which entails temptation, disobedience, guilt, bad conscience, and punishment. Sin as alienation refers to the depth and breadth of the whole human condition of brokenness. If we think about sin in the context of the greatest claim of Scripture, that all human beings are created through covenant to serve the well-being of each other, then the lack of faith in God, unfaith, involves more than the individual self before God in disobedience, guilty and liable to punishment unless forgiven. Sin involves all of us who live within its structures, including its victims and the many forms of estrangement beyond individual pride.

Closely related is the insight that this Hydra monster also has the face of shame. Sin is as easily the rejection of the image of God as it is overestimation of ourselves as the image of God. Shame is the cry of disbelief that God believes in us. Like the diffusion of the self, shame is the feeling of inadequacy or failure to live up to the social ideals about what people should be able to do, be, know, look like, or feel.[43] In sharp contrast to a healthy pride based on our capacity to live up to these ideals, shame arises when our perception of ourselves does not live up to them, so that a diminished self-esteem results along with feelings of inferiority, inadequacy, incompetence, and weakness.[44] Emptiness instead of arrogance describes this kind of brokenness. As Adam and Eve experienced in the Garden, we feel naked, exposed, needing to hide or cover ourselves, rejected by God and the community, abandoned, without any self-regard. Shame is a profound sense of unworthiness when things we want to hide are exposed, a sense of weakness in the face of a challenge, failure in competition, messiness, physical defects, mental defects, losing control of

---

43. Lyn Bechtel, "Shame," in *Dictionary of Feminist Theology,* ed. Letty Russell and J. Shannon Clarkson (Louisville: Westminster/John Knox, 1996), pp. 259-60.

44. Shame is about the self — its inadequacy, its defectiveness, and its unworthiness — whereas guilt is about self-judgment and remorse about violating rules and principles or consciously injuring others. "Guilt is about something I have done or contemplated doing; shame is about something I am (or am not)." In guilt, we need to follow the example of Jesus of naming specific acts or patterns for which we need to repent rather than emphasizing our general unworthiness. James Fowler, "Shame: Toward a Practical Theological Understanding," *Christian Century,* August 25–September 1, 1993, p. 816.

our bodily functions and feelings, sexual impulses, aggressive impulses, the sense that there is "something wrong" with us.[45]

Shame performs its destructive work on our selves through its capacity to make premature judgments about ourselves. The redemption needed is not so much the forgiveness of individual sin and guilt but the overcoming of our dishonorable status, the acceptance of the unacceptable, being made worthy human beings. In the ancient world of honor and competition, Paul declares in Romans 1:16-17 that the power of God is revealed in his shameful gospel. God reverses the stereotypes of honor and shame his hearers were subjected to. Robert Jewett puts it this way:

> The message of Christ crucified shatters the unrighteous precedence given to the strong over the weak, the free and well-educated over slaves and the ill-educated, the Greeks and Romans over the barbarians. If the gospel that the world considers shameful has divine power, it will prevail and achieve a new form of honor for those who have not earned it, an honor consistent with divine righteousness.[46]

This is not the triumph of grace as forgiveness of guilt. It is the triumph of grace over a shameful status.

Along with original sin as guilt there exists an original shame that is part of the structures into which we are born. To understand sin only as individual pride, and injustice as simply the consequence of that pride, omits an awareness of the sociohistorical reality of sin. Racism, classism, and sexism are not merely the *consequences* of the sin of the disobedient, isolated self who stands before God as guilty and subsequently becomes an oppressor. These "isms" *are themselves* an original sin. The "wretched of the earth" are born into a psychological and sociological context of shame and bitterness independent of the sin of guilt of the isolated individual. The shamed need release or liberation, not simply forgiveness. This situation of brokenness is referred to by Minjung theologians as *han*.[47] They understand sin as pride to be inadequate for dealing with the depth of human suffering and injustice. Brokenness is not simply individual pride and guilt; it is also a sinful condition within which victims of sin live. Sin and *han* must be treated together if the depth of

---

45. Leroy Howe, *The Image of God: A Theology for Pastoral Care and Counseling* (Nashville: Abingdon, 1995), p. 158.

46. Robert Jewett, *St. Paul Returns to the Movies: Triumph Over Shame* (Grand Rapids: Eerdmans, 1999), p. 18.

47. Andrew Park, *The Wounded Heart of God: The Asian Concept of Han and the Christian Doctrine of Sin* (Nashville: Abingdon, 1993), chapters 1-3.

human separation is to be understood and if the full redemptive significance of Jesus' suffering and death is to be grasped. Sin and *han,* then, are entangled realities; they must be discussed together; they interpenetrate and shape each other.

Human sin and brokenness consists of the pride of the sinner but also the pain of the victims of sin, who experience the condition of brokenness as helplessness and bitterness. *Han* is the critical wound of the heart generated by unjust psychosomatic repression as well as by social, political, economic, and cultural repression. Sin includes not only the moral agency of the sinner and his standing before God, but also the victims of sin and their pain. While sin and guilt belong to the oppressor, *han* and pain belong to the oppressed. The two realities overlap, exist side by side, and often exist within the same individuals and groups. Most people experience both sin and *han;* these are "indivisible in their cause-effect relationship."[48] Salvation is not only the healing of the sinner before God from the guilt of sin and fear of death, but also the healing of the victims of sin through awakening, understanding, a vision of a new world, and the redemptive power of God through the guilt and shame of the crucified and resurrected Christ. Thus, for Christians the primary thing to say about human nature is that the creature created in the image of God who exists in a state of alienation from God is redeemable.

V. Redeemed Humanity

One of the most egregious misrepresentations of the faith of the church is the claim that it teaches a pessimistic view of human nature. This perception is correct in the sense that Christian anthropology is a realistic assessment of the breadth and depth of the human capacity for evil, which it locates at the broken center of each human self and in every human society and social structure. This insight, formulated in the doctrine of original sin, emphasizes how estranged we are from ourselves, each other, nature, and God in our day-to-day existence. Anyone who lived through much of the history of genocide of the twentieth century knows that the concept of a sinful humanity is the most empirical of all Christian doctrines. Christians take sin seriously.

They do not take it too seriously, however. Obsession with sin is a complete distortion of the Christian faith. The Christian concept of sin is bracketed by the two optimistic doctrines that human beings are created in the image of God and are redeemable and redeemed. Surrounding the pessimistic

48. Park, *Wounded Heart of God,* p. 70.

strand of Christian anthropology is the optimistic promise that humanity as the image of God is redeemed by Jesus Christ and will be made into the image of God through the grace of justification and sanctification in this life and the next. If sin is taken too seriously, as a reality so entrenched that it is insuperable, then human nature is paralyzed. This is the ultimate pessimism. The Christian gospel, however, is optimistic. There is another reality, the kingdom of God and power of the resurrection, which is irrevocably established, and this power is already at work in the world every day and will be fully completed in due time. Any denial, or subordination, of these two doctrines that humanity is the image of God and redeemed is a negation of the Christian gospel.

Human beings are sinners and saints, destructive and creative, a bundle of tensions. Christian faith is neither completely optimistic (we can save ourselves by ourselves from our anxieties and hates) nor completely pessimistic (we can be saved only by being part of those predestined for salvation). Sin is a condition to be healed, not punished or forgiven.[49] The ultimate claim in Christian anthropology is that human beings are redeemable and redeemed. The fall does not say we are utterly sinful, basically wicked, and incapable of good. We are not evil by nature, but are good creatures of a good God who live in a brokenness which needs to be healed. Perhaps we should say that human beings are fallen, not that human nature is fallen. If we say our nature is essentially sinful, then salvation is impossible, or at best would be an annihilation of our nature, not a restoration (Augustine) or a fulfillment (Irenaeus) of the human way of being. We are *redeemable* in the sense that we can be repaired and completed as the image of God. Salvation or healing, either the restoration of our perfection or the fulfillment of our potential given in the creation, is possible. As there is original sin, so there is original righteousness in the sense that we long for release from our sin and for the fulfillment of our lives. It is impossible to determine how much of this is natural and how much of it is grace (that debate has preoccupied theologians for centuries), but there is a drive or a call, a continuing yearning for our restoration or fulfillment as the image of God. The fall means that we live under the systems of domination which pervert and destroy us, but the fall has not revoked our vocation to live humanly.[50]

Therefore, the central claim of a Christian anthropology is that we are *redeemable and redeemed.* The powers that pervert and destroy us can be, are be-

---

49. Rita Brock, *Journeys by Heart: A Christology of Erotic Power* (New York: Crossroad, 1988), p. 7.

50. Wink, *Engaging the Powers*, p. 73.

ing, and will be transformed by grace. There is nothing we can ruin that God cannot redeem. What has been perverted in time can be redeemed in time. God intends us for better things. When we receive the good news of the gospel, the news of justification and sanctification, and are reconciled to God, we regain our rightful role in the creation. We are set free to enjoy the creation and move forward in hope.[51] Redemption is not making us something other than what we are. It is restoring or fulfilling us to be what we essentially were or are, the image of God. The gospel is a message not of salvation from the world but of the transformation of the world, right down to its basic structures, which are liberated from the oppression of the powers that enslave and destroy us.[52] The distorted human potential is fulfilled in a redeemed humanity.

Jesus Christ is true humanity, humanity as it was created to be. Jesus Christ, not Adam and Eve, defines what it is to be the image of God. He is not humanity restored to the image of God. He is the new humanity, humanity as God calls humanity to be. In him humanity as the image of God has now become fully realized in history. The prototype of human nature is defined by Christ rather than by an original righteousness with which humans were endowed in the beginning by their Creator. Christ as the incarnate Word "from above" reveals the love and mercy of God and through identification with us restores or completes our human being, which is now disfigured by sin, as the likeness of God. The Word incarnate results in an insuperable dignity to every human being, leaving no human being unaffected, giving every human being an unsurpassed worth and intrinsic equality.

> "In the final analysis, God does not so much want something *of* us as want to be *with* us. . . . an incarnation-centered Christology emphasizes the fact that God does not so much require something of us as want to give something to us."
>
> **KATHRYN TANNER**

Jesus as the incarnate Word "from below" embodied and enacted the values of the reign of God in his discipleship, calling humanity to be the instrument of the reign of God in history through peace, justice, and well-being.[53] In Jesus Christ we know humanity from below as complete humanity. For the Christian faith, human nature is no longer thought of as its original form (an original perfection or historical potential at the beginning of the species), but is the new humanity both modeled in the image of God made flesh and re-

---

51. Williamson, *Way of Blessing, Way of Life*, p. 168.

52. Wink, *Engaging the Powers*, p. 73.

53. Johnson, *Consider Jesus*, pp. 71, 76.

deemed by Christ as the image of God.[54] In spite of all other conditioning factors, in spite of how real and intractable our estrangement is, no matter how reduced or compromised our responsibility for each other is, Christian faith does not give up on humanity. Our freedom to be the image of God can be restored or fulfilled through grace when we become a new creation in Christ.[55] Salvation is being conformed to Christ as the image of God and the new humanity. It is the establishment and fulfillment of our true nature. Christ is both the basis of redeemed humanity and the model of true humanity. He is himself the grace of God incarnate with us, for us, and in us. We cannot be saved from the power of sin by anything in ourselves or in the systems of alienation and oppression in which we live. We can be saved only by something that transcends us, by a good not our own which comes to us as the sweet sounds of amazing grace. Sinners though we are, we are redeemed sinners, part of the order of creation that nothing on earth, not even our sin, can separate us from. Anxiety and pride, diffusion and worthlessness, and shame and *han* are put to route in the presence and power of the one who always believes in us more fully than we believe in ourselves, in whose presence there is mercy from everlasting to everlasting.[56]

The redeemed humanity, the new humanity, the new creation is the beginning of a new freedom from bondage to sin and for partnership with God and each other through the grace present in the full humanity of Jesus Christ.[57] He is the pioneer of the new humanity (Heb. 12:1-2). "The fact that human beings really do have courage and hope, really do play and love, and can do so soberly and without illusions," writes Peter Hodgson, "suggests that the reality of redemption has already inscribed itself on the structural possibilities of human existence and is discernable there before and apart from an explicit theology of redemption, a Christology, and pneumatology. That inscription, however, remains ambiguous and obscure, subject to varying interpretations."[58] The question, to which we now turn, then, is how we are to think of Jesus Christ as the true image of God, as God with us in human form, and as the power of a redeemed humanity.

---

54. Howe, *Image of God*, p. 51.

55. Linda Mercadante, "Sin, Addiction, and Freedom," in *Reconstructing Christian Theology*, ed. Rebecca Chopp and Mark Taylor (Minneapolis: Fortress, 1994), p. 236.

56. Howe, *Image of God*, pp. 171, 176.

57. Migliore, *Faith Seeking Understanding*, pp. 136-38.

58. Peter Hodgson, *Christian Faith: A Brief Introduction* (Louisville: Westminster/John Knox, 2001), p. 87.

CHAPTER EIGHT

Faith in Jesus Christ

I. The Ministry of Jesus of Nazareth

For Christians faith in God is christomorphic (Christ-shaped). Faith is Christian when Jesus Christ is decisive for faith in God. The primary christological claim is that "in Christ God was reconciling the world to himself" (2 Cor. 5:19). Christology is the affirmation that Jesus reveals God to us, that he is the bearer of salvation in his life, death, and resurrection, and that he defines the shape of the Christian life.[1] Christology is the elaboration of the claims that Jesus was God incarnate (the person of Christ) and that Jesus saves us (the work of Christ).

The primary source of our knowledge about Jesus, the New Testament, is not interested in Jesus in the same way we might be interested in Julius Caesar or Abraham Lincoln as historical figures. The New Testament has a christological agenda. "But these are written so that you may come to believe that Jesus is the Messiah, the Son of God" (John 20:31). It is not interested in a biography of Jesus but in the claim that he is the Word incarnate. It presents us with a Jesus who is understood to be God with us. "And the Word became flesh and dwelt among us" (John 1:14 RSV). Christology affirms simultaneously that the Word of God was Jesus and that Jesus was the Word of God.

If we are talking about a real human being, then what can we say about him as a figure of history? One of the baffling questions for beginning students is why there is so much controversy among theologians about the historical Jesus. To ask this question seems odd to many Christians. They read in

---

1. Alister McGrath, *Christian Theology: An Introduction* (Oxford: Blackwell, 1994), pp. 273-75.

popular news magazines about "the quest for the historical Jesus" by members of the Jesus Seminar and wonder what about the story of Jesus in the New Testament is so debatable. They share the premodern view that Jesus of Nazareth, the portrait of Jesus in the four Gospels, and the Christ confessed in the creeds are identical. If an ABC reporter had been on the spot with a camcorder, she would have recorded exactly what is written in the four Gospels. The Gospels are history, biography, and theology all in one.

The problem for contemporary christology, however, is that this instinctive presumption is not so obvious to many modern Christians.[2] The great divide over Jesus among Christians in the late modern West has been shaped by the Enlightenment and its criteria of historical knowledge.[3] How reliable are the biblical documents as history? Those who accept this modern question have been involved in three "quests for the historical Jesus" throughout the modern period: The first began in the late eighteenth century and ended when Albert Schweitzer discredited it in his *Quest for the Historical Jesus* (1909). The quest was then resumed in the early 1950s with Ernst Kasemann's research. The third quest came about when the question was revived in the 1980s by the Jesus Seminar, and it has captured public interest through the mass media magazines and television.

It is notable, however, that a number of theologians have moved beyond the modern to a postmodern view of Jesus. They build their beliefs about Jesus either on the kerygma — the preaching — of the earliest church (Rudolf Bultmann and Schubert Ogden) or on the Jesus of the texts of the canon that are received as authoritative (Hans Frei). Jesus of Nazareth is the object of faith, but we do not have faith in him because modern historical research can establish reliable knowledge about him. We believe the kerygma or the narratives of the canon about him as God with us. In some important and ironic ways, then, the radically different premodern and postmodern perspectives

2. For a longer discussion of this problem, see chapter one of my *The Many Faces of Christology* (Nashville: Abingdon, 2001), esp. pp 25-36.

3. Modern views of Jesus in the last two hundred years have been shaped by criteria which have resulted, to one degree or another, in skepticism about our knowledge of the "facts" about the Jesus who lies behind the faith of the church. Modern historiography assumes we should bring a critical attitude to every document we read because what is reported in any document is not necessarily what happened. There is a tendency of the imagination, for any number of reasons, to embellish or "overinterpret" any historical event. Furthermore, all historical knowledge must be evaluated in the light of what our modern view of reality tells us is possible in history. Miracles, exceptional cases, complete novelty, and events of supernatural origin should give way to "natural" explanations of the events of history. We can recognize many of the stories and claims about Jesus as christological claims by the church about his salvific significance, but they cannot be admitted uncritically as knowledge about the historical Jesus.

converge against modern theologians on the role of the modern historical method in our knowledge about the Jesus who is the object of faith. "There is no getting behind the church's faith in Christ to a historical Jesus prior to or separate from the faith of the Christian community," writes Michael Jinkins. "From the beginning we are confronted with a unified reality, and this unified reality is Jesus whom we believe to be the Christ of God."[4]

Some beginning students in christology, therefore, are caught in the dilemma about how to decide what to believe about Jesus of Nazareth. This is not an easy quandary for them to resolve. Their backgrounds and instincts are premodern, and they are aware of the delusions that underwrite an uncritical Enlightenment historicism. On the other hand, few theologians believe anymore that modern historical method can provide purely objective knowledge about any historical figure or event. But I believe the reason for the modern quest for the historical Jesus is deeper than a debate about objective historical knowledge. The motivation is at its core theological.

The issue is not a choice between the modern search for the historical Jesus and a postmodern view of the Jesus of the kerygma or the text. No one can reconstruct an objectively certain picture of Jesus using modern historical methods. All postmodernists are correct on this point. Nevertheless, I think we must continue the modern quest for the historical Jesus for theological reasons. First, much christology, ancient and modern, has been implicitly or borderline docetic. It denies the full humanity of Jesus. It does not recognize a truly human person within first-century Judaism. The historical quest is important, therefore, because the gospel affirms something about a real historical figure. "By confessing this doctrine [incarnation], the church 'lays upon itself the obligation to do history.' Otherwise, Christians will be docetists, believing in Jesus only as a divine figure, not as the human (historical) representation of God," writes Mark Allan Powell.[5] Thus, "it is the concern of the kerygma for the historicity of Jesus which necessitates a new quest. For how can the indispensable historicity of Jesus be affirmed, while at the same time maintaining the irrelevance of what a historical encounter with him would mean, once this has become a real possibility due to the rise of modern historiography?"[6]

The quest must be pursued, second, for the sake of Christian life and practice. The historical Jesus is decisive because he shapes Christian praxis. Christology is not only proclamation about Jesus as the Christ in the light of his

---

4. Michael Jinkins, *Invitation to Theology: A Guide to Study, Conversation, and Practice* (Downers Grove, Ill.: InterVarsity, 2001), p. 102.

5. Mark Allan Powell, *Jesus As a Figure in History: How Modern Historians View the Man from Galilee* (Louisville: Westminster/John Knox, 1998), p. 183.

6. Powell, *Jesus As a Figure in History*, p. 88.

cross and resurrection; it is also a way of life which embodies his particular kind of praxis. The Christian life is not wide open to simply any kind of practice. The way Christians are to live is connected to Jesus' own "kingdom way of life." If it turned out, say, that Jesus was really a political revolutionary who wanted to kill as many Romans as possible, or that he was dragged screaming and kicking to the cross, it would radically alter how Christians are called to live. "One should attempt historical reconstructions of Jesus' life and practice not simply as a moral example but also as an individual historical communicative and critical praxis," writes Francis Schüssler Fiorenza.[7] The historical Jesus both deconstructs false, distorted, or inadequate ways of Christian life and provides a positive picture of love, justice, and forgiveness.

> "If [*The Last Temptation of Christ*] makes Jesus 'too human' for us, then it is our christology rather than the film that is flawed."
>
> BRYAN STONE

Modern New Testament scholarship has by no means left us with utter skepticism about knowing anything about Jesus. "Neither Jesus nor his message would have been remembered unless he was indeed the kind of person portrayed in the Gospels," notes John Macquarrie.[8] Scholars who inhabit a middle ground between utter skepticism and a premodern view believe we can, indeed, paint a portrait (although we do not have a photograph) of the historical Jesus.[9] Jesus (*Joshua* [Hebrew], *Yeshua ha Notzri* [Aramaic]) lived

7. Francis Schüssler Fiorenza, "Christian Redemption between Colonialism and Pluralism," in *Reconstructing Christian Theology,* ed. Rebecca Chopp and Mark Lewis Taylor (Minneapolis: Fortress, 1994), p. 295.

8. John Macquarrie, *Principles of Christian Theology* (New York: Scribners, 1977), p. 277. This claim, of course, stands in stark contrast to the notion that the true Jesus was the gnostic Jesus of the "secret Gospels" instead of the eschatological Jesus of the canonical Gospels. The claim that the gnostic Jesus is the true Jesus, who was completely and intentionally misrepresented by the church in its efforts to overturn the "pagan" worship of the goddess of fertility, is now a part of our mainstream culture in the widely read, thoroughly enjoyable, and positively reviewed novel by Ron Brown, *The Da Vinci Code* (New York: Doubleday, 2003). The book is an exciting murder mystery with long didactic passages informing the reader about the "real" historical Jesus whom we know from the original, dependable, but "secret" Gospels which present the real Jesus prior to the later propagandistic and anti-goddess Gospels of the New Testament.

9. I am referring to a broad consensus from relatively conservative to relatively liberal scholars, such as the more conservative Ben Witherington and N. T. Wright, the more radical John Dominic Crossan and Marcus Borg, and the more moderate John Meier, Raymond Brown, Paula Fredriksen, and E. P. Sanders. For two brief summaries of "consensus" portraits of Jesus, see Paula Fredriksen, *From Jesus to Christ: The Origins of the New Testament Images of Jesus* (New Haven: Yale University Press, 1988), pp. 127-30, and E. P. Sanders, *The Historical Figure of Jesus* (London: Penguin, 1993), pp. 10-11.

within, was involved with, and responded to the religious, social, political, and economic context of the first half of the first century in the land of Israel [*eretz Yisrael*]. He lived in Israel during the *Pax Romana,* a time period built around a social structure intended to protect the interests of the privileged classes of Romans. An abysmal gulf existed between the upper classes (perhaps 10 percent of the population) and the vast majority of the disenfranchised lower classes.[10]

As a first-century Galilean Jew, Jesus was a wandering teacher, faithful to the Torah, committed to the renewal of Judaism under the Torah.[11] All his teachings and actions fall within the range of the Judaism of his time. He was closest to the Pharisees, especially the liberal Pharisees of the Hillel party, who were less concerned than the Shammai party about the way the purity laws established and maintained social boundaries. He practiced a politics of compassion for the victims of the social and religious institutions of his day. Through his preaching, teaching, and healings he overcame the social ostracism of the discarded nobodies. He was partisan toward marginalized people, a fact most evident in the new kind of table fellowship he practiced. There were two kingdoms with two banquets, and his banquet, which was the reverse image of Caesar's, included the poor, the hungry, and the mourners, who were treated like royalty. At the core of his teaching was the call to love, which he manifested and to which he called his followers.

> "Today's most avid enthusiasts of the unfettered market are conservative Christians, followers of a homeless preacher whose disciples held their possessions in common, and who declared it 'easier for a camel to pass through the eye of a needle than for a rich man to enter the kingdom of God.'"
>
> **DANIEL BROOK**

Four points in particular must be noted:

1. "Repent, for the kingdom of heaven has come near" (Matt. 4:17). Jesus was, first, a Jewish eschatological prophet who announced the coming reign

10. For example, 1 percent of the people owned 50 percent of the land; there was massive landlessness and unemployment. On top were the rulers and governors (1 percent of the population), then the priests (who controlled 15 percent of the land), then the generals and bureaucrats, then the merchants. Below them were the peasant farmers, who paid two-thirds of the crops to the upper classes. Below them were the artisans and carpenters. At the bottom were the expendables — the beggars, the outlaws, the hustlers, the day laborers, the prostitutes, and the slaves. This was a period of massive social and political turmoil in Palestine. See Clark Williamson, *Way of Blessing, Way of Life: A Christian Theology* (St. Louis: Chalice, 1999), pp. 185-97.

11. For a description of Jesus' Judaism, see Williamson, *Way of Blessing, Way of Life,* pp. 222-25.

of God's love and warned of consequences for Jerusalem and the temple if his summons was ignored. The very center of his mission and message was the coming reign of God. There are 114 references to the kingdom of God or heaven in the Synoptics, and 34 in the remainder of the New Testament. God's kingdom, however, is not a place in some other world where God rules but is the reign of God's peace, justice, and well-being on earth. His preaching announces that reign is near. He finally "turned his face toward Jerusalem" to preach the imminence of God's reign through his words and deeds. Although his proclamation of the coming kingdom did not center on himself and his own role, it is probable he thought he had something to do with its coming. His preaching was not a political program in the strict sense, however, but rather had to do with God's dawning new age of peace in Israel's history. His prophetic preaching and deeds, especially with respect to the temple, brought down the wrath of a few in the religious and political establishment in Jerusalem and led to his death at the hands of the Romans on the grounds of political subversion.

2. "The kingdom of heaven is like a mustard seed that someone took and sowed in his field" (Matt. 13:31). Jesus was, second, a teacher. He taught that God wills our well-being, which consists of justice, healing, and peace. His Sermon on the Mount and his parables describe what life under the reign of God on earth is like when God's love and will for the well-being of the creation is accepted. He taught this primarily in parables. His teachings in the Sermon on the Mount and his parables were not a new legalism but rather describe what the reign of God looks like when God is recognized as the one in whom we should place our trust. He taught how his followers will live a life of love and forgiveness when God's rule dawns. God's rule, he thought, was already present but also would be fully manifest in the near future (the degree to which he was an apocalypticist is doubtful but debatable). His sayings and teaching were not primarily ethical rules but illustrations of what human relationships are like when the reign of God is established. His radical demands did not provide conditions *for* entrance into the kingdom but signs *of* the presence of the kingdom already dawning.

3. "But if it is by the finger of God that I cast out the demons, then the kingdom of God has come to you" (Luke 11:20). Jesus was, third, a healer. Inexplicable and remarkable things happened when he was present. He conveyed the power of God by healing the sick and forgiving sins. The most characteristic miracles in the Synoptics were exorcisms. Hardly anyone then or now can be skeptical that such healings occurred and that these were one of Jesus' characteristic activities. The issue then as now is how to interpret them. Are they the work of the Devil or of God? Some of his followers understood

them to be signs that the eschatological kingdom was breaking in or was being inaugurated in these healings.

4. "He came to his hometown and began to teach the people in their synagogue, so that they were astounded and said, 'Where did this man get this wisdom and these deeds of power?'" (Matt. 13:54). Jesus was, fourth, a Jewish sage. He was a representative of the Jewish wisdom tradition as well as Jewish prophetism. The most constructive recent contribution to the portrait of Jesus as an eschatological prophet has been the addition of the sapiential (wisdom) or ethical/political component to Jesus' teaching. Jesus was a prophetic sapiential sage.[12] His mode of public discourse used one or another form of wisdom speech, including riddles, parables, aphorisms, personifications, and beatitudes, in contrast to John the Baptist who was a more traditional apocalyptic prophet. In his short sayings and stories Jesus taught an alternative and subversive wisdom in contrast to conventional wisdom. Contrary to the conventional wisdom which centered around family, wealth, honor, and religious practice, he embodied a new kind of community, represented most clearly in the kind of people he had table fellowship with, which was based on acceptance instead of honor and shame.

II. The Birth and Death of Jesus

It is difficult to separate Jesus' own pre-resurrection understanding of his relationship to the reign of God and the post-Easter church's understanding of it. Did he understand himself to be the announcer of God's new reign, or did his preaching, teaching, healing, and wisdom inaugurate that rule? These, of course, are not mutually exclusive. Clearly he understood himself in the first sense before his death, and clearly the church understood him in the second sense following his resurrection. He spoke directly to God as Abba; he claimed he had authority to forgive sins. The imminent reign of God was intimately connected with his message and mission. Although he did not claim to be God in the sense that subsequent texts and creeds did, he claimed his mission was rooted in God's own power and authority. "You have heard it said . . . but I say to you." His mission was an "instantiation" of God's reign.[13]

Following his passion, death, and resurrection, some followers confessed

12. For a summary of this argument, see Ben Witherington III, *Jesus the Sage: The Pilgrimage of Wisdom* (Minneapolis: Fortress, 1994). See also his *The Jesus Quest: The Third Search for the Jew of Nazareth* (Downers Grove, Ill.: InterVarsity, 1995), pp. 185ff.

13. Marjorie Suchocki, *God, Christ, Church: A Practical Guide to Process Theology* (New York: Crossroad, 1982), p. 97.

him to be God's promised one. God had vindicated him, confirmed him, through his resurrection as the Christ. "He who formerly had been the *bearer* of the message was drawn into it and became its essential *content*," notes Rudolf Bultmann. "The proclaimer became the proclaimed."[14] Some followers understood the post-Easter Jesus to be the power and presence of God in such a decisive way that they confessed him to be Emmanuel, God with us. Jesus was proclaimed as the Christ of faith. His preaching, teachings, parables, healings, and death are told from this point of view. This is especially apparent in the church's account of the major "moments" in his life, notably his birth, baptism, temptations, transfiguration, passion, resurrection, and ascension.[15] They are presented as events of theological significance, evidence of the claim that God is incarnate in Jesus.

"Who Was Conceived by the Holy Spirit, Born of the Virgin Mary"

Only Matthew (1:18-25) and Luke (1:26-38) show any knowledge of (or interest in) Jesus' conception and birth. Their claim is that "[Mary] was found to be with child from the Holy Spirit" and "the Holy Spirit will come upon [Mary]." These two references have become the basis for the doctrine of "the virgin birth." The claim, however, is not that Jesus' birth was miraculous in the sense that he appeared without the normal birth processes, or that Mary was perpetually a virgin. It seems, rather, to be the biological claim that Jesus was conceived in the womb of a virgin without any contribution from a human father. The power of God through the Holy Spirit is the cause of Jesus' conception along with the genes and chromosomes of Mary.

This doctrine is part of the creeds of the church. It has also become a shibboleth among many modern Christians, a litmus test to distinguish the true believer from the heretic. For many Christians the power and presence of God in Jesus depend upon Mary's virginity during his conception. Incarnation is impossible without his virginal conception. After seventeen hundred years of unquestioned belief, however, the historicity of this event has become difficult for some modern Christians to affirm. When the Apostles' Creed is affirmed, this article is affirmed with fingers crossed. The reason is that the modern worldview, based on science and a natural explanation of all things human,

---

14. Rudolf Bultmann, *Theology of the New Testament*, vol. 1 (New York: Scribners, 1951), p. 33. Italics in the original.

15. Macquarrie, *Principles of Christian Theology*, pp. 279-90.

has made the conception of a human being apart from female and male genes and chromosomes implausible. Rationalistic efforts to defend the idea do not work. Animal parthogenesis (development of an egg without fertilization), experimental embryology (cloning), and evolution (the first two human beings had no parents) are all random or human calculations. Furthermore, the notion that God is the father of Jesus in the biological sense quickly reduces to the absurdity that God is a divine male with divine genes and chromosomes.

Beyond this, however, there are other problems with the importance of the doctrine. Most of the New Testament, including the earliest writings of Paul, know nothing about the claim, or at least do not derive any theological significance from it. While Matthew and Luke begin with the virginal conception instead of the pre-existence of Christ, Paul and John begin with the pre-existence of Christ. Furthermore, even if virginal conception is a biological fact, the fact does not prove the divinity (or at least uniqueness) of Jesus at all. There are many parallel stories of the virginal conceptions of many great men, especially religious figures. The Buddha, Krishna, the son of Zoroaster, some Pharaohs, Augustus, and Plato were all allegedly born by way of virginal conceptions.

The New Testament is not interested in the virginal conception of Jesus primarily as a biological fact. Neither should we be. It is an item of the faith of the church only to the extent that it is one way the church has made the theological claim about Jesus as the incarnation of God. Our concern should focus on the meaning of this story, not the biology of it. The reasons one affirms or does not affirm "the virgin birth" are more important than the actual affirmation or refusal to make it.[16] If you accept it as a biological fact, you should accept it for the appropriate theological reasons. It is, of course, possible for contemporary Christians to believe that the conception of Jesus was a miracle, on the basis that God, who is not bound by the natural laws of conception and genetics, can do anything God wants to do. If you take the belief to mean this, you do not have to mean that the Holy Spirit was the biological father of Jesus but rather that Jesus had no human father at all. There is no biological explanation of how Jesus is God incarnate. The analogy is not the physical process of procreation but the process of God's creation in the beginning when God spoke and it was done.[17]

16. John Leith, *Basic Christian Doctrine* (Louisville: Westminster/John Knox, 1993), p. 147.

17. Some who affirm the biological origins of Jesus defend his virginal conception as historical on the grounds that because they believe in the resurrection of Jesus and the incarnation of Jesus, they also believe in the virgin birth of Jesus as part of the entire story of Jesus. N. T. Wright, *The Meaning of Jesus: Two Visions* (San Francisco: HarperSanFrancisco, 1999), pp. 177-78.

Even if you think the virginal conception of Jesus as a biological claim is implausible or unnecessary in order to believe in the divinity of Jesus, there are, nevertheless, reasons to retain the doctrine of the virgin birth as the faith of the church as a symbol or a metaphor which makes the church's basic claim about Jesus. The primary affirmation of the creed is the mystery of the person of Christ, the union in him of true divinity and true humanity. When we affirm that Jesus was "from the Holy Spirit" (Matthew) and that "the Holy Spirit will come upon Mary" (Luke), we use an odd language to affirm, first and foremost, the divine initiative in the origins of Jesus' life and ministry. His birth is the beginning of God's miraculous project of re-creating the world. Jesus' birth, purpose, mission, and destiny did not originate primarily in the will of men and women, but in the will and power of God. The appearance of Jesus was "of God." This story of his conception arises out of an ancient way of expressing the belief that Jesus was God's choice. It was and remains one symbolic way of signifying God's grace which comes in the form of Jesus the Christ.

"Suffered under Pontius Pilate, Was Crucified, Dead, and Buried"

Who killed Jesus? In some New Testament texts and in common Christian belief, "the Jews" killed Jesus. All the passion narratives concur that the Roman governor Pilate judged Jesus to be innocent and that his death was due to the insistence of "the Jews." This charge of Jewish culpability — sometimes blatant and crude, sometimes subtle and sophisticated — continues to be made by Christians. The church claims to be a displacement of the Jewish people from the original covenantal relationship with God, and the church's gospel is seen as the replacement of the Jewish Torah.[18]

Probably a few Jews, most notably some chief priests among the rulers of the temple who gladly would do away with a troublesome wandering preacher, collaborated in the crucifixion of Jesus. He was brought to trial before a Sanhedrin, a council of high priests, which was a political, not a religious, body, and which was presided over by the high priest Caiaphas, a Sadducee who had been appointed by the procurator.[19] These rulers wanted to

---

18. John Pawlikowski, "Christology, Anti-Semitism, and Jewish-Christian Bonding," in *Reconstructing Christian Theology,* ed. Chopp and Taylor, pp. 254-55.

19. "Pharisees," *Interpreter's Dictionary of the Bible,* supplementary volume, ed. Keith Crim (New York: Abingdon, 1976), p. 663.

get rid of this person who enacted God's way of ruling, which stood in direct contrast to their own rule. Jesus was thus put to death by some conjunction of Jewish and Roman authority.[20] Whatever is the most proper answer to our question, however, "the Jews" did not kill Jesus. Why was he killed? His preaching and teaching about an alternative kingdom, and his demonstration at the temple at Passover under the nose of the Tenth Legion, gave these rulers grounds for claiming he was inciting insurrection and therefore was guilty of sedition. His ministry was interpreted as a challenge to Roman authority.

In terms of the immediate cause of the crucifixion of Jesus, writes John Dominic Crossan, the

> best historical reconstruction concludes that what led immediately to Jesus' arrest and execution in Jerusalem at Passover was that act of symbolic destruction, in deed and word, against the Temple. That sacred edifice represented in one central place all that his vision and program had fought against among the peasantry of Lower Galilee. In Jerusalem, quite possibly for the first and only time, he acted according to that program.[21]

The cause of his death was not his controversy with "the Jews" in general or "the Pharisees" in particular. It was in fact Rome that put Jesus to death. If we must put the blame on someone, Pilate had Jesus crucified.[22] Crucifixion was a Roman, not a Jewish, penalty. It was the Roman law, procurator, troops, execution, scourging, and cross that killed Jesus. The Sanhedrin could carry out capital punishment only by stoning, burning, decapitation, and strangulation. It was thus not because of a Jewish religious indictment but because of a secular accusation that Jesus was sentenced to die on a Roman cross.[23]

It is neither historically accurate nor theologically meaningful to say "the Jews" killed Jesus. Christians have claimed that for centuries, beginning with their canon, especially Matthew and John, and many continue to claim it today. The Gospels exonerate Pilate, and, in part, represent the Jews as responsible for Jesus' death for a specific reason: The Gospels are not only a proclamation of a new gospel. They are also an apologetic and even polemical

20. John Dominic Crossan, *Who Killed Jesus? Exposing the Roots of Anti-Semitism in the Gospel Story of the Death of Jesus* (San Francisco: HarperSanFrancisco, 1995), p. 147.

21. Crossan, *Who Killed Jesus?* p. 65.

22. "Probably, some individual Pharisees bore a measure of responsibility for this, but in both cases the principal, and certainly the ultimate, guilt lay with the representatives of the political establishment — Herod Antipas and his supporters in Galilee, and the chief priests and Pilate in the capital," Geza Vermes, *Jesus the Jew* (Philadelphia: Fortress, 1981), p. 36.

23. Vermes, *Jesus the Jew,* p. 37.

literature against the synagogue and Judaism. They were written at the end of the first century when the church and the synagogue were attempting to establish their own distinct identity and to separate from each other. Written after the destruction of the temple in 70 CE, the Gospels provide a rationale for this separation. In exonerating Pilate, the church made "a daring act of public relations belief in the destiny of Christianity not within Judaism but with the Roman Empire."[24] Since Christianity is "the true Judaism," it should be granted legitimate status in the Empire.[25]

If Christians need to assess responsibility for the death of God's Messiah, they must seek the best historical answer to the question they can establish. What and who killed Jesus? For a deeper answer to the question, we must turn to theological insight into Jesus' death. He was killed because of and by the power of human sinfulness. And that condition is the reality in which we all participate. This answer is best expressed in words from the hymn "Ah, Dearest Jesus": "Who was the guilty? Who brought this upon thee?/Alas, my treason, Jesus, hath undone thee!/'Twas I, Lord Jesus, I it was denied thee;/I crucified thee." Pilate, Caiaphas, some Pharisees, some Jews, and some Romans participated then no more and no less than we all participate now in the structures of violence and death which killed the prophet from Nazareth.[26]

III. The Resurrection of Jesus

"If Christ has not been raised, then our proclamation has been in vain" (1 Cor. 15:14). The New Testament rests upon the assumption of the resurrection of

---

24. Crossan, *Who Killed Jesus?* p. 159.

25. We today can recognize that this propaganda ploy to establish the Christian case was relatively innocent and harmless at the end of the first century. "But, once the Roman Empire became Christian, that fiction turned lethal. . . . it is no longer possible in retrospect to think of that passion fiction as relatively benign propaganda. . . . its repetition has now become the longest lie, and, for our own integrity, we Christians must at last name it such." Crossan, *Who Killed Jesus?* p. 152. The idea and language of first-century Jewish responsibility have consequences for which Christians are morally responsible today. Christians need to watch their language. To say "the Jews" killed Jesus and are "Christ-killers" only feeds the flames of the Holocaust and continues Hitler's work. Such rhetoric is the epitome of moral rubbish, indeed, outrage, and Christians ought to stop it.

26. Furthermore, the death of Jesus is no reason to conclude that God has abandoned God's people, the Jews. We can understand the gospel either as a new covenant from God which now includes the church as a parallel covenant (a double covenant theory), or as the good news which incorporates Gentiles into the original covenant of Yahweh with Abraham (a single covenant theory).

Jesus. In some twenty passages, using a series of verbs, the New Testament proclaims that God raised Jesus from the dead. God transformed the crucified Jesus to new life; God confirmed the pre-Easter authority of Jesus, his message, and his mission; God vindicated him against the death-dealing ways of the world; God exalted him to heaven. His resurrection ratified that God had been present and working all along. It was a sign of God's power to defeat death and create us as new beings in this life and the next. The general resurrection of the dead in the eschaton had already begun. He is the first to be raised; the rest of us will follow him at the end of history.[27]

The New Testament does not speak of the resurrection directly. No one saw the resurrection. When and how God raised Jesus is hidden from everyone's view. What the New Testament reports is the results of the resurrection. Paul provides the earliest written account in 1 Corinthians 15. Christ was buried and raised by God on the third day. He appeared to Cephas, then the twelve, then the five hundred, then James, then the apostles, and finally to Paul. Paul believes there are different kinds of bodies. The resurrection body is a particular kind of body ("not all flesh is alike"). There is an earthly body and a heavenly body, a perishable body and an imperishable body, a "physical body" and a "spiritual body." Likewise, the Gospels report the resurrected Jesus as some sort of body. The body these witnesses see is Jesus and they recognize him (Matthew); he is recognized by Mary Magdalene and the eleven (Mark). He has hands and feet with holes in them, he has flesh and bones, he eats fish and bread (Luke). His hands and side are pierced, he cooks and eats fish and bread (John). At the same time, he appears as lightning; his clothes are snow white (Matthew). He is in "another form" (Mark). The disciples do not recognize him after many hours; he is recognized only in the Eucharist, and they thought he was a ghost (Luke). Mary mistakes him for the gardener and is told not to touch him because he is "not yet ascended"; he walks through doors and they do not recognize him on the shore of Galilee (John).

It is crucial in understanding the idea of Jesus' resurrection to distinguish between resurrection and resuscitation. Jesus was not resuscitated; he was resurrected. He did not simply stand up after three days, his body reanimated as if he had been administered artificial respiration. Unlike Lazarus, who was reanimated and would die again, Jesus was raised from the dead as a transformed spiritual body as the first sign of the age to come. Furthermore, the idea of the resurrection is different from the idea of the immortality of the soul. Jesus' immortal soul did not escape an earthly body in which it was tem-

27. Ted Peters, *God — The World's Future: Systematic Theology for a New Era,* second ed. (Minneapolis: Fortress, 2000), pp. 197-200.

porarily trapped in order to return to heaven. He was raised from the dead as the "first fruits" of the new creation.

The crucifixion of Jesus brought disillusionment to the disciples. They fled back to Galilee in fear. All they had hoped for was negated by his death. Their hope that the reign of God was near had proven to be naive and false. Yet they came to believe that "Jesus lives!" (cf. Rom. 14:9 and 2 Cor. 13:4). Resurrection from the grave is not the only language they employed to claim Jesus triumphed over death. The Gospel writers also used the language of ascension, exaltation, and glorification (Acts 3:13; 5:30-31; Eph. 1:20; 1 Peter 1:21) to claim God's vindication of Jesus. Although the language of the general resurrection of the dead was available in first-century Palestine, especially among the Pharisees, it is, perhaps, too close to the language of resuscitation to be the only language used. That language, if used alone, could mislead someone seeking to understand the depth of the transformation that took place in God's confirmation of Jesus. Nevertheless, "resurrection" is the primary word the early church used.

For many Christians, the resurrection of Jesus is not an item of belief about which they have any problem. They believe the raising of Jesus from the dead was a miracle. The difficulty I find with most students is that they have little idea of how subtle the texts are when they portray the resurrection. As noted, the New Testament is not utterly clear about the idea. The resurrection is an inference; no one saw it. The New Testament infers something happened to the body between Jesus' burial and his appearances to his disciples, but it does not describe what happened. Many believers simply assume that Jesus was the object of divine CPR. The theological problem with this assumption, however, is not only that all resuscitated people eventually die (Lazarus, the child of the widow of Nain, Jairus's daughter). The idea of resuscitation completely misses the theological meaning of the resurrection. Therefore, even if belief in the resurrection is not a problem for premodern or postmodern Christians, they still need to explain what resurrection means and why it is the center of their theological affirmation about Jesus. The demand to interpret the meaning of the resurrection cannot be bypassed simply by saying that we refuse to accept modern ideas about what can and cannot happen to dead people.

"An event" happened which convinced the early believers that God had vindicated the life, teachings, and death of Jesus and confirmed that God's full reign had been inaugurated in him. What was new was this: the final resurrection of the dead had taken place within history, and it was associated with this figure of history. The great transformation had begun with him, a transformation which brought the power of God's future right into history.

The Jesus whom God raised and who appeared to the new community is the Jesus who was dead and buried. Resurrection language is important because it stresses the continuity between the transformed body of the risen Christ and the body of the Jesus who had been with them before his death. His post-Easter body was not identical with his pre-Easter body, but it was the body of the Jesus who had been buried. Although the body of Jesus and the body of the risen Christ were not identical, there was a *continuity of identity* between the one who died and the one raised.

> "I do think there are all sorts of odd things that happen in the world. And there are several stories in the Gospels — the resurrection is the main one — which have the flavor of people saying: Look here, you're not going to believe this, but this is what happened."
>
> **N. T. WRIGHT**

"The event," then, consists of (1) the appearance of a transformed body from the eschatological future (2) within history now. The New Testament uses "visual" images and experiences to describe what happened to Jesus. The risen Jesus *appeared* to his followers. He did not appear in his pre-Easter body. His body was a transformed body, a notion that has led some to conclude that the resurrection was a spiritual experience — such as a hallucination, an apparition, a vision, or an inner experience — rather than the perception of a physical body. But regardless of the different ways in which a body can be described as corporeal or spiritual, it was Jesus they saw. It was his body *transformed from one mode of existence to another*, a new mode of physicality or a new mode of corporeality. Paul called it a transformation from a terrestrial to a celestial body. N. T. Wright puts it this way:

> Granted that the resurrection body is of course physical, what sort of physicality is it? It is . . . a transformed physicality, with new properties and attributes but still concrete and physical. . . . The contrast is not so much between physical and nonphysical, but rather between a body animated by "soul" (the present natural body, which will, like those of animals, die and decay), and a body animated by "spirit," presumably God's spirit, which will therefore possess a quality of life that transcends the present decaying existence.[28]

The resurrection of Jesus is our evidence of a previously unfamiliar dimension of reality, the end and goal of history, which now we have seen in

28. Wright, *The Meaning of Jesus: Two Visions,* p. 120.

history. What is new is its timing, not its nature, for it is an anticipation of the destiny of all humanity. The resurrection of Jesus Christ is the beginning of God's great work of redemptive transformation, the seed from which the new creation begins to grow.[29] The raising of the dead which was supposed to happen on the last day has already begun with Jesus. His resurrection is the beginning, foretaste, and guarantee of the new mode of being God has in store for us at the end of history.[30] The deepest meaning of the resurrection, then, has to do with the promise of the renewal of the creation, the future which is already present. God does not annihilate the past and death but transforms them, releases new power, makes them into a new creation.[31] Christians believe God was in Christ because God raised him from among the dead as a continuing presence and promise of God's reign in the life of the church and the believer.

Is the resurrection historical?[32] There are, of course, people who believe the resurrection is a "non-event" because women and men don't rise now and didn't rise then. There is no analogy in our experience for such a claim. Clearly, however, something happened that caused the faith of the disciples to arise. Some interpret the resurrection as the rise of faith in Jesus, as a subjective (an existential) event through the preaching of the saving efficacy of his cross; what happened happened to the disciples and not to Jesus. Others doubt that the resurrection of Jesus is historical not because they doubt that God has the power to create new life but because the resurrection is not something that happened within history; it happened beyond history. Though not a purely subjective event, it happened outside our dimensions of space and time. It is life which arises within the transcendent dimension of God's own space and time. Therefore, we know the resurrection only through the eyes of faith as we hear the saving significance and power of the cross and resurrection preached within our space-time world.

To speak of the resurrection as eschatological, however, is not to speak of it as if the resurrection is unconnected to history. In the resurrection God's eschaton has already begun to touch the lives of men and women because it has appeared in history ahead of time in Christ.[33] This claim is essential to the theological interpretation of the meaning of the resurrection. According to John Cobb, "The real past event of the crucifixion and resurrection of Jesus,

---

29. John Polkinghorne, *Serious Talk: Science and Religion in Dialogue* (Harrisburg, Pa.: Trinity Press International, 1995), p. 103.

30. Polkinghorne, *Serious Talk*, p. 102.

31. Suchocki, *God, Christ, Church*, p. 112.

32. For another discussion of this question see McGrath, *Christian Theology*, pp. 327-34.

33. Peters, *God — The World's Future*, pp. 200-204.

involving his total being, has objectively established a sphere of effectiveness or a field of force into which people can enter."[34] This field of force is one of the most powerful among the other influences of history, and continues to have personal, cultural, social, and political influence. Though exactly what happened is beyond our understanding, it is an event affecting history.

One can, of course, believe in resurrection as a possibility, including the resurrection of Jesus, as some Jews do, but not necessarily believe Jesus is the Messiah.[35] What makes him the Messiah for Christians is our claim that the eschaton has already arrived as a foretaste, a power from, and a promise about the future. Jews await that future by remaining faithful to the Torah. Christians believe the Messiah is the risen Christ. Although his resurrection is from the future, it is also embedded within history in the present. This power is evident above all in what happened to Jesus. God elevated Jesus out of death from the future.

future – past, if there is no time than it just is.

IV. Jesus the Christ

In the decades following Jesus' crucifixion and resurrection, the church made explicit what they saw implicit in his ministry and his person in the light of his cross and resurrection. The New Testament is christology in the broad sense that it tells the story of Jesus from the point of view of faith that he is Emmanuel, God with us. It is not christology in the narrow sense that it presents a doctrine of Christ affirming and explaining how he is God. The New Testament presents the preaching, teaching, and healing of Jesus as a sign of the imminent reign of God; his birth, baptism, transfiguration, passion, death, resurrection, and ascension convey the purpose and destiny of his life. Hymns are sung about him (John 1; Phil. 2:5-11; Col. 1:15-20). Old Testament and other images are used to interpret his life and work as part of God's purpose (prophet, lawgiver, priest, servant, king, redeemer). It remained the task of the church throughout the next three and a half centuries (100-458), however, through its theologians (Justin Martyr, Melito of Sardis, Irenaeus of Lyons, Tertullian of Carthage, Origen of Alexandria, Arius, Apollinarius of Laodicea, Theodore of Mopsuestia, Cyril, Nestorius, Athanasius) and its ecumenical councils to produce formulas about how Jesus is related to God (Nicea, 325) and how to speak of his humanity and divinity (Chalcedon, 458).

---

34. John Cobb, *Christ in a Pluralistic Age* (Philadelphia: Westminster, 1975), p. 117.

35. For an extended discussion of the resurrection and Judaism, see my *Many Faces of Christology*, chapter 7, esp. pp. 176ff.

The early church used a series of honorific titles to make high claims about Jesus' relation to God. The primary New Testament symbol is Jesus as the Christ. Over five hundred times he is called the Messiah (Hebrew *mashiach*) or Christ (English form of the Greek translation of *maschiach* as *christos*) [for example, 1 Cor. 1:1; Gal. 1:1]). He is God's anointed one, the one who carries the authority of the divine commissioning, the one who completes, fulfills, and transforms the expectations of Israel (Acts 2:36; 5:42; 9:22; 18:5, 28). Also, over five hundred times he is called *kyrios* or Lord (for example, Acts 2:34; 16:31; 1 Cor. 12:3; Phil. 2:11). He has divine superiority, authority, and power. He is the representative of God's lordship over the world and the church (Phil. 2:11). Furthermore, he is the *logos* or Word of God (John 1), God's communication with the world; he is himself the source of true life. Along with other titles, such as the son of David (Matt. 1:1; Luke 20:41) and the Son of Man (a reference to a humiliated and suffering eschatological redeemer, which is the only title Jesus applies to himself [Mark 2:10; 2:28; 10:45]), he is called the Son of God, an idea ranging from a person having a close relationship with God to a distinct office or function in salvation history (Matt. 14:33; 16:16; Luke 1:35; John 3:16ff.; 5:23; 10:36; Acts 9:20; 13:33).

Eventually these titles were developed into metaphysical categories by which to understand the person of Jesus Christ as God incarnate. This claim is at the heart of the faith of the church and is the central christological category. It does not mean Jesus was God or a god and not truly human (Docetism), or that Jesus was some kind of intermediary being (subordinationism), or that Jesus was God or the Son of God inhabiting a human body (Apollinarianism), or that Jesus began as a man but was adopted or chosen by God to become the divine Son of God (adoptionism), or that Jesus was God changed into a man for thirty years.[36] Jesus is the answer to death, ignorance, and sin because he is the life of the world (who delivers us from death), the light of the world (who brings true knowledge), the savior of the world (who redeems us from sin) — because he is God incarnate. The divinity incarnate in Jesus is true divinity and the humanity of Jesus in which divinity is incarnate is true humanity (Nicea). He was both humanity and divinity in one person (Chalcedon). These formulas were agreed upon by the church in its ecumenical councils before the breaches between the Roman Catholic and Eastern Orthodox churches (eleventh century) and the Roman Catholic and Protestant churches (sixteenth century) occurred, and that consensus has remained even after these breaches.

Christians, however, must be careful in explaining what they mean when

36. Donald Baillie, *God Was in Christ* (New York: Scribners, 1948), pp. 79-84.

they say Jesus is God. "Jesus" and "God" are not convertible terms. Nor does "Christ" exhaust the meaning of "God." If it meant that, it would be an outright denial of the triune God. Christians mean, rather, that Jesus Christ is the unique incarnation of the Logos or Sophia of God, the enfleshment of the mode of the divine being through which the world is made. Robert Neville writes that "Jesus Christ is . . . fully divine by virtue of the divinity of the Logos, fully human as the person in whom the Logos is incarnate,"[37] and Kathryn Tanner explains that incarnation means simply that "in Jesus, unity with God takes a perfect form; here humanity has become God's own."[38] Technically this is called the hypostatic union. Lest we think Christ is less than God, Nicea affirmed he is "of one substance" with the Father. Lest we think God in Christ is not a real human being, Nicea affirmed Christ in his complete humanity. Lest we think these substances are unconnected, Chalcedon affirmed the two substances are in perfect unity in one person.[39] The creeds, however, do not *explain* any of these claims. They simply deny distortions of the formula: adoptionism, Apollinarianism, Monophysitism (Christ had only one nature, not both a divine and a human nature), Monoletism (God masquerading in human form), Nestorianism (Jesus was two separate persons as well as two natures), and Arianism (a subordinationist position that Jesus was the highest created being but did not share the same substance as God the Father) . The formula is not a metaphysical and theological explanation of how the two basic claims can be held together. Rather, it provides the linguistic rules which are the criteria for a proper christological language if one is going to affirm Christ with the orthodox church.[40] One must speak of him as divine substance and human substance united in one person.

After declaring the full divinity and full humanity of Jesus Christ at Nicea (325) — thus settling the Arian controversy — the church was left with the question of how they belong together. Were not humanity and divinity so different in kind that no one could be both with full integrity at the same time? Following the Council of Nicea, nearly a century of strenuous debate on this subject began in the Greek-speaking lands, with the Alexandrians on one side arguing that there was one nature only in Christ, and the Antiochenes on the

---

37. Robert Neville, *A Theology Primer* (Albany: State University of New York Press, 1991), p. 141.

38. Kathryn Tanner, *Jesus, Humanity, and the Trinity: A Brief Systematic Theology* (Minneapolis: Fortress, 2001), p. 9.

39. Owen Thomas, *Introduction to Theology*, revised ed. (Wilton, Conn.: Morehouse-Barlow, 1983), pp. 148-49.

40. Richard Norris, *The Christological Controversy* (Philadelphia: Fortress, 1980), pp. 30-31.

other maintaining that there were two parallel natures.[41] The church had to decide between these two, or offer an alternative, or provide a way to resolve the differences.

Apollinarius clearly denied that Christ had a human soul. Christ had a human body, but in him the divine mind, the Logos, replaced his human mind. "He may be proclaimed as flesh because of his union with the flesh, yet according to the apostle he is not a human being."[42] God is his spirit or intellect, and so he is not a full human being. When Theodore, a theologian from Antioch, claimed that Christ had a human mind as well as a human body, Apollinarius conceded that Christ had a human mind in its "lower parts" (emotions), but in its "higher parts" (reason) the human reason was replaced by the divine reason. But for Theodore, if that were the case, then Christ could redeem only that part of the human being and not all of it. So Christ must be fully human in all respects if he is to redeem the whole human being.[43] On the other hand, Nestorius, a member of the Antiochene school, claimed that Christ is the name applied to the two natures together. But the two natures simply existed side by side; they were not united in one person.

The Council of Chalcedon, held in 451, had six hundred bishops in attendance. The first half of the council's creed affirms the one Lord, Jesus Christ, who is both God and human: truly God and truly human, perfect in his divinity and in his humanity, consubstantial with the Father and with us. There are two natures, human and divine, which coexist in one person, and the oneness of the person makes it appropriate to apply the predicates of either nature to the other. The second half of the creed stresses the unity of the person, namely, two natures in one person without any commingling or change, division or separation. Thus the orthodox formulation is that Jesus Christ is two natures, there being no commingling or change of the natures which continue to be preserved in their specific character (against Alexandrian monophysites), and one person, there being no division or separation of the natures which are united in one person (against Antiochene Nestorians).

41. Richard Rubenstein, *When Jesus Became God: The Epic Fight over Christ's Divinity in the Last Days of Rome* (New York: Harcourt Brace, 1999), pp. 228-29. The logos-flesh christology of Alexandria, pushed to its extreme, became "Apollinarianism," while the two natures christology of Antioch, pushed to its extreme, became "Nestorianism."

42. Apollinarius of Laodicia, "On the Union in Christ of the Body with the Godhead," in Norris's *The Christological Controversy*, p. 104.

43. His great critics were the Cappadocians, toward the middle and end of the fourth century, who stressed the need for a human soul and psyche in Christ. At this point they stand in line with the anthropos/word school of Antioch. The Council of Constantinople in 381 ratified Nicea on Arius and condemned Apollinarius.

The language of the creeds is not without its problems, however. Above all others, these creeds were expressed within metaphysical concepts that undercut the idea of incarnation. Chalcedon used the metaphysical concepts of Middle Platonism to talk about divine and human natures. To understand something is to know what it *is,* that is, to what kind of category it belongs. Since the world is composed of different kinds of substances, the creed talks about incarnation by appealing to two underlying but different kinds of substances, hypostases, or natures. Divine substance is completely transcendent, impassible, and immutable; human substance is the reverse. Since the concept of will (or relationship) was ruled out as inadequate, the only available terms were nature and substance. Chalcedon lacked an adequate concept of personhood or personal life to speak of divinity.[44] Notably, instead of a formal and abstract language of substance, the Gospel narrative simply speaks of a personal God who in love has acted in human life to redeem the world.[45] Today, I think, we can question whether substantialist rather than interpersonal or relational language is adequate to affirm that "God was in Christ" reconciling the world to Godself.

If categories of person and relationship replace categories of substance, the incarnation can be described in language closer to the Gospel story. Unlike classical metaphysics, a thing can be known by what it *does* instead of what it *is.* This is especially true of persons, both divine and human, whose "natures" are their relationships and acts, not their fixed substances.[46] God's will and action — dynamic and relational categories — are fully present in Jesus. The attitudes, commitments, intentions, and activity of Jesus are God's. *Homoousia* in a relational context means Jesus' love toward people is not simply like God's love toward them or a mere reflection of God's love toward them but is *identical* with God's love.[47] Jesus' love is God's love. Within an interpersonal framework, the infinite and the finite are interrelated. A space for a substance does not need to be carved out; they can mutually inhere within each other. Jesus' activity, power, and purpose were his own and God's, even though this was not the whole of the divine activity in the creation. God and the world are interdependent, through mutual relationships, or through the dynamics of love, not unmixable substances like oil and water which are simply asserted to be united. If a person reveals the nature, purpose, presence,

---

44. Thomas, *Introduction to Theology,* pp. 151-55.

45. See Daniel Migliore, *Faith Seeking Understanding: An Introduction to Christian Theology* (Grand Rapids: Eerdmans, 1991), and Catherine Mowry LaCugna, *God for Us: The Trinity and Christian Life* (San Francisco: HarperSanFrancisco, 1991).

46. Robert Neville, *A Theology Primer,* p. 128.

47. Thomas, *Introduction to Theology,* pp. 151-55.

and power of God completely, we can call this person Emmanuel, God with us. That person is God incarnate.[48]

The incarnation, then, might be understood through the language of a Trinitarian ontology or a process metaphysics instead of through a Neo-Platonic metaphysics.[49] In such a relational understanding of the world, our way of thinking about incarnation changes.[50] A "trinitarian ontology . . . overturns the primacy of substance in the sense of determining what something is in itself," writes Catherine Mowry LaCugna. "Trinitarian ontology affirms instead that person, not substance, is the ultimate ontological category."[51] God is not a divine substance. God is what God does in God's activity, power, purposes, and presence. God can be fully incarnate in Jesus Christ in the sense that God's activity and presence constitute Christ's identity just as God's activity constitutes Godself. God's purpose, activity, and power are incarnate completely, fully, distinctly, uniquely in Jesus, who is the full image of God. If God's purposes and character are perfectly expressed in this particular person, then in this particular person the divine and the human exist together in unity.[52]

V. Jesus Christ Liberator

Throughout the history of christology there have been many models for understanding God's incarnation in Christ.[53] The Council of Chalcedon estab-

48. "We must say that in the perfect life of Him who was 'always doing the things that are pleasing to God,' this divine prevenience was nothing short of Incarnation, and He lived as He did because he was God incarnate. Thus the dilemma disappears when we frankly recognize that in the doctrine of the Incarnation there is a paradox which cannot be rationalized but which can in some small measure be understood in the light of the 'paradox of grace.'" Donald Baillie, *God Was In Christ* (New York: Scribners, 1948), p. 131.

49. In a process christology, the initial aim of God for Jesus was fully to communicate the nature of God, and this initial aim is fully adopted by Jesus. See Suchocki, *God, Christ, Church*, pp. 95-96; David Griffin, *A Process Christology* (Philadelphia: Westminster, 1973), chapter 9; and John Cobb and David Griffin, *Process Theology: An Introductory Exposition* (Philadelphia: Westminster, 1976), chapter 6. The key to a process christology is the claim that "whereas Christ is incarnate in everyone, Jesus is Christ because the incarnation is constitutive of his very selfhood," Cobb and Griffin, *Process Theology*, p. 105. For my summary of process christology, see my *Many Faces of Christology*, chapter 4.

50. Delwin Brown, *Theological Crossfire: An Evangelical/Liberal Dialogue* (Grand Rapids: Zondervan, 1990), pp. 167-68.

51. LaCugna, *God for Us*, pp. 248-49.

52. Macquarrie, *Principles of Christian Theology*, p. 299.

53. Jaroslav Pelikan describes eighteen faces of christology: the rabbi, the turning point of history, the light of the Gentiles, the king of kings, the cosmic Christ, the Son of Man, the true image, Christ crucified, the monk who rules the world, the bridegroom of the soul, the divine and

lished a standard, however, which Alister McGrath in his *Christian Theology* articulates thus: "Provided that it is recognized that Jesus Christ is both truly human and truly divine, the precise manner in which this is articulated or explored is not of fundamental importance."[54] *That* he is God with us, not *how*, is the key to the faith of the church. The primary claim is that Jesus Christ is the saving presence of God. The difference between the many faces of christology is how to adequately affirm and explain this claim.

Modern christologies (since the Enlightenment) have attempted to redress the dualism and Docetism characteristic of so much traditional christology. They have done this by insisting on the real humanity of Jesus, typically beginning with the Jesus of history, then moving "from below" by way of an "ascending christology" to affirm the incarnation. Modern christology reverses a "descending christology," which begins with the pre-existing Logos who then had to be conceived as taking on a body and appearing as a human being. Modern christology assumed it could do this because a degree of continuity exists between God and humanity — there is some point of contact, some affinity, some mutual relationship between the divine and the human. The paradigms of modern christology have been the liberal christologies of the eighteenth, nineteenth, and much of the twentieth centuries.[55]

> "Golgotha, the place of the skull, where nails smashed through the wrists and feet of Jesus ... can stand for the skulls of every genocide. Betrayal by friends, self-preserving denial, making sport with prisoners, the mockery of crowds, spectators drawn to the spectacle, the soldiers doing their duty and dicing for His clothes, a mother in agony, and a knot of women helplessly looking on — it happens time, and time, and time again."
>
> **RICHARD JOHN NEUHAUS**

---

human model, the universal man, the mirror of the eternal, the prince of peace, the teacher of common sense, the poet of the spirit, the liberator, the man who belongs to the world. *Jesus through the Centuries: His Place in the History of Culture* (New Haven: Yale University Press, 1985). Alister McGrath rehearses seven: the example of the godly life (Abelard), the symbolic presence of the divine (Tillich), the mediator (Justin Martyr, Brunner), the presence of the Spirit (adoptionism), the revelational presence of God (Barth, Moltmann), the substantial presence of God (creeds), the kenotic presence of God. McGrath, *Christian Theology*, pp. 294-308. Glenn Chestnut portrays eight: the sacrifice on the cross, the messiah, the Word of God, the Vision of God, the humanity of Christ, the divine man, the redeemed humanity, the Easter faith. Glenn Chestnut, *Images of Christ: An Introduction to Christology* (New York: Seabury, 1984). The list is indefinite.

54. McGrath, *Christian Theology*, p. 295.

55. For a summary of the great modern christologies, see John Macquarrie, *Jesus Christ in Modern Thought* (Philadelphia: Trinity Press International, 1990).

With the beginning of the breakdown of Christendom in the West in the seventeenth and eighteenth centuries, liberal christology shifted from pre-modern to modern ways of thinking. Jesus was interpreted as the re-issuer of the religious beliefs common to all humanity (rationalists), or the one whose moral insights inspire his followers to imitate him (moralists), or a friend who lives in the heart of the believer (pietists). The defining characteristic of modernity was the will to be liberated from the coercion of external authority and to focus on inner experience.[56] Faith was located in the autonomous knowing and acting human "subject." Liberal theology, consequently, based its beliefs on the life of the Spirit known through reason (Hegel), or on the inner experience of the individual, by which our knowledge of God is mediated through our moral sense of duty (Kant), or our feeling of absolute dependence (Schleiermacher), or our experience of value (Ritschl), or our born-again experience (evangelicalism). God in Christ is known in experience.

Modern christology continues to be a significant voice today through both process christologies (described in the last three paragraphs of the previous section) and evangelical christologies. Simultaneously and reciprocally, evangelicalism appeals, on the one hand, to the objective truth about Christ in Scripture and creeds, and, on the other, to the ultimate authority of the inner life of the knowing subject, that is, to the authority of the born-again experience, the experience of Jesus in the heart of the believer. Evangelicalism accepts the thoroughly modern notion about how one knows what one knows.[57] The truth of Christ is, in part, rooted in the subjective life of the believer. One cannot inherit, or even learn, one's family's or community's faith in Christ. Faith in Christ must be self-chosen, internalized, and confirmed in the inner life for it to be real and true. As much as evangelicals appeal to the authority of Scripture and creeds, it is not the authority of tradition which is finally normative. One knows the truth through the authority of "the heart."[58]

Christologies of religious experience, however, liberal or evangelical, inevitably encounter the threat of subjectivism. In their more extreme variations modern christologies have a difficult time maintaining the distinction between the reality of Christ and the religious consciousness of the believer.

---

56. Bernard Meland, "Liberalism, Theological," *Encyclopedia Britannica*, 14th ed., vol. 13, pp. 1020-22.

57. For an earlier form of my argument, see my "What Liberals and Fundamentalists Have in Common," in *Fundamentalism Today: What Makes It So Attractive?* ed. Marla Selvidge (Elgin, Ill.: Brethren, 1984), pp. 85-89.

58. For an eighteenth-century version of this evangelical theme, see John Wesley, "The Witness of the Spirit I," and "The Witness of the Spirit II," *John Wesley's Sermons*, ed. Albert Outler and Richard Heitzenrater (Nashville: Abingdon, 1991), pp. 145-56 and 393-404.

Liberals face this problem when they shift from Jesus as the one *in* whom they believe with the apostles to the one *with* whom they believe through his perfect God-consciousness.[59] Evangelicals face the problem of subjectivism once they lose the balance between the objectivity of their beliefs (the language about Jesus Christ in Scripture and creeds) and the subjectivity of their own inner experience (the authority of the experience of the heart). When moderns become so oriented to the inner world of the believer that their own moral consciousness, or their own spirituality, or their own born-again experience becomes what is sought as well as the grounds of their faith, the distinction between the Christian faith and one's own experience becomes hard to maintain.

Some twentieth-century christology, however, has been postmodern, and there are at least three different postmodern forms, specifically, neo-orthodox, postliberal, and liberationist. The neo-orthodox development began with Barth in the 1920s, and continued through the existentialist christologies of Bultmann and Tillich. These theologians did not identify faith with the subjective experience of the believer but with "the eyes of faith" through which we see or with "hearing the Word of God" as the objective Word in Jesus Christ addressed to us through the written word of Scripture and the proclaimed word of the church through its preaching and sacraments. Christ is mediated to the believer through the Word addressed to us, which liberates us from both the inner and the outer bondages in which we are trapped.

The second form of postmodern christology, a continuation of the neo-orthodox emphasis on the Word addressed to us, appeared in the postliberal christologies of the last two or three decades. Scripture and the church's language (stories, creeds, liturgies, practices, and doctrine) stand prior to the believer as a story or a narrative or a language which we learn and into which we are drawn and formed as the metanarrative of Jesus Christ. The power and authority of Christ is the story of the church, which authors and interprets our experience; the authority does not come from an inner life of the believers that precedes, authenticates, and interprets the church's story.

A third form of postmodern theology is the variety of liberation theologies of the last three or four decades. One of the many criticisms of liberal christologies is that they focused christology not only on subjective experience but also on the abstract problem of the relation of humanity and divinity, instead of on the concrete importance of Jesus for a Christian practice of liberation. Although most recent African-American, Latin American, and Asian christologies presuppose, and eventually reaffirm, a high doctrine of

---

59. Williamson, *Way of Blessing, Way of Life*, pp. 213-14.

the incarnation, they typically focus their christologies on the significance of Jesus for contemporary oppressed communities around the world. These christologies have provided a trenchant criticism of the social injustices of the modern world. They aim christology toward emancipation from oppression and toward the full humanity of groups who have been exploited by the power structures of modernity.

Jesus Christ as Liberator, then, has been a dominant theme in all forms of modern and postmodern christology. To be sure, all forms of christology — ancient, classical, liberal, evangelical, neo-orthodox, postliberal, as well as liberationist (feminist, African-American, Latin American, Minjung, gay) — have understood God to be present in Jesus Christ as Liberator. What has happened in recent decades, however, is that the concept of Liberator has been expanded in the various modern and postmodern christologies to the social as well as the individual's world. Ancient and classical christologies understood Jesus as the Deliverer of humanity from the consequences of sin, death, and ignorance. Modern liberalism understood him as the Liberator from the authoritarianism of religion and the state, the giver of the freedom of the individual from the authority of tradition. Many theologians of the last part of the twentieth century, however, have understood him as Liberator from many other forms of social oppression. God in Christ liberates us in this world from the oppressive structures of cultural hegemony, bureaucratic manipulation, economic exploitation, and sexual and racial oppression.

> "The social context for Black christology is the Black experience of oppression and the struggle against it. Christology is irrelevant if it does not take this into account."
>
> JACQUELYN GRANT

Both liberal and postliberal theologians agree that Christianity must be joined to the modern project of freedom, but there are some basic differences between the way these two types of christology understand Jesus Christ as Liberator. Jon Sobrino distinguishes between European (liberal) and Latin American (liberation) theologies of liberation, which are two distinct types of theology based on "two distinct phases of the Enlightenment" (represented by Kant and Marx).[60] While both liberal and liberation theology share the thoroughly modern goal of *freedom*, the agenda of freedom differs with each. The first phase of the Enlightenment was interested in the liberation of rea-

---

60. Jon Sobrino, "Theological Understanding in European and Latin American Theology," in his *The True Church and the Poor*, translated from the Spanish by Matthew J. O'Connell (Maryknoll, N.Y.: Orbis, 1984), pp. 7-83.

son from all authority, and the freedom of individuals from every form of dogmatism, from all authoritarianism, from historical errors, from myths, and from obscure meanings. The second phase is concerned with social liberation, namely, a change from the wretched conditions of the real world. These two agendas of christology, then, distinguish between concern for autonomy and concern for transformation. In the former, the question for christology is more the truth of the incarnation at the bar of natural and historical reason and concern for the meaning of faith in Christ in a situation in which each individual self had become obscured. The latter discerns a new kind of problem, the problem of the contemporary situation of injustice and oppression, and the task of transforming reality so that the meaning of Christ for faith in a context of injustice and oppression may be recovered. For recent liberation christologies the primary question is what Jesus has to do with liberation from the chains of modernity (its injustice in the many forms of gender, racial, economic oppression), not with the inner subjective world.

When you read postliberal christologies closely, however, you will notice that the shift is more a reorientation of christology to soteriology than it is a denial of Chalcedon. For both liberal and liberationist christologies, the question, "How is Jesus God?" is typically set within the context of the prior question, "Is Jesus the worker of our salvation today, and if so, how?" What is new in the various liberation christologies is not so much christology proper. What *is* new is the expansion of the meaning of liberation from the inner life of the individual to gender, racial, and economic structures of oppressed communities. Liberation christologies differ from other modern christologies not so much over the meaning of incarnation as in their understanding of where to start "from below." They continue the modern (and ancient Antiochene) strategy of approaching christology from below,[61] but in liberation christologies, "below" refers both to Jesus as one of "the low" and to "the low" among the wretched of the earth. For postliberal christologies Jesus is constitutive of the liberation from various oppressions of social communities. The christologies of the (late) modern world, therefore, have opened up both the question and the answers to our question, how do we benefit from and participate in the salvation which is offered to us by the God who was in Christ reconciling the world to Godself?

61. For another example of this location of liberation theology within the liberal tradition in the West, see Schubert Ogden, *Faith and Freedom: Toward a Theology of Liberation* (Nashville: Abingdon, 1989), chapter 1.

_____

CHAPTER NINE

Saving Faith

I. "He Was Crucified, Dead, and Buried": The Cross and Atonement

The faith Christians receive from the church is received as saving faith. Saving faith is the aspect of christology which theologians call soteriology (Gr. *sozein,* to save). Broadly speaking, christology consists of an interpretation of the person of Christ — who he was and is (the incarnation) — and the work of Christ — what he did and does for us (the atonement). Atonement as the redeeming, reconciling, and liberating work of God in Christ stands at the center of the Christian faith. The most fundamental claim of saving faith is that Christ reconciles estranged creatures and God. Atonement is the explanation of how this reconciliation is accomplished by Jesus Christ through his death on the cross and his resurrection.[1]

_____

1. It is common in modern theology to invert the order of the two poles of christology or even to eliminate the distinction between them. This is because the effects of Christ are the only grounds for talking about him as God with us in the first place. The New Testament texts read backward from the resurrection their picture of Jesus as Messiah and Lord, and the church reads backward from its experience of redemption in him the claim that he is God incarnate. The question of who Jesus was and is is not primarily a speculative question about the person of Jesus, but a question about the meaning of Jesus for us. Cf. Schubert Ogden, *The Point of Christology* (San Francisco: Harper and Row, 1982). Christology begins with talk about how the cross of Jesus saves us (atonement) and how we participate in it (salvation). In the order of logic, Chapter Eight precedes Chapter Nine, but in the order of Christian experience and life, this chapter could precede Chapter Eight. Chapter Eight answers the question, what must we say about Jesus when as a result of him we have been brought to the experience of God which is our lot as Christians? In order to underscore the inseparable relationship between christology and soteriology, I have formulated what I have called my "principle of christological construction." It says that in our

The cross is the primary visual symbol of the Christian faith. It marks the outside of a building as a church and the inside table as sacred space. In Chapter Eight I discussed the cross in the context of Jesus' ministry, who killed him, and why he was killed — the cross as a historical reality. Now I ask the theological question about the significance of the cross for faith. How does the death of Jesus reconcile us to God, and how do we participate in his death on the cross as our salvation? The cross was an embarrassment to the early church. A crucified Messiah was not only a disappointment; it was an oxymoron. Yet they believed the cross was not simply another tragedy in which a hero fell victim to the powers of evil. They saw it as the work of God to redeem the world. How could his unseemly death save the world? Soteriology explains how the death and resurrection of Jesus reconciles us to God.

Earlier I described sin as a Hydra-headed monster. Because alienation from God has been experienced in a number of ways in Scripture and in different times and places, the church has used many metaphors to describe the work of Christ in overcoming sin in its many forms. Every atonement theory depends on two things. First, it depends on a particular understanding of the human problem, such as death, finitude, disobedience, rebellion, pride, guilt, bondage, oppression, injustice, ignorance, unfulfilled potential, lack of awareness of our true self, or meaninglessness. Second, it depends on a theory to explain how the cross reconciles us with God by overcoming sin. The church has offered at least six different theories to give an account of how the cross of Christ is our salvation.[2] But we should remember that "no council has fixed an atonement dogma."[3]

The dominant New Testament metaphor is the cross as the *sacrifice* of Jesus for our sins (Heb. 9:6-15).[4] The framework for this interpretation is the

---

theology we will not let Jesus Christ be anything less than we think we need for our salvation, regardless of what the New Testament or the tradition say about him, lest salvation not be possible through him, and we will not let Jesus Christ be anything more than we need for our salvation, regardless of what the New Testament and the tradition say about him, lest he be irrelevant to our salvation because he has no identity with us. These are in fact, I think, the criteria by which the church determined its creeds.

2. The models of this section are my organization and description of the models summarized in chapter 7 of Ted Peters's *God — The World's Future: Systematic Theology for a Postmodern Era*, second ed. (Minneapolis: Fortress, 2000). My description of the six models draws heavily on my discussion in *The Many Faces of Christology* (Nashville: Abingdon, 2002), chapter 6, section 2.

3. Peters, *God — The World's Future*, p. 206n.

4. There were several kinds of sacrifice in the Bible, however, and different understandings of what these sacrifices accomplish. There were communion sacrifices, where worshipers shared a feast with God and offered praise and thanksgiving; there were gift sacrifices, which were bribes or offerings of praise and thanksgiving; there were sin offerings, which were propitiatory

ancient belief that the shedding of blood could remit sins and reestablish at-one-ment between God and the people.[5] The New Testament uses other metaphors as well, however. Jesus is the suffering servant of God (John 4:34; 6:38; 10:17-18; Phil. 2:7-8). His death on the cross is an act of obedience and by his obedience we are made righteous (Rom. 5:19; Heb 7:27; 8:3; 9:14, 23-28). He is our ransom (Mark 10:45; Rom. 5–8), our reconciliation (Rom. 5:10; 2 Cor. 5:18; Eph. 2:16; Col. 1:20-22). His cross is our acquittal, propitiation, expiation, purchase, and redemption. It is a victory over sin and death (John 12:31; Eph. 6:12; Col. 2:15; Heb. 2:14; 1 John 3:8). From these metaphors, ritual practices, and social patterns the church developed a variety of models to explain how his death reconciles us to God.

Classical Models of Atonement

There are two classical models of atonement, which have been the dominant ones in interpreting salvation as our participation in Jesus' death and resurrection as our liberation.

Jesus As Victor   Victory over Devil v death

Widely known as *Christus Victor*,[6] this theory was advocated by such theologians as Origen, Irenaeus, Gregory of Nyssa, and Augustine. It describes our rescue by Christ from bondage. Through his death on the cross and his resurrection, Christ frees us by defeating the powers of darkness. The primary human problem is our enslavement or bondage to the powers of sin, death, and

---

sacrifices (to placate the anger of the offended deity), aversion sacrifices (offered to ward off evil), or expiatory sacrifices (a means of wiping away sin and removing pollution). The church spiritualized these sacrifices through first-fruit offerings, offerings of worship, and offerings of self; through fellowship meals and Eucharist; and through baptism, spiritual progress, and martyrdom. All of these were used in the New Testament to interpret the sacrifice of Christ. Cf. Frances Young, *Sacrifice and the Death of Christ* (Philadelphia: Westminster, 1975), chapter 4, especially pp. 80-82. Jesus as the perfect sacrifice who was our substitute to appease God's anger is too narrow a summary of the biblical idea.

5. Young, *Sacrifice and the Death of Christ*. See also Gerhard von Rad, *Old Testament Theology*, trans. D. M. G. Stalker, vol. 1 (New York: Harper, 1962); Alan Richardson, "The Atonement Wrought by Christ," in his *An Introduction to the Theology of the New Testament* (New York: Harper, 1958), pp. 215-41; and Timothy Gorringe, *God's Just Vengeance: Crime, Violence and the Rhetoric of Salvation* (Cambridge: Cambridge University Press, 1996), part 2.

6. Gustav Aulén, *Christus Victor: An Historical Study of the Three Main Types of the Idea of Atonement* (New York: Macmillan, 1966).

the Devil. God in Christ battles these powers on the cross and defeats them in his resurrection. This model has been appropriated by contemporary liberation theologians, who interpret the victory of the cross as our liberation. We can think of Jesus as the liberator from the demonic power of political, social, and economic forms of oppression as well as from the threat of cosmic powers, death, and guilt. Among contemporary advocates of this theory, "Christ the victor" and the "moral influence" models converge through the example and influence of the historical Jesus and his resistance and defeat of the powers of death and destruction through his cross and resurrection.

Jesus As Scapegoat

Central to the sacrificial system in the Scripture is the notion of the scapegoat, a person or animal on whom the sins of the people are placed in order to restore the divine favor. This biblical imagery has been developed in contemporary theology into a theory of atonement by René Girard. The fundamental human problem is violence. Why are we so prone to the rivalry and conflict which lead to violence? We are prone to it because we compete with rivals for a perceived good. This violence can be reduced, however, when we converge on a single victim, whereby the violent energy is dissipated and a relative peace restored.[7] Scapegoating was so effective that it was ritualized in religion through the sacrificial system. Myths arose to declare scapegoating a divine requirement. Sacrifice, therefore, was sacralized violence to establish social tranquility.

In the New Testament, however, the death of Jesus is given a different interpretation. It is, first of all, a revelation of the bankruptcy of the scapegoating mechanism, an exposure of the scheme as contrary to the will of God. The suffering and death of the Son become "inevitable because of the inability of the world to receive God or his Son, not because God's justice demands violence or the Son relishes the prospect of a horrible execution."[8] Furthermore, the New Testament pictures a "God without sacred violence, God without scapegoating."[9] Jesus' passion is seen as "the willingness to give oneself to others and to commit oneself to God, not for sadomasochistic purposes (i.e., to inflict injury on others or oneself, ostensibly for the sake of faith), but out of love and faithfulness to the other."[10] His death reveals something about God. "To say that Jesus dies, not as a sacrifice, but in order that there may be

7. René Girard, "The Surrogate Victim," in *The Girard Reader*, ed. James G. Williams (New York: Crossroad, 1996), pp. 20-29.

8. James G. Williams, "Glossary: Sacrifice," in *Girard Reader*, p. 293.

9. Girard, "Epilogue," in *Girard Reader*, p. 282.

10. Williams, "Glossary: Sacrifice," in *Girard Reader*, p. 292.

no more sacrifices, is to recognize in him the Word of God. . . . Rather than become the slave to violence, as our own word necessarily does, the Word of God says no to violence."[11] Jesus' death and resurrection put an end to communities founded on scapegoating.

Exemplar Models of Atonement

There are also two exemplar models of atonement. These two models interpret salvation as our participation in and benefit from the death and resurrection of Jesus as our sanctification.

Jesus As a Teacher

In the early church, the apologists, and especially the Gnostics, saw Jesus as the revealer of the true knowledge of God and of ourselves.[12] They diverge in the sense that the apologists understood Jesus as a mediator of true knowledge from God, while the Gnostics considered him an incidental occasion for our discovery of ourselves as a Christ. Since the fundamental human problem is ignorance of a transcendent knowledge of our true selves, salvation is gained through the achievement of true knowledge about the cosmos and ourselves. We need a teacher who teaches us perfect knowledge about the divine law, or who provides an example of how we can imitate the pattern of the Logos in Jesus, or who prompts our mystical intuition into the transcendental truths of God and our inner selves. What is common in this model is that Jesus is understood as a mediator or teacher of the way to true knowledge. He is the premier mediator or occasion for it. Although this model depends on Jesus showing us the way, salvation does not occur until we discover the true knowledge about or within ourselves. The story of the cross is significant because it is an allegory of the deeper spiritual death to ignorance which we must undergo in our pursuit of spiritual knowledge. This theory of atonement is characteristic of contemporary New Age doctrines, in which salvation consists of enlightenment about one's true self and the cosmos.[13]

---

11. Girard, "Surrogate Victim," in *Girard Reader,* p. 184.

12. For selections from the early Christian apologists and early Gnostic texts, see Bart Ehrman, *After the New Testament: A Reader in Early Christianity* (New York: Oxford University Press, 1999), pp. 54-93, 146-92.

13. See, for example, Philip Lee, *Against the Protestant Gnostics* (New York: Oxford University Press, 1987), and Harold Bloom, *The American Religion: The Emergence of the Post-Christian Nation* (New York: Simon and Schuster, 1992).

Jesus As Example

This theory has affinities with the previous one, but it focuses more on the power of Jesus' moral example for our restored relationship with God. We are out of complete fellowship with God and need to be motivated to respond to and emulate the love which characterizes God as it is re-presented by Jesus, especially his self-giving love on the cross. Jesus' example of going to death on the cross reminds us of the depth of God's love and forgiveness. It also inspires our emulation of his sacrificial love. Usually identified with Peter Abelard in the twelfth century, this theory rejects a radical doctrine of original sin. We need simply to know what is good (God's love and forgiveness), and to resolve to live by it. Our awareness and response are aroused by the example of Jesus' life and death on the cross which exhibits divine love. The atoning significance of Jesus' death is his capacity to provide us with an inspiring, even compelling, example to follow. When we follow him, empowered by his example, love between God and us is restored and reconciliation occurs. His ideal love motivates and empowers us to emulate it. Reconciliation comes as a result of our effort to follow Jesus' example.

Legal Models of Atonement

Finally, there are two legal models of atonement. These models have been the two dominant ones in interpreting salvation as our benefit from the death of Jesus as our justification.

Jesus As Satisfaction

The atonement theory that has dominated the West, especially its liturgy and theology, assumes that the basic human problem is a disordered life which dishonors God. The divine order that governs the world has been disrupted by sin, and the honor of the governor of the world has been besmirched by this disorder. Consequently, God had to reestablish the divine honor. The requirements of the moral order and God's honor are satisfied by Jesus' death because justice is fulfilled, honor is restored, and reconciliation is accomplished. The great representative of this theory is Anselm of Canterbury (1033-1109) in his book *Cur Deus Homo? (Why Did God Become Incarnate?)* For Anselm, perfect happiness requires total and voluntary harmony between God's will and ours. Since we disobeyed and fractured the cosmic harmony, that disharmony can be restored either by punishment (the denial of our happiness) or by an act of satisfaction (an offering that is greater than the act of disobedience and which restores God's justice and honor).

Unconditional forgiveness is not an option, since this would introduce even further irregularity into God's universe and the world would be even more unjust and God more dishonored. Furthermore, no human can offer adequate satisfaction because each human is already obligated to be totally obedient. If a human offered himself or herself in order to pay the price to restore honor, there would be no extra spiritual capital available to render just satisfaction. God is capable of making such an offering for the sins of the world, but God's incarnation as human was necessary if this plan was to work. That is, satisfaction had to be made by a human, so we know *cur deus homo*, why the God-man. The incarnate Son offered his sinless life, to die on the cross as satisfaction to restore the honor of God. Because that death was unwarranted, since he was both human and God, and so cannot go unrewarded, and because the Son needed nothing for himself, the reward accrues to those for whom he dies. Justice and order have been restored.

> **"Do you suppose if a wound goes so deep, the healing of it might hurt as bad as what caused it?"**
>
> **PERCY TALBOT, *THE SPITFIRE GRILL***

Satisfy God's honor

Jesus As Substitute *Pay our debts.*

The penal substitute theory, represented most notably by the Reformer John Calvin, is in large part a further development of Anselm's theory of satisfaction. The difference between Anselm and Calvin is this: whereas the restoration of order is central for Anselm, Calvin is more concerned with the vindication of the law, which stems from the righteousness which is God's own being.[14] Anselm's Christ pays our debts; Calvin's Christ bears our punishment. Instead of compensation for personal injury (Anselm), the cross is punishment for the violation of the law (Calvin). A righteous God cannot endure disobedience. A debt is owed to God because of our iniquity; it must be punished. Christ the mediator steps in as our substitute and takes the pain and the penalties of sin unto himself. His death is our punishment, our payment, for our sin, because he serves as our substitute.

The fulfillment of the divine law can be accomplished only when the offender and offense have been punished. Christ simultaneously fulfills the law and suffers the punishment for our sin. He becomes the victim of the wrath

14. Gorringe, *God's Just Vengeance*, p. 139.

of God in our place. Although he fulfilled the law and so deserved no punishment, he, nevertheless, suffered the punishment the law pronounces against transgressors: God's wrath. He suffers God's condemnation for us, receives the just punishment for our capital offenses, and by doing so he satisfies the law as our substitute and frees us from God's wrath. Christ assumes the just penalty, and in exchange, bestows upon us his justice and his resurrected life. The righteousness of Christ is transferred to us in what is called the "wonderful exchange." Many evangelical Protestants consider this substitutionary theory of the atonement to be the one that must be believed by a Christian who affirms the faith of the church.

II. Cross Purposes: Interpreting the Atonement

Each model has its strengths and weaknesses. The strength of the classical models is that they address the problem of our enslavement to our many idols, which restricts our freedom to live by faith in God. The flaw is that most forms of this model are highly mythological, envisioning a cosmic battle between supernatural powers, a divine trickster, and a God who owes something to someone, either the Devil or Godself. The power of the exemplar models is that they see the cross as part of the whole life of Christ. His characteristic self-giving love which climaxed in his death represents the ideal of love of God and neighbor. Their deficiency is that they do not provide the power we need to be released from the power of sin. Given the depth of our alienation from God and the power of our bondage, we need something more than an inspiring example; we need a liberating power which comes as a gift of God's grace through the Spirit. The appeal of the legal models is that they take with utter seriousness our experiences of stain, guilt, and sin. They assume a moral order of justice and stress the costliness of God's work to accomplish our redemption. And they recognize the complete adequacy of God's work in Christ apart from any works on our part of righteousness, merit, and reward.[15]

The legal models leave the impression, however, that salvation is a strictly forensic or declarative pronouncement by God of our innocence in a purely formal matter.[16] And above all, they focus Christ's redemptive work primarily on his suffering death and not on his life and resurrection. The question about this kind of atonement theory is whether an interpretation of the cross

15. Peters, *God — The World's Future*, pp. 230-31.
16. Peters, *God — The World's Future*, pp. 230-31.

as our suffering substitute is an answer to the problem of sin or a contribution to it.[17] Juridical theories are not only offensive to our moral sensibilities; they appear to many Christians to unwittingly contribute to an ideology of violence. This may seem like a very odd, indeed, outrageous accusation against a theology of God's love and grace through the cross. For some Christians, however, juridical theologies of the cross serve, willy-nilly, as a charter for oppression and abuse.[18] The juridical way of thinking about the cross has been used to legitimate gender, familial, ecclesiastical, and societal values and patterns that create and sustain nonassertiveness, passivity, and diminishment of the self, especially among women and the powerless.[19] Because suffering is redemptive, the suffering of the innocent person is justified theologically, both the suffering of God's Messiah and the suffering of those called to emulate him in his cross. As the suffering of Christ is required for salvation, those who participate in its benefits are called to suffer in their own life.[20]

17. This section draws heavily on sections three, four, and five of the chapter on atonement in my *The Many Faces of Christology*, pp. 150-64.

18. Some of the most persistent critics of juridical models have been womanist and feminist theologians. Their critiques are focused on the social consequences of atonement theories. Because Jesus died on the cross in place of humans, he represents "the ultimate surrogate figure." "Surrogacy, attached to this divine personage, thus takes on an aura of the sacred. It is therefore fitting and proper for black women to ask whether the image of a surrogate-God has salvific power for black women or whether this image supports and reinforces the exploitation that has accompanied their experience with surrogacy. If black women accept this idea of redemption, can they not also passively accept the exploitation that surrogacy brings?" Delores Williams, *Sisters in the Wilderness: The Challenge of Womanist God-Talk* (Maryknoll, N.Y.: Orbis, 1993), p. 162. The primary point feminist critics offer is that by celebrating the suffering and death on the cross as the feature of the cross that makes it atonement for our sins, the cross functions to justify and reinforce the suffering and acceptance of abuse by all Christians, and especially by women. Atonement theory has been the primary force in shaping Christian women's acceptance of abuse. Internalization of this theology traps women in an almost unbreakable cycle of abuse by accepting suffering and surrogacy as redemptive. As Rosemary Ruether puts it, Christian women are in a "double bind": they deserve suffering for guilt and they receive the promise of becoming a Christlike agent of redemption for their victimizers through innocent suffering. Rosemary Ruether, *Introducing Redemption in Christian Feminism* (Sheffield: Sheffield Academic Press, 1998), p. 100.

19. Anne Carr, *Transforming Grace: Christian Tradition and Women's Experience* (San Francisco: HarperSanFrancisco, 1988), p. 174.

20. Even in the classical model suffering is a necessary prelude to triumph of the plan of God; in the humanistic models, suffering is the only way to illustrate the love of God and move us to a decision; in the juridical models, God demands and carries out the death of his own obedient son in order to free us from the guilt of our sin. Joanne Carlson Brown and Rebecca Parker, "For God So Loved the World?" in *Christianity, Patriarchy, and Abuse: A Feminist Critique*, ed. Joanne Carlson Brown and Carole R. Bohn (New York: Pilgrim, 1990), pp. 4-13.

Is it possible to affirm the predominant atonement theology in the West in the light of such problems? Some have argued that interpreting atonement theory as an ideology of abuse or self-abuse depends upon a misunderstanding of the logic of this atonement theory and is a misuse of its social implications. A nonlibelous defense of it is possible. God's justice (God gives everyone her due) requires the punishment of sin and the sinner because sin is an assault on God's holiness. Christ on the cross endured our punishment in our place, however. Although this was undeserved because he was the sinless Son of God, he was made sin for our sake, subject to the full brunt of the divine wrath that hung over sin. The core of the defense is the claim that because it is the incarnate God who pays the price, the theory is not subject to the charges of divine child abuse and the sacralization of abuse itself because it is God who suffers redemptively, not a victim upon whom God decrees suffering as redemptive.

I think it is not possible to salvage the satisfaction and substitutionary theories of atonement even in this way, however. The internal logic of the framework remains constant. Redemption is possible only when a surrogate is put to death as punishment for sin. Even if it is God who is punished by God — some kind of divine masochism instead of sadism? — it is still suffering as punishment that is redemptive. Even though sophisticated caveats do reduce the charge of sacralized child abuse, they nevertheless maintain the *framework* of suffering and punishment as necessary for salvation. Suffering as punishment is the core of what constitutes redemption. *a consequence*

Problematic as that assumption is, the cross, nevertheless, *is* central to any Christian understanding of salvation. There can be no christology which stands anywhere within the bounds of "the faith of the church" which does not interpret the cross as decisive for our redemption from sin, suffering, and evil. The cross is not only a historical fact; it is theologically definitive of what we know about God and the work of God for our redemption. We must retain sacrificial imagery at least in the sense that Christ takes on the affliction of sin through his death. But sacrifice does not have to be interpreted as punishment administered by God on a final scapegoat. The cross can be interpreted as redemptive in ways that avoid, even reject, the liabilities of the satisfaction and substitutionary views of sacrifice. It can be reframed in such a way that reconciliation is accomplished through the cross without requiring us to sustain a spiral of violence, suffering, and death within God's economy. How can we interpret Jesus' death as the atonement for our sin without getting caught in sacralizing suffering and violence?

First, Jesus' death on the cross unmasks our fundamental human condition. The cross is unambiguous evidence that the world stands in need of redemption. As unbridled violence against the innocent one, the cross lays completely bare the darkness of the human heart, the truth about our bent toward violence, our unconscious projection of our own aggressions on someone else, and the mechanism of scapegoating we employ to do this.[21] The one who taught us to love one another, even the enemy, calls the hand of abusive power by revealing in his death the mechanism of violence which motivates it. Jesus' death exposes the deep-seated tensions present in our established ways of containing our uncontrolled rage by projecting it onto the innocent victim. The death of Jesus is the *end* of sacrifice, not the final sacrifice. God raised Jesus from the dead, not to reward him as the final scapegoat in a scheme of (divine) blood vengeance, but to end all sacrifice by vindicating Jesus' nonviolent, pure, unbounded love. The cross breaks the power of sin, in part, by showing us ourselves in our estranged relationships through collective delusion from the one whose name is Love. As Raymund Schwager, drawing on Hebrews 9, puts it, "by erasing the sins of all with his own blood, Jesus put an end to ritual sacrifices in which it was always the blood of another that was shed."[22] His death ends our need to project our violence onto anyone, including God. The very act of embracing the consequences of sin began his resurrection as victory over the cross, suffering, and death.[23]

Second, the cross does not stand alone as our redemption. The cross does not make possible the love of God; it represents and re-presents the love of God. Jesus' death itself does not redeem us, nor is his death to be glorified as God's means of overcoming sin and evil. It is Jesus' death on the cross as a moment *within the scope of the entire redemptive life and work of Jesus Christ* as God's work for our salvation that is the subject of atonement theory. "When one speaks of 'reconciliation,' or still more of 'atonement,' in Christian theology . . . our attention will indeed be focused on the death of the cross, but only because this is the finish and culmination of Christ's work. It has its significance only in the context of Christ's life as its climax and summation," writes John Macquarrie.[24] Jesus' cross belongs within the context of his nativity, baptism, temptations, transfiguration, passion, resurrection, as-

21. Raymund Schwager, *Must There Be Scapegoats? Violence and Redemption in the Bible*, trans. Maria L. Assad (San Francisco: Harper and Row, 1987), pp. 146-57.

22. Schwager, *Must There Be Scapegoats?* p. 202.

23. Schwager, *Must There Be Scapegoats?* p. 156. Note such cinematic Christ-figures as Sister Helen Prejean in *Dead Man Walking*, R. R. McMurphy in *One Flew Over the Cuckoo's Nest*, Luke Jackson in *Cool Hand Luke*, and Percy Talbot in *Spitfire Grill*.

24. John Macquarrie, *Principles of Christian Theology*, second ed. (New York: Scribners, 1977), pp. 311-12.

cension, and promised return.[25] When Calvin in his 1541 Geneva Catechism asked why the creed moves immediately from Jesus' birth to his death, passing over the whole history of his life, he answered, "Because nothing is said [in the creed] but what pertains properly to the substance of our redemption."[26] Karl Barth, however, replies, "I take the liberty of saying that here Calvin is wrong. How can anyone say that the rest of Jesus' life is not substantially for our redemption? . . . I should think that there is involved in the *whole* of Jesus' life the thing that takes its beginning in the article, 'He suffered.'"[27]

Third, a theology of the cross is above all a claim about who God is and how God engages our sin and suffering. Jesus' death is not a moment of transaction within the Godhead between the Father and the Son which enables the Father to forgive us. The cross tells us something about the very identity of God. The crucified Jesus is also "the crucified God" (Luther). Because Christians speak of Jesus Christ as the incarnation of God, our claim is that the self-giving of Jesus Christ "is continuous with the self-giving of God, and the whole work of atonement is God's."[28] Jesus' death is not only the consummation of his message about the coming kingdom of God. It is, also, the self-identification of God with and for the world in all its frailty, vulnerability, suffering, and death. The cross shows that the reestablishment of love and trust costs God the vulnerability to suffering and death.[29] God is willing to die for us, to bear our sins in this particular way, because we need to be delivered from the sin of violence. As S. Mark Heim notes, "God breaks the grip of scapegoating by stepping into the place of a victim, and by being a victim who cannot be hidden or mythologized. God acts not to affirm the suffering of the innocent victim as the price of peace, but to reverse it. God is not just feeding a bigger and better victim into this machinery to get a bigger pay off. . . ."[30] Exemplar atonement theories which assume that God loves and forgives with no cost, and that all we have to do is to see God's unfailing and unconditional love, are inadequate.[31] God endures even death on the cross to identify with the world in love. God undergoes Jesus' suffering and death. It is God incarnate who is "sacrificed" through the power of

25. "Soteriologically speaking, nothing is created on Golgotha which was not there before. The taking away of the sins of the world already begins directly on the incarnation of the Word. It is not necessary here to wait for the death of Christ on the cross." C. J. Den Heyer, *Jesus and the Doctrine of the Atonement* (Harrisburg, Pa.: Trinity, 1998), p. 106.

26. Quoted in Bryan P. Stone, *Faith and Film* (St. Louis: Chalice, 2000), p. 91.

27. Karl Barth, *Dogmatics in Outline* (New York: Harper Torchbooks, 1959), p. 101.

28. Macquarrie, *Principles of Christian Theology*, p. 320.

29. David Wheeler, *A Relational View of the Atonement* (New York: Peter Lang, 1989), p. 193.

30. S. Mark Heim, "Visible Victim," *Christian Century*, March 14, 2001, p. 21.

31. Heim, "Visible Victim," p. 19.

identification, resistance, and transformation of sin and suffering. *It is the incarnation, not the cross,* which redeems us from our sin.

The cross, as the near side of the resurrection, shows us how far God goes — even to "empty" Godself or to "sacrifice" Godself or to "die" — to identify completely with the world and through the power of the cross and resurrection to justify and sanctify us. The God who raised Jesus from the dead despised the death of Jesus on the cross. Apart from the power of the resurrection, the cross means nothing but one more human tragedy. God turns human violence around and uses it against itself. The compassionate and transformative power that makes for life is liberated from the violent and retributive power that makes for death.[32] God's boundless love negates the vicious circle of destructiveness. The cross and resurrection together is God's power unto salvation. No one had to pay — Jesus to God the Father, God to the Devil, God to Godself. Rather, God's compassion and lovingkindness redeems us as God undergoes the suffering caused by our sin and raises to new life those who participate in a power that is strong enough to promise the end of evil and the completion of the creation in relationship with God. Grace, grace, all is grace.

> "God is not just feeding a bigger and better victim into this machinery to get a bigger pay off, as the theory of substitutionary atonement might seem to suggest. Jesus' open proclamation of forgiveness (without sacrifice) before his death and the fact of his resurrection after it are the ways that God reveals and rejects what Girard terms the 'victimage mechanism.'"
>
> **S. MARK HEIM**

III. Amazing Grace: The Christian Idea of Salvation

The Christian faith is a religion of grace. The beginning and empowerment of the restoration or completion of human life as the image of God depends on God. Our salvation is a gift, not an achievement. There is nothing we can do

---

32. The cross understood in this sense is rejection of oppression and abuse of the powerless, the poor, and the marginalized. In a world that regards them as nobodies, the cross is the most powerful affirmation of their worth. "[T]hat God was willing to suffer and die for them is a message of hope and self-respect that can hardly be measured and that transforms their lives. That God has become one of the broken and despised ones of history is the unshakable reference point from which to resist the mental colonization that accepts God as belonging to the oppressors." S. Mark Heim, "Christ Crucified," *Christian Century,* March 7, 2001, p. 14.

to earn it. The core of the gospel is that our relationship with God depends upon God's relationship with us. This emphasis on grace is most obvious in the doctrine of justification by grace through faith alone. But this grace is also expressed through election, conviction of sin, repentance, regeneration, assurance, liberation, and sanctification. Most Christians, however, find it difficult to live on the basis of grace. We want to replace trust in God's grace with our search for signs of salvation, such as believing the faith of the church, having a born-again experience, attending upon the sacraments, or leading an upright life. We replace grace with works that convince us that God will accept us when we earn God's favor. "Works righteousness" replaces the mystery of the sheer grace of God's lovingkindness.

Grace, however, is not only a difficult idea to accept and live by. Salvation itself is a complex theological concept that explains how we benefit from and partake of God's work in Christ, that is, how we are saved from sin, how we enter into the way of life inaugurated by Christ, how we become Christians. To be sure, the major Christian traditions emphasize different dimensions of salvation. Eastern Orthodox and Roman Catholic churches typically describe salvation as *theosis* or deification or divinization (our participation in the energies of God's life through the power of the Spirit), while Protestant churches typically describe salvation as the restoration of a personal relationship with God, that is, as a change in our status before God through forgiveness.

Regardless of emphasis, however, most Christians agree that salvation is a complex process involving many dimensions of grace. One of the most egregious mistakes Christians make is to succumb to the temptation to identify salvation with only one form of grace, such as "being baptized," or "having a born-again experience," or "speaking in tongues," or "following Jesus." The *ordo salutis* (the order of salvation), sometimes referred to as the *via salutis* (the way of salvation), describes God's work as *the whole process* through which the image of God is completed in us. It begins with our incorporation into Christ and ends in our glorification in him. It is neither a conversion experience nor a sequence of other moments we complete to earn our salvation. Salvation is a holistic concept in which we appropriate grace as (1) election, (2) conviction of sin, (3) repentance, (4) justification by grace, (5) regeneration, (6) assurance, (7) liberation, and (8) sanctification. Its "two grand branches" are justification and sanctification.[33]

---

33. John Wesley, "On Working Out Our Own Salvation," *John Wesley's Sermons*, p. 204.

Election

"We love [God] because he first loved us" (1 John 4:19). Salvation begins with God. We are saved because God has chosen us. Since we can do nothing to earn salvation, we are saved by grace alone. In some Calvinistic traditions, grace as God choosing us is interpreted as predestination. Before the foundations of the world, God chose to redeem a few out of the mass of perdition. Christ died for those who are elect. The majority of humanity whom God did not elect are doomed to punishment (double predestination). They witness to the glory of God through their punishment. Many modern Christians have reacted to the determinism and the absence of divine mercy for the majority of humanity implied in the idea of predestination in one of two ways. First, some have understood God's elect to be all humanity (universalism), arguing for either the election of all humanity in Jesus Christ (Barth) or God's will and power ultimately to save everyone (liberalism). Second, some claim that God chooses those who choose God (Pelagianism). God cannot save anyone until we decide to chose God.[34]

There is, however, another interpretation of election, which theologians from Augustine through John Wesley have called "prevenient grace." Wesley rejects both predestination and synergism (the belief that salvation is half our work and half God's, the belief that we work our way up to God through our righteousness to earn God's favor). To be sure, for Wesley there is no salvation apart from our "cooperation." Salvation consists of our freely responding in faith to God's mercy. But our freedom and faith are neither possible nor actual until they have been *restored* enough by God's grace and *empowered* enough by God's Spirit that we can freely respond to God's call to us. Wesley replaces predestination with prevenient grace. Although we cooperate with God, we cannot do anything to cooperate apart from the preceding grace of God. The *first* word in salvation is the prevenience, priority, power, and perseverance of God's grace.

Conviction of Sin

This, too, is the work of the Holy Spirit, and so is an act of grace. "Salvation begins with what is usually termed preventing [prevenient] grace; including first the wish to please God, the first dawn of light concerning his will, and

---

34. The problem with any Pelagian idea is that it denies both the primacy of God's grace and the adequacy of God's grace.

the first slight transient conviction of having sinned against him," writes Wesley.[35] In light of Jesus Christ, we become aware of the disruption of human existence. It is important to note that conviction of sin is not the same thing as neurotic guilt.[36] It is not regret at having violated the moral law or disobeyed our parents or teachers. It is, rather, an awareness through the work of the Spirit of how fractured and unfulfilled our lives are, when we get a glimmer of God's love for us in Christ and hear God's call on our lives in light of our possibilities as the image of God. Conviction of sin is the work of the Spirit showing us, apart from our neuroses or psychological vulnerabilities, how inauthentic our lives are apart from our relationship with God.

Repentance

Repentance, also, is a soteriological term, not a psychological one.[37] It is not regret based on an introspective conscience. Rather, the biblical term for repentance is *metanoia*, which means "turning around." Although it includes our self-awareness, it is above all the maturing of the seeds of conviction through the power of the Spirit. It is our knowledge of the dire nature of our sin and our alienation from God, our heartfelt longing for God, our desire and decision to be what we really are meant to be in light of Jesus' preaching and teaching about the reign of God. It is our 180-degree turn toward the reign of God. Repentance begins our dying to sin and our accepting the challenge of God's call. It is the turning of the self away from sin (pride, egocentricity, inertia, shame, and *han*) toward God in faith. This, too, is not something we can do of our own insight and power. Repentance, also, is a gift of grace through the power of the Spirit.

Justification by Grace

Justification by grace through faith is the first "great branch" of salvation. I will discuss this in more detail in the following section.

35. Wesley, "On Working Out Our Own Salvation," in *John Wesley's Sermons*, p. 488.
36. On the distinction between psychological guilt and conviction of sin, see Paul Tillich's distinction between neurotic guilt and ontological guilt in *Courage to Be* (New Haven: Yale University Press, 1952).
37. "Salvation is carried on by convincing grace, usually in Scripture termed repentance, which brings a larger measure of self-knowledge and a farther deliverance from a heart of stone." Wesley, "On Working Out Our Own Salvation," p. 488.

Regeneration

The priority of justification and the primacy of faith cannot ignore the new birth and good works as part of the Christian life. But these *follow* from justification; they do not contribute to our justification. Nevertheless, we can ask to what extent, if any, justification and regeneration are interdependent. In one sense, most Christians agree that justification is not dependent on our inner renewal. As Luther emphasized, justification is dependent on the faithfulness of God and our faith in God's promise, not on an inner sense of renewal or on subjective experience or assurance of divine grace. Most theologians agree, however, that justification and regeneration are simultaneous. Therefore, Calvin and Wesley emphasized that salvation is not identified with justification alone but includes together the two great branches of justification and sanctification. Within this context, justification is emphasized as the moment the new life which restores us to the image of God begins as obedience to God's law or holiness.

The forgiveness of sins and the renewal of life, then, are simultaneous. The work of Christ for us and the work of Christ in us are fused. In the Reformed tradition, regeneration is the instantaneous and irresistible transformation of sinners from the fallen state, in which they are incapable of repentance, faith, and good works, to a new life where repentance, faith, and good works are natural. In the Wesleyan tradition, there are "degrees of regeneration" that range from the rejuvenation of our spiritual faculties in the new birth to the gradual renewal of our image of God in sanctification. The new birth is the gate or the beginning of sanctification.[38] Both Calvin and Wesley thought that sanctification is the goal of the Christian life. But Calvin never thought of regeneration and sanctification as separate doctrines with a distinct set of problems (such as the relation of justification to sanctification) in the way Wesley did. The purpose of regeneration is the sanctified life of the believer through the empowerment of the Holy Spirit.

> "To be saved does not just mean to be a little encouraged, a little comforted, a little relieved. It means to be pulled out like a log from a burning fire."
>
> **KARL BARTH**

---

38. Randy Maddox, *Responsible Grace: John Wesley's Practical Theology* (Nashville: Kingswood, 1994), p. 159.

Assurance

Wesley made a great deal of the importance of assurance in the Christian life. For him God's Spirit witnesses to our spirit that we are a child of God. Calvin, however, never made much of the quest for an inner assurance that we are a child of God. In response to people who tried to figure out by careful introspection if they were saved, Calvin remarked that "we shall not find assurance of our election in ourselves" but only in "Christ, the mirror wherein we must, and without self-deception may, contemplate our election." For him certainty does not lie in a subjective sense of assurance that God loves us. Certainty resides in faith's "firm and certain knowledge of God's benevolence toward us . . . both revealed to our minds and sealed upon our hearts through the Holy Spirit."[39] *Faith itself* as recognition and trust *is* our assurance. We do not find it in our subjective feeling of being loved, which can set us on a disastrous search for our certainty of forgiveness and great anxiety when feelings do not confirm the love of God for us.

Liberation

Salvation includes liberation from sin and for love. From the moment when by faith we have entered into contact with Christ, we are free to participate in the life of Christ. Salvation frees us *from* the guilt of sin, the threat of death, fear, frustration, futurelessness, and meaninglessness. It frees us *from* the power of sin. Salvation also frees us *for* a life of personal and social holiness.[40] Christ frees us from "the principalities and powers" for service to the reign of God. Saving grace not only redeems believers from their guilt and shame; it frees them to love God and neighbor. Regenerating grace liberates, motivates, and empowers the believer and the church to seek justice for everyone, especially the dispossessed whom Jesus privileged in the coming reign of God, to serve the well-being of all creatures great and small, to engage the powers by turning upside down the structures of Caesar's kingdom so we can live within the reign of God as preached, taught, and enacted by Jesus. "I am saved" means I have been freed to serve my family, neighbors, the human community, and our whole environment in the kind of love that reverses the in-

---

39. John Calvin, *Institutes of the Christian Religion,* 2 vols., ed. John T. McNeill, trans. Ford Lewis Battles (Philadelphia: Westminster, 1960), vol. 1, p. 551 (3.2.7).

40. See Schubert M. Ogden, *Faith and Freedom: Toward a Theology of Liberation* (Nashville: Abingdon, 1979).

grained political, economic, racial, and gender patterns of injustice, oppression, and exploitation that bind us to serve the realm of evil.

Sanctification

Justification by grace through faith should not be interpreted in such a way as to render sanctification unnecessary, tangential, or merely consequential to real salvation. The purpose of the Christian life is not justification but our completion as the image of God. Although the divine grace that restores our relationship to God is the first word, and a necessary word, it does not encompass the whole of the realm of redemption. Salvation means to be saved from the power as well as from the guilt of sin. It is the fulfillment of the image of God in the sinful creature. I will discuss this other great branch of salvation in some detail below.

IV. "You Are Accepted": Justification

The first great branch of the Christian understanding of salvation is justification. Forgiveness of sins is at the heart of the gospel. "For by grace you have been saved through faith, and this is not your own doing; it is the gift of God — not the result of works, so that no one may boast" (Eph. 2:8-9). Clearly in Scripture the word "justification" means both to account someone as righteous and to make someone righteous. Understanding the etymology of the word, however, does not settle the theological issue at stake in the controversy about justification. The issue is whether we are justified by grace alone (*sola gratia*), or whether we are justified when we are made righteous by the work of the Holy Spirit. In the former case — which is the emphasis of the Protestant Reformers — we are justified when we are pardoned by God. Its sole condition is faith; its ground is the righteousness of Christ imputed to us; its fruits are good works.[41] We are so alienated from God because of sin that on our own we face only the wrath of God. "Justification," writes Thomas Oden, "is the declaration of God that one who trusts in Christ's atoning work, however sinful, is treated or accounted as righteous. This credited righteousness is received by faith."[42]

Justification, however, is not merely a legal fiction in God's mind. It is a

---

41. Thomas Oden, *The Justification Reader* (Grand Rapids: Eerdmans, 2002), p. 3.
42. Oden, *The Justification Reader*, p. 36.

divine act of reversal of God's judgment against the sinner whereby the sinner is no longer under God's wrath. We are pardoned, acquitted, freed from wrath, released. We are accepted. We are restored to God's favor. We are declared righteous, or credited as righteous, on the basis of Christ's work on the cross. Our righteousness is a pronounced righteousness, an imputed righteousness. It is a change in our status before God. Using a bookkeeping analogy, our debt balance is charged to Christ; his plus balance is credited to us.[43] As summarized by the Westminster Confession of Faith,

> Those whom God effectually calleth, he also freely justifieth: not by infusing righteousness into them, but by pardoning their sins, and by accounting and accepting their persons as righteous; not for anything wrought in them, or done by them, but for Christ's sake alone; not by imputing faith itself, the act of believing, or any other evangelical obedience to them, as their righteousness; but by imputing the obedience and satisfaction of Christ unto them, they receiving and resting on him and his righteousness by faith; which faith they have not of themselves, it is the gift of God.[44]

This Protestant emphasis on justification as imputed righteousness is intended to be a rejection of the idea that our salvation is a reward for the infused righteousness of our increasing love and obedience to God. Salvation is an act of sheer grace, of God's mercy toward us. Justification is accepting the fact that we are accepted by God. Tillich has stated the idea of justification in everyday language:

> Sometimes at that moment [of despair] a wave of light breaks into our darkness, and it is as though a voice were saying: "You are accepted. *You are accepted,* accepted by that which is greater than you, and the name of which you do not know. Do not ask for the name now; perhaps you will find it later. Do not try to do anything now; perhaps later you will do much. Do not seek for anything; do not perform anything; do not intend anything. *Simply accept the fact that you are accepted!*" If that happens to us, we experience grace.[45]

---

43. Oden, *The Justification Reader,* p. 92.

44. "The Westminster Confession of Faith," *The Constitution of the Presbyterian Church (U.S.A.), Part I, Book of Confessions,* "Of Justification"(Louisville: Office of the General Assembly, 1996), p. 139 (number 6.068).

45. Paul Tillich, "You Are Accepted," *The Shaking of the Foundations* (New York: C. Scribner's Sons, 1948), p. 162.

Grace is God's kindness, goodness, favor, goodwill, and generosity offered to those who do not deserve it and can never earn it. The sinner is forgiven, the accused is pardoned, the offense is remitted. We are viewed by God through the lens of Christ "as if" we are righteous, because Christ's righteousness is credited to us by God. The alternative to justification is that we are made righteous through an actual transformation from the state of sinfulness to a state of righteousness. In this view of salvation, regeneration precedes justification. The reason God declares us righteous is that we actually become righteous and therefore acceptable to God, are in a proper relationship with God, and thereby deserve God's acceptance. For Luther, the great theologian of justification, however, our salvation cannot be both a credited and an instilled righteousness. Such an understanding makes us co-determiners of our salvation, an impossibility given the depth of our sin and guilt and the wrath of God. If we must look to ourselves and our inner renewal in any way to co-determine our standing as guilty sinners before God, we will wallow in our own works-righteousness for our salvation.[46] We can do nothing to become righteous enough to overcome our sin and separation from God.

> "Separation which is fate *and* guilt constitutes the meaning of the word 'sin.' . . . In grace something is overcome; grace occurs 'in spite of' something; grace occurs in spite of separation and estrangement. . . . Sometimes at that moment a wave of light breaks into our darkness, and it is as though a voice were saying: 'You are accepted. *You are accepted. . . . Simply accept the fact that you are accepted!'*"
>
> **PAUL TILLICH**

How normative is this Protestant view of justification for the gospel of grace and reconciliation? I want to emphasize here that justification by grace through faith is *an essential article* of the faith of the church. "Whatever you talk about do in such a way that the justification your words open to your hearers is the justification that faith apprehends rather than the justification your works apprehend," says Robert Jenson.[47] It is a plumb line by which the church's teachings and practices must be measured. No article of faith can undercut or diminish divine mercy and acceptance. The primacy of this affirmation is no longer a controversy between Roman Catholic and Protestant Christians. All agree that it is "grace alone" that leads to salva-

---

46. Carl Braaten, *Justification: The Article by which the Church Stands or Falls* (Minneapolis: Fortress, 1990), p. 116.

47. Robert Jenson, *Lutheranism*, quoted in Braaten, *Justification*, pp. 15-16.

tion.[48] Each agrees that justification is the first and indispensable moment in our reconciliation with God. We become "right with God" because Jesus effects our salvation through his life, death, and resurrection. Salvation is not something we can earn. Both agree that "by grace alone, in faith in Christ's saving work and not because of our own merit, we are accepted by God and receive the Holy Spirit, who renews our hearts while equipping and calling us to do good works."[49]

Although forgiveness of sins is necessary in a Christian understanding of grace, there is no reason to make the doctrine of justification a cartel in the economy of salvation. If justification by grace through faith alone is a shorthand formula for the whole range of the biblical message about God's grace, then the term does deserve to have a monopoly on the idea of salvation. But if it refers only to the turning away of the wrath of God against the guilty sinner through sheer declaration, then justification is not a synonym for the biblical idea of the mercy and lovingkindness of God. Prior to the Reformation, the doctrine never received the primal significance for the Christian faith it received then, and it has never since assumed such significance again.[50] As I argued in Chapter Seven, guilt and wrath are not the only problems God's grace addresses as our reconciliation. Death, ignorance, shame, bondage, injustice, *han,* despair, and meaninglessness also separate us from God. The idea of justification usually addresses only the problems of guilt and the wrath of God. Apart from the extreme Protestant insistence that justification is *the* article on which the faith of the Christian church stands or falls, most Eastern Orthodox, Roman Catholic, Anglican, Reformed, Methodist, Baptist, evangelical, and pentecostal Christians understand salvation to be a more comprehensive concept.

Even Lutherans acknowledge there is a sense in which justification is not the sole word of the gospel.[51] Lutherans stress justification in order to reject any notion that salvation is dependent upon our earning it, either by an objective process of believing the doctrines of the church or by our own subjective processes of inner renewal or religious experience. There cannot be a true theology of grace without a clear and prominent doctrine of justification. What is essential to the Lutheran view is that we not get the cart before the

---

48. See the "Joint Declaration on the Doctrine of Justification" by the Roman Catholic Church and the Lutheran World Federation on June 10, 1999. *Christian Century,* June 30–July 7, 1999, pp. 669-70.

49. "Joint Declaration," *Christian Century,* June 30–July 7, 1999, pp. 669-70.

50. Alister E. McGrath, *Iustitia Dei: A History of the Christian Doctrine of Justification* (Cambridge: Cambridge University Press, 1986), p. xii.

51. Braaten, *Justification,* pp. 68-69.

horse. Love and good works *follow from* justification, they do not *contribute to* justification.[52] Justification becomes the only word when it must be stressed against any doctrine of self-salvation. Even for Wesley, for whom good works are required for the Christian life as a condition of our final salvation, justification as pardon and restoration is not contingent upon our prior sanctification by which we earn the grace of God.

Even though all agree that we are justified by grace alone and not by our own works, the role of good works, nevertheless, remains an issue between "Catholic" and "Protestant" views of salvation. The Catholic *emphasis* has always been that justification is something that happens at the end of a process that involves not only the forgiveness of sins but also the sanctification of the believer through our cooperation with the grace of God by the empowerment of the Spirit. Many theologians teach that our reconciliation with God *includes* our regeneration (Calvin), our sanctification (Wesley), or our sanctification and our calling (Barth).[53] Justification is one aspect of the larger doctrine of reconciliation, which includes our actual change. Many Protestants stand with Orthodox and Catholic Christians in this larger view of reconciliation, notes Carl Braaten, "only without the complicated ecclesiastical system to monitor the process of salvation."[54]

There is a sense in which both Calvin and Wesley, the two great Protestant "theologians of sanctification,"[55] also stress with Luther the primacy of justification as pardon even while they understand salvation in the larger sense. Calvin clearly affirms a forensic concept of justification. (In other words, he believes God "declares" rather than "makes" a sinner righteous.) He also understands salvation through justification as the personal union of Christ with the believer, however. Alister McGrath explains Calvin's position this way:

> Calvin speaks of the believer being "grafted into Christ," so that the concept of *incorporation* becomes central to his understanding of justification. . . . Calvin is actually concerned not so much with justification, as with incorporation into Christ. . . . [H]e emphasizes the recognition that the question of justification was essentially an aspect of the greater question of man's relation to God in Christ, which need not be discussed exclusively in terms of the category of justification.[56]

---

52. Braaten, *Justification*, pp. 104, 116, 122-23.
53. Karl Barth, *Church Dogmatics*, IV/1 (New York: Charles Scribner's Sons, 1936).
54. Braaten, *Justification*, p. 125.
55. John Leith, *Basic Christian Doctrine* (Louisville: Westminster/John Knox, 1993), p. 190.
56. McGrath, *Iustitia Dei*, pp. 3-8.

The concepts of justification and regeneration are more closely connected in Calvin's evangelical faith than in Luther's.

In Wesley's case, even though salvation consists of the "two great branches," justification alone is sufficient for our salvation. The benefits of Christ's work are adequate for our salvation, and we are reconciled to God fully and completely by what Christ has done for us. What we do is to contribute to the development of that relationship of renewal which begins at the moment of justification. We do not pursue that relationship as our justification.[57] But Wesley distinguished between initial and final justification.[58] Justification is immediately salvific if one dies following the moment of justification. "If there is not time" to come to the full image of God, the Christian has been justified through Christ and so lives or dies within the mercy of God. Wesley retains a Reformation view of grace, however, by transposing the idea of justification by grace through faith alone into his doctrine of sanctification by grace through faith as well. Sanctification does not earn our salvation. We cannot on our own do anything to earn it. But the fullness of salvation depends on both the justifying and sanctifying grace of God.

fullness of salvation

V. "Be Perfect, Therefore": Sanctification

The other major branch of the Christian concept of salvation is sanctification. Salvation is *both* an instantaneous and a gradual process. It is important not to distort Luther's doctrine of justification. He also taught sanctification. But he made a distinction between our standing *before God,* which is through imputed righteousness, and our standing *before each other,* which entails getting our relationships right. The latter is our *response in gratitude* for our justification. New life in the Spirit and sanctification are the *consequence* of justification. Important as the Christian life is, we remain nothing but justified sinners throughout our entire Christian life. There is no "actual righteousness," only "faith righteousness," because we still deserve condemnation. We are forever justified anew. Instead, holiness of life results from our desire to serve God's law in gratitude and obedience.

Calvin and Wesley, however, were closer to each other than to Luther in their understanding of salvation as both justification *and* sanctification. Both accept Luther's doctrine of justification by grace through faith alone. There is no salvation apart from it. But they were also great theologians of sanctifica-

57. Peters, *God — The World's Future*, p. 231.
58. Maddox, *Responsible Grace*, pp. 171-72.

tion. They stressed the importance of regeneration and growth in the Christian life. The object of the Christian life is not to be forgiven but to be transformed into the likeness of God, to love righteousness and search for a rightly ordered life. Though justification and sanctification cannot be confused with each other, there is no justification apart from sanctification, and vice versa.[59]

It is significant that in his *Institutes* Calvin offers no explicit discussion of the relationship between justification and sanctification.[60] He teaches salvation as "two graces," first, the grace which reconciles us to God through Christ's blamelessness, and, second, the grace which sanctifies us by Christ's Spirit, which we cultivate for purity of life. Equally significant is the fact that in Book 3 of the *Institutes,* which is about the way we receive the grace of Christ, Calvin does not discuss justification by faith until chapter 11, *following* his discussion of faith, regeneration, and "the Christian life" (chapters 6-10). For Calvin, regeneration and sanctification are nearly synonymous terms.[61] Regeneration consists of the love of righteousness and the rule of righteousness.[62]

Wesley, also, understands salvation to consist of the two great branches of justification and sanctification. The "threshold" to the Christian life is faith, repentance, justification, the new birth, and assurance. The "living room" is holiness, which he calls sanctification, from which he develops his own dis-

59. "Q.77. Wherein do justification and sanctification differ? A. Although sanctification be inseparably joined with justification, yet they differ in that God, in justification, imputeth the righteousness of Christ; in sanctification, his Spirit infuseth grace, and enableth to the exercise thereof; in the former, sin is pardoned; in the other, it is subdued; the one doth equally free all believers from the revenging wrath of God, and that perfectly in this life, that they never fall into condemnation; the other is neither equal in all, not in this life perfect in any way, but growing up to perfection." "The Larger Catechism," *The Constitution of the Presbyterian Church (USA), Part I: Book of Confessions* (Office of the General Assembly, 1996), p. 212.

60. While one can explicate Wesley's views on sanctification by reading his explicit discussion in such sermons and essays as "The Scripture Way of Salvation," "On Working Out Our Own Salvation," "Christian Perfection," "The Circumcision of the Heart," and "Thoughts on Christian Perfection," one can only piece together Calvin's understanding of sanctification as he treats it in Book 3 of the *Institutes* within his teaching about regeneration, which consists primarily of faith, repentance, and the Christian life. Calvin's views on sanctification are found in his *Institutes of the Christian Religion* 3.3.10-11, 14-15; 3.6.2-3; 3.11.1, 15; 3.14.9, 11; 3.22.12-13.

61. The great Calvin scholar François Wendel holds that Calvin never made a special distinction between the terms "regeneration" and "sanctification"; he speaks of "regeneration *or* sanctification." Wendel, *Calvin: The Origins and Development of His Religious Thought* (New York: Harper and Row, 1963), p. 242 (italics mine). Leith, likewise, says Calvin "spoke first of sanctification or, to use his language, repentance" (*Basic Christian Doctrine*, p. 187).

62. Calvin, *Institutes*, vol. 1, p. 685 (3.6). Calvin focuses on the Law (the Ten Commandments) and the righteousness defined there, whereas Wesley focuses on the "higher righteousness" of the law of love described in the Sermon on the Mount.

tinctive concept of "Christian perfection." Sanctification is primarily the renewal of the image of God and our growing into the likeness of God. It is the
process that begins by freeing us *from the power of sin,* that includes *the power
not to sin.* Negatively stated, sanctification means that sin is rooted out and we
no longer commit sin "properly so called" (an intentional violation of known
laws of God). Positively stated, Christian perfection means we are "being
made perfect in love" in this life, that we are empowered to love God and
neighbor with all our heart, soul, strength, and mind. For Wesley complete
sanctification ought to occur in this life. We can reach the stage where everything we say and do is governed by love.[63] "Pure love reigning alone in our
hearts and life. This is the whole of scriptural perfection," he writes.[64]

Contemporary Presbyterian and Methodist theologians agree that the primary meaning of sanctification is "growing in faith" or "growth in the Christian life" or "growing in holiness" *(hagiasmos).* John Leith, a Reformed theologian, speaks of justification and sanctification as "indissolubly united in one
experience of salvation" as forgiveness of sin, the call to be holy, and the transformation of life.[65] Although justification is an *act* of God that is complete and
final, sanctification is a *work* of the Holy Spirit in human life that is a process
of growth. "Sanctification does not add anything to forgiveness, but sanctification is the end for which we are forgiven."[66] It consists essentially of the formation of Christian character, of the good and virtuous person: in the actions,
but first in the freedom, disposition, intentions, and commitments, of the self
to God. Sanctification is characterized by trust in God, gratitude and humility,
openness, detachment from things, a deep sense of responsibility, embodying
the purposes of God, simplicity, and freedom. It is also life lived in the world
and includes the disposition, the attitudes, and political and social activities. It

63. Christian perfection does not for Wesley include, however, some possible meanings
others might include in their understanding of the phrase. It does not mean we are perfect in
knowledge (free from ignorance), free from mistakes, free from infirmities, or free from temptations. Wesley in some places says explicitly there is no *absolute* perfection on earth, for perfection does not mean we are no longer liable to the frailties of human nature. But when every
word and action spring from love, our weaknesses or infirmities are not properly called sin.
(Wesley, however, does not remain wholly consistent in this claim, as these mistakes of the
Christian still need the atonement of Christ [both sin properly so-called and sin improperly so-
called need the atonement], a claim he must make because he still seems to think we are guilty
of not fulfilling the "perfect law" by our mistakes and weaknesses.) But they are not sin properly
so-called if love is the sole principle of action.

64. Wesley, "Thoughts on Christian Perfection," in *John Wesley,* ed. Albert Outler (New
York: Oxford University Press, 1964), p. 293.

65. Leith, *Basic Christian Doctrine,* p. 187.

66. Leith, *Basic Christian Doctrine,* p. 191.

consists of a vision of a "holy commonwealth," life in the family and in the economic, social, and political spheres obedient to God. Sanctification accents our part in the mission of the church, our response to our vocation or calling, and the transforming power of Christ in the church and our society. Sanctification is possible, *but it is never complete in this life.*[67]

Many contemporary Methodist theologians interpret Wesley's notion of Christian perfection as dynamic and relational perfection instead of a static perfection.[68] Randy Maddox describes it as the therapeutic transformation of our lives following the new birth. Sanctification as Christian perfection refers to the gradual growth into the likeness of God. It is that dynamic level of maturity within a process in which Christians walk with the love of God and our neighbors ruling our passions, words, and actions. We take on the disposition of the mind of Christ and live that out within the constraints of our limitations and infirmities. Some critics of Wesley's teaching misunderstand his idea of perfection, says Maddox, "because they have read it from the Western Latin translation of *perfectio* (perfected perfection), an achieved state of perfection, rather than as *teleiotes* (perfecting perfection), as in the Eastern tradition, 'a never ending aspiration for all of love's fulness.'"[69] If one substitutes a relational (or therapeutic) concept in place of a substantialist (or juridical) understanding of perfection, then perhaps Christian perfection is not as implausible as critics say it is. "The best starting point for reinterpreting and reappropriating Wesley's doctrine of Christian perfection . . . is the perfection of God's love as we receive it from Christ through the Holy Spirit," writes Maddox.[70] Through *sanctifying grace* we receive God's love as the empowerment to reflect the divine love. We can interpret entire sanctification to be the claim that the Christian can come to the point in her or his life where love reigns. John Cobb puts it this way:

67. One rarely finds the term "perfection" used by Presbyterian theologians, and whenever it does enter the discussion, the term is almost always explicitly rejected. Any hope for the attainment of perfection in this life as the outcome of the process of sanctification is rejected. Sanctification is "never realized in history, only in glory." Leith, *Basic Christian Doctrine*, p. 192. Donald McKim, another Reformed theologian, says "perfection is associated only with justification, since the righteousness that is given to human beings in justification is the righteousness of God in Christ and therefore perfect. The holiness we acquire in sanctification . . . is always limited by our human inabilities and weakness and so cannot be termed 'perfection.'" Donald K. McKim, *Introducing the Reformed Faith* (Louisville: Westminster/John Knox, 2001), p. 156. While Christians are called to perfection, "they struggle daily with sin, and that entire or full sanctification is not possible in this life." Leith, *Basic Christian Doctrine*, p. 157. Perfection occurs only in heaven after death.

68. Maddox, *Responsible Grace*, p. 23.

69. Maddox, *Responsible Grace*, p. 91.

70. Maddox, *Responsible Grace*, p. 225.

Now in entire sanctification love has its way. One genuinely loves God with *all* one's heart, mind, soul, and strength. There are no competing motives. Hence one's actions flow directly from love. The time of strenuous self-discipline and effortful striving is over. One has attained perfect love.[71]

Nevertheless, some real differences remain between these two theologies of sanctification.[72] Everyone is (or should be) aware of the dangers of teaching any doctrine of entire sanctification. Methodists must grant that any doctrine of Christian perfection remains an ambiguous and dangerous teaching. As John Cobb notes, "The results are rarely, if ever, what is promised."[73] Furthermore, within a "hermeneutic of suspicion," the doctrine of sanctification is surely one of the most liable to the charge of "false consciousness," to the dangers of delusion, pretension, manipulation, and repression. Any teaching about perfection in private or public life leads almost inevitably to self-righteousness, fanaticism, and brutality.[74] Geniuses, crackpots, and dictators have throughout the ages followed the delusion of human perfectibility through visions of utopia sacred and secular.[75] While the dangers of utopian-

71. John Cobb, *Grace and Responsibility: A Wesleyan Theology for Today* (Nashville: Abingdon, 1995), p. 108.

72. The biggest difference is that Calvinists never teach a doctrine of Christian perfection. Calvin's successors have clearly repudiated the possibility of any such condition in this life. They speak against the illusion of perfection which he believed is not possible in this life but only when divested of our mortal bodies where sin "remains an inordinate desiring." Calvinists and Methodists differ, also, in part, in their use of the term "perfection." Presbyterians stress sanctification as obedience to the Law instead of sanctification as increase in the law of love. Consequently, Presbyterian theologians, following Calvin, make the Ten Commandments central to sanctification, while Methodist theologians, following Wesley, make the Sermon on the Mount definitive of sanctification. Presbyterian theologians, also, seem to use the term in its traditional Western sense of "perfected perfection," a perfect obedience that overcomes not only sin properly so-called but also the "sins" of finitude and ignorance. Methodists, on the other hand, seem to use the term in the more Eastern dynamic sense of "perfecting perfection," the state of perfect love that not only overcomes sin properly so-called but in which the fullness of the love of God and of the neighbor dominates the life of the Christian.

73. Cobb, *Grace and Responsibility*, p. 110.

74. Leith, *Basic Christian Doctrine*, p. 200.

75. "Utopia means conformity, a surrender of the individual will to the collective or the divine. . . . For God substitute adepts, the People, the Charismatic Leader, or any one of a number of beguiling gurus. . . . The Utopian state of mind indicates a yearning to be released from history, to shed the burdens of free will, failure, improvisation. . . . [Y]ou may think that to be deprived of a life in Utopia may be a loss, a sad failure of human potential. Until, that is, you consider how unspeakably awful the alternative would be." Review of "Utopia: The Search for the Ideal Society in the Western World," 2000-2001 exhibition at the New York Public Library, *Time*, November 6, 2000.

ism of any kind are evident throughout history, they are especially evident in the utopian pretensions and delusions of the twentieth century.

Yet some holiness churches continue to claim that although entire sanctification does not do away with competing interests, temptations, and passions, through the power of sanctifying grace love can become from day to day and year to year a stronger force in our lives, and other forces that limit and derail it can be weakened. Recognizing our weaknesses, resentments, demands for security, and repressed hostile feelings surely is necessary to any Christian life. None of this means, however, that "the goal of perfect love misdirects our energies. Nor does it mean that there is any necessary limit to the approximation of that goal that the Holy Spirit can work in us. . . . We need not be cynical about the possibility of perfect love. But we should rejoice in whatever move we actually find within us, not feeling guilty because it falls so short of perfection."[76]

How should one evaluate these real differences in teachings? There is no way to settle what Scripture teaches about sanctification. Christians differ on how they exegete biblical passages about perfection (Matt. 5:48; 1 Cor. 15:42-53; Phil. 1:9-11; Heb. 10:14). The better approach, I think, is to ask what pragmatic difference each church's teaching might make for the Christian life. Does one account motivate, direct, and enhance the religious life better than the other, or is one view more subversive or destructive of the Christian life than the other? Broadly speaking, Methodists tend to be uncomfortable with the "pessimistic" view of human nature rooted in a Reformed doctrine of depravity and the impossibility of perfection in this life, while Presbyterians tend to be uncomfortable with the "optimistic" view of human nature rooted in a concept of prevenient grace and of sanctification in this life.

Christians live under the promise and demand of personal and social holiness within our finite limits. The completion of this promise and demand depends primarily on the sanctifying grace of God which precedes and empowers our decisions, commitments, and efforts. Methodist doctrine teaches that love can have its way to the degree that there are finally no competing motives and our actions can flow from love. From day to day the Christian can become stronger in love of God and world. Calvinist doctrine teaches that there can be no such state in this life. Which is better for the Christian life — to be "idealistic" about human life and *overestimate* the possibility of living into the likeness of God where all we feel, do, and are is characterized by the love of God, or to be "realistic" about human life and *skeptical* about the power of grace to restore our passions and practices to the image of God in

---

76. Cobb, *Grace and Responsibility*, pp. 113-14.

love? The truth probably is that Christians whose beliefs align more with the Calvinist position, such as Lutherans and Presbyterians, and Christians whose beliefs fall on Wesley's side of the debate, such as Eastern Orthodox, Roman Catholics, and Methodists, need each other to correct the subtle but significant differences between these two traditions about what the Christian understanding of salvation means in the Christian life.

CHAPTER TEN

The Community of Faith

I. "The Lord and Giver of Life":
The Holy Spirit and the Christian Life

I begin with three observations. First, the Holy Spirit is one of the most nebulous and ambiguous concepts in Christian theology. For many Christians the Spirit is an oblong blur, like Casper the friendly ghost, a mysterious chiffon-like being floating around out there.

Second, the New Testament is as pneumocentric (Spirit-centered) as it is christocentric (Christ-centered). Much Protestant theology, however, especially in the twentieth century, has been so christocentric that it has left almost no place for the Spirit in God's work. Indeed, some Protestant theology has been functionally binitarian instead of Trinitarian, collapsing the work of creation, redemption, and consummation so completely into the work of the first two persons of the Trinity that there is nothing left for the Spirit to do.

> "For the Christian church, the experience of the Spirit is too often limited to a focus on the Holy Spirit as the Spirit of redemption and sanctification. It is given, that is, a specific Christological focus. There is too scant mention in Christian theology of the Spirit's presence in nature, in culture's activity, or even in human relationships."
>
> **ROBERT JOHNSON**

Third, the work of the Holy Spirit has for the most part been conceded by mainline Protestant churches to the new charismatic movements and denominations. Roman Catholic and Protestant churches have been challenged by the vitality and growth of the worldwide pentecostal movement, now barely a century old. A fourth great ecclesial family has emerged, alongside the Orthodox, Catholic, and mainline Protestant churches, throughout not only the United States but the world, especially in Africa, Latin America, and Asia. The future of Christianity as a worldwide phenomenon seems to lie with the Roman Catholic, charismatic, and pentecostal churches more than with the mainline Protestant churches.[1]

A theology of the Holy Spirit, however, is central to the faith of all Christian churches, for three reasons. First, there is no christology apart from pneumatology (doctrine of the Spirit). Without the power of the Spirit to make Christ present to the believer, he remains as a figure in the past without any significance other than as a historical example. Jesus Christ, who was raised by God, is alive in the church insofar as the Spirit instills and maintains his life in the community of his disciples.

Second, the concepts of the Holy Spirit and salvation are inseparable. Every church and every Christian is charismatic in the sense that there is no Christian life apart from the Spirit. No one can participate in Christ's saving work apart from the work of the Spirit. Our salvation — election, conviction of sin, repentance, forgiveness, new birth, sanctification, and liberation — is launched and sealed by the Holy Spirit, who unites us with Christ in faith. One of the church's earliest theologians, Irenaeus, notes, "Know thou that everyman is either empty or full. For if he has not the Holy Spirit, he has no knowledge of the creator; he has not received Jesus Christ the Life; he knows not the Father who is in heaven."[2] The Spirit turns the Tower of Babel into Pentecost.

Third, the church is created and maintained by the Holy Spirit from the time of the resurrection and Pentecost until all is complete. The church is not a product of human striving and aspiration. The Holy Spirit establishes, sustains, and reforms the community of disciples who live by their picture of Jesus and the love of God. Without the creation and preservation of the church as the instrument of God's mission and ministry from the resurrection until he comes again, the church is merely a human institution of like-minded people who assemble to hype themselves to feel good and live by their highest ideals. The church is a gift of God established at Pentecost and maintained as indefectible (faithful but not infallible!) by the Spirit.

A new appreciation of the importance of the Spirit is perhaps emerging even within mainline churches; since the 1960s many Catholic and Protestant churches have experienced charismatic renewal movements, characterized by

---

1. Philip Jenkins, "The Next Christianity," *Atlantic Monthly,* October 2002, pp. 53-68.
2. Irenaeus, *Fragments.*

intense experiences of the Spirit, renewed appreciation of spiritual gifts, and Spirit-filled singing, praying, and modes of worship. These have been supported by a variety of spiritual formation movements led by spiritual directors. The Spirit has been at work to renew and enliven the worship and lives of many mainline Christians.

The Spirit in Scripture

In the Scripture the concept of spirit has an extraordinary number of meanings. Wherever there is life there is the Spirit. In the Old Testament, "spirit" *(ruach)* refers both to distinctively human life and to the dynamic activity of God. The Spirit acts in creation; maintains human life; motivates leaders; imparts wisdom, discernment, and holiness; and inspires the prophets. The Spirit is the presence and power of God in the history of Israel. What is definitive in the Old Testament is the discernment of the Spirit in the context of God's dealing with the people of Israel according to the covenant.

In the New Testament, the Spirit *(pneuma)* is the motivating power in the birth, life, and resurrection of Jesus, is the power to which miracles are attributed, is given to believers with faith in Christ as a gift empowering the faithful to live free from sin, is continuous with the Spirit of Christ, is manifest in a new form of life characterized by joy and peace, is the author of special and diverse gifts, and is, above all, active in the love of the neighbor.[3] What is definitive in the New Testament is the claim that the Spirit is inseparable from Jesus Christ and the new covenant established between God and God's people through the mission of Jesus Christ.

The Spirit in the Creeds

In 325 the Council of Nicea followed the section of the Nicene Creed on "the One Lord, Jesus Christ" by affirming simply, "and we believe in the Holy Spirit." Nothing more was said about the third article. This, however, left a host of questions unanswered. Was the Spirit fully God, or was the Spirit a lesser, created being? The Council of Constantinople answered in 381, saying that the Spirit "proceeds from the Father through [or "and" in the Western

---

3. George Johnston, "Spirit, Holy Spirit," in *Theological Word Book of the Bible*, ed. Alan Richardson (New York: Macmillan, 1957), pp. 233-47, and G. W. H. Lampe, "Holy Spirit," in *Interpreter's Dictionary of the Bible*, vol. E-J (Nashville: Abingdon, 1962), pp. 626-39.

church] the Son." (The creed in use today that is commonly called the "Nicene Creed" is technically the Niceno-Constantinopolitan Creed, this modified and expanded version of the original formula from Nicea.) The theologians at Constantinople struggled to rank the Holy Spirit equal with the Father and the Son. Although none of them applied the word *homoousia* to the Spirit, they applied narrative language to affirm that the Spirit is fully and equally the Spirit of God. The Spirit is a mode of God's being, a way God is God.

To affirm the Holy Spirit as the Third Person of the Trinity is to make two fundamental affirmations about God. First, to affirm the Holy Spirit as a "person" completes the full meaning of the Christian idea of God. God is the Spirit; the Spirit is fully God. God in God's fullness includes the Spirit. God is present in every mode of life ("the Lord and Giver of Life") through the Holy Spirit. Second, the Holy Spirit is also an affirmation about the saving reality of Christ. Jesus Christ as risen Lord is present to the believer through the power of the Holy Spirit. The Holy Spirit, the Spirit of Jesus, the Spirit of Christ, and the risen Christ are one and the same reality.

If Nicea and Constantinople had stopped at the end of the second article, they would have provided an account of the old days when God was present and active in Israel and in the life of Jesus for a brief moment only to withdraw again into mystery and an indeterminate future. But the creed affirms that the work of God in its many dimensions is an everlasting, not a sequential, work. It does this by tying the work of the Father and the Son to the work of the Spirit. The creed affirms with utter clarity that God was, is, and will be present and active among us as the Spirit. God the Spirit was at work at Pentecost through the birth of the church and through our incorporation into Christ in baptism. God continues to be present with us as the Spirit of Christ, creating a new community, empowering the people of God, nurturing the church in faithfulness, and leading us into lives of joy, peace, and love. The Spirit makes Christ present to believers, unites believers to Christ, spans the gap between there and here, then and now. When we talk about the Christian life, we are talking about the work of the Spirit, and vice versa.

But the work of the Spirit is not limited to christology. The Spirit exists before the incarnation and outside the church. The work of the Spirit is as wide as creation itself. The Spirit (*ruach*, wind) works in the creation as "the Lord and Giver of life." The work of the Spirit is tied to the Sophia and Logos of God throughout the whole creation. Christians talk about the universal prevenience of God's grace not only on christological grounds but also on pneumatological grounds. The Spirit is at work in all the modes of God's activity, including the striving throughout the whole creation for unity, harmony, wholeness, and drawing out all potentialities.[4] The Spirit is tied to the providence of God as the principle of union, reunion, and communion.

The Spirit and Gifts

In addition to baptism in the Holy Spirit as our new birth through incorporation into the church as Christ's body, the Holy Spirit works through charismata, through special gifts and special types of experience. This aspect of the work of the Holy Spirit was effective throughout the early years of the church, reasserted itself throughout various periods of church history, and became throughout the twentieth century (and apparently will continue to be in the future) one feature of the Spirit's activity which accounts for the church's growth and vitality.

The term *charismata* has in the New Testament two significantly different aspects. The first is the ecclesiastical meaning, the second the pentecostal meaning. Charismata are, in the first sense, gifts given to the church for everyone — including apostles, prophets, evangelists, and teachers — for the building of the church. Everyone has a charism, a gift from God, given to him or her for the maintenance and mission of the life of the church.

Beyond the Spirit incorporating the believer into Christ through baptism and endowing the believer with power, however, there are special "pentecostal gifts," distinctive types of experience, such as being filled with the Spirit. Some Christians think of these as a second stage of salvation, called baptism in the Holy Spirit. This work of the Spirit may be accompanied by the fruit of the Spirit, such as Christian dispositions of joy, peace, or patience (Gal. 5:22), and by the gifts of the Spirit, such as tongues and interpretation of tongues, prophecy, healing, and deliverance from possession (1 Cor. 12:8-10). These gifts were never intended for private use but were for the edification of the church.

Denominations have appeared throughout the twentieth century that "specialize" in experiencing, employing, and interpreting these gifts of the Spirit. This is clearly the fastest growing form of Christianity throughout the world. Going beyond the primary interpretation of the work of the Spirit as the incorporation of the believer into the church and the Spirit's maintenance of the church through charisms, many mainline Protestant churches have become more charismatic as the Spirit prompts more enthusiasm or ecstasy by the use of praise songs in place of hymns and praise gestures (raised hands) in place of bowed heads. All but the most traditional worship services of most

4. John Macquarrie, *Principles of Christian Theology* (New York: Scribner's, 1977).

mainline Protestant denominations have become, to one degree or another, more charismatic in the tone, style, and content of their services as Christians search for a deeper spirituality, or ecstasy, or vitality, or wholeness, or a Spirit-filled worship and Christian life.

II. "In Used Pots and Pans" (2 Cor. 4:7; 1 Cor. 4:13): The Identity of the Church

Lifelessness is only one of many criticisms of the church. Its split into denominations, separation by race and class, unwieldy bureaucracy, bickering and strife over petty matters, and superficial activity confirm the claim that the church is full of hypocrites. Everyone can criticize something. The church is too self-centered or too involved in politics, too compromising or too intolerant, too conservative or too liberal, too chummy or too cold.[5] Any Christian who does not love and hate the church simultaneously probably does not know the church very well.

Believing Too Little or Too Much

The major danger in any ecclesiology (doctrine of the church) is believing too little or too much about the church.[6] Some Christians believe too little. People go to church; they do not understand themselves to *be* the church.[7] They do not distinguish between the church as an assembly and an event which consists of believers and the church as a building or institution in which the assembly and event occur. For them the church is a voluntary association of individuals who, after they have accepted Jesus as their Savior, decide to form a church in order to testify to their conversion experience and to support each other in their personal relationship with Christ. God does not call and form the church; God calls individuals to become Christians. The church is the consequence, not the context, of salvation.

Other Christians, conversely, believe too much about the church. They identify the church as the kingdom of God on earth. They think of the church as a purely spiritual reality, which exists above history and all the ambiguities

5. Shirley Guthrie, *Christian Doctrine* (Atlanta: John Knox, 1968), pp. 350-51.

6. Clark Williamson, *Way of Blessing, Way of Life* (St. Louis: Chalice, 1999), p. 255.

7. People go to church for many reasons: to escape the crowd, to connect with a group, to expose their children to moral teachings, to be with family, to enjoy the music, to be entertained by extravaganzas, to be alone with God.

of every institution. They distinguish between the true and the false church, the invisible and visible church, identifying the true church with the invisible church. The invisible church consists of the predestined few (Calvinism) or of those who can testify to a conversion experience (evangelicalism) or of the faithful disciples who obey the teachings of Jesus (sectarianism). The visible church is corrupt and consists of people who are not true Christians.

Is it possible to be a Christian without being a member of a church? In one sense, yes. Christ is more than the church; our relationship to the church is dependent on the church's relation to Christ. The church is *also* necessary in mediating our relationship with Christ, however. Ecclesiastical docetism will not do. To be a Christian is to be part of the body of Christ in history. The church consists of churches. "The church must be actual or it is nothing," writes Robert Neville. "[I]f the church is not actual, then Jesus Christ is not the actual savior."[8] Actual churches are those communities of believers identified as disciples of Jesus through the symbols of the church that mediate their relation to him. So the answer to my question is not either/or. The issue is a matter of priority.[9] To be a Christian is to be incorporated into the body of Christ. One does not become a Christian and then become part of the church; nor does the church exist apart from believers. The two belong together. As John Leith says, "To be a Christian and to be the church are one and the same existence."[10]

A Dialectical View of the Church

"Church" is not a New Testament word. The New Testament word is *ecclesia,* a word which in its secular usage means simply a meeting or gathering summoned for a particular purpose. In its Christian usage *ecclesia* refers to the body of believers gathered by God through Christ. The *ecclesia* refers to "the new community of believers gathered to praise and serve God in response to the life, death, and resurrection of Jesus and in the power of the Holy Spirit."[11] It is the people who believe in Jesus as Savior and are his disciples in the world.

8. Robert Neville, *A Theology Primer* (Albany: State University of New York Press, 1991), p. 153.

9. Carl Braaten, *Justification: The Article by Which the Church Stands or Falls* (Minneapolis: Fortress, 1990), p. 10.

10. John Leith, *Basic Christian Doctrine* (Louisville: Westminster/John Knox, 1993), p. 234.

11. Daniel Migliore, *Faith Seeking Understanding: An Introduction to Christian Theology* (Grand Rapids: Eerdmans, 1991), p. 189.

A theology of the church, then, requires a dialectical set of ideas. It is *both* a people (an abstract concept, a spiritual reality) and an institution (a concrete community). It is a theological reality and a human institution. On the one hand, its basic identity and unity as a people is transcendent. Christ transcends and unites various communities of believers into his universal community. But this community is not otherworldly. It does not exist outside history. It is the historically continuous body of believers known as Christians which exists prior to individual Christians and into which individual Christians are incorporated. Individuals are engrafted into a reality which exists prior to them. Its unity is made visible through its symbols and structures, primarily through its Scripture, sacraments, ministry, and polity. It is the community in which the gospel is preached and heard and the sacraments administered and received. The church is a provisional community between the resurrection and the eschaton, however. There is no church or temple in the vision of God's final reign in the book of Revelation, where the whole creation worships God.

There is no ideal essence of the church apart from the concrete forms of the church. The church has spatial and temporal dimensions. Like a nation, school, or association, it is an institution subject to the same kind of analysis as other organizations.[12] Like any institution, it meets the physical, emotional, economic, and educational needs of its members.[13] It is an organization that gathers in buildings and has social structures and political arrangements to conduct its affairs. It exists with all the messiness, politics, and meanness that all other institutions exhibit. Though the spiritual reality of the church cannot be identified with the empirical churches, there is a necessary connection between these two realities. Otherwise, the core claim of the incarnation is denied. The church is both a theological reality and a human institution; but it is a people with its institutions, not an institution that benefits people.[14]

12. James Gustafson, *Treasure in Earthen Vessels: The Church As a Human Community* (New York: Harper and Brothers, 1961), chapter 1.

13. How does the church differ from every other institution that serves the good of society? How does it differ from the Kiwanis Club or Red Cross? The church is distinctive in its purpose. Its sole purpose is to keep alive the story of Jesus and to serve as his disciples in the world. Its sole and unique purpose is to express and mediate faith in God through loyalty to Jesus Christ. It does this, in contrast to every other institution, through its distinctive language, stories, symbols, rituals, and style of life. When and where the story of Jesus and his significance is told, "where believers in Christ are assembled and the gospel is present, there is the church of Jesus Christ." Ted Peters, *God — The World's Future: Systematic Theology for a New Era*, second ed. (Minneapolis: Fortress, 2000), p. 267.

14. Joseph Haroutunian, *God With Us: A Theology of Transpersonal Life* (Philadelphia:

How essential is the church? I must be careful here. Ecclesiology does not answer the question of whether there is salvation apart from the church. Nothing said here about the church implies that God is limited to working only through the church. It is not the church but God who saves. While the church is bound to Christ, Christ is not confined to the church or trapped in the church. Christ came to express God's love for the whole world (John 3:16), not just for the church. Ecclesiology, rather, establishes *Christian* identity and the role of the church in that identity. The way *Christians* know, trust, and obey God in Christ is through the ministry of the church.[15]

The Church and the Triune God

There are many New Testament images of the church.[16] I will emphasize here how the identity of the church is rooted in the nature and work of the Trinity.[17] The church is, first of all, the *people of God.* This image is rooted in the

---

Westminster, 1965), chapter 2. A striking example of a layperson who understands this distinction was conveyed to me by my friend, Julie Carmean, who is pastor of a United Methodist congregation. A layperson in her congregation said to her following a planning session on the future of their church, "I want to be buried from here." Julie initially assumed he meant, "I want my funeral to be held in this building, so we must keep this building in good repair." In their ensuing conversation, he told her he meant, "I don't care what building I am buried from, but I want to be buried by these people in this community."

15. Guthrie, *Christian Doctrine,* pp. 357-58.

16. There are about one hundred cognates used in the New Testament to describe the *ecclesia,* which can be grouped into ten categories. The church is the saints and sanctified, viewed from the standpoint of God's action toward and upon us, those whom God has chosen; the believers and the faithful, viewed from the standpoint of personal and communal response to God's action; slaves and servants, viewed from the standpoint of the basic duties that the response entails; the people of God, viewed as the continuation and culmination of the covenant community of Israel; the kingdom and temple, viewed in terms of those two institutions long central to Israel's life, including kings and priests, a holy nation, a royal priesthood; a household and family, viewed as an eschatological gathering of God's family into a household; a new Exodus, viewed by way of typological comparison with a key epoch in Israel's history; vineyard and flock, viewed by way of agricultural analogies, stressing our dependence on God, the necessity of producing fruit, and the processes of judgment; one body in Christ or the body of Christ, stressing the solidarities in which all humankind participates, the destruction of the body of sin and the creation of the new body, and participation in the death and resurrection of Jesus; and, finally, the new humanity, in which Jesus Christ is the last Adam whose image we bear. Paul Minear, "Church, Idea of," *Interpreter's Dictionary of the Bible,* vol. A-D (Nashville: Abingdon, 1962), pp. 607-17.

17. There are many ways to describe the reality of the church. In addition to the Trinitarian model that I follow here, which follows Hans Küng's "Fundamental Structure of the Church" in

First Person of the triune God and the doctrine of creation. The church as the people of God emphasizes, first, that the church is "of God."[18] The initiative lies with God. Without electing grace there is no church. The church is not simply a human-generated association of like-minded religious people. It exists as God's elect; it is based on a covenant established by God.

This image emphasizes, second, that "the people" is wider than the Christian churches. The church is already implicit in the creation. The people of God is, in one sense, tied to all humanity (and perhaps beyond).[19] God's people is rooted in God's original intention and ultimate design to call all the creation out of isolation into covenant and communion with God and each other. There has always been a church; it was established "in the beginning," going back as far as God's covenant relationship with Adam and Eve, Abel, Enoch, and Noah (Heb. 11:4-7).

The image emphasizes, third, that the church is a continuation of God's

> "A church will not last long as merely a health club; other health clubs exist, and other, less demanding means for generating togetherness. The pith and poignancy of a church lies in its being a company of believers."
>
> JOHN UPDIKE

The Church, the other major format has been Avery Dulles's *Models of the Church,* which uses the typology of the church as institution (its visible structures, focusing on the rights and powers of offices within the church, where salvation is gained by getting people into the church, whose beneficiaries are its members); the church as mystical communion or people of God (focusing on the spiritual and interior communion of people and their bonds of union through the Holy Spirit, whose beneficiaries are its members who are led into communion with God); the church as sacrament (through which the world shares in the divine life and nature mediates supernatural signs of grace, whose beneficiaries are those able to articulate and live the life of faith thanks to the church and to purify and intensify people's response to the grace of Christ); the church as herald of the Word (where people are gathered and formed by the Word and faith is achieved through proclamation, whose beneficiaries are those who hear and participate in faith in Christ); and the church as servant (in which the church is in dialogue with the secular world and the bonds of the church are formed of the mutual brotherhood among those who join in Christian service, whose beneficiaries are the brothers and sisters of the world over who are helped and served wherever they are). An alternative typology has been offered by Keith Ward, *Religion and Community,* part 2 (Oxford: Clarendon, 2000), where the church is represented as a teaching community, as a charismatic community, as a sacramental community, and as a moral community (pp. 131-233). One might also note megachurch, metachurch, superchurch, woman church, base communities, mission church, charismatic church, or any other number of ways of designating types or dimensions of "the church."

18. For some of the ideas in these two paragraphs, see Hans Küng, *The Church* (Garden City, N.Y.: Image Books, 1976), pp. 147-200.

19. Paul Davies, "E.T. and God," *Atlantic Monthly,* November 2003, pp. 112-18.

covenant with Israel through Abraham and Moses (Heb. 11:8-38). God's mission for Israel was that the whole world would come to God. God established that covenant so that the whole of the gentile world could come to God. The church, therefore, is a continuation of God's covenant with Israel (Gal. 6:16). It is heresy as well as it is sinful that some Christians are unwilling to acknowledge our continuity with Judaism. They use the Old Testament for prophecy or inspiration but fail to recognize that the church is related to the election of Israel. The church is that part of humanity making a journey from Israel's covenant toward the future of God through incorporation in Christ.[20] But we remain in continuity with God's covenant with Israel as God's elect (Isa. 42:1; 62:12) and with all humanity as the people of God.[21]

The image emphasizes, finally, that the church is the whole people (the *laos*), not its institutional hierarchy. No one in the church ever becomes more than the *laos* (the people) of God. Any distinctions within the church arise within and among the whole people as a way of deploying its ministry. The church consists of all of the faithful and loyal people of God, not a particular caste, order, or offices within the fellowship of the believers.

Second, the church is the *body of Christ*. This image is rooted in the Second Person of the triune God and the doctrine of the incarnation. Ecclesiology is inseparable from christology. The body of Christ image emphasizes that this new people is constituted by Jesus Christ.[22] The crucified Jesus is present as the risen Lord of the church.[23] The church does not derive its life from what Christ did in the past but from his living presence in the community through the power of the Spirit. We must be careful here, however. We cannot identify Christ with the church. There is no ontic identity in which Christ and the church merge their identities.[24] Nevertheless, five New

---

20. God is Israel's God and Israel is God's people, even after Christ. The title is never withdrawn from Israel. Through faith in Jesus as the Messiah, the church is a new people of God (1 Peter 2:9-10). But we are not the only people of God or the replacement of Israel.

21. Macquarrie, *Principles of Christian Theology*, pp. 386-87, and his *Theology, Church, and Ministry* (New York: Crossroad, 1986), chapter 11.

22. Küng, *The Church*, pp. 266-337.

23. "The church cannot exist without Christ; Christ cannot be present without his church. . . . Thus they are mutually connected one with the other, and this reciprocity is essential. Christology and ecclesiology condition one another." Anders Nygren, *Christ and His Church* (1956), p. 31, quoted in Claude Welch, *The Reality of the Church* (New York: Scribner's, 1958), p. 27.

24. Küng, *The Church*, pp. 201ff. Christ is not present now in the incarnate way but rather through the Holy Spirit. Paul thinks of the glorified spiritual body of Christ existing in heaven, not on earth, at least until the parousia. "All this would lead not to the idea that the Church is a continuation or extension of the incarnation on earth but rather to the idea that we are now liv-

Testament Pauline writings do connect Christ and the idea of the body. They stress the harmonious relation of members, the subjection of the body to the head, the life which comes to the body through the head, and the reconciling unity of the body.[25] Jesus Christ is the head of the church. But this relationship is analogical, not literal or ontological.[26] Therefore, the church's existence is dialectical. It is the body of Christ insofar as it is subject to Christ and represents Christ, through its preaching and sacraments and through its healing and reconciling acts. But it is also a community of believers dependent on the faith of the believers and on the work of the Spirit within the community to create disciples of Jesus Christ.

The church as the body of Christ is also tied to soteriology. The church is the community of faith in Christ, the community in which humanity is consciously and intentionally being shaped and conformed to Christhood (2 Cor. 5:17).[27] The church as the body of Christ, therefore, emphasizes the union of the church with its Lord in the present and the union of its members as a community of disciples. To be in Christ is to be in the church and to be in the church is to be in Christ.[28] To become a Christian is to become a part of the community of believers who trust in Christ as Lord and seek to live in his way. There is no such thing as a purely individualistic relationship with Christ. Salvation comes through participation in Christ through the sacraments (Roman Catholic), through the proclamation and response to Word and sacraments (Protestant), through a new birth (evangelicalism), or through the gathering of true believers into a disciplined community of followers of Christ (Anabaptist). Salvation is the incorporation of persons into the realm of redemption through incorporation into the church as his community on earth.

Third, the church is the *community of the Holy Spirit.* This image is rooted in the Third Person of the triune God and the doctrines of sanctification and eschatology. Following his resurrection, Christ's followers experienced the sending of the Spirit at Pentecost as the life-giving Spirit of the church. "The Spirit is thus the earthly presence of the glorified Lord. In the Spirit Christ becomes Lord of His church, and in the Spirit the resurrected Lord acts both in the community and in the individual," writes Hans Küng.[29]

---

ing in an era when the incarnate life is no longer here but in heaven." Donald Baillie, *The Theology of the Sacraments* (New York: Scribner's, 1957), pp. 63-64. The church remains a fellowship of believers in Christ.

25. Welch, *Reality of the Church*, p. 148.

26. Welch, *Reality of the Church*, pp. 122-23.

27. Macquarrie, *Principles of Christian Theology*, pp. 388-90.

28. Guthrie, *Basic Christian Doctrine*, p. 356.

29. Küng, *The Church*, p. 221.

The Spirit opens up for the believer the saving work of Christ and incorporates the believer into the body of Christ.

As with christology, the church is not the Spirit. It is the creation of the Spirit and lives under the reign of the Spirit. The church is a community of the Spirit:[30] people on the way from sinful humanity to the kingdom of God, the community where the Spirit works to bring the saints to perfection, the new creation in which Christ's image is borne, the community where the eschatological promise of God's shalom is being fulfilled. The Holy Spirit keeps the church in truth and guides it.[31]

III. "One, Holy, Catholic, and Apostolic": The Marks of the Church

Whenever you say, "Now there is the church!" you assume a theology of the church. By saying a church is authentic, however, we do not refer to the ideal church that exists abstractly above history, or to the spiritual church in contrast to the church in history. There can be no dualism in ecclesiology as there can be none in christology. We cannot separate the intangible church and the empirical churches. It is invisible only to the extent that we are unable to set precisely the boundaries of the church. There may be many sheep outside the church and many goats inside the church who are known only to God. "It may well be that some members of the church are not or will not be saved and that some non-members are or will be, but that simply means being saved is not identical with being a member of the church," notes Owen Thomas.[32]

The judgment that "that was the church at work!" or "the church failed to be the church there!" is based on some criteria to describe what the church as the body of believers which exists in history looks like. An authentic church is

---

30. The church is a community of persons who live not by and for themselves according to the "flesh" but for others according to the Spirit (Rom. 8:4). Although the church is often a place of bondage (to sin, the law, authoritarianism, absolutism, personality cults, blind obedience), the church is constituted by a new freedom given as a gift of God through the work of the Spirit, who awakens a new freedom in us (2 Cor. 3:17). It is a sign and foretaste of the coming commonwealth of God, a new kind of life that is free from personal sin and guilt but also free to be for and with the other and the whole of humanity in a quite radical way. Susan Thistlethwaite and Peter Hodgson, "The Church, Classism, and Ecclesial Community," in *Reconstructing Christian Theology,* ed. Rebecca Chopp and Mark Taylor (Minneapolis: Fortress, 1994), p. 317.

31. *Baptism, Eucharist, and Ministry,* Faith and Order Paper No. 111 (Geneva: World Council of Churches, 1982), paragraph 20.

32. Owen Thomas, *Introduction to Theology,* revised ed. (Wilton, Conn.: Morehouse-Barlow, 1983), p. 238.

not characterized by the perfection of its members but by their faithfulness to Christ who is re-presented in the gospel preached and the sacraments administered by those who are called to witness to him.[33] What are the marks, qualities, or characteristics of the church which permit, even require, Christians to claim that what is said and done is said and done by the true church?

The Reformed emphasis on the church as *semper reformandum* (always reforming) reminds us how quickly ecclesiastical institutions become rigid and corrupt. There are inauthentic churches. The appearance of the German Christian Church during World War II, which Barth resisted in the "Barmen Declaration" and Bonhoeffer in his martyrdom, is a recent example. Beyond this, a monolithic institution with uniform beliefs and practices is not desirable. People differ in language, culture, history, practice, taste, style, temperament, and habit, and this adds to the richness of the church. Christians should celebrate and support our differences. We should not seek to stir all differences into a common melting pot. Unity and uniformity are not the same. How, then, do we identify a church as an authentic church? Since the Council of Constantinople in 381, the church has professed in its creed that "we believe . . . in the one, holy, catholic, and apostolic church."[34]

One

Desirable as diversity of the church is, this diversity often disintegrates into the sinful disunity of the church. The reconciling work of Christ in the cre-

---

33. Peters, *God — The World's Future,* p. 276.

34. It is not possible (or desirable) to establish a fixed set of criteria by which to make a judgment about an authentic church. In addition to the four "marks," the Reformed churches, for example, have subordinated these four to additional marks. The one essential of the church is the Word of God, so the church exists where the Word is rightly preached and heard, and where the sacraments are rightly administered. Reformed Christians have added ecclesiastical discipline, which is also a key mark in all Methodist ecclesiology. Many twentieth-century ecclesiologies have added a fourth, mission (Thomas, *Introduction to Theology,* p. 234), or a fifth, commitment to God's liberation of the poor (Juan Luis Segundo, *The Community Called Church,* trans. John Drury [Maryknoll, N.Y.: Orbis, 1973]). See also Curt Cadorette et al., eds., *Liberation Theology: An Introductory Reader* (Maryknoll, N.Y.: Orbis, 1992), esp. part 3, "The Church in Solidarity: Liberation Ecclesiology," including the following: "Introduction," by Marilyn J. Legge; "The Church: Sacrament of History," by Gustavo Gutiérrez; "Church Base Communities," by Dominique Barbe; "Women's Participation in the Church," by Maria Pilar Aquino; "New Ways of Being Church," by Yong Ting Jin; "Defining 'Women-Church,'" by Mary Hunt; and "A Struggle for the Church's Soul," by Charles Villa-Vicencio. See also James H. Cone, "Church, World, and Eschatology in Black Theology," in *A Black Theology of Liberation,* second ed. (Maryknoll, N.Y.: Orbis, 1986), pp. 129-42.

ation is blocked within the church itself by its barriers of race and class. The church is divided and separated on the basis of gender or ethnic origin.[35] Indeed, the idolatry of the churches today may be our ultimate loyalty to the golden calves of nation, class, and race. This is not only a scandal for effective mission; it is a denial the oneness of the church in Jesus Christ. There is but one church, the church of Jesus Christ, to which all Christians belong. There is one body and one Spirit, one Lord, one faith, one baptism, one hope (Eph. 4:4-6), one bread and cup (1 Cor. 10:16-17), one Spirit (1 Cor. 12:4-27). The church's diversity belongs within a given unity. This unity is not an achievement growing out of efforts to cooperate. The church is one community, a family that lives in the same household, eats together, and carries forward its mission to the world. The church is one so that the world might believe (John 17:20-21).

The visible symbol of this unity amidst all the diversity is the Bible.[36] Some "free-church" doctrines of the church interpret the church's unity as entirely spiritual and invisible. Since only one part of the visible church is the true church, namely, those who have had a born-again experience or who are disciples of Jesus in their pacifism and voluntary poverty, the church cannot be visibly one. For more "Catholic" and "reformed" ecclesiologies, in which the church consists of all of its members, some form of visible unity is essential to the oneness of the church. The oneness of the church includes its unity as denominations, associations, federations, and councils.[37] The church's unity must be visible in some form, such as a shared canon.

Holy

The church is the community where Christ is being formed among and within its members. The church is rooted in Christ, by whose life, death, and resurrec-

---

35. H. R. Niebuhr, *The Social Sources of Denominationalism* (New York: Henry Holt, 1929).

36. Macquarrie, *Principles of Christian Theology*, p. 404.

37. This includes the Roman Catholic Church and the various Orthodox churches; the denominations such as Episcopal, Presbyterian, Methodist, Baptist, and Assemblies of God; the Lutheran World Federation, the World Alliance of Reformed Churches, the Lambeth Assembly, and the United Methodist Council; the World Council of Churches, the National Council of Churches, and the National Association of Evangelicals; and the emerging Christian Churches Together in the USA, which have met in 2001 in Baltimore, in 2002 in Chicago, and in 2003 in Pasadena, and which consist of five traditions — Evangelical-Pentecostal, historic Protestant, Eastern Orthodox, racial/ethnic, and Roman Catholic — joined together "to enable churches and organizations to grow closer together in Christ in order to strengthen our Christian witness in the world."

tion believers are justified by grace and set on the path to sanctification.[38] The church is the assembly within which the Spirit works, through the appointed means of grace, to conform its members to Christ. The sacraments are the primary visible means in most Catholic and Protestant churches of our inclusion into the church and of the maintenance and growth of our life in Christ.[39]

Catholic

The church is a universal community spread throughout the world from one end of the earth to the other. This does not mean the church is one institution to which all Christians declare loyalty. It means, rather, that the church is whole or complete in the sense that it is present in all parts of the world, through all periods of history, and includes all kinds of people. Any church, including a local congregation, which does not intend to be catholic in the sense that it invites all manner of people — people of differing sexes, races, classes, sexual orientation, national origin, intelligence, skills, even odors — is not the church.

Some Christians, such as Roman Catholics, understand catholicity to consist of membership and loyalty to an institution. Its unity and authority are represented and sustained through a line of apostolic succession, embodied in the pope, bishops, and clergy of the church. Others, such as Presbyterians and Methodists, understand the local congregations, along with Presbytery and Synod or the General and Annual Conferences of the denomination, to be the church in its fullness. Still others, such as Anabaptists, understand each local congregation to be the church in its fullness. The church's universality is the spiritual unity of local congregations. Regardless of these different emphases in polity (church order), however, most Christians confess the church to be catholic or ecumenical in the sense that it inhabits the whole world and that the body consists of people from every political, economic, racial, and cultural group of every society.

Apostolic

The word "apostolic" for Protestants is nearly synonymous with "biblical." That is, to be apostolic is to be faithful to the gospel as it is preached in the New Testament. An apostolic church stands in continuity with the faith of the apos-

---

38. Migliore, *Faith Seeking Understanding*, p. 202.
39. Macquarrie, *Principles of Christian Theology*, pp. 458, 469.

tles and their proclamation. We can say that the church is apostolic when it has been kept faithful to its gospel by the Holy Spirit. Hans Küng has argued not for the "infallibility" of the church but for its "indefectability" precisely on this basis.[40] In Roman Catholic churches an apostolic church requires a belief in apostolic succession. Faithfulness to the gospel is represented and guaranteed by the college of bishops, who, in an unbroken line of succession from Peter, transfer the ministry of the apostles to the contemporary clergy. In some non-Roman churches as well, especially the Orthodox, Anglican, (some) Lutheran, and Methodist — episcopacy remains the primary visible symbol of apostolicity. In most Protestant churches, however, it is neither possible nor necessary to establish a direct line of continuity of ecclesiastical orders. Rather, a church is apostolic when all of its members, in all of their roles and offices, remain in continuity with the prophets, with the ministry of Jesus, and with the continuing apostolic witness of the New Testament in its proclamation of the gospel. Those who trust and obey Jesus Christ are in communion with the apostles. They form an unbroken succession of believers.[41] Reformed and Baptist churches believe the church to be apostolic through its faithfulness to the New Testament gospel in all of the roles and offices of the church.

IV. Our Ministry of Reconciliation (2 Cor. 5:18): The Mission of the Church

Ed Zeiders, the president of my school, served as a superintendent of United Methodist churches in central Pennsylvania before coming to the school. One of the pastors under his leadership called him one Monday morning to tell him about a family in the neighborhood who had lost everything they had accumulated over the years — their house, their furnishings, their memorabilia — in a disastrous fire. The pastor assembled the congregation in an official meeting to consider what the congregation might do for the family. A discussion ensued, then a debate broke out, and finally a vote was taken about whether or not to help the family. The vote was negative. Broken to the point of despair, the pastor called his superintendent to seek support and counsel. "Why, what reason could they possibly give for their vote?" Zeiders asked. The reply: "Because they had done nothing to help the church, the church voted to do nothing to help them."

---

40. Hans Küng, *Infallible? An Inquiry*, trans. Edward Quinn (New York: Image, 1972), pp. 163ff.

41. Leith, *Basic Christian Doctrine*, pp. 240-44.

The terms "mission" and "ministry" are sometimes used interchangeably, and with good reason. They are identical in the sense that both refer to the work of Christ for the redemption of the world. It is helpful here to note that there is no wall of separation between the church and the world. The church exists in the world (and the world in the church). The church is that part of the world where the story of Jesus is retold, where his death and resurrection are observed, where God's shalom is prepared for and enacted, and where the promise of his final victory is celebrated. In my usage the mission of the church refers to Christ's work of reconciliation in the world, while the ministry of the church refers to the church's remembering, celebrating, preparing for, and enacting Christ's ministry of reconciliation in the world.

The church exists as God's instrument of reconciliation. It does not exist as an end in itself. The church does not *have* a mission, it *is* a mission. Its mission is not to become a big and powerful institution, nor to impress the world about how good it is. Its purpose is not to make every person a member of the church. The purpose of the church is to be God's instrument to fulfill God's covenant with the whole creation.[42] It carries out its mission "by proclaiming the good news of God's grace and thus seeking the fulfillment of God's reign and realm in the world."[43] It exists in order to re-present and represent the gospel both outside (mission) and inside (ministry) the community of disciples. "To be reconciled to God," we read in the Constitution of the Presbyterian church, "is to be sent into the world as his reconciling community. This community, the church universal, is entrusted with God's message of reconciliation and shares his labor of healing the enmities which separate men from God and from each other."[44] The church does not bring salvation by saving people from the world; it seeks to make God known to the world and to realize God's will of justice and peace. The terms for mission vary: to promote reconciliation, gratitude for the forgiveness of sins, the realization of the kingdom of God, the power of the Spirit, the response to the gospel. Jesus presented to his followers our clearest mission statement: to increase the love of God and the neighbor.

Although the church is not the incarnation, it is analogous to the incarnation in the sense that as the body of Christ it is called to the same kind of worldliness that God assumed in Jesus. The church lives to serve the world.

---

42. Neville, *A Theology Primer,* p. 159.

43. Part 3, "The Ministry of All Christians," *The Book of Discipline of the United Methodist Church 2000* (Nashville: United Methodist Publishing House, 2000), p. 87.

44. "The Confession of 1967," *The Constitution of the Presbyterian Church (U.S.A.),* Part I, Book of Confessions (Louisville: Office of the General Assembly, 1996), 9.31.

There is no other reason for it to exist.[45] The church is placed in the world by God to be an instrument of reconciliation. A church separate from the world, relocated apart from and above the world in some spiritual realm beyond history, has no reality. The church, therefore, should seek neither to rule nor to renounce the world.[46] It should not seek to rule the world because it participates in sin just as the world does, and so is as corruptible, as unreliable, and as dangerous as any other institution in ruling the world. At the same time, the church cannot withdraw from the world because it is the community through which God wills to make the redemptive activity of Christ and the Spirit manifest. We are not only the church gathered for worship and study. We are the church at home, in the office, at the mall, in the voting booth, at the union meeting, at the bridge party, on the picket line, in a stockholders' meeting, in the soup kitchen, at the PTA, or wherever the gathered people are scattered in daily life.

"The church is the community called into being, built up, and sent into the world to serve in the name and power of the triune God," writes Daniel Migliore.[47] The church does not make Christ present in the world. Christ is already there, especially among the poor and oppressed, whom the church is called upon to recognize as Christ present and to join in solidarity (Matt. 25:31-46).[48] We represent Christ in the world by serving "the least of these" in their struggle for emancipation, justice, and peace. When the church exposes the conditions of injustice, calls for freedom and justice, works for the transformation of people and structures, as Bonhoeffer and Romero did in their struggle against evil in the world and in the church, the church participates in Christ's redemptive work. "Those who minister to the wretched of the earth minister to Christ," says Migliore.[49]

> "You've got self-righteous people on all sides arguing with other self-righteous people. God is saying No to . . . these little trivial debates we're having in the church while hundreds of thousands of people are starving to death."
>
> **SHIRLEY GUTHRIE**

Following Jesus who was *the* servant of God for the sake of the world, the church is a servant of God and the world (Matt. 20:25-28; Mark 8:34-35). It is a

45. Donald Messer, *Contemporary Images of Christian Ministry* (Nashville: Abingdon, 1989), p. 64.

46. Ward, *Religion and Community,* pp. 131-36.

47. Migliore, *Faith Seeking Understanding,* p. 200.

48. Cone, *Black Theology of Liberation,* pp. 130-31.

49. Migliore, *Faith Seeking Understanding,* p. 204.

servant of the world not in the sense that it is obedient to the world but in the way Christ was a servant to God's work for the redemption of the world. The church represents and re-presents the gospel outside the gathered community as a promise and a foretaste of God's reign through justice and peace. It is that part of the world where God's love and purpose of salvation are recognized, responded to, celebrated, and enacted. Its mission of reconciliation is never finished until the kingdom of this world becomes the kingdom of our Lord and of his Christ (Rev. 11:15), a kingdom of loving service, justice, well-being, and shalom. The church is also called to be itself a place where God's purpose for the world becomes visible in history as a sign to the world of its own destiny.[50] The church's mission, then, is also to itself. The maintenance of its liturgy and organization is part of its mission to the world. Its own programs and structures, therefore, should be missional, should facilitate the carrying on of the mission of Jesus in the world.[51] The church's service to the world, then, includes the worship of God, mutual edification, and pastoral oversight. The church's service as worship is absolutely central to the well-being of both the church and the world.

Is the church's mission spiritual or material? Should the church be more concerned with souls and their spiritual needs or with bodies and their physical and emotional needs? Should it look primarily to the individual or to society? The answer is that the church's mission is to people in their wholeness. Therefore, the question poses false alternatives.[52] The church is called to participate in God's purpose of bringing well-being to the whole creation,[53] and that includes the world in all of its dimensions — physical, emotional, cultural, political, economic, and spiritual. Persons are bodies and souls. There is no such thing as a soulless body or a bodyless soul. And we are each individuals and social beings embedded in society. We proclaim the Word in both word and deed. It would be nonsense to say that God loves you but doesn't care if you are hungry, or that God loves you but doesn't care about your fears and anxieties and prejudices and false gods. The mission of the church is a holistic one for the whole world.

Any talk about service to the world which does not begin with the church's learning, repeating, interpreting, and celebrating its own story and

---

50. Thomas, *Introduction to Theology,* pp. 234-35.

51. Mary Hines, "Community for Liberation," in *Freeing Theology: The Essentials of Theology in Feminist Perspective,* ed. Catherine Mowry LaCugna (San Francisco: HarperSanFrancisco, 1993), p. 166.

52. Tyron Inbody, "Mission and Worship: Basic Polarities But False Alternatives," *Lexington Theological Quarterly* 18, no. 2 (April 1983): 52-63.

53. Williamson, *Way of Blessing, Way of Life,* p. 255.

language and liturgy will eventually empty the church into a secular institution with no gospel. The church represents and re-presents this gospel within the community as a promise and foretaste to the world through its preaching and sacraments. Without this it has no language, no motivation, and no message to proclaim in and for the world. The ministry of reconciliation in the world includes keeping alive the story of Jesus by the community remaining faithful to its Scriptures and reciting its story faithfully in its worship, preaching, and sacraments. "The church has to learn how to tell its own story, teach its own faith, sing its own song, develop the skills to use its own language if it is going to survive as church," notes Clark Williamson.[54] The vocation of the church to make Christ present in the world depends on Word and sacrament, representing and conveying God's promise that salvation is offered to the whole of the creation. The church is not the kingdom of God, but as the community of reconciliation it proclaims and prefigures God's reign between the resurrection of Jesus and the eschaton.

V. "The Gifts He Gave . . . for the Work of Ministry" (Eph. 4:11): The Ministry of the Church

Christian ministry is the ministry of Christ. It is given by God to all those who are reconciled in Christ. "All this is from God, who reconciled us to himself through Christ, and has given us the ministry of reconciliation; that is, in Christ God was reconciling the world to himself, not counting their trespasses against them, and entrusting the message of reconciliation to us" (2 Cor. 5:18-19). This ministry is given to the whole church, the *laos*, the people of God. All Christians are ministers to each other and to the world. This is the meaning of the Reformation idea of the priesthood of all believers (not that we have our own private access to God apart from each other). In the United Methodist Church's *Book of Discipline* we read that "All Christians are called through their baptism to this ministry of servanthood in the world to the glory of God and for human fulfillment. . . . This means that all Christians are called to minister wherever Christ would have them serve and witness in deeds and words that heal and free."[55] Although I need to be very clear about what I do not mean, I might say that baptism is "ordination" to Christian ministry in the sense that it is our inclusion into Christ's one ministry of rec-

---

54. Williamson, *Way of Blessing, Way of Life*, p. 274.

55. Part 3, "The Ministry of All Christians," *The Book of Discipline of the United Methodist Church 2000*, p. 89.

onciliation. A more proper formulation would be that Christian ministry is "sealed" in and by our baptism; in other words, it is in the sacrament of baptism that Christians receive the gift of ministry.[56]

I took the risk of misusing the term "ordination" in order to underscore the claim that all Christians are called to the ministry of Christ. After reading "statements on ministry" for over twenty-five years, I am convinced that any theology of set-apart ministry which does not begin with the general ministry, *the ministry of all Christians,* is likely to move quickly to a view of ministry that sees the set-apart person or persons as a "super Christian," a "higher Christian," or an elite group with special authority over or apart from the *laos.* Every form of special ministry must be set within the context of the general ministry of all Christians. Otherwise, the temptation to spiritual or moral elitism is overwhelming. The consequences of this are numerous: the laity are deprived of their ministry; they submit to and are exploited by the clergy; the set-apart person has to maintain an image or endure unreasonable expectations, which too often leads to self-righteousness and delusion or to depression and burnout.

Although there is only one ministry of the church, there are, also, diverse gifts (charisms) of the Spirit within the ministry of Christ. "The gifts he gave were that some would be apostles, some prophets, some evangelists, some pastors and teachers, to equip the saints for the work of ministry, for building up the body of Christ, until all of us come to the unity of the faith and of the knowledge of the Son of God, to maturity, to the measure of the full stature of Christ" (Eph. 4:11-13). All ministry is based on charisms, gifts bestowed by the Spirit on *all* members of the church, for the edification of the church and for the church's mission to the world. Each depends on the other and contributes to the one ministry of Christ. These different gifts of ministry are the means by which the church prepares and deploys itself in its mission in, to, and for the world.

The New Testament does not describe, let alone proscribe, a single pattern for these various ministries within a single ministry. Following the second and third centuries, however, a threefold pattern of deacon, presbyter, and bishop emerged as the common pattern in Western churches, past and present,[57] although many Reformed and evangelical churches question the biblical grounds or necessity of this threefold pattern. Typically within Catholic and most Protestant churches, however, "specialized ministry," "called-out ministry," or "representative ministry" refers to some form of the three

56. Messer, *Contemporary Images of Christian Ministry,* p. 65.
57. *Baptism, Eucharist, and Ministry,* paragraph 21.

traditional orders, offices, or roles within the church. These include deacon ("love, justice, and service"), priest, presbyter, or elder ("Word and sacrament"), and bishop ("oversight").[58]

In those churches where the priesthood of all believers is emphasized and democratic forms of organizing the church (polity or order) predominate, such as Baptist churches, specialized ministry refers simply to the distinction between laypersons and the person ordained to preach and administer the sacraments. For them the church in its fullness exists in each local congregation. (We call this a "congregational polity.") The church does not require any other orders, offices, or ecclesiastical structures, such as presbyteries or conferences, to be the church. Local churches may decide voluntarily to join associations or conventions for practical purposes, but they are not necessary for the fullness of the church.

In Presbyterian churches, which also have a fairly democratic polity, specialized ministry refers to two offices. One is the office of deacon, into which one is ordained to a ministry of service, and the other is the office of presbyter or elder; presbyters are the group responsible for governing the session of the church and the presbytery, while elders have a distinctive responsibility for Word and sacrament.

In other denominations, such as Methodist, that are more "episcopal" in their structure, specialized ministry refers to the office of deacon and to the office of elder or pastor. The deacon's ministry is Word and service, namely, assisting in worship, administrative tasks, and representing the love of Christ to the world. The ministry of the office of elder or pastor is Word, sacrament, order, and service, namely, preaching and teaching, sacraments, pastoral care, and the discipline (discipleship) of the congregation. In Methodism this office includes the office of bishop, who is consecrated (not ordained) with responsibility for oversight. In churches with even more highly defined structures, such as Roman Catholic and Anglican, special ministry refers to the deacon, the pastor or priest (whose ministry is a sacramental order within the church), and the bishop (who is sacramentally ordained into a separate order which is a fuller ministry of the church and is responsible for oversight, continuity, and unity of the church's ministry). The church in its fullness does not exist without these three orders.

Regardless of what polity is followed, however — congregational, presbyterial, or episcopal — almost all Christians understand the church's ministry to include some form of called-out, special, or representative ministry within the general ministry of the church.

58. *Baptism, Eucharist, and Ministry,* paragraphs 19-32.

Call to Ministry

Most of my students begin their statements on Christian ministry with their personal call to ordained ministry. A few hear voices or see visions, but the majority of them describe a clear, unequivocal, and inescapable inner conviction that God has chosen and called them to ordained ministry. They have, finally, after much resistance or many roadblocks and detours, answered their call. Beginning here leads some to conclude that their call is their ordination. The laying on of hands is simply the church's acknowledgment of God's private ordination. The call to ordained ministry, however, involves other dimensions of a call about which the church must make a judgment before it ordains a person to representative ministry.

Ordained ministry is a calling, not a way to make a living, or an occupation, or a career, or even a profession. This calling consists,[59] first, of the call to be a Christian, the call to hear the Word of God, the call to discipleship, or the call to be baptized. It consists, second, of an inner persuasion that God has a special purpose for one's life and that one is summoned, even commanded, by God to obey that call. It includes, third, a providential call, which is sometimes referred to as "gifts and graces" for specialized ministry. These refer to the talents, temperament, motivations, and skills which have been given as a charism by the Spirit, along with the circumstances of time and place for exercising these gifts. A call includes, finally, an ecclesiastical call, an invitation extended by the church, through a congregational call or an episcopal appointment, to engage in the work of representative ministry. The church makes the judgment that the first three of these components of a call from God are present, and that the church needs these particular persons now for the church's ministry. The church recognizes and confirms the inner call, the gifts and graces, and the need of the candidate. The church is, of course, liable to impaired discernment, to prejudice, and to downright error. But its task, after much prayer, is to make a judgment.

Ordained Ministry

What does ordination *do?* The meaning of the act of ordination depends upon whether you have primarily an ontological or a functional understanding of ordination. In an ontological view, "the church and its ministry are

---

59. H. Richard Niebuhr, *The Purpose of the Church and Its Ministry: Reflections on the Aims of Theological Education* (New York: Harper, 1956), pp. 63-66.

equally primordial, the ministry belonging to the very structure of the church."[60] Though all Christians participate in the general ministry of Christ, ordained priests and bishops participate in a different way.[61] Ordination is a special grace, a different way of being the church, a different order within the people of God and the priesthood of Christ. It is a fuller ministry than the ministry of all baptized Christians. When a person is ordained through a sacrament administered by those who have the authority to administer sacraments, the ordinand receives an indelible character as a priest. This is a supernatural endowment bestowed upon the recipient by a bishop, not merely a setting apart by the community for a special ministry. The ordinand is not simply commissioned with authority to perform a function but is conferred with a special grace. Ordination belongs to the essence and structure of the church.

In the functional (or operational or instrumental) view of ordination, ordination belongs to the church's ordering of its ministry.[62] In its extreme (and cynical) form, a purely instrumental view of ordination speaks of it as a union card, a way to get into the ecclesiastical system so that one has an institutional vehicle to express one's own private call and to share in the authority, power, prestige, and pension plan of the church. In its more defensible form, functional views of ordination emphasize that clergy never cease to be laity, the people of God. It emphasizes that there is no biblical basis for thinking of ordination as a higher or fuller ministry in contrast to the ministry of all Christians. In this view, ordination has one purpose. It is the means by which the church deploys its service and servanthood most effectively and efficiently in its ministry and mission within the church and in and for the world. These *roles* are different forms of the one ministry of the church. Ordination is missiological rather than ontological.[63] To be ordained is to be commissioned and authorized by the church for the particular tasks of teaching doctrine, proclamation of Word and administration of sacraments, govern-

60. Macquarrie, *Principles of Christian Theology*, pp. 426-27.

61. Thus, Vatican II in its "Dogma on the Constitution of the Church," in chapter 2 on "The People of God," says, "Though they differ from one another in essence and not only in degree, the common priesthood of the faithful and the ministerial or hierarchical priesthood are nonetheless interrelated. . . . Each of them in its own special way is a participation in the one priesthood of Christ." Walter Abbott, ed., *Documents of Vatican II* (New York: Guild, 1966), p. 27.

62. Robert Clyde Johnson, "The Doctrine of the Ministry," in his *The Church and Its Changing Ministry: Study Material Prepared under the Direction of the General Assembly Special Committee on the Nature of the Ministry* (Philadelphia: Office of the General Assembly, United Presbyterian Church in the United States of America, 1961), pp. 97-106.

63. Migliore, *Faith Seeking Understanding*, p. 227.

ment of the church, and service to the sick, poor, and needy.[64] It is the general body of Christians who ordain, of which other clergy are representatives who pass on that representative role.

I said "primarily" two paragraphs above because few Christians understand ordination in a purely functional manner (as simply a role that the institution creates as an efficient way to administer the institution and its mission). Most Christians understand ordination in some sense as a gift of God to the church. God continues through the Spirit to choose and call persons into representative ministry. Ordained clergy are representatives to and of Christ's church.[65] They take a vow of obedience to God and the church to represent the message of reconciliation to the church and world as pastor, teacher, and leader.[66]

In some views, such as Roman Catholicism, the ordained person is also a priest who represents God. He belongs to the priestly order and serves as a sacrificing priest, representing God to the people and the people to God. In some forms of Protestantism, the ordained person is thought of as a representative in the sense that he or she is the person of God in the congregation. This person represents God by preaching the Word, and represents the congregation as the one who witnesses, prays, and reads the Scripture. Or the pastor is the person in the community who has the deepest experience of God and is therefore the model of the Christian life. Regardless of these differences — and many churches are a mixture of all of these, at least in practice — ordination calls, designates, and authorizes a person to be a representative of God and the church.

A theology of ordination as an *office* brings together the two poles which many Christians understand to be inadequate if they stand alone. Ordained ministry as an office embodies another dialectical idea. It includes, on the one hand, the emphasis that ministry as an order makes, namely, the dimensions of mystery, holiness, and sacrality in ordination, and, on the other hand, the emphasis that ordained ministry as a role accents, namely, the ministry of all Christians and the practicality and efficiency of the church's ordering of its one ministry.

As an office, ordination as a gift of God to the church does not establish the essence or identity of the church,[67] but it is central to the life of the

---

64. Leith, *Basic Christian Doctrine.*

65. Dennis Campbell, *The Yoke of Obedience: The Meaning of Ordination in Methodism* (Nashville: Abingdon, 1988), p. 100.

66. *Baptism, Eucharist, and Ministry,* paragraphs 21-22.

67. It is in principle conceivable that God could guard the indefectibility of the church by means of a different charism to order the life of the church. The idea of office implies that ordi-

church. God sets apart through call and ordination persons for the ministry of Word, sacrament, order, and service in the church. The Holy Spirit through the prayer of the church confers upon the ordinand the authority to exercise the power of the church in a responsible manner, especially to preach the Word of God, to consecrate and administer the sacraments, and to lead the congregation into the spiritual disciplines necessary for the church to carry out its mission. Ordination is the way the church authorizes the candidate for a special work of Word and service (deacon), or service, word, order, and sacrament (priest, presbyter, elder, or pastor), or oversight (bishop) in the community. This authority is from God and from the collegial and communal authority of the body of Christ.

The dialectical idea of office is also apparent when we think of the various actors in ordination through which the ordinand is acknowledged to possess the gifts of the Spirit and is authorized for representative ministry. The first actor is God. God has given the gift of ordained ministry to the church for the well-being of the church and the world. Although ordination is not a sacrament for Protestants, it is sacramental in the sense that it is a means of grace by which God calls, establishes, and maintains the Word, sacraments, and order of the church. God calls persons into this ministry through the Spirit, incorporating them into a set-apart ministry, and sustaining them through the power of the Spirit. God works through individual calls and through the structures of the church to set apart persons for the office of ministry.

The second actor is the candidate for ordination, who is involved by responding to the call. Ordinands respond to the call by committing themselves to this way of life in the church and by dedicating themselves through their vows of obedience before God and the church to live the life of ordained ministry. Ordination, in this dimension, refers to the personhood or personal identity of the ordained as well as to the office she fills and the duties she performs. "Ministry is a form of life and not just a role one plays or a job one does," notes Migliore.[68] It is a sacred calling to inhabit an office rooted in a deep commitment to God and a sincere desire to serve God, the church, and the world.

The third actor is the church. Ordained ministry arises from and belongs to the church. Although most Christians understand the church as an actor in ordination, the forms of the church which are involved differ from denomi-

---

nation belongs to the *bene esse* (well-being) but not the *esse* (essence) of the church. Christians who have a "higher" view of ordination will be scandalized by the idea of ordination as an office instead of an order. Christians with a "lower" view will see such an office as a bid for elite status and power.

68. Migliore, *Faith Seeking Understanding*, p. 228.

nation to denomination. The church as a community of believers is involved in the sense that it nurtures persons with gifts and graces for ministry, discerns and designates those persons who have the gifts and graces to fulfill this ministry, and encourages, supports, and evaluates the candidates through their preparation for representative ministry. The church is also involved through those who already have been ordained. In some denominations, the church is involved in ordination primarily through a bishop, who is understood either as the one to whom the fullest ministry has been given by God and through whom the continuity of the ordained ministry has been maintained (Orthodox, Roman Catholic, and Anglican), or as the one from among the ordained who is designated to represent the continuity and authority of specialized ministry (Methodist).[69] In denominations without bishops (Reformed, Baptist), the other clergy are involved in ordination, representing the continuity of ordained ministers and incorporating the candidate into the office or role of representative ministry. In many denominations representatives of local churches, laypersons, are involved in ordination, standing in support of the candidates, representing the churches from which they are called, symbolizing the whole church in its baptismal ministry or the call of a local congregation to representative ministry. In summary, there are several actors in a valid ordination.

A pressing issue in the church today is the place of women in ordained ministry. Throughout the last few decades I thought the Protestant churches had changed their minds about exclusion of women from ordained ministry. I was wrong. The church remains an institution in which there is a long line of ordained males with a few ordained women at the periphery. This constitutes an anomaly in the Christian church. All people in the church — women and men, rich and poor, black and white, straight and gay, brilliant and ordinary — stand before God and before each other in Christ. Exclusion from this office on one of these grounds is sinful and to be rejected.[70] We are all children created in the image of God, sinners saved by grace, members of the one body of Christ and one ministry.

Scripture, not natural rights, is the basis for an equal status of women in ordained ministry.[71] In the sweep of the canon, the work and word of God is

---

69. For a Methodist view of ordination, see Campbell, *The Yoke of Obedience.*

70. "The continued exclusion of women from the ministry of Word and sacrament by some churches under the pretext that God is masculine, or Jesus chose only male apostles, or that only a male can properly represent the person and work of Christ to the people of God is a great scandal to the gospel." Migliore, *Faith Seeking Understanding,* p. 230.

71. Elizabeth Achtemeier, "The Scriptural Basis for Women in Ministry," *reNews,* December 2000, pp. 10-11.

clear. Both male and female bear the image of God. In Christ there is no male or female, for all are one in Christ (Gal. 3:28), and Christ has restored women and men to equality (Eph. 2:14-22). In the Gospels women were among Jesus' disciples (Acts 1:13-14). John recognizes Mary Magdalene as the first apostle, as she is the first to see the risen Lord and the first to be commissioned by him. Women exercised ministerial authority in the New Testament. Priscilla (Acts 18:24-28) is a teacher of advanced theology, and Phoebe is a deacon (not a deaconess) of the church at Cenchreae, a title applied to Timothy (1 Tim. 4:6) and Paul (1 Cor. 3:5).[72] Women are candidates for ordained ministry if New Testament theology and practice are our norms.

72. The notorious passages, 1 Corinthians 14:33-36 and 1 Timothy 2:11-15, are seeking order in worship, not opposing female leadership as such.

CHAPTER ELEVEN

Initiating and Maintaining Faith

I. "Every Common Bush Afire with God": Worship in a Sacramental Universe

As a theologian I spend significant time in local churches teaching short-term courses on theology. Usually I attend the worship service of the church where I am teaching. One of the churches I visit regularly is a Presbyterian church in my area. The church has an exceptional choir and one of the finest organists in the country. Each worship service concludes with the organist playing a postlude while the congregation remains seated. One Sunday the minister preached a sermon on worship, concluding with the announcement that the congregation would no longer applaud the organist's postlude. "God is the audience," the minister said. "The choir and the organist are here to lead us in our worship. They sing and play on our behalf as we worship God through our hearing God's Word, our singing, and our prayers." The congregation usually follows the minister's directive. Occasionally, however, a spontaneous outburst of applause follows the conclusion of the postlude. Some in the congregation simply ignore the pastor's directive. They have been moved to express their enjoyment of the music of the organist. One Sunday I heard someone say, "This music is so inspiring. I don't care what the minister says. He should not try to prohibit me from expressing my appreciation of this wonderful music."

Is the focus of Christian worship God or my experience of God? These, of course, are not mutually exclusive. Nevertheless, the *primary* aim of worship shapes our worship practices. The debate about how to hold this dialectic together is at the heart of the disagreements in Protestant churches over contemporary patterns of worship. No one would admit that the focus of their worship was their experience instead of God. What one emphasizes, however, and how one understands the actors in worship, shapes our worship practices.

What is the purpose of Christian worship, specifically, of a Christian worship service? Is the purpose to worship God or to get something out of it? Clearly it is both. No one would attend a worship service if they did not find some kind of personal significance in attending it. A Roman Catholic confirmation service or an Episcopalian high church eucharistic service is as spiritually and emotionally powerful for its participants as is a Baptist revivalistic preaching service with an altar call or a megachurch contemporary seekers service with its praise songs to its participants. But where you begin and what you emphasize determines your theology of worship as well as the forms, patterns, style, and ethos of what you do in a worship service.

> "If you can't go to church and, for at least a moment, be given transcendence; if you can't go to church and pass briefly from this life into the next; then I can't see why anyone should go. Just a brief moment of transcendence causes you to come out of church a changed person."
>
> **GARRISON KEILLOR**

The place to begin, I think, is with the axiom that worship is God-focused. Worship is not entertainment, the church's contribution to the shopper's stimulation and excitement in a consumer culture. Worship is not like a Broadway musical in which the bulletin is the playbill, the choir is the orchestra, the liturgists are the actors, and the congregation is the audience. Rather, the ministers, liturgists, and choir are prompters. The members of the congregation are the performers, listening to God's Word, confessing their sins, lifting up their hearts, giving thanks to God. The audience is God.

Christians worship because God is worthy of our worship. Christian worship focuses on the priority, primacy, and objectivity — the otherness — of God, rather than on having an experience of God, which would make our inspiration the purpose of worship. This primary purpose is difficult to understand, let alone emphasize, in a culture where experience, subjectivity, stimulating media, and consumer satisfaction define reality and worth. In a consumer culture, people will not go to church if the service is not attractive, stimulating, and entertaining, or if it does not promise a religious experience. People who live in a Disneyland world, which idealizes (or idolizes?) entertainment and subjectivity, do not worship out of a sense of mystery, loyalty, obedience, duty, or liturgy (service). They worship to be inspired, to seek for answers about how to live, to find out how to feel a part of something bigger than themselves, to search for something meaningful. Above all, they worship "to have a worship experience." Songs and prayers are about my experience as much as they are about God.

This tension between the objective side of worship and the subjective side is one of the deepest tensions among Protestant theologies of worship. This is especially evident in the battle within the mainline Protestant churches over traditional versus contemporary forms of worship. The conflict, of course, is in part between older, more conservative traditionalists, who assume organs and brass and eighteenth- and nineteenth-century hymns with theological substance (Watts and Wesley) are the instruments God has provided for worship, and younger, postmodern, electronic-media-conscious contemporaries whose music is expressed through guitars, keyboards, bands, and drums and consists of repeated phrases. But the debate about "real" worship versus "meaningful" worship is underneath a debate over a theology of worship.

The word "worship" comes from the Saxon term "worthship," an attitude that recognizes the intrinsic worth of the person or thing to which homage is directed. When we worship we say that "God is of intrinsic and infinite value, and that as such God is the ultimate target of our praise, thanksgiving, and prayer."[1] We worship God because of God's worthship. The purpose of the church's liturgy is not to calm our frazzled nerves, to generate an emotional experience, to make converts, to motivate our participation in some worthy project. It is to worship God who is holy and who loves us. The key to understanding Christian worship, then, can be found in the very language we use to designate the activity. We refer to worship as a worship *service*. As in its everyday meaning, service is something we do for someone else.

Our worship as service to God, then, includes both the gathered worship in services of worship and our scattered service through our service to the world. Worship and ethics are distinguishable, but they are inseparable as our liturgy (service) to God. That is, our whole life is our liturgy, both in our worship services and as our service to the neighbor. Worship includes our service to God's justice, healing, and peace in the world. Our work for justice is part of our worship of God through our service to the neighbor and the stranger (Matt. 25:31-46).[2]

---

1. Ted Peters, *God — The World's Future: Systematic Theology for a New Era*, second ed. (Minneapolis: Fortress, 2000), p. 280.

2. See my "Mission and Worship: Basic Polarities But False Alternatives," *Lexington Theological Quarterly* 18, no. 2 (April 1983): 52-63.

The unique activity of the church as a gathered people is the self-conscious and explicit service of God by retelling, celebrating, and responding to what God has done for our salvation in Jesus Christ. This happens in a community which gathers to hear and respond to the Word (reading the Bible and preaching the gospel) and to celebrate the sacraments. God's Word is heard in the Scripture and the sermon and is seen and tasted in the sacraments. The place of the preaching of the Word is well-established in all forms of Protestant worship. The celebration of the sacraments, however, has become increasingly important in many Protestant churches after decades, even centuries, of marginalization.

I have already laid the groundwork for a theology of the sacraments in my earlier chapters on creation and on the incarnation and redemption. First of all, the meaning of the sacraments is cradled within a concept of "sacramentality."[3] There is a deep connection between nature and sacrament. We can even say that the most basic relationship between God the creator and the creature as creature is sacramental.[4] Because the world is created by God, the natural world is created to speak to us of God.[5] As has been said many times, nature, in many of its features, bears the fingerprints of God. It has sacramental significance because it conveys the presence of God as a common grace. It mediates God's power and nearness, expresses the divine love, faithfulness, and mercy in its very existence as well as in many of its features. Indeed, nothing could be a sacrament in the special sense unless everything in nature is sacramental, at least latently or potentially.

> "Despite the truth of the spiritual's lyrics, 'He's got the whole world in his hand,' we seldom notice God's sacramental presence in the ordinary experiences of life, including our movie-going."
>
> ROBERT JOHNSON

Therefore, what is concentrated in the sacraments is diffuse throughout nature. Natural objects can become bearers of transcendent power and meaning. There is something holy in nature itself. "Earth's crammed with heaven / And every common bush afire with God," Elizabeth Barrett Browning wrote.[6] Many things within nature represent God to us. The sky is transcendent, the

---

3. James F. White, *The Sacraments in Protestant Practice and Faith* (Nashville: Abingdon, 1999), chapter 1.

4. Owen Thomas and Ellen Wondra, *Introduction to Theology*, third ed. (Harrisburg, Pa.: Morehouse, 2002), p. 282.

5. Donald Baillie, *The Theology of the Sacraments* (New York: Scribners, 1957), Lecture 1, pp. 39-54.

6. Elizabeth Barrett Browning, "Aurora Leigh."

sun enlightens, water cleanses, grain nourishes, stones manifest permanence and power, the earth is fertile, plants regenerate, wind is mysterious and unpredictable, places mark the center of the world, time is renewed.[7] Furthermore, many features of nature, such as creativity, novelty, rebirth, and reunion reveal something of God's power to us. God is mediated to us through these things and characteristics of the natural world as well as through events of history. Thus, for Christians the world through its very being is sacramental in the sense that its ground and source, its creator, is apparent in nature. Creation itself is sacramental because it is a visible form of the invisible presence which is its source, ground, and goal.

Second, even more important for a Christian understanding of the sacraments is the fact that the Christian faith is an incarnational religion. In incarnational thinking, Spirit is not the antithesis of matter. They belong together as inseparable. The doctrine of the incarnation is the claim that God came to us in physical form, that God's presence was mediated to us in human form, that God as Spirit is God with us in the form of Jesus Christ as the Word made flesh. God, who is the mysterious source of the world, is *in* the world *through* places and events of the history of Israel. Above all, God comes to Christians primarily *through* the incarnation in Jesus Christ. An incarnational religion is inescapably a sacramental religion.

Since God comes to us through and in Christ, explains Theodore Runyon, "the mystical desire to transcend such mediation and fly to some pure immediacy not only is inevitably frustrated; in effect it attempts to bypass God's paradigmatic means of mediation, the Incarnation."[8] The most intensive sacramental relation in Christian faith, of course, is between God and Jesus.[9] Karl Barth, Karl Rahner, and Edward Schillebeeckx all speak of Jesus Christ as "the primal sacrament of God."[10] We know God through God's incarnation in Jesus Christ. The God who can be experienced in the inner life of each person is not the God who is known directly and privately in an unmediated way to each individual soul, but is the God who is mediated to us in the incarnation in Jesus and made near to us through the power of the Spirit. Assuming the centrality of the Word of God in worship in both its verbal and its visual forms, then, I concentrate now on the Word which is seen and touched and tasted as well as heard. What role do the sacraments

7. Mircea Eliade, *Patterns in Comparative Religion* (Cleveland: World, 1963).

8. Theodore Runyon, *The New Creation: John Wesley's Theology Today* (Nashville: Abingdon, 1998), p. 114.

9. Thomas and Wondra, *Introduction to Theology*, p. 282.

10. See, for example, E. Schillebeeckx, *Christ the Sacrament of the Encounter with God* (New York: Sheed and Ward, 1963).

play in mediating God to us in Christ and in our being incorporated and maintained in Christ?

II. Christian Sacraments

The Christian life is not given to us through our natural birth, nor is it achieved by us through our own efforts. It is a gift of grace through justification and sanctification to which we respond and with which we cooperate. This means that the Christian life depends on *means of grace* through which God's forgiveness, love, and empowerment are mediated to us. The consensus in both the Eastern and Western church is that a sacrament can be defined as "a visible sign of an invisible grace." Sacraments initiate us and sustain us in the Christian life. Physical things and acts become transparent vehicles of God's presence and activity. "The general sacramental principle is that there is a relation between a reality that can be perceived by the senses and a reality that cannot be so perceived."[11]

There are many means of grace. For the Christian, anything or anyone is a potential means of grace. Along with the omnipresence of God (there is nowhere from which God is completely absent), God is present in a special way with those who trust and obey God, and God is present with us more obviously at some times than at others ("where two or three are gathered together in Jesus' name" for worship and prayer, for example).

Among high liturgical churches, the seasons of the church calender (Advent, Christmastide, Epiphany, Lent, Eastertide, and Pentecost) and the rites of the church, such as marriage and funerals, are means of grace. For evangelical Christians the technology of the revival meeting is a primary means of grace. In the Reformed tradition (as well as many others), preaching and prayer as well as the sacraments are recognized as means of grace. These are "outward signs, words, and actions ordained by God and appointed to this end — to be the ordinary channels where he might convey to men preventing, justifying, and sanctifying grace."[12] Some Reformed theologians even include church suppers, conversation, church meetings, and ministries of compassion among the means of grace.[13] For Methodists, Wesley lists three chief ordinary channels of grace — prayer, searching the Scriptures, and the Lord's Supper — while his General Rules include attendance to the ordinances, pub-

---

11. Thomas and Wondra, *Introduction to Theology*, p. 281.

12. John Wesley, "The Means of Grace," in *John Wesley's Sermons: An Anthology*, ed. Albert Outler and Richard Heitzenrater (Nashville: Abingdon, 1991), p. 160.

13. John Leith, *Basic Christian Doctrine* (Louisville: Westminster/John Knox, 1993), p. 251.

lic worship, ministry of the Word, the Lord's Supper, private and family prayer, searching the Scripture, and fasting or abstinence.[14] Other Methodists have named visiting the societies by preachers, camp meetings and revivals, love feasts, and watchnight services as means of grace.[15]

In designating two or seven sacraments, the church is not overlooking these "sacramentals." Rather, it is simply recognizing that there are different degrees or modes of divine activity and presence in the church. The church has selected two or seven of these many means as gifts of God to the church which re-present in a distinctive way the good news of Jesus Christ addressed to us in oral and visible as well as in written form. God is especially present to the believer in the sacraments. "The chief distinction between the sacraments and the other sign-acts used in worship," explains James White, "is the church's long-standing history of the experience of both God and human beings working in those sign-acts called sacraments."[16]

What do sacraments do? The sacraments, first, *represent and re-present the Word of God,* that is, the gospel of God's gracious love for us. In many Protestant churches, the pulpit has had priority over the table; preaching overshadows the sacraments. The church is constituted by the Word of God, and this threefold Word is the living Word (Jesus Christ), the written Word (Scripture), and the proclaimed Word (preaching).[17] A theology of the sacraments, however, assumes that the Word is not only heard through preaching but also seen, touched, and tasted through the sacraments. The Word of God as God's personal communication and presence to us comes not only through reading and hearing the Word in preaching but also through seeing and tasting the Word through the tangible symbols of the sacraments. The sacraments are forms of expression of God's self-giving.[18] They are dramatic

14. John Wesley, "Means of Grace," pp. 158-71, and "General Rules," *Book of Discipline of the United Methodist Church 2000* (Nashville: United Methodist Publishing House, 2000), pp. 48-49.

15. Ted A. Campbell, *Methodist Doctrine: The Essentials* (Nashville: Abingdon, 1999), pp. 70-71.

16. James F. White, *Sacraments As God's Self-Giving* (Nashville: Abingdon, 2001), p. 22.

17. Karl Barth, *Church Dogmatics,* vol. 1, *The Doctrine of the Word of God* (New York: Charles Scribner's Sons, 1936), pp. 98-135.

18. James F. White, *Sacraments As God's Self-Giving,* pp. 13-14. God uses the same means for self-giving as people do. God did not come to us primarily through words. God came to us in the Word, by becoming one of us by incarnation in Christ. God became visible as well as audible. Christ became the *primal* sacrament of God. After the incarnation, God *continues* to be in our midst, audibly in the preaching about Christ, and audibly and visibly in the sacraments. The sacraments are not merely an audio-visual aid but sign-events that brings to us, by the power of the Holy Spirit, the very reality they proclaim. Through the sacraments the promises and presence and power of God are conveyed to us.

enactments of the gospel of God's graciousness, which preaching proclaims and explains. As Daniel Migliore puts it, they act out "the gospel by means of which the Spirit of God communicates to us the forgiving, renewing, and promising love of God in Jesus Christ."[19]

Second, as visible signs the sacraments are *channels or instruments of God's presence.* They are ways God's personal presence and power are mediated to us. The sacraments are not pipelines of a substance called grace, mechanical means to convey a divine substance which is infused (injected or ingested) into our soul through the sacraments. Rather, sacraments mediate God's presence to us. Grace is the presence of God in us through a living, personal relationship. They are signs by which God's intimate nearness and strength are made evident through the power of the Holy Spirit. As a "visible Word," sacraments are testimony to God's presence for, with, and in us. As Calvin put it, "We have in the sacraments another aid to our faith related to the preaching of the gospel."[20] Through them God's presence is re-presented anew to us. They show forth the grace of God, confer the grace of God, and testify to the faith and commitment of the recipient.

Third, the sacraments are a *seal of God's promise.* In sacraments, the church not only looks backward to the death and resurrection of Jesus, which are remembered, but also forward in promise, anticipation, and rehearsal to the fulfillment of the reign of God. This theme is emphasized by Calvin: "It seems to me that a simple and proper definition would be to say that [a sacrament] is an outward sign by which the Lord seals on our consciences the promises of his good will toward us in order to sustain the weakness of our faith."[21] The Holy Spirit seals this memory and promise through the sacraments.

There remains, however, a fundamental disagreement in the Protestant churches about the sacraments. Almost all Christians, with a few exceptions, such as Quakers, *practice* baptism and the Lord's Supper. Eastern Orthodox, Roman Catholic, Reformation Protestant, Anabaptist, evangelical, and pentecostal Christians all baptize and partake of the meal. Most agree that Christ is present to us *in some way* and that the Spirit accomplishes this communion between Christ and the believer.[22] Indeed, during the past two decades, many Protestants have undergone a sacramental renewal through the development of new liturgical texts, weekly or monthly celebration of the Eucharist, and the

19. Daniel Migliore, *Faith Seeking Understanding: An Introduction to Christian Theology* (Grand Rapids: Eerdmans, 1991), p. 212.

20. John Calvin, *Institutes of the Christian Religion*, 2 vols., ed. John T. McNeill, trans. Ford Lewis Battles (Philadelphia: Westminster, 1960), p. 1276 (4.14.1).

21. Calvin, *Institutes of the Christian Religion*, p. 1277 (4.14.1).

22. Peters, *God — The World's Future*, pp. 298-303.

placement of the font in the middle of the sanctuary, all indicating that the sacraments have taken on a deeper significance for many Protestants. At the same time, the debate about the sacraments has intensified within some Protestant denominations, as the church growth movement has tended to see the sacraments as a barrier to attracting new members.

Protestant Christians, even though most refer to the two rituals as sacraments, differ in their theological understanding of these ritual acts. Are they "sacraments" or "ordinances"? I want to be careful here not to fuel the fires of theological controversy unnecessarily. There are various alliances between these two perspectives. Many churches are closer to each other than they acknowledge. Although some churches seem thoroughly divided over baptism and the Lord's Supper, it becomes clearer upon closer examination that often these differences are matters of priority and emphasis rather than either/or choices between contradictory views. Furthermore, these differences exist within denominations, within local churches, and even between individuals. For the sake of brevity and clarity, I am going to oversimplify the issues surrounding the distinction between sacraments and ordinances so you can decide what you need to emphasize and why.

The theological difference between a sacrament and an ordinance is not a difference between Orthodox, Catholic, Protestant, Anabaptist, and pentecostal churches but between traditional and modern understandings of the sacraments.[23] Although some meanings of the sacraments are shared by most of these traditions, there is within many Anabaptist Protestant churches a modern in contrast to a traditional view of the two rituals. Deeply shaped by the Enlightenment view of the importance of human feeling and activity, the modern view stresses our role in the sacraments.[24] They are a public testimony to our born-again experience (evangelicalism)[25] and our pledge to live

23. My discussion here is shaped by James White, *Christian Worship in Transition* (Nashville: Abingdon, 1976), pp. 32-40.

24. The modern, "non-sacramental view" of the sacraments began with Zwingli, the Protestant Reformer who emphasized that the sacraments were dedications and pledges on our part. Although moderns may use the word "sacraments," they do not believe that these rituals mediate the grace of God more than any other means of grace. Rather, they are ordinances, or memorials, or pledges we make to God.

25. This Enlightenment emphasis on ourselves has deeply influenced American revivalism, which frequently offers a modern view of the sacraments. With revivalism's focus on our experience of Christ, the sacraments as the mediation of the presence of Christ has been replaced by revivalism as the means of grace. The presence of Christ is mediated to the heart of the believer through the revival technology which makes Christ present to the believer through a conversion experience. Most evangelicals still practice the sacraments, but they interpret them as memorials, recollections of the truly effective sacrament, the revivalistic conversion experience which is

a kingdom-of-God lifestyle (Anabaptist). Their power depends on our ability to use them to remember and witness to what God did for us in Christ. They stimulate our memories of God's acts, excite our feelings, and signify our being chosen and commissioned for God's mission in the world and our covenanting with God and our sisters and brothers to perform this mission.[26] They are our pledge to God. To be sure, they are not completely human acts; the Spirit works in ordinances. But the emphasis is on our personal experience of Christ and our dedication to his kingdom.

In a sacramental view of the sacraments, these rituals are enactments of God's self-giving. They are means of grace, signs of grace, vehicles of grace. They are a gift of God to the church for the establishment and maintenance of the Christian life. We are recipients of what God does through the sacraments for us and our salvation. The sacraments contain and confer grace in the sense that God comes to us graciously through these signs. God not only changes our thoughts and our feelings; God changes our very being through the operation of this grace (Roman Catholic), or God imputes to us the benefits of Christ promised to us in Scripture (Luther), or God grafts us into the body of Christ and raises us to feed on Christ (Calvin), or God uses them as a means of grace (Wesley).

The easiest way to determine whether you understand baptism and the Lord's Supper as a sacrament or an ordinance is to answer this question: Who is the chief actor? In a sacramental theology, we begin with the divine side, with God's grace, God's gift, God's presence, God's acts toward us. Sacraments tell us God's story from the creation to the consummation through these signs. God is the chief agent; the priest or minister is God's instrument. The emphasis is on God's graciousness, God's initiative, God's promise. In the memorialist view, we are the chief actor. For memorialists we perform these acts because they were commanded by Jesus. They are valid and efficacious if they succeed in stimulating our memory, feelings, and commitment. But again, the question is a matter of emphasis.

A theology of sacraments, like most other theological puzzles, especially those which focus on the importance of grace, raises the problem of the relation of divine act and human freedom. What is the role of faith in the grace

---

now memorialized ritually by the believer. The challenge many American evangelicals face is that although they have retained the idea of sacrament, they have replaced the two sacraments with an alternative sacrament, the conversion experience in the revivalistic mode. The so-called sacraments serve as memorials and public testimony of the one real sacrament, the conversion experience.

26. Vernard Eller, *In Place of Sacraments: A Study of Baptism and the Lord's Supper* (Grand Rapids: Eerdmans, 1972), p. 67.

mediated through the sacraments? No one teaches the absence of faith in the efficacy of the sacraments. Roman Catholics teach that there must be no obstacle in the soul in the reception of the sacrament, and Protestants teach the necessary role of the faith of the community and the recipients in making them valid. But the modern emphasis on our faith as the grounds for an efficacious sacrament is inadequate. Although faith is essential to sacraments as a means of grace, to suggest that faith is first, that it is the prerequisite for a sacrament, forgets the prevenience of God's grace, not only in the grace of creation, or in saving grace, but also in sacramental grace. God's grace creates and awakens our faith by means of the sacraments. It is *through* subsequent faith throughout our life, not because of our faith, that the sacraments are efficacious and the channels of God's grace.[27] The basic principle is that God's presence and power precedes our faith. Our faith follows God's presence to us in the sacraments.

III. The Sacrament of Initiation into the Christian Life: Baptism

Almost all Christian churches baptize. Across the spectrum, from Orthodox to Roman Catholic to mainline Protestant churches (Lutheran, Reformed, Anglican, Methodist, United Church of Christ, Disciples of Christ, and Baptist) to nondenominational evangelical churches and pentecostal churches, baptism with water in the name of the triune God is central to the Christian faith. Assuming that we cannot know the limits of God's grace among all humans and cannot know what happens between any individual and God, the only objective answer we can give to the question, "Who is a Christian?" is that a Christian is one who has been baptized.[28] In this sense, there are only "nominal" Christians. Baptism is the way we enter the Christian community and are named. Regardless of the explanations each church gives of how baptism is central to the Christian life — why we baptize, what baptism does, who is eligible for baptism, and the role of faith in baptism — most churches agree that to be a Christian is to be baptized.[29]

27. Baillie, *A Theology of the Sacraments*, p. 89. "A sacrament is a sacred sign which God uses for the quickening of our faith" (p. 88).

28. Laurence Hull Stookey, *Baptism: Christ's Act in the Church* (Nashville: Abingdon, 1982), p. 90.

29. Assuming this as my beginning point, I will explore here how the two basic understandings of sacraments developed above work out in the various churches' explanations of the role of baptism in Christian faith and practice. My purpose is not to trash one view or the other,

I begin at the beginning. Why do churches baptize in the first place? Most Christians share at least one answer. Baptism was commanded by the New Testament Jesus. This is called "dominical institution," the belief that Jesus our Lord *(Dominus)* commanded his followers to baptize in the name of the triune God (Matt. 28:18-20). These references are few, however, and exegetical problems cannot be answered with any degree of certainty.[30]

A second answer to the question is, tradition. How compelling you find this reason will depend on how you answer the question I raised in Chapter Two about theological method. How authoritative is the tradition of the church in what you believe and what you practice? The Catholic side of this discussion will find this a decisive reason in itself to practice baptism. The Protestant side of the discussion also, in practice if not in theory, accepts this as a compelling reason. We baptize because the church has practiced it for nearly two thousand years. Even if modern scholarship could show that in all probability baptism was an early church practice and did not originate with Jesus himself before his death, most Christians would continue to practice it.

> **"Remember your baptism and be thankful. Amen."**
>
> *THE UNITED METHODIST HYMNAL*

What does baptism do? The difference between the modern and the traditional views comes into focus in answering this question. In the modern

---

although it should be obvious that this theology advocates the sacramental side of the debate. Rather, my purpose is to explain the implications of the two general perspectives, and to show that the differences between the modern and traditional views are not necessarily exclusive choices. If you accept that both sides affirm some work of God and of our faith in the sacraments, then the differences are matters of emphasis. To be sure, these differences have consequences for practice. But the double-mindedness of many Protestants about the sacraments may rest on a sound intuition that both sides have something to say about the sacraments. We may be able to integrate the wisdom of the other side into my own theology of baptism. That, at least, is my goal in an irenic theology of baptism.

30. Most modern scholarship agrees it is very difficult to determine in the New Testament just what is the relationship between the baptism of John, in which Jesus participated, and Jesus' command to baptize, and whether Jesus commanded water baptism or the early church originated the practice and formula. It is historically probable that baptism and the baptismal formula originated very early in the church and was connected with the Jewish practice of proselyte baptism and John's preaching and practice of repentance in the light of his eschatological expectations. If you are going to build a theology of baptism on biblical grounds, however, you are going to have to do this on the grounds of a deeper understanding of the whole New Testament message, not on exegetical certainty about a small set of texts. Narrowly considered, the point is that in the New Testament Jesus commands baptism, and the church has followed the command of this Jesus in developing its faith and practice.

view of baptism emphasis falls on our faith and our action. Baptism is our public testimony of our response to the gospel, our conversion experience, and our commitment to Jesus and to his kingdom lifestyle. Christian baptism is similar to John's baptism of repentance. In the traditional view of baptism, on the other hand, which we might call baptism with the Holy Spirit, emphasis is on God's choice of us and work for us. Baptism is the means by which God incorporates us into Christ, making us citizens of Christ's kingdom, members of the household of faith. God's promise and work are emphasized.

Set within this stark contrast, a theology of baptism appears to be an either/or choice between the modern and traditional views. When we examine New Testament views of baptism, along with the historic churches' ideas of what baptism does, and a very important ecumenical consensus about baptism,[31] however, we begin to see that both sides of this debate contribute significant points for an adequate theology of baptism. These theologies are not mutually exclusive. The debate can be about what one should emphasize — God's work or ours — and what the implications of that emphasis are for faith and practice. The key to an irenic theology of baptism, however, is to recognize that baptism does not signify just one thing; baptism signifies many things. It does several things which overlap and complement each other:

1. Baptism is *a sign of the coming reign of God.* Like the baptism of John, it calls the world, the state, the church, and each of us to repent. It is an eschatological sign of a break with the principalities and powers of the present age. It is, also, a sign of commitment and loyalty to Christ's kingdom.[32] It makes us part of the disciplined community which is moving from the old age into the new. This has been the primary emphasis in the Anabaptist view of baptism. It is also central to the Reformed understanding of baptism as vocation, our calling to participate in the vision of God's commonwealth in our family, economic, social, and political lives.[33]

2. Baptism is a sign of pardon, *cleansing from sin,* conversion. The connection between baptism and the forgiveness of sin is a New Testament emphasis.[34] This image was central to the medieval Catholic and the Lutheran

---

31. *Baptism, Eucharist, and Ministry,* Faith and Order Paper No. 111 (Geneva: World Council of Churches, 1982), paragraphs 2-7.

32. Eller, *In Place of Sacraments,* p. 67.

33. Migliore, *Faith Seeking Understanding,* pp. 182-84, 215-16; Leith, *Basic Christian Doctrine,* pp. 254-56. This theme has also been included in *Baptism, Eucharist, and Ministry,* paragraphs 2-3; White, *Sacraments in Protestant Practice and Faith,* chapter 3; Peters, *God — The World's Future,* pp. 288-89.

34. "Those baptized are pardoned, cleansed, and sanctified by Christ." *Baptism, Eucharist, and Ministry,* paragraph 2.

views of baptism, in which baptism washed away the guilt of original sin and canceled the guilt of actual sin. The emphasis is on God's act in Christ to forgive us and to establish a new relationship with sinful humanity.[35]

3. Baptism is our *participation in Christ's death and resurrection*. It is a sign of our rebirth through our union with Christ's death and resurrection (Rom. 6:3; Col. 2:12). We are called not only to be like Jesus but to be "in Christ" by the power of the Spirit.[36] This is a strong emphasis in Luther's, Calvin's, and Anabaptist theologies of baptism.[37] Whether baptism is causative or declarative,[38] that is, causes forgiveness of sin or declares what has already occurred, most Christians understand there to be some relationship between baptism and regeneration.[39]

4. By baptism we are *incorporated into the church as the body of Christ* (1 Cor. 12:13).[40] Through baptism we become part of the church. It is a sign and seal of our incorporation into the visible and invisible church, or, in the Anabaptist understanding, of the pure and undefiled believers' church. Baptism is analogous to circumcision, which was reception into the original covenant with Abraham. Through baptism we are received into the new covenant in Christ. This theme has been emphasized by all of the Reformation churches, including descendants of Zwingli as well as the Anabaptists.

5. Baptism is *a gift of the Spirit's presence*. Our reception into the church is through the power of the Spirit, through baptism with the Holy Spirit. Pentecostal Christians are not the only Christians who declare and experience the work of the Holy Spirit. Through baptism the Spirit "marks [Christians] with a seal and implants in their hearts the first installment of their inheritance as sons and daughters of God."[41]

For whom does baptism do all of these things? Who is eligible to receive

---

35. Although most theologians, beginning at least with John Wesley, and reaffirmed by evangelical and liberal Protestants today, do not consider anyone guilty of Adam and Eve's original sin and punishable by damnation in the way Augustine and the medieval church did, baptism remains the basic sign of God's forgiveness of our sin.

36. Stookey, *Baptism: Christ's Act in the Church*, p. 27.

37. "By baptism Christians are immersed in the liberating death of Christ where their sins are buried." *Baptism, Eucharist, and Ministry*, paragraph 2.

38. For a good description of this distinction see Alister McGrath, *Christian Theology: An Introduction* (Oxford: Blackwell, 1994), p. 446.

39. By being buried with Christ in his death and by rising with him in his resurrection to newness of life through baptism, we share in his death (Luther), are united to Christ himself (Calvin), and are "engrafted into Christ" (Westminster Confession).

40. "Christians are brought into union with Christ, with each other and with the Church of every time and place." *Baptism, Eucharist, and Ministry*, paragraph 3.

41. *Baptism, Eucharist, and Ministry*, paragraph 3.

baptism? In many American churches, baptism of infants is one of the most intensely debated practices of the church. It is the symbolic issue over which so many other debates — the meaning of salvation, the nature of the church, the meaning of the sacraments — come to a head. In the ordination examinations in my denomination, infant baptism is a litmus test about whether the candidate will fulfill the vows to practice the ministry offered by my particular denomination. The issue is this: must, should, can the church baptize infants, or is baptism reserved for believing adults?

Although this is a five-hundred-year-old debate between Catholics and Anabaptists, with most Protestant churches somewhat befuddled about what they really believe, the debate today is not between these historic rivals. There are good reasons, old and new, for all Christians to question the permissibility of infant baptism.[42] The case against it is not groundless. First, the exegetical case for it (or against it) is impossible to make.[43] The primary objections are social and ethical. Infant baptism, it is argued, is a major source and means of the corruption of the church. In a post-Constantinian church, it is used as a means to preserve the national church or denomination. It doesn't challenge Christendom and its union of church and state.[44] In addition, for many Enlightenment Christians, infant baptism is magic or superstition. It is primarily a spiritual life insurance policy for newborns. Finally, for evangelicals it deludes people into thinking they are Christians because they were baptized rather than because they have had a conversion experience.

One way to acknowledge these criticisms, but to bridge the chasm between the Catholic and Anabaptist views, and to maintain a dialectic between God's act and our act in baptism, is to elaborate three themes common to any good theology of baptism. First, both sides affirm that baptism marks the entry of individuals into the church as the community of Christ on earth. No

---

42. The case against infant baptism is not a case made only by Anabaptists today. Karl Barth and Emil Brunner were persistent critics of the practice of infant baptism, as is Jürgen Moltmann today.

43. There are only three verses which might indicate infants were baptized. Acts 16:15 refers to the baptism of the household, as does 1 Corinthians 1:16, and Acts 16:33 refers to the baptism of the whole family. Of course, these do not determine for us whether or not the church practiced infant baptism. Any case in the New Testament for the baptism of infants can rest only on larger themes of the gospel, namely, on God's grace that goes ahead of us preparing the way for faith, on the corporate nature of faith, and on the relation of the Holy Spirit to the whole body of believers. Stookey, *Baptism: Christ's Act in the Church*, p. 46.

44. Barth and Brunner, strong critics in the 1930s, were responding to the social fact that nearly everyone in Europe was baptized and it did not seem to make any difference; many of the killers in Auschwitz were baptized Christians. Clark Williamson, *Way of Blessing, Way of Life* (St. Louis: Chalice, 1999), pp. 284-87.

one teaches that just anyone should be baptized. Baptism is open to those who respond affirmatively to the call of God and God's promises through Christ on their lives. The question is whether children of believing parents fall under that call and promise and therefore have a place as members within the church of Christ, or are outsiders until they make their own decision and profession of faith, whereupon they can become members of Christ's body.[45]

Second, adult baptism is normative for the meaning of Christian baptism. No defender of infant baptism teaches that infants have faith in the same way mature adults have it. Baptism of children is derivative from adult baptism into a community. Children cannot be baptized until there exists a covenant community of adults in which they can be incorporated and nurtured. Therefore, baptism of adults declares most fully what is implied in all baptism.[46] The claim, rather, is that baptism is available to all in the living community of professing believers along with their children, who are part of the new covenant. Infant baptism rejects the idea that the children of believers are heathen and stand outside God's promises until they reach a certain age.

Third, faith is an essential component of baptism. The efficacy of baptism depends on faith. But it is important to understand this relationship in the proper sense and in the proper order. All Christians teach the necessity of faith in baptism. The question is whose faith, the one who is baptized (Anabaptist view) or the parents or sponsors and community (the Catholic view)? In the latter view, baptism is still believers' baptism. The belief of the parents and congregation is on behalf of the infant.[47] Infant baptism, writes Oscar Cullmann, depends on

---

45. I need to be fair here. Neither side of this debate teaches — or needs to teach — that children who are not baptized are condemned to hell. The lack of baptism means only that an individual is not part of the earthly body of Christ, not necessarily that they are outside or beyond the grace of God. Baptism does not determine who is saved and who is lost. It determines who is incorporated into the church. Most Christians today teach that God does not damn infants and children on the basis of inherited guilt: Most evangelicals teach either that infants are not guilty of sin until they commit their own actual sin, or that they are covered by the grace of redemption until the age of accountability. Liberal universalists teach that all persons, including infants, are loved by God and are ultimately saved, while Barthian universalists teach that all persons, including infants, are beneficiaries of the universal atonement of Christ which redeemed all. Barth's case against infant baptism was that all people received a general baptism on Good Friday and Easter, an act of God carried out without our cooperation and faith, so all the world was baptized by the sovereign act of God in Christ. Church baptism is to inform us and make us aware of Christ's work. We cannot know of Christ's death and resurrection as an infant but only as an adult. Karl Barth, *The Teaching of the Church Regarding Baptism* (London: SCM, 1959).

46. Stookey, *Baptism: Christ's Act in the Church*, pp. 48-49.

47. Peters, *God — The World's Future*, p. 290. For advocates of believer's baptism, it is not clear how an infant receives grace in faith or confesses that faith before a congregation. In infant

the faith of the congregation assembled for the baptism . . . if faith were lacking in the congregation assembled for Baptism, it would not be a congregation; and then the Holy Spirit would be absent. But where the believing congregation is, there the Holy Spirit, operating within it and knowing no limitations, has the power to draw an infant into his sphere, just as in the case of all baptized persons who, according to Paul, are "by one Spirit . . . baptized into one body of Christ."[48]

Finally, faith is required of all recipients, adult and infant, but not as a precondition of God's work. God is faithful and so what happens in God's promise and seal cannot be contested. But faith is necessary *after* baptism. It is what results from baptism throughout the life of the person who is baptized, adult or infant. As in natural birth, so in the new birth we are talking about a beginning, which is in itself a reality, but is not the whole reality of life. Birth and the new birth are not in doubt. But subsequent life depends on what the recipient of both the first and second birth do. Faith after baptism is required of all persons. It is as if to say, "You have been redeemed, now live like it!" But there must be no indiscriminate baptism where there is no sign suggesting the prospect of living out one's baptism within a community of faith.

In the end, the question is whether the church may baptize infants as well as adults as recipients of God's grace and claim. Because there is only one baptism, these two forms of practice are complementary rather than exclusive. "It can be argued that the two forms of baptism — infant and adult — together express the full meaning of baptism better than each would alone," suggests Migliore.[49] When the church baptizes infants, the act signifies God's gracious initiative in creation and redemption, our human solidarity in the presence of God, and our covenantal responsibility as a Christian community.[50] I think the church may continue to baptize the infants of believing adults because that practice is a key symbolic act by which we affirm the priority and primacy of grace. The strongest case for infant baptism is that it makes utterly clear the prevenient character of God's grace in every baptism. We love God because God first loves us.

---

baptism the faith of the church, both the parents' faith and that of the gathered congregation, is necessary and is present during baptism. Oscar Cullmann, *Baptism in the New Testament* (Chicago: Henry Regnery, 1950), pp. 42-43, 47, 54-55.

48. Cullmann, *Baptism in the New Testament*, pp. 42-43.

49. Migliore, *Faith Seeking Understanding*, p. 217.

50. Migliore, *Faith Seeking Understanding*, p. 219.

IV. The Sacrament of Maintenance
of the Christian Life: Eucharist

Almost all churches partake of the Lord's Supper. As baptism is the sacrament of initiation into the Christian life, the Lord's Supper is the sacrament of maintenance of the Christian life. Here, again, the differences between the modern and the traditional perspectives shape our understanding. The modern outlook emphasizes following the command of Jesus, our recollection of his life, death, and resurrection, and our dedication to the lifestyle of the reign of God he preached. The traditional view emphasizes God as the primary actor and the promise of God to come to us through the bread and the wine. No one maintains that this is the only sacramental means through which Christ maintains the life of the church. Nevertheless, most Christians agree that, in some way, the Lord's Supper is commanded by Jesus and/or the church and is the one common means of our remembrance and of Christ's presence. It is the ordinary means by which Christ is present in the church today and the church is nourished by him for its life and ministry.

Most churches agree that we appear at the Lord's Supper because it was instituted by Jesus ("dominical institution") and commanded by him of his followers (Matt. 26:26-29; Mark 14:17-25; Luke 22:14-23). "Take, eat . . . drink . . . do this in remembrance of me." The question of dominical institution, however, is not primarily the question of whether Jesus himself directly commanded this practice with these words or the church followed his practice of table fellowship with his followers and his "last supper" in this way. It is dominical because it is rooted in the life and ministry of Jesus. What is crucial is that the church in its Scripture and its two-thousand-year-old practice understands this sacrament to be founded on the reality of what God did in Christ, in his life, words, and works, in his cross and resurrection, through the gift of the Spirit. A Christian "love feast," which uses spontaneous prayers, colas, and potato chips, may be a means of grace; but it is not a sacrament because it is not one of the two "instituted" and "ordinary" means of grace established by the Scripture and by the tradition of the church.

As a sacrament the meal is oriented simultaneously toward the past, present, and future. It is a meal which recalls the past, but this memory is an *anamnesis*, a remembrance in the sense of making the past present as a meal of fellowship and of covenant with the reality which is remembered. The supper is also oriented toward the future, an *anticipation* which enacts the promised eschatological meal with the Messiah.[51]

---

51. Hans Küng, *The Church* (Garden City: Image, 1976), pp. 283-84.

The very term you use to designate the ritual will indicate what you emphasize. The four traditional names — the Mass, the Lord's Supper, the Holy Communion, and the Eucharist — highlight four different themes in a complete interpretation of the meal.[52] If you call it "the Lord's Supper," you emphasize the gathering at the table as a fellowship meal. The supper is rooted in the Passover meal, Jesus' table fellowship throughout his ministry, and his last meal with his disciples before his death. It recalls his life and his death. The modern emphasis on the supper as a commemoration interprets it primarily as a narration of salvation history, a recital of what God did in Christ, God's saving acts from creation to consummation. When seen strictly as an ordinance, the emphasis falls on our recollection, our public testimony of our commitment and loyalty to the life of Christ and to his preaching and teaching of the kingdom of God. This emphasis takes a more sacramental meaning when the gathering and reenactment of the supper is thought of as *anamnesis,* a way to experience anew the reality of Christ, to relive his life, death, and resurrection as the power to save and to free us.

If you call the supper "the Mass," you emphasize the sacrifice of Christ on the cross, which is done again and again for the sake of our sins. The traditional Roman Catholic emphasis on the sacrament as a mass emphasizes its sacrificial significance (Matt. 26:28). The Catholic church historically has understood the sacrament as a re-doing of the propitiatory sacrifice of Christ by which we find favor with God. It is the means through which we appropriate the benefits of Christ's death on our behalf. Sometimes this has been interpreted as an offering of us to God instead of God's free gift to us. Protestants who do not understand the meal as a sacrifice, however, stress the sufficiency of what God did for us in Christ, and so speak of it as a recollection of Christ's "full, perfect, and sufficient sacrifice," as well as our sacrifice of praise and thanksgiving.

If you call it "the Holy Communion," the sacramental significance of the meal as a communion between the believer and the risen Christ and among the members of the church is emphasized. Both moderns and traditionalists can be united in their understanding of the meal as a communion with Christ in and with the whole church (1 Cor. 10:16-17). The stress, however, is not on the meal as a private communion between the soul of the individual and Christ, but rather on our common liturgy, the communion of the whole community with its Lord in its singing, praying, and hearing the Word of God together around the table.

If you call it "the Eucharist," the meal is a thanksgiving to God for our

---

52. White, *The Sacraments in Protestant Practice and Faith,* chapter 5.

salvation in Christ. This term and emphasis, which has become more common among Protestants, has always been primary among Orthodox Christians, and it is reflected also in some Catholic theology today. The meal is a meal of thanksgiving. The emphasis does not fall on our unworthiness but on God's supreme gift. We highlight God's gift of grace in Christ whom we receive through the Holy Spirit, and our gratitude for God's grace. The joyful aspect of thanksgiving is most apparent in the Great Prayer of Thanksgiving, which invokes the presence of Christ through the Spirit in (or on or through or with) the elements.

Regardless of what is emphasized by these four names, what makes the meal a sacrament is the presence of Christ to and in the community. The major debate among Christians, causing them to interpret the meal as an ordinance or a sacrament, is *how* Christ is present. The language of miracle and mystery is surely appropriate here, as Orthodox Christians make clear when they refer to the Eucharist as a Mystery. Roman Catholics and Protestants have not been content with this term, however. Since the Middle Ages and the Reformation they have tried to explain how Christ is present in this mystery. Is Christ's presence a "real presence," or is he present "only" symbolically, or "only" through our memory of him? If his presence is "real," is he present as body and blood, or spiritually present, or present in our memory of his life and death?

> **"Though thoughts were not reconcilable, thinkers were, or might be. (It is an awkward truth that social life is the antidote to scholarly paranoia; it drains intellectual differences of their drama. The cure for the acrimony of intellectuals is dinner.)"**
>
> **ADAM GOPNIK**

Transubstantiation

In Roman Catholic teaching, the priest, through his priestly powers, makes the bread and the wine the literal body and blood of Christ. Christ is corporeally present because the essence of the bread and the wine have been changed into body and blood through the sacramental office of the priest. Using the categories of Aristotle to explain this miracle, the priest turns the substance of the bread and wine into the body and blood of Christ, but by another miracle the bread and wine retain their accidents or appearances and so look, feel, taste, and smell like bread and wine. We eat the body and blood of Christ when we partake of the bread and wine.

Consubstantiation

Luther denied transubstantiation, but he did not deny that the bread and the wine are the body and blood of Christ. The elements are both bread and wine *and* body and blood at the same time. The body and blood are "under" the form of the bread and wine, so both the divine and human natures of Christ are in the bread and wine. He is corporeally present in, with, or under the bread and wine.

Memorialism

Memorialism does not need to be interpreted as simply our memory. Through our remembrance Christ is present, but it is a strictly spiritual presence. For Zwingli, for example, a sign and what it signifies are quite distinct. So he taught that Christ was present only in a spiritual fashion. That is, Christ is present in his divine nature, and we feed on him spiritually. For him the sacrament was a symbolic memorial of Christ's presence, or what Heinrich Bullinger described as a symbolic parallelism between the elements and Christ's spiritual presence.

Virtualism

Calvin and Wesley fall somewhere between Luther and Zwingli. According to their view, the Lord's Supper is an encounter with Christ. Christ is objectively present; to say that he is present only subjectively would to be say that we only imagine Christ to be there but really he is not. Christ's presence is a "real presence," but it is not the presence of his flesh and blood. Christ's risen body is in heaven. The elements are *signs* through which the reality of Christ is joined to the visible symbols and to us. Some theologians call this "transignification," on the basis that a change in context and use of words, acts, and symbols changes the meaning of a sign itself. The Eucharist becomes a "sign-act" or "sign-event" of God's presence, analogous to the way human communication is dependent on visible signs and gestures (eating together, drinking together, a handshake, a kiss, a ring). Sign-acts have the power to mediate the presence of the risen Christ to us just as sign-acts mediate us to each other. Sign-acts, to be sure, include church suppers, foot washing, the kiss of peace, and laying on of hands. But preeminently the sign-acts for Christ's presence are baptism and the Lord's Supper. By the *virtue* (the power) of the Holy Spirit, our spirits are joined to Christ, raising us to heaven to feed on Christ (Calvin), or, reversing the direction, bringing Christ down from heaven to feed us (Wesley).[53]

V. FAQs

Your theology of the sacraments is unlikely to begin, as I did, with a discussion of sacramentalism, sacraments, baptism, and the Lord's Supper. More likely, your interpretation will be implicit in your answers to a set of questions about church practices. My procedure now will be to review a dozen of the most frequently asked questions in churches and classrooms, and to offer my answers in the light of the theology of sacraments outlined above.

Q1: How many sacraments are there?

A1: Protestants have two sacraments, Roman Catholics seven. Why two or seven? Why not four or seventeen? The answer to that question is primarily, if not exclusively, tradition. For many reasons it is impossible to establish with certainty the New Testament teaching on this question. During the first eight hundred years of the church there were no systematic treatises on the sacraments, and for nearly twelve hundred years no consensus on the number of sacraments.[54] Augustine mentioned several dozen, including the baptismal font, the creed, and the Lord's Prayer. By the twelfth century some thirty sacraments made it into the list compiled by Hugh of St. Victor, a list reduced to seven by Peter Lombard's *Sentences* (1150), the best-selling theology text of the time. This list has held ever since in Roman Catholic theology, including that of St. Thomas (1225-1274). It was dogmatically defined in the fifteenth-century Council of Florence (1439) and reaffirmed in the sixteenth-century Council of Trent (1545-63). Protestants reduced the number to two on the argument that only these two were instituted by Christ.

Q2: Can other rituals be sacraments?

A2: It is possible, of course, to use the word "sacrament" for any act or thing that mediates God's presence to the community. If we do this, the number can be nearly limitless. The better option is to acknowledge that the tradition of the church is to designate two or seven sacraments, and that there are other "sacramentals" — rites, rituals, and ceremonies that have *sacramental signifi-*

---

53. Runyon, *The New Creation*, pp. 129-30. "Jesus Christ is truly present in a spiritual and personal, not a physical, way." Leith, *Basic Christian Doctrine*, p. 253.

54. White, *Sacraments in Protestant Practice and Faith*, pp. 15-16.

cance for making Christ present. Although most Protestants have only two sacraments, marriage, burial, confirmation, ordination, and other rites without question serve as sacramentals in the life of the Christian. Furthermore, many denominations have begun to develop rituals and ceremonies that serve to give sacramental significance to the passages throughout human life, especially crisis periods of transition, such as naming a child, dying, divorce, vocational change, and various other endings and beginnings.[55]

Q3: What makes a sacrament valid and efficacious?

A3: We call a sacrament valid if it is properly administered by a duly appointed officer of the church; that is, if she or he institutes the elements of the sacrament, the water, bread, and wine, as a sign-act of God's grace through the invocation of the Holy Spirit in prayer and the language of the triune God. If one holds ordination to be to an office instead of an order, then the presbyter or elder is necessary to preside at the sacraments, but aside from the issue of order, ordination does not have any intrinsic relation to the sacraments.[56] We call a sacrament efficacious if it mediates God to the believer and is received in faith with thanksgiving. Validity depends on our performing the rite correctly, efficacy depends upon God doing what God has promised to do for us through the sacraments. The sacraments do not have any intrinsic power in themselves, and they do not depend on our worthiness, sentiments, or comprehension. Christ is the "meritorious cause" of their efficacy. Our faith has a role, in the sense that we can resist and accept them. But our faith follows as our trust that God accomplishes God's purpose and promise in this way.

> "A couple of decades ago — in the wake of the first scandals in the [contemporary Christian music] field — the industry revisited the Donatist controversy: Can the Holy Spirit minister through songs performed by unholy vessels?"
>
> **MARK ALLAN POWELL**

Q4: May I be rebaptized?

A4: This is one of the most frequently asked and hotly debated questions among many American Christians. People want to be rebaptized because it is a mark of denominational identity, or they were baptized at an early age and don't remember it, or it must be administered in a certain way, or it testifies to a recent conversion experience.[57] But this is one of the easiest questions to an-

---

55. See Hoyt Hickman, *Ritual in a New Day: An Invitation* (Nashville: Abingdon, 1976).
56. White, *Sacraments in Protestant Practice and Faith* (Nashville: Abingdon, 1999).
57. Stookey, *Baptism: Christ's Act in the Church* (Nashville: Abingdon, 1982), p. 12.

swer, and the answer depends wholly on whether you have a sacramental or ordinantial view of baptism. If you hold a sacramental view of baptism, rebaptism is at best a meaningless concept and at worst a blasphemous act. "Rebaptism" asserts that God was not trustworthy to do what God promised, to make God's seal on this life. It implies that the validity and efficacy of baptism depend on me, my understanding, my decision, my commitment, as in an ordinance, not on the faithfulness of God, as in a sacrament. If, on the other hand, you hold an ordinantial view, then rebaptism is permissible and may even be seen as necessary.

Q5: What is the place of confirmation in the idea of baptism as a sacrament?

A5: If one understands the sacraments in relation to faith as I described above, then confirmation has a role to play in the Christian life. I consider it to be unfortunate that some denominations, in order to emphasize baptism as regeneration, have eliminated or reduced the significance of confirmation as one of the sacramentals in the life of the church. There are some reasons to do this, in order not to imply that two halves are necessary for an efficacious baptism. But to eliminate it undercuts our affirmation of the role of faith in the sacraments. The church, in my opinion, should keep confirmation as a sacramental. This does not mean the Spirit is given for the first time in confirmation; rather, the Spirit is given in baptism and "increased in confirmation."[58] The liability can be reduced if one provides for "baptismal renewal" as a part of one's understanding of baptism. We live into our baptism by a regular renewal of our baptismal vows, a practice that has become part of the ritual of the sacrament of baptism in some Protestant denominations. Christians who have had a special experience can renew their vows in a service of baptismal renewal instead of by rebaptism, reaffirming their renewed faith in the context of the priority of God's grace and promises.

Q6: What is the proper mode of baptism?

A6: The case for immersion as the practice in the New Testament and in the earliest church is a good one. Furthermore, the New Testament clearly connects baptism with the death and resurrection of Jesus, for which the practice of entering into and arising out of the water is obviously the most dramatic representation. This is only one New Testament image among others for interpreting baptism, however. Baptism is also a cleansing, a forgiveness of sin, and a liberation, for which sprinkling and pouring are appropriate expressions. It is also an outpouring of the Holy Spirit, which is probably better rep-

---

58. Thomas and Wondra, *Introduction to Theology*, p. 286.

resented by sprinkling and pouring than by immersion. The point is that the three forms are one and the same reality, aspects of the renewal of life and of newness of life.

Q7: Should I believe in baptismal regeneration?

A7: Among the metaphors for what baptism does, another controversy in the American churches is over baptismal regeneration. Baptism is clearly related to the new birth (John 3:3; Titus 3:5). In some churches (Orthodox, Roman Catholic, Lutheran, and Anglican) baptism itself *is* the means of justification and regeneration. Those who are baptized *are* justified and born again. In other churches (Anabaptist and evangelical) baptism is an outward sign which follows upon the private relationship between the believer and God's forgiving grace. It follows regeneration as a witness to a rebirth. In other Protestant churches (Reformed, Methodist) there is a link between justification and regeneration, but not automatically. These *may* be different moments.[59] The differences diminish if we do not understand regeneration as a mechanical act, but as a dialectic between God's prevenient grace and our responsive faith which brings newness of life.

Q8: Can we lose the efficacy of our baptism?

A8: Unless one is a strict Calvinist or a strict Pelagian, this is a tough question to answer. In strict Calvinism, with its doctrines of election as predestination and preservation of the saints, the person who has been baptized as part of the elect cannot lose the efficacy of his or her baptism. Otherwise God's election would be called into question. In strict Pelagianism, in which salvation depends as much on us as on God, we can lose our salvation if we don't keep up our half of the commitment. If, however, some dialectic exists between God's act (grace) and our response (faith) — though in the proper sequence — the answer is determined by what you want to emphasize. If all is divine grace, the answer is no. If grace and faith belong together, the answer is yes. Wesley tried to hold together both the priority of grace and necessity of faith in baptism. He says that "baptism does now save us if we live answerable thereto."[60] In his view, however, we can lose the efficacy of baptism if we don't live out our baptism. Since we don't, we must be reborn. In practice, then, since these are matters of emphasis, we cannot determine a dogmatic answer to the questions about whether we can lose the grace of our baptismal regen-

---

59. Campbell, *Methodist Doctrine*, pp. 19-72.

60. John Wesley, "On Baptism," in *John Wesley's Sermons,* ed. Outler and Heitzenrater, p. 323.

eration. Perhaps the best answer is that Christians, infant and adult, are called to live out their baptism and to depend upon the grace of God in all the stages and states of their new life in Christ.

Q9: Can we practice private baptism?

A9: If baptism is God's act of our inclusion into the church as the body of Christ, and if the efficacy of baptism requires the faith of the community (and, by anticipation, the response in faith of the individual, adult and infant), then there is no such thing as a private baptism. Baptism is an act of the community on behalf of the community for incorporation into the community. Of course, this does not imply at all that the grace of God is not effective beyond the community. If persons have not been baptized — infants, the dead, those who have never heard — it means only that they have not been included in the church. It does not mean they have no way of knowing the grace of God. Baptism is the "regular means," the "standard practice" of the church for incorporation into the church, not a theological definition of the boundaries of grace. Beyond this, there are, of course, special cases where baptism may be administered outside the standard practice. Pastoral considerations might take precedence over routine practice. For example, where no clergy are available, where the imminent death of a newborn presents an emergency, or where other special cases appear, it might be more important to respond in grace than by policy. If baptism speaks foremost of the graciousness of God, then some extraordinary practice which deviates from ordinary practice may best convey the graciousness of God. God's grace cannot be confined to textbook accounts like mine.

Q10: How frequently should we partake of the Lord's Supper?

A10: The church's practice has varied extensively throughout history. The Protestant Reformers made a major change from the medieval practice of daily mass in the parishes, which was attended only on Sunday by the villagers. Protestants eventually marginalized the sacrament from the weekly service to an occasional practice, varying from once a year to quarterly or monthly, although Luther advised "frequently" or every Sunday, as did Calvin, and subsequently the Disciples of Christ. Wesley advised "the duty of constant communion," which meant two to three times a week. There has been no standard practice in the Western church, however. "As often as possible" would be, in my experience and the experience of many of my students, and increasingly in the case of many of the Protestant churches, a sensible guideline, which, of course, varies from context to context. Contrary to the caution I used to hear, that too-frequent a practice denigrates the sacrament, I have found that the more frequent the celebration of the Eucharist, the more significant as a means of grace it becomes in the life of the church.

Q11: To whom is the Eucharist offered?

A11: Some Christians have argued that the Eucharist should be open to everyone, not only to all Christians regardless of denomination but even to non-Christians. The grounds for an invitation to all are, first, that the grace of Christ is offered to everyone, and, second, that the sacrament can be a converting sacrament as well as a sacrament of maintenance. At the other extreme, the pope has recently warned Roman Catholics against taking communion in non–Roman Catholic churches. Communion is "closed" on the grounds that the sacrament is valid and efficacious only when it is performed by those who can make it a valid and efficacious sacrament and when it is received in a doctrinally pure church. The proper answer, however, it seems to me, is that as there is only one baptism, one Lord, and one faith, so there is one supper which should be offered across denominational lines to all who present themselves to receive it (even if they have not been baptized), assuming that God's mysterious work within the Christian may be equally mysterious among the nonbaptized. In my view no one is ever barred from the table. Furthermore, the Eucharist should never be offered on the basis of worthiness. No one is worthy but comes to the feast of forgiveness and acceptance as a foretaste of God's kingdom, which is open to all sinners. Indeed, no one should come to the table who feels they are worthy. I also believe that children should not be excluded from the table. An analogy from our civil religion may make this clear: I would never think of excluding my children or grandchildren from our November Thanksgiving dinner at home because they were not aware of, did not understand, or could not explain the mythology of the first Thanksgiving. Every member of the family is included, the most mature along with those with special needs, infants, and children. Indeed, such persons make it most clear to us who think we are so sophisticated that we all come to the table by sheer grace and with thanksgiving.

Q12: Is there such a thing as a private Eucharist?

A12: As with baptism, the Eucharist is an act by the community within the community on behalf of the community for the benefit of the community of Christ in the world. Its validity and efficacy reside within this context. Therefore, it is never a private act between the clergy and God or the individual and God. Of course, there are, again, special cases where emergency or restricting circumstances prevent the reception of the Eucharist within the gathered congregation. The elements used in these special circumstances should come from the regular eucharistic service, however, and a lay representative of the congregation should, if possible, be present to make visible the communal nature of what is occurring in the sacrament. The controlling principle, as always, however, is the graciousness of God's promise which we recite in anticipation as we pray, "Even so, come, Lord Jesus."

CHAPTER TWELVE

The Fulfillment of Faith

I. What Can Christians Hope For?
Eschatology and Apocalypticism

What will happen to the creation, to history, and to me at the end of time?[1] Eschatology is the doctrine of "the last things." It is important, however, to recognize that "there is in the Bible no time called 'the end of the world.'"[2] The Bible offers a much richer vision of hope than an apocalyptic end. Its language of hope consists of a family of symbols, including kingdom of God, kingdom of heaven, parousia, final judgment, new creation, new heaven and earth, new Jerusalem, resurrection of the dead, resurrection of the body, and eternal life.

Old Testament prophetic eschatology is primarily a this-worldly hope. It is the hope for the survival and flourishing of the covenant people, the promise of the salvation of the community. God promises the continuation of the nation. Through judgment and repentance, God will restore Israel to the covenant and will establish God's reign over the whole earth. Eschatology is the fulfillment of history through granting the people the ideal state of affairs of justice, peace, good government, and prosperity by means of an ideal ruler, which Second Isaiah extends to a universal hope of peace.[3] Toward the inter-

---

1. Will the God who creates the world save that world from death and despair by transporting souls to heaven after their death, by resurrecting the dead at the end of time, by establishing God's reign on earth through a community of justice and peace, by evolutionary progress within history, by retaining us in God's everlasting memory, or some other means?

2. Catherine Keller, "Eschatology, Ecology, and a Green Ecumenacy," in *Reconstructing Christian Theology,* ed. Rebecca Chopp and Mark Lewis Taylor (Minneapolis: Fortress, 1996), p. 337.

3. "Salvation will be something to see; the earth will be extremely fruitful, people will be

testamental period, however, prophetic eschatology broke down and was replaced by apocalyptic eschatology. This form of hope was alive in Palestine, the Israelite diaspora, and the early Christian church between 200 BCE and AD 100. Instead of the intervention of God into history to establish justice and peace, they now expected God to destroy this world and establish a new eon. Apocalypticism is apparent in certain texts in Daniel, Mark 13, and Revelation, which appear to be a disclosure of hidden knowledge about the end of this world and a heavenly state at the end of time.

Biblical eschatology cannot be identified with apocalypticism, however. The primary significance of what Jesus said and did was the inbreaking of the reign of God. Although Jesus was not a strict apocalypticist, his message and activity made present the power of the future of God's reign in an apparent way. Furthermore, Paul's and John's eschatology differs from the Seer (Revelation). For Paul the cross and resurrection constitute the turning point of the ages, but he emphasizes also the "not yet" of salvation. We live "between the times," both in the present (old eon) and in the future (new eon), which will be completed when the parousia brings to completion the cosmic redemption of Christ. John seems to expect an end, but he stresses that salvation is already realized in the present and that believers already possess "eternal life" (John 5:24).[4]

The early church soon lost its sense of an imminent end. The mainstream of Christian thought has retained an idea of a final end, a "judgment day," which it puts off into the indefinite future. But what they hope for is that when they die, their soul will go to heaven, and they will be prepared to spend eternity in heaven following the judgment day. Nevertheless, apocalypticism has recurred throughout church history. Indeed, there has been a strong resurgence of apocalyptic fervor in American fundamentalism, a movement that has had a deep impact on American Protestantism through the influence of John Nelson Darby, an Irish preacher who introduced dispensationalism through the Niagara Conferences into American fundamentalism. In fact, many Americans, even in the mainline churches, think the book of Revelation

---

inwardly renewed, society will become righteous, and the nations will be at peace. Israel, the least of the nations, will be exalted above all the others, provided the people remain faithful to the ancient covenant." Carl Braaten, "The Kingdom of God and Life Everlasting," in *Christian Theology*, ed. Peter C. Hodgson and Robert H. King (Philadelphia: Fortress, 1982), p. 277.

4. Scholars have described the eschatology of the New Testament as futuristic (the principal events are yet in the future), as consistent (an apocalyptic end of the present order), as realized (the eschaton has arrived in Jesus), as inaugurated (fulfillment began with the resurrection but is yet to take place fully), and as symbolic (a reminder and promise that our fulfillment is trans-historical).

is the most important book in the Bible, and its apocalypticism defines Christian hope.[5]

There are, however, two things I want to emphasize about apocalypticism.

First, there are two ways to interpret apocalyptic literature. The meaning of the literature depends on which hermeneutical road you take. Is apocalyptic literature a preview of the end of history, or is it a literature of encouragement and promise in a period when faithfulness to Christ is challenged?

The first road interprets the book as a preview to coming attractions. "Bible prophecy is history written in advance," we read in *Left Behind*.[6] Apocalypticists, Hal Lindsey explains, search for "the prophecies which are related to the specific pattern of world events which are precisely predicted as coming together shortly before the coming of the Messiah the second time — coming in power to rule the earth."[7] Revelation provides information from God hidden in symbols and visions with encoded data about the end of history. The primary audience is the twenty-first-century reader, whose task is to discover the skeleton key that unlocks the hidden information about when and how the world will end.[8]

---

5. Apocalypticism has been brought back into mainstream Protestantism since 1970 by Hal Lindsey, who wrote the best-selling "nonfiction" book of the decade *(The Late Great Planet Earth)*. Interest was revived in 1995 by Tim LaHaye and Jerry Jenkins in the *Left Behind* series of ten novels, which sold fifty million copies by January 2002. In a Time/CNN poll, 59 percent of Americans say they believe the events in Revelation will come true. My experience in my classes and in churches confirms that many American Christians equate eschatology with apocalypticism. For fundamentalists and evangelicals, Christian hope is determined by the signs and portents of "the end times." Most of them teach "premillennialism," the belief that Christ will return to establish his kingdom, which is defined by the views of Darby, Scofield, Lindsey, and LaHaye, who teach "pre-tribulation dispensational millennialism," in which Christ will return to rapture the church, which will meet him up in the air in the clouds to be taken to heaven, followed by a seven-year tribulation period, during which the remainder have a chance to repent, after which Christ returns to earth to rule from Jerusalem for one thousand years, and then the final judgment. Furthermore, many liberals agree that eschatology has to do with this belief, and so simply choose to disregard biblical eschatology and believe that their hope is that they will go to heaven when they die.

6. Tim LaHaye and Jerry B. Jenkins, *Left Behind: A Novel of the Earth's Last Days* (Wheaton, Ill.: Tyndale House, 1995), p. 214.

7. Hal Lindsey, *The Late Great Planet Earth* (New York: Bantam, 1970), p. 31.

8. Those who follow this road today claim the outlook and imagery of the apocalyptic literature "literally." I put quotation marks around "literally" because the book cannot be interpreted "literally," and no one ever does. "Literal" interpreters find all sorts of secret, hidden references and meanings in the text. Apocalyptic is a literary *genre* or form. It is a literature loaded with images, symbols, colors, numbers, animals, and visions, as well as hundreds of Old Testament references. The basic pattern of apocalyptic literature is dualistic and eschatological. The dualism is not so much a metaphysical dualism between spirit and matter as it is a cosmic dual-

If, however, you interpret apocalyptic as a genre written for the historical context in which it was first read and heard, then apocalyptic literature represents a different kind of hope. On this hermeneutical road, the book of Revelation deals with the first-century culture wars between the church and the state. Through the use of dramatic imagery, visions, and symbolism (the Lamb = Jesus, the dragon = Satan, the Beast = the Empire, the seven heads = the seven emperors, Babylon = Rome), the book is a kind of "Hallelujah Chorus," affirming that God, not Caesar, rules over human affairs. In this book that would have been read to the seven churches who were undergoing a period of persecution in Western Asia Minor at the end of the first century (probably around the end of the rule of the Emperor Domitian [81-96]), the Seer is encouraging the churches to remain loyal to Christ by his reassurance through dramatic images of the triumph of the power of God amidst a threat to their loyalty to Christ. Clark Williamson paraphrases the message this way: "God will bring an end to Roman oppression, but do not expect Caesar to go gently from the scene. He will leave destruction in his wake. Yet the oppression will end."[9] John's message to his hearers and to us is that in the midst of conflict and struggle, Jesus' death and resurrection marks the beginning of the defeat of the forces of evil. The illegitimate power of Rome is overcome by the power of the Lamb. Christians must remain faithful to the power of Christ instead of the power of the cult of imperial Rome.[10] As in the first century, so in the twenty-first, we are called to

> "Mainline Christianity has never made very much of the apocalyptic and eschatological elements in the New Testament because, as mainline and established, it doesn't have much interest in changing the status quo."
>
> JOHN KILLINGER

ism of two opposing forces in the universe, a good god and a bad god. It is eschatological in the sense that both time and beyond-time are involved, and there are two distinct ages, the second growing out of the first as a new creation. Secondary features include visions, pseudonymity, a messiah, angelology and demonology, animal symbolism, numerology, predicted woes, and astral influences. By its very nature it is a dramatic and open body of literature, a sort of Rorschach ink blot onto which anyone with clever imagination can project an almost infinite number of schemes of interpretation of the end of history. If you doubt this, read Lindsey's and LaHaye's books. We get from them a scheme about the end of history in our time based on their access to the secret code, which interprets (the end of) history in advance.

9. Clark Williamson, *Way of Blessing, Way of Life* (St. Louis: Chalice, 1999), p. 298.

10. Adela Yarbro Collins, *The Apocalypse* (Wilmington, Del.: Michael Glazier, 1979). For another interpretation of the book of Revelation in this context, see Wes Howard-Brook and Anthony Gwyther, *Unveiling Empire: Reading Revelation Then and Now* (Maryknoll, N.Y.: Orbis, 2003).

be loyal to Christ instead of to the empire of our time, the nation state and the marketplace.

The second thing I want to emphasize about apocalypticism is that there is a sense in which an apocalyptic note is important to Christian hope. It is a language of crisis, of negation of the ultimacy of the present principalities and power. Specifically, it expresses in dramatic form the difference between the current age and the reign of God and the crisis created by that tension. Its dramatic symbolism reveals the perversion of the present and the grasp of a future of revolutionary transformation. Apocalyptic language is important to faith because, as Carl Braaten puts it, it makes clear "the power of the future entering the present through creative negation,"[11] through liberation from the power of our present bondage to powers of repression, exploitation, and destruction. To put it bluntly, apocalyptic imagery affirms that Jesus is Lord, Caesar is not!

Eschatology is the affirmation about the completion of the creation through an interpretation of a whole family of symbols expressing Christian hope. We do not know the content of our hope through some special revealed gnosis (knowledge) about how and when history will end. "Symbols, images, and metaphors of heaven, life after death, and the resurrected life are best understood as ways of talking about God rather than as knowledge statements about what we have not experienced," writes Williamson.[12] What we know is based on the symbols, images, and metaphors which express the faith of the church grounded in the church's belief in the resurrection of Christ.

There is, however, a danger we must avoid in any eschatology. It is the danger of claiming to know too much. We must remember Jesus' comment that "about that day or hour no one knows, neither the angels in heaven, nor the Son, but only the Father" (Mark 13:32). We also should recall Paul's reminder that "for now we see in a mirror dimly" (1 Cor. 13:12), and John's warning that "what we will be has not yet been revealed" (1 John 3:2). Too many Christians want to know too much about the end.[13]

---

11. Carl Braaten, *Christ and Counter-Christ: Apocalyptic Themes in Theology and Culture* (Philadelphia: Fortress, 1971), p. 9. "Apocalyptic future brings new reality through negation" (p. 11).

12. Clark Williamson, *Way of Blessing, Way of Life*, p. 315.

13. You will notice, of course, the irony of this caution. I am writing a chapter similar in length and assertions to all of the other eleven chapters. Although this is extrapolation and speculation, it is shaped by and shapes what has been said up to this point. Faith from the beginning gives us hope and confidence that the purposes of God ultimately will be fulfilled; and that hope from the beginning has been the foundation for and shapes what has been said up to this point.

Eschatology interprets the nature and the grounds of hope in the face of despair about human history. Instead of seeing history as terror, the Christian sees history as promise because its fulfillment is guided by divine providence and inaugurated by the resurrection of Christ. Therefore, eschatology is not only the last doctrine in an introduction to theology; it stands at the heart of the gospel. The creating, redeeming, and consummating work of God are inseparable works of the triune God. The eschatological affirmation is that the God who is creator and Lord, and who has revealed the divine purposes in Jesus, will fulfill these purposes at the end (both terminus and telos) of history.[14]

The content of our hope, then, is an extrapolation from what other beliefs imply or suggest about the future. The first context for an interpretation of eschatological symbols is God's providence. The future is not simply the outcome of the past; the future is the future of God's providence. As I discussed in the chapter on creation, the future is created by God as an open future within God's purposes. Such a view of providence does not mean that God controls the future so that regardless of what we decide the future is set. Rather, providence means that God is the ground, source, and resource of the future of our existence and our freedom. Past and present are destiny (given to us), not fate (overriding determinism).[15] The future is open but destined for fulfillment.

But the primary context for our interpretation of eschatological symbols is the resurrection of Jesus.[16] Hope begins at Easter where the end appeared ahead of time.[17] Eschatology ponders the ultimate significance of the work of Christ, a work that is not yet complete. "Easter cannot be understood rightly except as prolepsis, except as an anticipation in Jesus's person of what God will do to transform and renew the whole creation," writes Ted Peters.[18] Jews are right, there is no coming of the Messiah without the time of liberation, peace, and blessing. The only way Christians can affirm Jesus is the Messiah is to affirm that he will come again to complete his work. The resurrection of Jesus is the first evidence ("the first fruits"), the confirmation, of that messianic reign. It is the promise and seal of God's shalom (peace). The negation of

---

14. Owen Thomas, *Introduction to Theology,* revised ed. (Wilton, Conn.: Morehouse-Barlow, 1983), p. 222.

15. Paul Tillich, *Systematic Theology,* vol. 1 (Chicago: University of Chicago Press, 1951).

16. One of the most important discussions of the relation of eschatology and resurrection is Jürgen Moltmann's "Promise and History" and "The Resurrection and the Future of Jesus Christ," in *Theology of Hope: On the Ground and the Implications of a Christian Eschatology* (New York: Harper and Row, 1967), chapters 2-3.

17. Ted Peters, *God — The World's Future: Systematic Theology for a New Era,* second ed. (Minneapolis: Fortress, 2000), p. 318.

18. Peters, *God — The World's Future,* p. 319.

the evil powers of the present age is impossible without the affirmation of the power of the future which is the resurrection. In the resurrection of Jesus, says Peters, "somehow the everlasting future was collapsed and compressed and appeared in seed form within the soil of that temporal moment."[19] God comes as the power of promise from the future and guarantees the future as promise through the cross and resurrection. The eschatological future has entered into death and conquered it inside its own stronghold.[20]

The resurrection is the confirmation of the reliability of the God of the future. God is doing a new thing, a new kind of humanity, a new creation. One symbol is a new heaven and a new earth. Hope is not based on optimism about the future but on the promise of resurrection. We do not defend the past or acquiesce to the present but understand the past and present in the light of the future as God's future. True revolution has nothing to do with violence but with the change that occurs in turning from the old order — the values and ways we are used to — to a new order which comes from the future as shock and promise.[21]

II. What Is the Goal of History?

Eschatological hope is in part earth-bound. It has to do with "the future of and in this world."[22] We might even say that eschatology is broadly political. It asks what Christians can hope for within history. Is there improvement or progress, even fulfillment or perfection, within history, or is historical progress an illusion because human beings and institutions remain sinful, evil, and hopeless to the end? Is our hope for some kind of fulfillment within history, or is our hope wholly "beyond history"? Do apocalyptic visions of the end refer to the end of history as we know it or to the end of earthly injustice and violence within the reign of God's peace?[23]

---

19. Peters, *God — The World's Future*, p. 321.

20. Braaten, *Christ and Counter-Christ*, p. 49.

21. Braaten, *Christ and Counter-Christ*, p. 102. There is no consensus about how one should interpret the eschatology of the church. Is it otherworldly and future (traditional), or otherworldly and present (dialectical theology), or this-worldly and present (existentialist theology), or this-worldly and future (liberation theology)? Braaten, "The Kingdom of God and Life Everlasting," in *Christian Theology*, ed. Hodgson and King, p. 278. But our hope is not in our certainty about any of them. It rests on God's promise from God's future.

22. Williamson, *Way of Blessing, Way of Life*, p. 310.

23. By "history" I mean the events in time which result from human decisions and acts. It is the irreversible and unforeseeable course of human events directed toward a future end. History is the new and novel events which humans imagine, choose, and enact. History is the accumula-

Is the future of history, both its proximate future and it ultimate future, menace or promise? In the modern Western world, especially in the eighteenth and nineteenth centuries, promise was rooted in the inevitable progress of history as it moved increasingly toward improvement. The kingdom of God was being established gradually but inevitably on earth. Through evolutionary progress (survival of the fittest), science (knowledge that leads to power and control), technology (ever improved ease and comfort), democracy (increase of individual control over one's destiny), medicine (health, organ transplants, and gene therapy), capitalism (increased wealth), empire (spread of British and American liberalism around the globe), education (knowledge), inherent individual rights (inalienable equality for all), there is an ever increasing improvement of every facet of human life, including our material, political, moral, and spiritual well-being — or so the argument went.

> "I believe, in fact, that we are on the verge of the best period in human history. Over the last twenty-five years we have made great advances in the sciences, in education and health care, in protecting the environment, and in securing a more peaceful economic order, and I have reason to believe we will do even better over the next twenty-five years."
>
> GEORGE McGOVERN

Modern this-worldly hope was grounded in evolutionary eschatologies (the liberal doctrine of progress) or revolution (Marxist doctrines of revolution). Hope was found in progress, which depends on evolutionary development or revolutionary change of all social institutions. Evolutionary or revolutionary progress has led to an increase in freedom, education, democracy, science, technology, the successes of capitalist competition or socialist planning. In liberal Christianity, the kingdom of God was seen as a vital power at work in history, energizing humanity to act in behalf of our common humanity through the progressive reign of justice and love in human affairs. Any resistance to increasing improvement was based on our lack of knowledge or technique. The future, with a few variations, it was believed, will be an extension of the technological, bourgeois, pragmatic, nonideological, affluent, sensate, diversified, and relatively stable present world of the Western way of life.

But throughout the twentieth century, the future approached us more as a storm, as a constant threat of barbarism. A nearly constant state of war,

---

tion of human deeds through time in the movement from the past to the future, as well as the recollection of these events in our memory.

someone calculated, killed an average of over a hundred people an hour throughout the twentieth century. The barrage of confidence-shaking events and attitudinal changes, such as World War I, the great worldwide depression, World War II, the Vietnam War, violence in the streets, race riots, world poverty, drugs, assassinations, and terrorist attacks seemed to lie outside our rational control and to have made a mockery of middle class gentility and security. The continuation of this barbarism into the twenty-first century has prolonged the twentieth century and forced us to ask whether the liberal version of hope is adequate. In the twentieth and twenty-first centuries, we have had to reconsider the doctrines of sin, original sin, and even total depravity.

Responses to history as a threat as much as a promise vary. Some argue that in the long run there is no fundamental threat to this hope because the preceding analysis is shortsighted, questionable, and probably wrong. In the long haul, progress is inevitable. Furthermore, throughout the past century we saw significant improvements in history through the rise of great movements of liberation, the worldwide women's movement, and the struggle for freedom and human rights everywhere. Although there may be a genuine crisis in the late modern world, the question about the future of history is long-range, and science and technology will solve all of these problems through the discovery of new resources and methods of control, either forced or voluntary, and through education. Skeptics, however, argue we really do not know and cannot care that much about the future. We can live only in the now, and live the now to the fullest, since the only meaning we can know is our own personal meaning. We cannot even imagine posterity beyond two or three generations. Extreme cynics, religious (apocalypticists) and secular, argue that we should give up hope for history; there is no hope in history. Hope in this life itself is evil (secular) or sinful (apocalypticists) because it is an illusion or misunderstands God's promise.

Even though there are clearly steps forward as well as backward in history, it is clear that history is not continual progress. There is genuine loss and tragedy in a history that is open and risky. Eschatology, therefore, expresses dissatisfaction with the present world. Eschatological hope consists in part of a challenge to the present order. The present order is not all that God intends for history. "We know what the end is when we face it head-on by refusing, at the risk of death, to tolerate present injustice," writes James Cone.[24] Therefore, the Christian cannot abandon hope for history. Eschatology includes hope for liberation within history, the promise that the fight for freedom, jus-

---

24. James Cone, *A Black Theology of Liberation* (Maryknoll, N.Y.: Orbis, 1986 [1970]), p. 137.

tice, and peace is not futile. Christians hope for the kingdom of God as a liberated and liberating human community within history. Not only is such hope built into our bodily responses through our genes, as a "life instinct" or a "will to live"; the central symbols of our faith demand and promise hope for the future of history. The future is, in part, menace, and this should not be news to Christians who understand us as creatures liable to finitude and sin; but the route of the future toward the end as purpose and meaning is something God has put into the hearts and hands of humans, and something that has been confirmed in the story of Jesus.

The end of history as purpose and promise, then, is not the abolition of history but the healing of history. "The 'end' of which we are speaking," notes Paul Fiddes, "can only be a decisive shifting of creation into a new level of existence, not an absolute end, if God's being is indeed in the process of becoming."[25] Christian eschatological symbols, therefore, prevent us from seeing the future, both proximate and ultimate, as menace only. Symbols of hope within history are not tacked onto the Christian faith. They are at the heart of faith. The proximate future is ambiguous, but it is not hopeless. Our faith provides us with symbols of hope for the reign of God in history as freedom, justice, and peace.

The eschatology of history is the hope that God will establish justice and peace on earth, that God's will will be done "on earth as it is in heaven." One of the things Christians hope for, then, is that however history ends (terminus), history will move toward its end (telos), when God establishes a new earth of justice and peace as a new creation. God saves history by inaugurating and bringing to fulfillment God's reign within a humane community of equity, harmony, and love. God's reign is the transformation of human society through good government and peace, the well-being of all in community with each other. The kingdom of heaven, in part, is God's reign in time when the whole established world is overturned through a reversal of our accustomed values of kingship as domination.[26] "The end" of human history includes "the ends" of justice and love toward which God works. The end (terminus, termination) of history is when the end (telos, goal) of history is accomplished.

But eschatological hope for history does not exhaust the Christian hope, and, indeed, it cannot stand alone apart from the personal and cosmic hope. The problem with limiting hope to history is that we are left with a tension

25. Paul Fiddes, *The Creative Suffering of God* (Oxford: Clarendon, 1988), p. 106.
26. Marjorie Suchocki, *God, Christ, Church: A Practical Guide to Process Theology*, new revised ed. (New York: Crossroad, 1989), p. 187.

which is not resolvable apart from hope in the final resurrection. In contrast to the Hebrew prophetic expectations and modern secular eschatologies, I would agree with Rosemary Radford Ruether, who writes, "I do not expect that we can finally develop or transform life on earth into a final, perfect state. This notion of final perfection is itself a contradiction of the finite nature of existence."[27] The other side of the tension, then, a dialectical truth, is that the transformation of historical existence is possible only on the basis of an idea larger than the promise of the perfection of history itself. All hope, for Christians, rests, ultimately, in the promise of the final resurrection. That means the fulfillment of history is intimately tied to the hope of personal and cosmic fulfillment.

In the light of the resurrection as the central eschatological symbol, then, our hope for history is that God will create a *new* earth and a *new* heaven. God's power to resurrect the whole creation will triumph. Justice will prevail over injustice, love over hatred and greed, peace over hostility, humanity over inhumanity, the kingdom of God over the kingdom of evil. This triumph includes judgment, to be sure, but the judge is Christ, the Lamb, the one who loves us and gave his life for sinners. In the new heaven and the new earth there will be no more church. The whole human community will be a heavenly throng where there is no more hating, destroying hostilities, self-centeredness or alienation, loneliness or suffering. What we affirm at Easter, that Christ is the exalted one, that Jesus is King and Caesar is not, that Christ is Lord and the emperor is not, and what we affirm at Christmas, that Christ is coming again, and again, and again in many ways, will be complete. His kingdom will have come and his will will be done, on earth as it is in heaven. Hope for history cannot be separated from personal and cosmic fulfillment.

III. Dying We Live: Do We Survive Our Death?

The majority of Christians have been and still are amillennialists. They expect to go to heaven when they die. Eschatology is primarily the hope for individual survival. After a day of final judgment in the far distant future, they will live forever with God and the saints.

Will I survive my death? If I do, what is my destiny? Eschatology deals, in

---

27. Rosemary Radford Ruether, "Eschatology and Feminism," in *Lift Every Voice: Constructing Christian Theologies from the Underside,* ed. Susan Brooks Thistlethwaite and Mary Potter Engel (San Francisco: Harper and Row, 1990), p. 121.

part, with the fate of individuals following their death. Our desire to survive is a deep longing within the human heart. This craving is expressed by Terry McGovern, a Manhattan Irish Catholic attorney, whose mother died in the World Trade Center terrorist attacks.

> How could this happen? Is this really it? Is that it for my mother? I mean, she dies like that? You know? I think on some very deep level, I want the church's teachings on the spiritual life after death to be true. I need them to be true. And frankly, the church since September 11 has comforted me.[28]

Obviously we do survive in some respects, at least in the memories and dreams of family and friends, in the genes and behaviors we pass on, and for a few, in the history books. But such memory is hard to imagine, let alone sustain, beyond two or three generations. And even those remembered in the history books are fated to be dropped out as the books get thicker and thicker. Are we destined to be forgotten or lost to everyone in the end? Are death and loss the last words?

The concept of individual survival has a long history. Belief in a soul which continues to exist after death in some kind of shadowy mode of existence appears in many religions. There are allusions in the Old Testament to persons (semi)existing after death in Sheol, which ancient Judaism identified with the grave, but there was no future *life* of individuals beyond the grave because persons are psychosomatic unities. During the Maccabean period (second and first centuries BCE), however, the idea of a future resurrection entered Jewish thought (Dan. 12:2). During the first

> "If history is all you get, there's too much evil that triumphs over good, and too much evil that triumphs over God."
>
> MARJORIE SUCHOCKI

century BCE, the Platonic idea of the soul as an eternal metaphysical entity also entered Judaism, probably by way of Philo and Alexandrian Hellenistic philosophy, and influenced early Christian writings with ideas of deathlessness and imperishability (Rom. 2:7; 1 Cor. 15:53). But during the intertestamental and New Testament periods, the predominant idea was the resurrection of the dead. Only God is eternal and immortal.

Philosophical criticisms of the idea of personal survival[29] can be coun-

---

28. Terry McGovern, 9/4/02, http://www.pbs.org/wgbh/pages/frontline/shows/faith/questions/religion.html, page 3.

29. I refer to such criticisms as the following: that belief in personal survival is too self-

tered with other philosophical arguments for believing that we survive our deaths.[30] But for Christians, what we believe and why we believe in individual survival is not dependent on philosophical arguments. Belief is rooted in christology. On the basis of the resurrection of Jesus, the church affirms individual survival as one part of our hope.

To understand what we believe, we must recognize that there are two contrasting ideas at the heart of the Christian belief in individual survival[31] (although I will try to bring these two together in some kind of consistency).

---

centered and egotistical an idea ("the apogee of male individualism and egoism," Rosemary Radford Ruether, *Sexism and God-Talk: Toward a Feminist Theology* [Boston: Beacon, 1983], p. 235); that our faith is in God, not in our ego or our personal survival; that only God is eternal or everlasting; that belief in personal survival denies the full significance of this world by focusing on the next; that such belief is a character defect of the weak, insecure, and fearful, or males; that survival is an empty phrase, since people survive catastrophes or escape death but cannot survive death; that there is no spiritual or mental life apart from our cerebral system, no spirit or personality or self apart from a body; that spirit and mind are biologically based concepts within the evolutionary process, emergents and functions of bodies and brains, not eternal metaphysical entities; that disembodied existence is a meaningless idea, since the word "person" is intelligible only insofar as it refers to concrete embodiments or physical and mental characteristics; and that personal identity depends on spatiotemporal continuity, so incorporeal souls do not have the sufficient conditions necessary for identity.

30. I refer to such arguments as this: First, the idea of the soul surviving death, even if the soul is an emergent within the evolutionary process and not an eternal metaphysical entity, is not impossible. The mind may depend on the brain, but the mind also transcends the brain in the sense that we can distinguish between mental experience and brain processes. Mind is more than the brain or central nervous system. It is not unthinkable that the mind or soul or person, as I will describe below, survives the death of the brain. We might even see suggestive evidence for this in out-of-body experiences, reports of individuals "returning from the dead," parapsychology, and especially in contemporary psychic research. Second, in a world of change, every state is generated from its opposite, otherwise reality would be lopsided or all reality would cease (death and life arise out of each other) [Plato]. Third, the soul is by its nature immortal (the soul is simple and spiritual and so cannot die; only composite things can die). Fourth, the soul is our link with the intelligible world of incorporeality, and shares in what it knows [Augustine]. Fifth, moral experience requires God, freedom, and immortality [Kant]. Sixth, it is not obvious we cannot talk meaningfully about an essential part of us surviving our death, since spatiotemporal continuity is not necessary (memory more than substance may be what establishes our continuity). Seventh, spatiotemporal conditions of identity may not operate under all conceivable circumstances, that is, in all possible worlds. Eighth, psychical research and parapsychology provide some evidence of our surviving our death. And finally, precisely because God is love and because God achieves a good through personalized existence which is good in itself, it may be that God preserves that personalized agency by which this good was achieved [process philosophy].

31. Oscar Cullmann, *Immortality of the Soul or Resurrection of the Body?* (New York: Macmillan, 1958).

The first idea, the resurrection of the body, is rooted in the Hebrew idea of the person as a psycho-physical unity. A person perishes at death, but is resurrected (re-created) by God in the future. This idea is grounded in the resurrection of Jesus. His resurrection is not belief that his eternal soul went on to live forever after his crucifixion. Rather, he was raised by God as a transformed, spiritual body. "Resurrection hope does not really mean a life after death," says Wolfhart Pannenberg, "but a new life that is given to the dead person by God."[32] The primary hope for a personal destiny with God, then, rests not on the resuscitation of our corpse or the immortality of our soul (a "soulectomy")[33] but on the resurrected body, which is a new creation. Although we must fall back on the words of 1 Corinthians that admit the fullness of this vision is beyond our comprehension, we can use the imagery of resurrection "to express a mighty transition from a finite subjectivity that is alone with itself to that same subjectivity within the presence of God."[34] The primary basis for our hope for survival is Christ: As God raised Jesus from the dead, so God will raise us.

Christians frequently have attached to this primary grounds of hope, however, another very different idea, the immortality of the soul. This concept was developed most clearly in the *Phaedo,* by Plato, who understood the person to be a soul, which by its very nature is immortal. I (my soul) am temporarily trapped in this body until I am released by death to return to the eternal realm. I will live in that eternal realm until I am again trapped in another body (reincarnation). Death, therefore, is not a threat but is welcomed because it frees me (my soul) from this body in which I am temporarily trapped to return to heaven or to God. My soul — one more little flower — is finally released to go home — transplanted back to heaven, which is its real home. (When you speak about death, do you say the person "died," or do you say the person "passed on"?)

When we think of our personal survival as the resurrection of our body and the immortality of our soul — as in the Apostles' Creed — we are affirming both the continuity and the discontinuity with our present "self." Salvation is the salvation of the whole person, who is body and soul, so only if the body is re-created will the person be restored to life with God and each other. We can reduce the tension between these two contrasting ideas by affirming that in our resurrection we will be transformed as part of the new creation.

---

32. Wolfhart Pannenberg, "History and Resurrection in Christianity," in *Progress, Apocalypse, and Completion of History and Life after Death of the Human Person in the World Religions,* ed. Peter Koslowski (Dordrecht: Kluwer Academic, 2002), p. 85.

33. Peters, *God — The World's Future,* p. 325.

34. Suchocki, *God, Christ, Church,* p. 205.

We will be embodied in the "matter" of the new creation, which will be "located" in God's "space" and "time." Here Paul's idea of the body as a form which can exist with one or another "substance," either flesh or spirit, is helpful.[35] God will re-create us in the form of "a spiritual body," a form which we cannot even begin to understand as part of the old creation, but which is continuous with our current "self," which is both our body and our soul.

We also can reduce the tension between resurrection and immortality with the speculative hypothesis that the soul as well as the body establishes continuity as well as discontinuity between our present self and our resurrected self. The old idea of the soul as the form of the body means that it is possible, as John Polkinghorne writes, that "at death that human 'pattern' is held in the divine memory, to be re-embodied in the 'space-time matter' of the new creation."[36] The soul that lives after the death of the individual might bridge the gap between the death of the person and the future resurrection of the body.[37] Continuity of identity of the person who exists physically at a particular time and the person resurrected from the dead in the future might be maintained through the idea of the soul as "the program of the physical reality of the human person."[38] Polkinghorne and Welker summarize this idea when they say that this "revival of the notion (as old as Aristotle and Thomas) of the soul as the form (information-bearing pattern) of the body may offer a credible concept serving to carry across identity from the life of this world to the life of the world to come."[39] It is possible that the soul remains present to the God who created the whole person until in the end the person is resurrected or re-created as a new person. If the world to come is free from death and decay, the "matter-energy" of that world will certainly be different in its "physical" properties from the matter-energy of the present world. "The matter of the new creation," writes Polkinghorne, "will be divinely transmuted matter."[40]

Finally, I suggest it makes no ultimate difference in terms of the question of personal survival whether God bestows life after death by creating us initially as immortal souls (at our conception or birth or development as a self) or by re-creating us individually through a new ensouled body at the end of

---

35. Peters, *God — The World's Future*, p. 326.

36. John Polkinghorne, "Eschatology and the Sciences," in *The End of the World and the Ends of God*, ed. Polkinghorne and Michael Welker (Harrisburg, Pa.: Trinity Press International, 2000), p. 17.

37. Pannenberg, "History and Resurrection in Christianity," p. 85.

38. Pannenberg, "History and Resurrection in Christianity," p. 86.

39. Polkinghorne and Welker, "Science and Theology on the End of the World and the Ends of God," in *The End of the World and the Ends of God*, ed. Polkinghorne and Welker, pp. 12-13.

40. Polkinghorne, "Eschatology and the Sciences," p. 39.

history. The basic issue is to what extent our hope depends on Christ and his resurrection (1 Cor. 15, the resurrection of the body), and to what extent it depends on a natural immortality which we possess quite apart from the grace of God (the immortality of the soul). The most fundamental point of all is that either or both must be seen as a gift of God, not something we possess as immortal beings. Only God is immortal. Any Christian idea of immortality must understand both the body and the soul as gifts of God in creation (and re-creation). What saves a Christian idea of the soul from Platonism (we and God are equally immortal) is the concept of traducianism, the idea that the soul is propagated along with the body at conception, birth, or the development of the self, or the concept of creationism, the idea that God creates out of nothing a new soul for each individual when they are conceived, born, or become a self. Both are gifts of God, and both depend on the power of God to establish personal identity from one life to the next. I prefer the language of the resurrection of the body, though, because it roots the hope for our personal survival in Christ, specifically, in the resurrection of Christ.

All of this said, it is important here to be theologically agnostic. Our faith is not in our speculations about our survival but in God who is the source and guarantor of our final destinies. Christians believe that our destiny is by, for, and with God. We do not know in detail what that destiny is like. Ted Peters makes the point nicely:

> That our identity is yet to be determined by our relationship to the whole of God's creation through our relationship to Christ is the destiny into which the gracious God is drawing us. Just what that identity is will be forged by us through the course of our actual life stories as they converge into the one cosmic story. . . . our destiny will be the result of the intertwining of the divine life with the creative world process.[41]

IV. What Are God's Ultimate Purposes?

Eschatology, then, finally, has to do with the future of the whole creation, time after human history ends, the creation as a whole in all its modes of existence. If Christ's work in history is all there is, then redemption is only partial, for the cosmos as a whole remains distorted, fragmentary, and incomplete. If God's purposes are completed, the whole cosmos must be redeemed, the end of evil must be affirmed. "The gospel reaches backwards and forwards all

41. Peters, *God — The World's Future*, p. 344.

along the line from creation to consummation, because Christ is the eschatological revelation of God already at the beginning of things," writes Carl Braaten.[42] God's purposes include the new heaven as well as the new earth. God's reign includes the renewal of the creation, which extends beyond human history. God fulfills all finite space and time, the cosmos as a whole, within God's own space and time.

When cosmologists speculate about the future, their speculations usually end in inevitable futility rather than in promised fulfillment. Within that perspective the world began with a "big bang" fifteen to twenty billion years ago, when a single bit of reality began to expand at lightning speed, which is still flying, and will end when the explosion has exhausted its energy and the dissipation of heat is complete. Not only do humans die; the universe is doomed to physical decay. According to entropy (the second law of thermodynamics), heat flows from a hot source to cold. Heat energy will no longer be available to work, and so will come to a complete equilibrium and final dissipation (though some subsystems provisionally increase energy at the macro level).[43]

Christians do not have to concede to cosmic despair even if they accept the framework of modern cosmology, however. Cosmological despair does not take seriously enough the transcendent purposes and power of God. God's power does not depend on the continuation of *this* cosmic epoch. There are possibilities of transformation of the cosmos beyond what we can envision or understand in our space-time epoch. Indeed, if we make the resurrection the key to eschatology, we have an answer to cosmic despair in our theology of hope. The center of that hope does not rest on our assurance that scientific cosmologies are wrong about our cosmic era. Hope rests in our trust in the power of fulfillment by the faithful God of any and every cosmic epoch. "Christian hope is not a consoling fantasy that somehow death is an illusion," note Polkinghorne and Welker. "Death is real, but death is not ultimate. Only God is ultimate. The Christian hope is death and resurrection."[44] The heart of Christian hope is belief in the resurrection of Jesus Christ, whose resurrection redeems the old creation's bondage to death and decay through every cosmic era.

Throughout the New Testament the work of Christ is significant for the whole creation. Christ's redemption is also a cosmic redemption. Christ came not only for individuals but for the whole world (cosmos). Personal redemp-

---

42. Carl Braaten, *Justification: The Article by which the Church Stands or Falls* (Minneapolis: Fortress, 1990), p. 95.

43. For a popular discussion of this idea, see "The End," *Time*, June 25, 2001, pp. 48-55.

44. Polkinghorne and Welker, "Science and Theology on the End of the World and the Ends of God," p. 12.

tion and cosmic redemption are not two separate things but correlative aspects of one and the same redemption by Christ. If faith is redemptive, then, because of the problem of evil, it must either expand the idea of redemption to encompass the whole of the environment, or become an other-worldly concept according to which redemption is an escape from the environment.[45] Instead of a gnostic escape from the world, the New Testament claims that Christ's work is universally effective in all of creation (John 1 and Col. 2). As the divine wisdom or logos is immanent in the creation (the person of Christ), so the work of Christ redeems the whole creation. The evils that are associated with our space-time world, and, indeed, with any cosmic order whatsoever, are redeemed by Christ. "In [the church's] efforts to interpret the significance of the Christ in relation to the world," Allan Galloway writes, "she has been forced to see in Him and His work either the simple condemnation of the whole natural order, or else the revelation and fulfillment of a meaning already latent in the natural order, however partial or obscure it may have been."[45]

The whole structure of the world, then, has been transformed by Christ. In his cross he confronted the principalities and powers of domination and destruction, unmasking, resisting, and defeating them through his cross as the power of the new creation (Col. 2:13-15). The whole creation is now destined to be restored in Christ. Galloway puts it this way:

> The ultimate destiny of the Church is to become the whole cosmos, so that there shall be no more Church: "For there shall be no temple therein: for the Lord God Almighty and the Lamb are the temple of it. And the city shall have no need of the sun, neither of the moon, to shine in it; for the glory of God shall lighten it, and the Lamb shall be the light thereof" (Rev 21:22-23). So Christ shall be truly "the fulness of Him that filleth all in all" (Eph 1:23).[46]

The key to the completion of the creation is the resurrection of Christ. We don't know when and how, but we have the promise and the confirmation of its fulfillment. Eschatology is not the hope that God will wipe the cosmic slate clean and start again. The completion is God's transformation and renewal of the world as a "new creation," a "new heaven and earth." Renewal includes not only the inner world of the divided self and the historical world of human purposes and deeds. It includes, also, nature and the cosmos. The new

---

45. Allan Galloway, *The Cosmic Christ* (New York: Harper and Brothers, 1951), p. 238.
46. Galloway, *The Cosmic Christ*, p. 259.

creation is possible only by the power of God who is the creator of all things. Such a holistic hope is imaginatively expressed by Marjorie Suchocki as

> a home in God, a home for the whole universe. In that home, multiplicity finally achieves unity, and fragmentation is embraced in wholeness. The unity and wholeness receiving and transforming each part is more than the sum of them all, for the unity is the ever-living God, drawing upon the divine resources of infinite possibility to blend all reality into the giving and receiving of the whole.[47]

Within this framework, what is heaven? Seventy-six percent of all Americans believe in heaven. Although they believe for any number of reasons, the primary reason is this: the ultimate threat to existence is not the threat of death but the threat of meaninglessness. Heaven, whatever and wherever it is, is our most basic symbol of our confidence that the threat to our sense of self and the meaning of history and the cosmos is answered by God's ultimate triumph over the power of sin and death within us, within history, and within the cosmos. Heaven is the new order that redeems the old order of sin and death. It is the realm of God's reign, on earth and in heaven.

Where is heaven? Seventy-one percent of Americans believe heaven is a physical, concrete place somewhere up in the sky, a place as real as Chicago or London. It is, for them, apparently, a place in some galaxy out there. Unfazed by Jesus' reticence in describing heaven, Ann Graham Lotz describes it as a cube of fifteen hundred miles on each side, with twenty billion inhabitants, each with a dream home on a seventy-five-acre plot.[48] Other Christians prefer to follow Plato. For them, heaven is our real home in the realm of eternal ideas or forms, a sort of abstract, spiritual realm above the physical world to which souls or spirits go when they die. A few modern Christians believe heaven is life on earth here and now; this life is all the heaven we need to know. It is either the condition of my own happiness and satisfaction, or the condition of peace and justice that reigns within the human community.

I understand heaven to be a metaphor or a symbol of our ever growing experience of and communion with God in this life and beyond. Heaven is the symbol that represents "the transformed reality promised by the resurrection of Jesus," conveyed in other symbols such as the ecstasy of worship, the vision of God, the garden of paradise, and the new Jerusalem.[49] It is the symbol of

---

47. Suchocki, *God, Christ, Church,* p. 216.
48. Ann Graham Lotz, *Heaven: My Father's House* (Waco: Word, 2001).
49. Peters, *God — The World's Future,* p. 331.

our communion with God. Heaven symbolizes the overcoming of the death and despair which separate us from God. Heaven is not a place up in the sky, forty miles or four hundred million miles or someplace beyond the galaxies. It refers to our relationship with God, our abiding life in communion with God, and our fellowship as a community together in Christ.

What about hell? Hell, also, is a persisting idea in our culture. Sixty-four percent of Americans say they believe in hell, and only twenty-five percent say they do not. It is the subject of one of the best-known pieces of American literature read by every high school student, Jonathan Edwards's "Sinners in the Hands of an Angry God." As with heaven, many Christians think of hell as a physical place, a kind of inky inferno deep beneath the surface of the earth with an address. It is a place of torment, a pit, a lake of fire and brimstone with flames and a red-suited devil with a pitchfork. A few think of it only in the here and now. We create our own hell on earth through the suffering we create, such as with the Holocaust, Hiroshima, and the Twin Towers bombings.[50]

There is an alternative view of hell which takes the idea seriously but does not take bits of biblical imagery, or the imagery of our poets, literally. Hell is the absence of God, a symbol of the final absence of God. Hell is a state of being, a condition in which we live, here and hereafter, expressed through the imagery and symbols we all know. It is the state of being cut off from God, unaware of God anymore. As Pope John Paul II has said, heaven "is neither an abstraction nor a physical place in the clouds but a living and personal relationship with the Holy Trinity." Hell is not a physical place but "the state of those who freely and definitively separate themselves from God, the source of all life and joy."[51] Any Godforsaken condition is hell. Even Jesus knew this experience ("he descended into hell"), the depths and dregs of the most negative experience of separation from God we can imagine. Hell is any anguished state of existence apart from God and from those whom God loves. It is the suffering which results from our deprivation of the presence of God. It is the

---

50. Hell has a history, beginning in the Old Testament with the idea of Sheol, a place of semi-existence where all the dead go. It is then melded with the idea of Hades, which is a temporary abode of the wicked, and finally becomes the place where the wicked are condemned in a lake of fire. In the early church it referred variously to eternal death (Jerome), to a place of spiritual suffering or remorse and separation from God (Gregory of Nyssa), or to both (Augustine). Most Christians assume that what the Bible teaches is in fact what our Western poets have taught, that it is a multi-leveled subterranean chamber of horrors below ground, with nine circles at the earth's center in which Satan lives (Dante, elaborated by Milton and Blake). Calvin and Luther thought it was a place, but that the fiery torments are figurative, since the worst agonies are the terror and utter despair of spending eternity without God.

51. Quoted in Hanna Rosin, "Pope, Evangelicals Collide on View of Heaven, Hell," *Washington Post*, August 17, 1999, p. A2.

state in which no one praises God, where God's love is not known, where God's faithfulness is unknown, where God is not with us. We have a foretaste of hell as a dreadful condition when we experience the absence of God from our lives.

The idea of an eternal hell is, however, a deeply problematic idea for the Christian faith. Not only is it a dangerous ideology, a tool we can use to terrorize children, threaten those we are trying to control, or dismiss those of whom we disapprove; belief in hell as an eternal condition leaves us with the ultimate theodicy problem, namely, a God who has abandoned the vast majority of humanity hopelessly in their sins without providing any means for their salvation. Fortunately, even some conservative Christians today have tried to moderate the theodicy problem either through a doctrine of annihilationism, in which God simply withdraws the providential power to be from those who are not redeemed, so they are not eternally punished (Ezek. 18:4; 2 Tim. 1:9; Rev. 20:14), or through belief in their opportunity to know God after death.[52] In more liberal perspectives, God's love will ultimately lure all creatures to fellowship with God (universalism). But for modern Christians of all stripes, the most liberal to the most conservative, our belief in freedom seems to necessitate belief in a realm that eternally rejects God's love and grace.[53] I will deal in more detail below with the question of an everlasting hell.

V. Is Jesus the Only Way to God?

What happens to those who have never heard of Jesus Christ? Or to those who have heard and not responded in faith? Or to those who have responded positively to another faith? Within Christian hope, what is the destiny of persons of other faiths or of no faith at all?

Throughout most of its history the church has taught *exclusivism*. Salvation is possible only through Jesus Christ and the church. Most pre–Vatican II Roman Catholic theologians and most Protestant theologians have taught that Christianity is the one true religion. They interpret a handful of New Testament texts as teaching that Jesus is the only way to God: "The one who believes and is baptized will be saved; but the one who does not believe will be

---

52. Gabriel Fackre, "Divine Perseverance," in *What About Those Who Have Never Heard?: Three Views of the Destiny of the Unevangelized,* by Gabriel Fackre, Ronald H. Nash, and John Sanders, ed. John Sanders (Downers Grove, Ill.: InterVarsity, 1995), pp. 71-106.

53. Peters, *God — The World's Future,* p. 337.

condemned" (Mark 16:16). "No one comes to the Father except through me" (John 14:6). "There is salvation in no one else, for there is no other name under heaven given among mortals by which we must be saved" (Acts 4:12). These show, write Dennis Ockhold and W. Gary Phillips, "a consistent pattern of 'fewness' in redemption and 'wideness in judgment.'"[54] The majority of humanity is lost because they do not know Jesus as their Savior.

Exegetical questions surround these specific texts.[55] The question, however, is whether we should use these isolated texts or the logic of the gospel of God's love and mercy to answer our question. Stating the issue in this way, of course, implies that exclusivism finally stands in conflict with the Christian understanding of God's character, purposes, and power. I first raise a practical question. What are the consequences of the exclusivist position? Of the world's population, 67 percent is not Christian, and 94.7 percent is not Protestant. This means that either 67 percent or 95 percent of all humanity living today is lost. Is this conclusion consistent with belief in an all-loving God, who is "not willing that one should be lost," and an all-powerful God, who will fulfill God's sovereign will? A success rate of .333, which is exceptional in baseball where failure is the norm, or .075, is a less than impressive average for an all-loving and all-powerful God.

Beyond this quaint numbers game, however, the most telling case against exclusivism is that it is the most extreme form of the problem of evil.[56] Exclusivists assume every human being faces a predicament. All persons since Adam and Eve live in lack of faith in God. Without election or prevenient grace, there can be no faith and therefore no salvation. But the vast majority of humanity was and is trapped in double jeopardy. If this is the case, then, writes Schubert Ogden, "Through no fault of their own, by far most human beings have been allowed to remain in their sin without any prospect of salvation."[57] They had not or have not heard about Jesus Christ. So, as a conse-

---

54. Dennis Ockhold and W. Gary Phillips, "A Particularist View: An Evidentialist Approach," in *Four Views of Salvation in a Pluralistic World*, ed. Ockhold and Phillips (Grand Rapids: Zondervan, 1995), p. 238. See also Ronald Nash, *Is Jesus the Only Savior?* (Downers Grove, Ill.: InterVarsity, 1994), pp. 16-18.

55. See, for example, the significant differences between John Sanders's interpretation of the so-called exclusivist texts and the interpretation of Ronald Nash in *What About Those Who Have Never Heard?*, pp. 21-55 and 107-39. Furthermore, we can ask whether these texts teach philosophical and theological doctrine about the effectiveness of the religions, negating all religions apart from Christianity, or whether they are confessions of faith affirming the universal importance of what God did in Christ for both the church and the whole world.

56. Schubert Ogden, *Is There One True Religion, or Are There Many?* (Dallas: Southern Methodist University Press, 1992), pp. 50-52.

57. Ogden, *Is There One True Religion?* p. 51.

quence of their sin but also of their fate (they were by sheer accident born in the wrong place and time), they are abandoned by God to their own useless devices and are lost.

The horror of this kind of eschatology has prompted many Christians to look at other biblical and theological perspectives.[58] Their predicament has been stated in a personal account of one of my students:

> Late one night I was studying and conversing with a group of friends, none of whom happened to be Christian. We began to talk about our own belief systems and eventually the subject of hell become the focus of our discussions. By the end of the evening, my friend Mike leaned across the table, looked me in the eye, and asked, "Do you think *I'm* going to hell?" I realized that the only honest answer to his question was, yes, and that I had never been forced to look someone in the eye and say that before. The conversation ended, and we all returned to our rooms. When I arrived back at my room, I literally fell to my knees and wept at the reality that my theological perspective meant that some people, maybe even a lot of people, would spend eternity in terrible suffering and separation from God. I just couldn't bear that reality, and I spent the next three years looking for other plausible theological frameworks.[59]

The predominant plausible alternative framework today for many Christians is called *inclusivism*. There are New Testament texts which seem to interpret Christ's work as inclusive (John 12:32; Rom. 5:18; 1 Cor. 15:22-28; 1 Tim. 4:10; 2 Peter 3:9; and 1 John 2:2) and universally effective (Rom. 11:25-26; Eph. 1:9-10; Phil. 2:9-11; Col. 1:18-20; 1 Tim. 2:3-4; 1 John 2:2). Inclusivism is the claim that

---

58. Many have tried to mute the implications and consequences of exclusivism. A few have adopted a viewpoint called annihilationism, while others have adopted a view called "divine perseverance" into the next life. Others, however, maintain a traditional Calvinist version of sovereignty, omniscience, and election. The majority of humanity either have not or would not have chosen Christ if freely given the choice, and, therefore, they are rightly condemned forever. "It is equally plausible philosophically that God knows that all individuals who never hear the gospel are individuals who would not believe if they were to hear the gospel." Ockhold and Phillips, "A Particularist View," p. 270. Ronald Nash reflects the extreme Calvinist view: "God could conceivably desire all kinds of things to happen and still allow those things not to happen for some good reason, whether or not he chose to reveal the reason to us." Nash, *Is Jesus the Only Savior?* p. 135. Damnation is not unjust, according to such a view, since God defines justice, and predestines or permits the vast majority of humans to everlasting inhabitation of hell for God's own just reasons and to God's glory.

59. Amelia Fulbright Howard, Union Theological Seminary core group autobiography paper, 3.

there are other paths to God, but that the truth of the other religions is established by Christ and measured by him as the norm. Salvation outside the church is included within the efficaciousness of Christ's work. Inclusivists hold to the ontological necessity of the work of Christ for salvation (no one can be saved without him), but question the epistemological necessity of it (awareness of his work in order to benefit from him). Saved non-Christians participate in the one salvation constituted by Jesus Christ. Saving grace is a universally effective power of Christ through the Holy Spirit that touches individuals through some form of mystical awareness, moral consciousness, or knowledge of the truth by following their own conscience or by following faithfully the practices of their own religion. Non-Christians are saved through implicit faith in Christ, and so are imperfect, latent, hidden, or anonymous Christians.

> "I don't have this liberal, rational certainty, thank God, that once you die you die, and that's the end of it."
>
> NORMAN MAILER

Most Roman Catholic and some evangelical theologians have adopted some form of inclusivism. The watershed for inclusivism was Vatican II (1962-1965), which is now the official teaching of the Catholic church through its "Declaration on the Relationship of the Church to Non-Christian Religions."[60] Increasingly, evangelical Protestants — such as Sir Norman Anderson, Clark Pinnock, and John Sanders — have adopted a form of inclusivism as well.[61] According to such a view, it is only through Christ that anyone can be saved and only through his death and resurrection that salvation is possible. In the pre-Christian era, including Old Testament times, people were saved because they anticipated, and so expressed saving faith in, the redemption that was finally made effective in Christ. Furthermore, God has worked in the hearts of the followers of other religions through the Spirit to bring them to the realization of their sins, to repentance, and to throwing themselves on the mercy of God, through which they benefit from the propitiation of Christ.[62]

The strength of inclusivism is that it is not simply an ethics of civility within an increasingly vicious world. It is a way to maintain the finality of Christ while viewing the other religions as possible ways to God. The major

---

60. "Declaration on the Relationship of the Church to Non-Christian Religions," *Documents of Vatican II* (New York: Guild, 1966), pp. 660-68.

61. Clark Pinnock and John Sanders have even argued that certain biblical texts teach inclusivism, and that there are theological grounds for Christians to affirm the inclusive effectiveness of the work of Christ.

62. Sir Norman Anderson, *Christianity and the World Religions* (Downers Grove, Ill.: InterVarsity, 1984).

weakness, however, is that inclusivism is still one form of exclusivism. Non-Christians are saved by including them in the work of Christ as the only grounds for their salvation. "For it, too," writes Ogden, "there not only is but can be only one true religion, in the sense that Christianity alone can validly claim to be formally true."[63] It does not permit the other religions to define the truth in the way they understand the truth. It finally eliminates their truth by subsuming their truth under the definitive truth of the Christian faith.

The other major alternative today is called *pluralism*. Pluralists avoid the dangers of imperialism by teaching that there are many true religions. The other religions not only might be true but are true on a basis other than Christ. They are true on their own grounds. Christianity is one true religion among many true religions. We live in a theocentric universe where God is the infinite, mysterious, incomprehensible One. There are many ways to salvation, for the Ultimate Reality has no one exclusive way to salvation. People who worship in a church, synagogue, mosque, and temple worship the same Ultimate Reality or Really Real under different names, such as Yahweh, Trinity, Allah, Rama, and Krishna. Pluralists, however, do not claim that just any or every religion is true. They judge the truth of other religions on pragmatic grounds ("by their fruits"). Religions are each authentic spheres of salvation insofar as they are effective means of ultimate transformation from self-centeredness to a new orientation toward Ultimate Reality manifested in their fruits of spiritual, moral, and political transformation. When they produce good fruits, they lead their adherents to Ultimate Reality and are therefore true paths of salvation.

Here is the rub for pluralism, however. If you distinguish between true and false, better or worse, profound and trivial, according to how successful religions are, you have to have some criteria by which to judge what is good fruits and what is Ultimate Reality. The move from christocentrism to theocentrism is no improvement over exclusivism and inclusivism as forms of imperialism. Among the many world religions, theocentric and pragmatic views of God, truth, and goodness are at least as controversial as are exclusive or inclusive christocentric views. Theisms of any sort — Yahweh, Allah, Trinitarian, classical, process, or even Neoplatonic versions — are culturally situated views of God. A Neoplatonic theocentric view of reality is as distinctive to a certain kind of liberal Christian theology as is a christocentric view of reality to neo-orthodox or conservative Protestant strands of Christian theology.

This is why I recommend a viewpoint I call *confessional pluralism*. By that

---

63. Ogden, *Is There One True Religion?* p. 32.

I mean to affirm pluralism from a self-consciously Christian perspective. I speak within a community which confesses its faith as belief, trust, and loyalty to God in Christ and speaks about hope within the symbolic and doctrinal context of the faith of the church. I recommend confessional pluralism as a framework for a Christian theology of the world religions for three reasons.

First, there is no God's-eye view of anything. We have no transcendent grounds on which to say we know with certainty that other religions are true or false. We have no standpoint beyond our confessional communities — Jewish, Christian, Muslim, Buddhist, scientific, secular, humanistic, or atheistic. What I say is said from a Christian viewpoint. I accept not only the fact of relativity of perspectives and beliefs but the truth about the contextual nature of all our language, knowledge, social reality, and, indeed, reality itself.

Second, confessional pluralism makes strong claims about the universal significance of Christ. Christ is the icon and incarnation of God who is the creator, redeemer, and fulfiller of the whole world. Along with the other religions, which also can — and should, if they want — make claims about the universal significance of their religion, I make universal claims — though not absolute or exclusive ones — about the boundless significance of Christ. Christ is significant, available, effective, and normative for the whole world. As a Christian I witness to the unlimited significance of Christ's reality for everyone's forms of salvation.

Third, as a confessional pluralist, I can claim that the other religions can be, might be, or even are true from a Christian point of view. Each person of the triune God gives me grounds to affirm the ubiquitous work of God. The First Person, the creator and providential ruler of the whole world, creates and lures all creatures to the fulfillment of God's purposes for the creation. The Second Person, the Sophia or Logos of God, is incarnate in all of the creation, from beginning to end, including the many religions, and so works to transform all of the creation into the divine image. The Third Person, the Spirit, the Lord and Giver of Life, works through many means, including the religions of the world, to bring the creation to its completion.

Who will be saved in the end? Will the majority of humanity in the end be lost, or will all be saved? This is one of the most difficult quandaries to resolve in Christian theology today. In the New Testament itself, there are three irreconcilable positions.[64] It teaches, first, that salvation applies to some and not to others on the basis of who has faith (John 3:16; Rom. 1:16), or, second, that salvation applies to some and not to others on the basis of who does good works (Matt. 25). Third, it teaches the salvation of all by grace alone

64. Peters, *God — The World's Future*, p. 367.

(Rom. 5:18; 2 Cor. 5:15). An evangelical interpretation of the gospel as divine love and mercy directed toward all can lead to the "hypothesis" that salvation will be universal and hell cannot last forever, although the New Testament is not conclusive.[65]

In the end, the fundamental issue is whether we give the primary weight to the power of human freedom to turn away from God's love or to the power of God's love to lure all people freely to the love of God. If we affirm the ultimacy of God's love and power, we have the problem of how free the creature is, how genuine the fellowship is which does not depend on the free response of persons. If we affirm the genuineness of human freedom, however, we end up with the worst of the theodicy problem: the final defeat of the will and power of God, who was unable to complete what God began.[66] There is no knock-down solution to this dilemma!

The unthinkableness of one side of the quandary, however, led to a position in the early church known as *apokatastasis* (the universal restoration of all things). Not only *can* all be saved; ultimately, all *will* be saved in fellowship with God. If hell is everlasting, then Christians cannot avoid the conclusion that the creation is one vast cosmic tragedy. This conclusion can be avoided only by affirming that hell serves the glory of God, either as part of a decree for each person from eternity (double predestination), or because each person's freedom to deny God's love glorifies God through his or her choice for eternal damnation. Either way, their damnation glorifies God. Universalism is preferable to this horrific understanding of the glory of God!

Universalism has usually been considered a heresy. Nevertheless, it continues to attract many Christians today. And there are good theological reasons to teach it. Because God is love, wills the salvation of all, and is omnipotent (or at least sovereign), somehow, sometime, somewhere God's love will accomplish God's purposes. In this view, hell is temporally provisional, and purgative, and in the end all beings, angels, devils, women, and men will be complete in their fellowship with God because as free creatures they will turn toward God. Many Christians of whatever stripe believe that God wills this, but nevertheless believe that God cannot accomplish this because of human freedom. Let me be clear. The issue is not the reality of judgment and even hell within God's economy. The New Testament clearly teaches a future punishment because of sin. But it does not clearly teach that punishment is everlasting (Matt. 5:26; 18:34-35; 23:14; Luke 6:23-26). The issue is whether the righteous and sovereign God abandons most of the creatures to eternal pun-

---

65. Peters, *God — The World's Future*, p. 368.
66. Thomas, *Introduction to Theology*, p. 224.

ishment in hell, a punishment which apparently is for sheer retribution, or is at least pointless and useless (unless eternal punishment is a bizarre form of the glory of God).

Here I face one of the most irresolvable problems of theology. I must admit that I cannot affirm universalism as a *logical necessity* of Christian faith. On the basis of the ideas of creatural freedom and the limits of God's power, which I have defended throughout this book, I must grant that everlasting separation from God must be taught as a logical possibility. Instead, the fulfillment of God's will is *a hope and a promise* based upon the love and power of God as revealed in Jesus Christ.[67] If God is the God incarnate in Christ, the God of pure unbounded love, whose love is everlastingly faithful, and whose power is the power of the new creation, then we have all the grounds we need to affirm our hope and confidence that in the end that love and power will draw all creatures to God in God's own time and place.

Whether any of these speculations is the truth about the fate of the creature created in the image of God we do not know because we cannot know. The limits to the certainty of our claims, however, do not limit our faith in the power of God to transform the whole creation. Whatever the details of our hope do and do not entail, our hope is rooted in our faith — our belief, trust, and loyalty — in God. Our confidence is that God can and will complete what God began, a confidence that our lives are not lost in a meaningless mist of nothingness but are ultimately complete with God. We live in such hope and promise. The last thing to say is that the fate of the creation is in God's hands. We can affirm with Julian of Norwich that "all shall be well and all shall be well and all manner of thing shall be well."[68] That is part of the faith of the Christian church.

---

67. John Hick, *Evil and the God of Love*, revised ed. (New York: Harper, 1978), pp. 341-45.

68. Julian of Norwich, *Revelations of Divine Love* (New York: Penguin, 1998), pp. 24, 25, 83, 85, 86, 89. Originally published in the fourteenth century.

Glossary

Abelard, Peter (1079-1142) — Twelfth-century theologian most noted (apart from the love story) for his moral influence theory of atonement in which the cross teaches us about God's love, mercy, and forgiveness and inspires us to live our lives in terms of the love of God and neighbor.

Absolute/absolute — A term used by Christians to refer to God as a static, unconditioned, changeless, ultimate reality unaffected by finite being. Many today also use the term to refer to ultimate, unconditioned, and fixed truths contained in cognitive and moral propositions.

Adam and Eve — The primeval parents of the human race, understood by some as the first two human beings, of whom all other human beings are heirs and by whom the boundaries of human knowledge and freedom are set. Many understand them to have been created by God as complete and perfect human beings. Others understand them to be the two primary symbols of every man and every woman who emerged as human creatures (Heb. *'adam*) from the processes of the natural world (dust of the ground, Heb. *'adamah*).

adoptionism — The belief that Jesus was human in every way but was different in his superior righteousness, such that God appointed him or adopted him to be the Son of God either at his baptism, his temptations, or his suffering on the cross.

affections — Feelings; refers not merely to subjectivity but to basic sensibilities and intuitions which make the believer aware of God. Jonathan Edwards and John Wesley are two modern theologians who have made affections central to their understanding of Christian faith.

agapē — The completely unmotivated, self-giving love of God, which is to be distinguished from friendship *(filia)* and erotic love *(erōs),* which are motivated in part by the attractiveness of the other.

agnosticism — Literally, not to know. The term usually refers to skepticism about the existence of God based on our inability to know one way or the other. It is also used to refer to our inability to know with clarity or certainty many other claims.

amillennialism — An eschatological view which claims either that we cannot know the details of the end times or that there is not a scheme dividing history into a series of ages or time periods or stages which culminates in an apocalyptic end of history.

Anabaptist — Free church traditions which derive their historical origins from the "left wing" or Radical Reformation of the Protestant churches in Europe; refers to such denominations as the Mennonite, Brethren, and Baptist churches today.

analogy/analogical — A way of thinking and speaking in which one tries to show how our knowledge or talk about one thing is similar to and at the same time different from our knowledge or talk about something else. God-talk is analogical, for instance, in the sense that there are ways in which we can say God's knowledge is similar to ours (God knows the truth about the world) but at the same time that God's knowledge is unlike ours (God's knowledge of the world is infinite).

anamnesis — To remember, not only in the sense of recalling the past as a fact from the past but of participating in the recalled event so as to share its meaning and power in the present.

annihilationism — The eschatological doctrine that instead of condemning sinners to an everlasting punishment, God mercifully withdraws God's providential power to sustain the existence of these individuals, and they simply cease to exist instead of existing in an everlasting hell.

Anselm of Canterbury (1033-1109) — Eleventh-century British theologian best known for his view of theology as "faith seeking understanding" and his satisfaction theory of atonement, according to which the cross of Jesus satisfies (reestablishes and fulfills) the demands of justice and cosmic harmony by paying the price of restitution and thereby restoring God's honor.

anthropocentric — Human-centered thinking and valuing; all thought is oriented primarily if not exclusively to human perspectives and interests.

anthropomorphism — Describing God (or, in a larger context, talk about anything) according to the human framework; using language about the finite human creature to describe God.

Antichrist/antichrist — In contemporary apocalyptic theory, an evil figure who will roam the earth, threatening to control it until finally defeated by Christ in the battle of Armageddon. In its larger usage, a figure, power, or principle that stands counter to Christ, his gospel, and his way of life.

apatheia — Greek term used to describe God meaning that he is apathetic, not in the sense of not caring or unmotivated but in the sense that God's being is changeless in every respect (absolute) and therefore cannot be affected by anything that happens in the world.

apocalyptic/apocalypticism — A form of eschatology which presumes a dualistic cosmic conflict between the force(s) of good and the force(s) of evil in which the former wins a battle carried on within history; God has revealed through a vision what will happen in the near future when God intervenes through a cataclysm in the existing world to destroy the evil through violence and establish the kingdom of God. Many contemporary Christians believe we are living in the end times, which will culminate in the rapture (the return of Christ on the clouds to rescue the saints), followed by a cosmic struggle prior to the end of history and the day of judgment.

apokatastasis — An ancient doctrine of the church which teaches the universal restoration of all things to their original perfection or final unity or fulfillment.

Apollinarianism — A form of christology shaped by the thought of Apollinarius, who denied the two natures of Christ, divine and human, and thought of Christ as a divine being who in the incarnation took on a human body rather than full human nature.

apologetics — The effort to build an apology (a defense) of the Christian faith for skeptics based on an argument for the rationality of Christian belief and practice.

apophatic theology — A kind of theology which teaches that God is absolute mystery, is so transcendent and infinite and so radically different from any finite reality that when we make any statement about God we must follow the way of negation *(via negativa)* and say what God is not. See, in contrast, cataphatic theology.

Apostles' Creed — One of the earliest creeds of the church, and based on an ancient Western baptismal confession, its present form is usually dated from the ninth century in the Middle Ages. It continues to be the creed which almost all Christians in the West know and teach. (Some do not memorize it or repeat it publicly in worship but they still teach the content.)

apostolic — The faith of the church founded by the apostles, in the sense that the faith is derived either directly from the eyewitness testimony of the earliest apostles or from the witness of the earliest church as it is recorded in the canon.

apotheosis — Our deification or divinization, not in the sense of our being made into a god ourselves or becoming a part of the being of God but in the sense of infusion of the human with the divine energies or the process of the union of the human and the divine which is completed with the resurrection of the dead.

Aristotle (384-322 BCE) — Early Greek philosopher, who, along with Plato, had the most influence on Christian theology from its classical period up until modern times. He became a major influence in medieval theology and the key philosopher in Catholic theology from the Middle Ages up to modern times. He was most influential in theology by way of his logic and his emphasis on beginning the search for knowledge through empiricism and science instead of the realm of ideas. His teachings are known as Aristotelianism.

Arius (250-336) — A central figure in the christological controversy of the fourth century, Arius was declared to be a heretic by the Council of Nicea (325) for teaching that Christ was a created and therefore temporal being subordinate to God the Father, that Christ is the firstborn of all creation and therefore not of the same substance *(homoousia)* but rather of a similar substance *(homoiousia)* as the Father. Arius's teachings are called Arianism.

Armageddon — In contemporary apocalyptic theory, a place in Palestine, the city of Megiddo in the ancient Plain of Esdraelon, twenty miles southeast of Haifa, where Jesus will fight a cosmic battle with the antichrist and win, ushering in a thousand-year reign of Christ.

Arminianism — The belief taught by James Arminius (1560-1609) that God intends the salvation of all people, that Christ died for all humans (unlimited atonement), and that human free will is compatible with divine sovereignty; stress is therefore placed on the human response to the gospel. Arminianism had a strong influence on Wesleyanism.

aseity — Attribute of God which describes him as self-existent, depending on no one or nothing for existence.

Athanasius (296-377) — Key figure in the christological controversy responsible for establishing orthodox christology at Nicea in 325. Athanasius argued against Arius by maintaining that Jesus Christ must be both fully God (of the same substance as the Father) and fully human (of the same substance as human beings) or else salvation would not be possible.

atheism — Literally, no theism. In the strictest sense atheism is the denial that the kind of God described by theism exists; in the larger sense, it is the denial of the reality of any kind of divinity.

atonement — At-one-ment; an interpretation of how Jesus' life, and especially his cross and resurrection, effects our reconciliation with God. The dominant interpretations are *christus victor,* moral example, satisfaction, and substitution.

attributes of God — Qualities or characteristics of God, such as all-knowing, all-loving, all-powerful.

Augustine (354-430) — Late-fourth-century and early-fifth-century North African theologian who is perhaps the most influential theologian in the Western church, both Protestant and Catholic. Although a thoroughly Catholic theologian in his many of his concepts, such as the Trinity, christology, and the church, he is best known in Protestant theology for the influence of his anthropology, namely, his doctrine of original sin.

authority — The basis or criterion by which judgment of belief about the truth and rightness of practice is made. In Protestant theology, Scripture is usually held to have a unique authority (*sola Scriptura,* primacy, sufficiency), although the relation of Scripture to tradition, experience, and reason appears in any discussion of authority in theology.

baptism — One of the two (Protestant) or seven (Catholic) sacraments of the church, it is a ritual entailing the use of water and a formula, which serves as the vehicle or means of grace by which individuals are incorporated into the universal church as the body of Christ. Some Christians believe baptism washes away the guilt of original sin; others believe it is our public confession of faith in Christ; others believe it is the means of initiation into the church.

Barmen Declaration (1934) — A confession of faith written primarily by Karl Barth for the Confessing Church in Germany (which consisted of members of the Lutheran, Reformed, and United churches of Germany), declaring the Lordship of Jesus Christ for Christians instead of loyalty to *Der Führer* (Hitler) and calling on the Confessing Church to stand against the German Christian accommodation to National Socialism. It can be found in the ninth confession of faith in the Presbyterian Book of Confessions.

Barth, Karl (1886-1968) — A Swiss-German Protestant theologian, and the most influential Protestant theologian of the twentieth century (along, perhaps, with Paul Tillich), who was known as the father of dialectical or neo-orthodox theology from the 1930s through the 1960s. Barth was one of the most christocentric theologians in the history of Christian theology, claiming that theology is the proclamation and interpretation of the Word of God only, which is incarnate in Jesus Christ, written in the Scriptures, and proclaimed by the church; theology is not grounded in human experience or reason (philosophy) but in God's revelation. Barth remains a very influential theologian today in the work of the postliberal and narrative theologians.

being/Being — The most basic concept in Western philosophy, being is the most fundamental characteristic of anything that can be said to exist (it possesses being or the power of being). When capitalized as Being or Being-itself, the concept is the abstract reference to God, the ultimate reality (Being-itself), or the ultimate power of the world (the power to be); Paul Tillich is the great modern representative of this form of theology.

Bible — The name applied to the collection of books (for Protestants thirty-nine Old Testament and twenty-seven New Testament) which constitute the Scripture or canon of the church. Debates about the nature of the authority of Scripture in the church and in theology center around discussions of the meaning of the Bible as the word of God, and whether or how it is inspired, infallible, inerrant, primary, or sufficient for belief and practice.

biblical criticism — The critical approach to Scripture which uses modern methods of the scientific study of texts to understand the original texts (lower criticism), the historical origins of the texts, the original meaning of the authors of the texts (higher criticism), or the meaning and use of the texts by the original readers or the contemporary readers of the texts (canon criticism).

biblical theology — A twentieth-century movement in biblical studies and theology for which the Bible is the source and norm for theological ideas, developed through tracing either theological doctrines or major themes in the texts for use in systematic theology. Sometimes the categories of systematic theology are used to organize and interpret biblical stories, symbols, and themes.

black theology — A North American liberation theology, begun by James Cone in 1969, in which the gospel is interpreted within the context of black oppression and for the liberation of black people (and the liberation of all oppressed people).

Bonhoeffer, Dietrich (1906-1945) — A student of Karl Barth who published works on the church, christology, and ethics, and a twentieth-century martyr to Nazism because of his resistance. Bonhoeffer was one of the promising theologians in Germany who returned from the United States to Germany in the 1930s to train pastors for the Confessing Church in Germany.

born again — A phrase used by many evangelical Christians to describe an experience of conversion they have undergone. Also, in the larger sense, the regeneration which occurs at baptism in which the spiritual life is renewed and set on the path toward sanctification.

Bultmann, Rudolf (1884-1976) — Twentieth-century German Protestant biblical scholar and theologian who is most noted for his form-critical study of the Bible, for his program of demythologizing Scripture (interpreting its mythical language in modern language), and for his existential interpretation (using the language of existential philosophy as the modern language for interpreting the meaning of myth and of the gospel).

Calvin, John (1509-1564) — Sixteenth-century Swiss Reformer theologian whose *Institutes of the Christian Religion* constituted the first full statement of Protestant theology. Calvin was most noted for his emphasis on the grace of God through his interpretation of the sovereignty of God (which resulted in his doctrine of divine election, which he interprets as predestination), for his emphasis on the total depravity of human nature (the way in which sin corrupts the entire range of human activity, including religion), and for his substitutionary theory of the atonement; salvation is also a major theme, through which he provided a Protestant interpretation of justification and sanctification.

canon — The books of the Bible, which are used as the primary source and final norm for the church's faith and practice. The first known reference to the twenty-seven books that now make up the New Testament canon came from Athanasius, bishop of Alexandria, in a letter to the churches throughout Egypt, also proscribing the reading of books we now refer to as noncanonical, such as the Nag Hammadi texts.

cataphatic theology — A type of theology which teaches that God and the world share enough affinity (being) that we can build what we say about God on the basis of God's being the ultimate expression or form of things we say about the world; God is power, knowledge, and wisdom, but is the limitless or ultimate form of these finite things we know. See, in contrast, apophatic theology.

catholic/Catholic — When used with a lowercase "c," refers to the teachings and practices of the church universal. When used with a capital "C," especially when used by Protestants, refers to the Roman Catholic Church, to be distinguished from the Orthodox (Eastern, Russian, Greek, or others) Church as well as from the various Protestant churches.

Chalcedon — The fifth ecumenical church council which, in 451, reaffirmed Nicea and Constantinople and also declared the doctrine that Jesus Christ is one person in two natures, human and divine, which are united but not mixed in the one person.

charismata — Gifts of grace, freely bestowed gifts of the Holy Spirit given to the believer. There are various gifts of the Spirit named in the New Testament, ranging from unremarkable gifts, such as knowledge and wisdom, to remarkable gifts such as miraculous healing, prophecy, tongues, and interpretation of tongues, to fruits of the Spirit, such as love, joy, and peace; some of these are viewed as given to some but not to others in the church for some useful purpose to the church.

Christ — A title, *Christos* is the Greek word for the Jewish idea of Messiah. The term is applied to Jesus in the New Testament to describe his special relationship with God. When used in the name "Jesus Christ," the term points to Jesus who is the Christ or Jesus who is called the Christ by the earliest church.

Christendom — Those post-Constantinian societies or cultures that have been shaped predominantly by the Christian church and its symbols, ecclesiastical structures, and power. Today the term is frequently used pejoratively to indicate a Western culture that has co-opted and corrupted the true gospel and the church's message and mission; many Christians celebrate the end of Christendom in light of their understanding of the gospel, while others are attempting to restore their understanding of the church and its symbols, moral values, and purpose.

christocentric/christocentrism — Christ-centered. The neo-orthodox theology of the twentieth century was perhaps the most thoroughly Christ-centered theology in the history of the church in the sense that its proponents claimed that all doctrines are derived from or completely dependent upon christology for their basis and meaning. (Barth's theology is frequently described as a christocentric theology.) Christocentric theology can be distinguished from a christomorphic (Christ-shaped) theology or a theology which is christological (Christ is a decisive center though not the only source or norm of the theology).

christology — The theological study of the significance and meaning of Jesus as God with us and of the way he is significant for our salvation.

christology from above — A christology which begins from above, that is, from the Johannine theology of the Word made flesh or from the christological creeds of the church, and then moves to a consideration of the human Jesus or the humanity of Jesus who was God incarnate.

christology from below — A christology which begins from below, that is, from the Jesus of history (as constructed by historical scholarship) or from the earliest church's recollection of Jesus and testimony to him, and moves then to ask how we can speak of him as God or the Word of God incarnate.

Christus Victor — The atonement theory in which Christ is victor over the powers of sin, death, and the Devil, the powers that enslave us, by defeating them through his victory on the cross and resurrection, thereby freeing us from the power of sin and death. Liberation theologians provide a variation on this theory by understanding the powers we are freed from to be political, social, and economic oppression, such that Jesus is more a liberator from these powers than a military victor and we are to follow his example and carry out his work of liberation of the oppressed.

Church Fathers — The early church theologians of the first five centuries, which is sometimes called the patristic period; they usually include the pre- and post-Nicene theologians who set the course and direction for the theology of the Orthodox, Catholic, and Protestant churches. The Church Fathers include the apostolic fathers, the apologists, Origen, Tertullian, Cyprian, Athanasius, and culminate with John of Damascus in the Orthodox Church and Isidore of Seville in the Catholic church.

classical — The dominant theological tradition in the church, usually referring to the earlier period of the history of the church, most especially to the period of the development of the creeds. The term also refers to the mainstream tradition of beliefs and practices which has continued throughout the history of all of the major branches of the Christian churches; it is sometimes used as a synonym for traditional or orthodox beliefs.

common grace — The grace of God, which is part of the creation itself. It may be the "residue" of grace which survived the fall and is still faintly known by all creatures apart from or independent of saving grace (through justification and sanctification), or it may be the "restoration" of the grace of creation and human freedom given to all creatures through benefits of Christ (prevenient grace).

confession of faith — In the most general sense, the confession (I/we declare) of faith in Jesus Christ as Lord and savior; also the adherence to the broad traditions of the faith of the church; finally, the written confessions of faith of the various denominations, especially the documents of the various denominations which declare their understanding of the gospel and their distinctive beliefs.

conservative/conservatism — As a noun, refers to a person who wants to preserve or to return to traditional beliefs. As an adjective, refers to a particular temperament, namely, a desire to be in continuity with the past and to preserve the past in the present. Theological conservatism is an effort to preserve the doctrines and practices of Scripture and the mainstream of the Christian church, specifically, the beliefs and practices which most Christians accept as derived from Scripture and embodied in the traditions of the church. Conservative Christians might be described both temperamentally and substantively as traditionalists in the style and content of their beliefs and practices.

constructive theology/constructivism — A type of theology which maintains that the task of theology is not to repeat the past interpretations of the symbols and beliefs of the church but to construct contemporary meanings of these symbols and beliefs for the contemporary believer.

cosmology — A study of the origin, development, and structure of the cosmos as a whole. Sometimes the term is used loosely to refer to the worldview or the large perspective of a particular era; the cosmology of the biblical period(s) is different from the cosmology of the modern scientific era.

covenant — An agreement between two parties, either between equals (as in a modern contract) or between unequals (in which case the superior party elects the inferior party and the latter agrees to be faithfully obedient to the former, as in the biblical notion of covenant).

creatio ex nihilo — Latin for creation out of nothing. The term can mean creation out of nothingness, the state in which nothing exists, or can mean creation of a structured world out of a pre-existing chaos, in which no thing exists. There is a debate about which is the biblical view, and even about how Genesis 1 is properly interpreted amidst other biblical views of creation, although many hold that the former view is central to Christian faith, regardless of how Scripture is exegeted.

creation, doctrine of — The doctrine that the world in its origins, structure, and purposes is ultimately dependent on the power, will, and purposes of God. Christians today disagree on whether modern science, and especially Big Bang theory and evolution, are compatible with a doctrine of creation or not; all agree that the doctrine affirms the dependence of the world on God and the goodness of the creation as the work of God.

creation science/creationism — Late-twentieth-century view among some evangelicals and fundamentalists that the creation stories in the Bible are a factual account of origins; its proponents claim that evolution is "only a theory" (a hypothesis) with no proof to confirm it, and that the biblical story of a ten-thousand-year-old, six-day creation and of a special human creation is just as compatible with the scientific "facts" and therefore must be taught as an alternative plausible scientific theory. This view has been institutionalized in the Creation Science Institute in San Diego, California, and its many publications, including alternative science textbooks in secondary schools and colleges.

creeds — Documents declared by church councils to be official teachings of the catholic church; sometimes creeds are referred to as dogmas. For most Christians the creeds of the church derive from the first six or seven ecumenical councils prior to the "split" within Christendom in the Middle Ages. The most familiar creed to almost all Christians is the Apostles' Creed, though most accept (at least the content of) the Nicene and Chalcedonian creeds as statements of the true faith of the Christian church.

critical thinking — A way of thinking and speaking which analyzes language, including images, symbols, sentences, and comprehensive views, with an effort to understand the meaning and truth of the language. To think critically does not mean to deny or to denigrate beliefs but rather to be analytical in order to interpret, understand, justify, or revise as well as reject ideas.

death of God theology — A theological movement in the 1960s in which various theologians (Gabriel Vahanian, William Hamilton, Thomas Altizer, Paul van Buren, Richard Rubenstein) argued that God, or at least the concept of God, was no longer alive at the end of modern world; also referred to as "radical theology."

deconstruction — A late-twentieth-century term in philosophy and literary criticism derived from the French philosopher Jacques Derrida; a strategy of analysis which deconstructs classical beliefs by stressing the bias, limited perspective, arbitrariness, exploitation, and oppression involved in texts and modes of thinking. Deconstructionism denies any epistemological certainty or transcendental or unconditioned truth in any belief or practice.

deification — Another term for *apotheosis* (divinization).

deism — The concept of God according to which God created the world and since then has withdrawn from any active participation, allowing the world to run on its own power, principles, and structures without any divine intervention, determination, or direction since it was set in motion.

demonic — Refers to powers and structures of the world which are beyond individuals, and to personal decisions or actions which enslave, oppress, and destroy; many identify demonic powers with the Devil, while others hold that while there may not be devils or demonic beings which occupy and control the earth or the air, there are powers, forces, or structures of evil which transcend individual and personal decisions and work destruction and despair within the creation.

demythologize — To interpret the biblical language of myth, including its cosmology of a three-story universe in which demons and angels traffic between heaven, earth, and the underworld to interfere with human existence, into another kind of language, usually the language of philosophy. Rudolf Bultmann, for example, translated the language of myth into the language of existentialist philosophy (freedom, decision, and commitment).

dialectic/dialectical — Reasoning method according to which the truth or full reality of an idea consists of both the affirmation and the negation of the idea, which results in a new synthesis; the idea that both sides or poles of an idea, a conflict, or a distinction are necessary to the whole truth of the belief.

dispensationalism — A theory of history which divides time into discrete time periods, typically seven of them from creation to the present evil age; we are living in the last period (the end times), before the sweep of this history will be completed and judged.

divided self — Paul's doctrine that the self is so conflicted at its center that what we want to do we do not do and what we do not want to do we do (Rom. 7:18-19). The central problematic of soteriology in much Protestant theology has been shaped by this Pauline doctrine.

Docetism — The heresy that Jesus was not human but only appeared to have human flesh and blood, emotions, fallibilities, and ability to die. (In the Greek, the term means "to seem" or "to appear.") Nicea and Chalcedon repudiated any form of docetism.

doctrine — An agreed-upon teaching of the church which has been declared to be an official teaching in some kind of assembly (council or conference), resulting in some kind of document(s). In some Protestant churches that claim to be nondoctrinal, doctrine is established and conveyed through less formal means, such as sermons, hymns, liturgy, Bible study, or prayer groups.

dogma/dogmatic theology — An official teaching of the catholic church set forth in creedal form through a church council. Dogmatic theology is theology based on and restricted to the subject matter and the guidelines of the dogmas of the church.

dualism — The doctrine that there are two ultimate realities, a good Spirit or power or unseen reality and a bad Spirit or power or unseen reality; these are in a cosmic conflict with each other until one prevails. Dualism also refers to the doctrine that human beings consist of two dissimilar substances (which somehow are mysteriously conjoined during life until the one is released from the other at death), one, mind, and the other, body or matter; this doctrine from Greek philosophy stands in contrast to the Hebrew teaching that humans constitute one reality, which includes body, spirit, and soul.

ecclesiology — The study of or theological doctrine relating to the church.

Economic Trinity — An interpretation of the triune name and formula as a summary of the three ways we experience the creative and redemptive work of God; Father, Son, and Holy Spirit refer to the divine economy, to how God's work is experienced by us as creating, redeeming, and sanctifying, so we speak of God as creator, redeemer, and sanctifier.

ecumenical — Relating to the unity of the church. The Ecumenical Movement in the twentieth century attempted to make visible the spiritual unity of the church in various concrete and symbolic forms.

election — The idea that God has chose certain individuals (the elect), who are ultimately unknown to and unknowable by us, from among the mass of sinners to be saved and to carry out God's purposes in the world; or the idea that all humanity has been elected by God through Jesus Christ (Karl Barth).

Emmanuel — A name for Christ meaning "God with us." This designation is frequently used to summarize what is the core of the affirmation about the incarnation of God in Christ.

empiricism — A kind of philosophy or theology which appeals to experience as the source and norm of beliefs. Empiricism in philosophy sometimes takes the form of a philosophical naturalism, in which evolutionary naturalism and a scientific understanding of the natural world provide the viewpoint and definition of what there is to know and how we know it. In some theological naturalism, the breadth and depth of human experience are appealed to, not simply sense data but experience of relations and values (William James, for example). Some theologians, such as John Wesley, have an empirical orientation because they believe that we know God in experience in the sense that we have, in addition to the five senses, a spiritual sense, by means of which we know God.

Enlightenment — The movement in modern Western culture from the mid-seventeenth through the mid-twentieth century which rejected the authority of tradition and affirmed a body of attitudes and ideas which appealed to critical reason, in both its deductive and its inductive forms, and to an experimental power of the mind as the basis of clarity and certainty and therefore of all knowledge. The movement includes, also, a wide range of additional values which have become characteristic of modernity, such as individuality, autonomy, subjectivity of the self, analysis, control, objectivity of nature and knowledge, science, technology, linear progress, and domination of nature.

episcopacy — Form of church government (polity) in which bishops are essential. Churches with this form of government are said to have an episcopal polity.

epistemology — Theory of how we know what we know, either through authority, intuition, faith, reason, experience, experiment, science, wager, subjectivity, or some other means.

eschatology — The doctrine of "last things"; in theology eschatology encompasses the larger question, "What is it that Christians can hope for?" Eschatology may take the form of apocalyptic, progress, or various other forms.

Essentialist Trinity — An interpretation of the doctrine of the Trinity which understands the triune name and formula as describing the inner essence or being of God; the godhead or divine essence consists of three Persons and their eternal relationships, and theology attempts to describe the nature and economy of these relationships, or to affirm that the Trinity is a mystery.

eternal decrees — Decisions laid down by God before or at the beginning of time. The term can refer to a wide range of reality, such as the structure of the world and how the world operates, or it can refer to what will happen in history, in every detail or in the overall sweep of history, and what will happen in the life of each individual, including her birth, details of every event in her life, and her eternal destiny. In the most technical sense, the idea refers to whether or not the individual is among the elect.

eternity — A realm or mode of being that includes unchanging forms and immutable realities, including God, that exist outside of time, beyond time, untouched by what happens within time. The eternal is unaffected by time and so changeless, immutable, impassible; negatively stated, the concept of time does not apply to eternity, or, positively stated, in eternity the perceptions and conceptions of past, present, and future are simultaneous.

Eucharist — A term for the sacrament of bread and wine that emphasizes thanksgiving.

evangelical — Particularly on the Continent, the term is used to refer to a Protestant in distinction from a Roman Catholic Christian. In America, the term is used to describe Christians who locate the source, norm, and center of their faith in the New Testament gospel or "good news"; most Protestant theologians would consider themselves evangelical in this sense. Finally, in North America and England, "evangelical" can refer to Christians who emphasize the internal appropriation of the gospel through an experience of being "born again." Evangelicalism is formed by such movements as pietism, Puritanism, Methodism, and a series of revivalistic movements which have developed a kind of "religious technology" along with a particular understanding of salvation and a set of doctrines considered central to Scripture and salvation; doctrinally evangelicals claim to represent the mainstream teachings of the orthodox church throughout the ages, which are believed to be derived from the Bible.

exclusivism — The teaching that all who do not know Jesus Christ are doomed to everlasting punishment, either because they are not among the elect or because they do not elect God during their lifetime; salvation is exclusive to Christians.

exegesis — The interpretation or explanation of the meaning of texts; in theology, exegesis is the explanation of the meanings of the words, verses, and chapters of the Bible. Hermeneutics is the set of principles by which one exegetes texts.

existentialism — A twentieth-century philosophical movement in the West in which anxiety and despair that are the result of our being "thrown toward death" at our birth are emphasized; the reality, freedom, and necessity of our having to make choices or decisions of how to live in the midst of this situation are also stressed. Religious existentialism is characterized by an understanding of God as the call to decision and the basis of our security by which we are free to live in faith in God. Rudolf Bultmann and Paul Tillich are the major representatives of religious existentialism in the twentieth century.

expiation — An interpretation of the Old Testament sacrificial system and the cross in the New Testament in which the forgiveness of sin or the removal of sin from the sight of God, and the means by which this is accomplished, is emphasized.

faith — The way we know God in which assent (believing that a teaching of the Scripture or the church is true), or trust (confidence in God's grace, mercy, and acceptance is felt and expressed), or loyalty (faithfulness to Christ and his way of life) are stressed.

fall, the — Adam's and Eve's free decision to disobey the command of God, as a result of which they "fell" from their state of perfection or original righteousness. As a result of the fall, human nature was corrupted, making all humans now prone to sin until redeemed; the consequences of the fall include guilt, suffering, and death.

feminist theology — One of the forms of contemporary liberation theology which, first, begins as a hermeneutic of suspicion to uncover the patriarchal character of classical Christian theology and practice, and, second, follows with an attempt to interpret or reconstruct the meaning of Christian symbols, practices, and beliefs in a revolutionary way that supports the full humanity of women (and ultimately all humanity). In its more radical forms (non-Christian or marginally Christian), feminist theology attempts to construct religion and religious symbols on the basis of women's experience alone, with no appeal to the authority or even the language of the Christian faith.

fideism — An epistemology which asserts that we do not know or believe the Christian faith on the bases of any evidence or proof or any other basis than sheer belief.

filioque — Latin for "and the Son." This phrase was added to the Niceno-Constantinopolitan Creed at the Council of Toledo (589) to say that the Holy Spirit proceeds from both the Father and the Son (rather than from the Father alone). It was inserted in part as a strategy in the Western church's struggle for papal dominance, and was rejected by the Eastern church. Arguments against it include, first, that it is a violation of the ecumenical principle in determining the faith of the church through a council of the whole church, and second, that it can be interpreted as subordinationism of the Holy Spirit. Arguments for it include, first, that it ties the Holy Spirit closely to Christ, and, second, that it upholds the principle of the unity of the Trinity.

first-order language — The primary language of faith learned and used prior to any judgment, interpretation, or critical analysis of that language; examples include "Jesus Christ is Lord," the biblical stories and symbols, the Apostles' Creed, and the language of liturgy of the church.

foundationalism — The belief that the truth of an idea depends upon being able to establish the clarity, assured grounds, and certainty of the idea or belief. Foundations are sought in theology through logical necessity, empirical verification or falsification, universal human experience, or some experience or document or teaching that is taken to be revealed.

free will/freedom — The capacity of human beings to make decisions and to choose. The debate in theology is whether humans are inherently free, and whether they have any freedom after the fall (either as a result of some freedom remaining after the fall or as a result of it being restored on the basis of the prevenient grace of God as a result of the work of Christ).

free-will theism — A contemporary form of evangelical theology which emphasizes the self-limitation of divine omnipotence and therefore the (provisional) reality and importance of human free will in understanding sin and evil and salvation. Free-will theism has several affinities with process theology on the nature of human freedom and the limits of divine power; it is strongly countered among other evangelicals in persisting forms of Calvinism.

fundamentalism — A specific twentieth-century form of evangelicalism. It is, first, an attitude and mentality which perceives the modern world as an enemy that is to be challenged and resisted as a persistent antagonist of Christian faith. It is also a specific social and theological movement that has waxed and waned throughout the twentieth century as an effort to demarcate Christians sharply from the modern world and to combat modernity's influence on Christian doctrine by formulating a distinct body of beliefs and practices which are identified as the true Christian beliefs ("the fundamentals"). The typical identifying mark of fundamentalism is the claim that the Bible is "infallible" or "inerrant."

general revelation — *See* revelation, general.

Gnosticism/Gnostic — A movement in the early church, especially in the second and third centuries, that emphasized the need for true knowledge for salvation and claimed that Jesus was a revealer of special knowledge *(gnosis),* either an esoteric knowledge of another real world which leads to the salvation of those who know it, or the true self-knowledge that God is within us or we are part of God. Gnostics were considered to be heretics by those who determined the canonical Gospels and those who defined orthodox doctrine. Gnostic ideas have reappeared in the church as a result of the discovery of the extracanonical Gospels and the New Age revival of interest in the "divine spark" that lies dormant within the religiously sensitive person; salvation is thought to be the attainment of true knowledge of ourselves, our divine natures (or spark or potential), and our oneness with the cosmos as a whole.

gospel/Gospel — "Good news." Spelled with a lowercase "g," the word refers to the content of the primary witness and interpretation of Jesus as God with us. Capitalized, the term refers to a literary form, namely, the four Gospels in the New Testament and/or other early Gospels not included in the canon.

grace — God's graciousness toward and God's presence with us either through the creation itself, through Jesus Christ, or through the sacraments of the church. "Grace" refers to the divine power through the divine presence in contrast to human effort or power.

han — A Korean term, developed in Minjung theology, used to describe to the condition of exploitation, repression, and oppression of the poor, both individuals and groups, and the pain of unjustly oppressed persons and groups. Its major contribution to contemporary theology is the argument that the Christian understanding of sin in the West is too narrow because it confines the understanding of sin to individual sin and the guilt of the individual sinner and her condemnation and forgiveness (with injustice as simply the consequence of individual sin and guilt). In Minjung theology, the concept of sin must include the sinned-against, her pain and bitterness and sense of helplessness, so that salvation includes not simply the forgiveness of the sinner but also the establishment of justice for the sinned-against.

heaven — A place, state, or condition of fellowship with God in soul or body, usually thought of as being obtained as a result of either justification or sanctification. Heaven is usually thought of as everlasting.

hell — A place, state, or condition of anguished existence following death or the final judgment. Many think of it as the condition of separation from God, although it is more typically thought of as a place where people suffer fiery torments as punishment for their wickedness or unredeemed status before God. Hell is usually thought of as everlasting.

henotheism — The belief that there are many gods but one supreme God. Much of the Old Testament was henotheistic rather than monotheistic: the Israelites recognized the existence of other deities but believed that Yahweh, their God, was supreme.

heresy — False teaching; a view contrary to the official teaching of the church.

heretic — A person who denies one of the orthodox teachings of the church either by refusing to accept it or by repudiating it. Most heretics, however, have been declared such because they were one-sided in their talk about a particular doctrine or failed to affirm the full truth of the doctrines of the church. In wider usage, "heretic" refers to someone who does not speak the true or the whole gospel; sometimes the term is used to mean little more than someone who disagrees with my beliefs.

hermeneutics — In general usage, the process of interpretation of texts. More technically used, though, the term refers to the theory or principles of interpretation which undergird, inform, and guide the process of interpretation the interpreter is using; theology as hermeneutics understands theology to be only the interpretation of biblical texts.

hermeneutics of suspicion — A term used to point out that since the interpretation of a text is shaped by the presuppositions, past experiences, contemporary experiences, community interests, expectations, desires, interests, and social location of the interpreter, these influences, either consciously or unconsciously, shape the way we interpret the meaning of a text; therefore, we should approach a text with an awareness of a gap in meaning between the text and our interests. A hermeneutic of suspicion should thus make us aware of the way our interpretations mask an ideology that reflects and preserves the power and interests of the social group of interpreters, especially their race, gender, and class.

historical Jesus — A term to describe Jesus of Nazareth, the actual Jesus of past history, as he existed prior to his resurrection and the church's interpretation of him as the Christ, insofar as he is knowable through reconstruction by way of empirical research, that is, by modern historical methods and conclusions of modern scholarship (the Jesus of history). More broadly, the term refers to the claim that the Jesus who is the object of faith is not a mythical figure but an actual historical figure from history, regardless of what detailed historical knowledge we do or do not have of him.

historical theology — The branch of theology that studies the history of theological doctrines in their context. Much historical theology is done with an eye to why and how the past history of theology can and should shape contemporary theology as both a source and a norm for belief today.

history — In the broadest sense, time and the change over time (so nature has a history); more typically, refers specifically to the realm of human decisions and acts and their consequences (so to human history); also refers to events in the past (history); finally, refers to the study of the past and the results of that study in order to interpret it (historiography).

Hodge, Charles (1797-1878) — Nineteenth-century Calvinist theologian who provided the theological foundations of modern American fundamentalism through his "Princeton theology," an interpretation of the Scriptures as the word of God that provides theology with the data it then puts in systematic form. The Bible serves for theology what data serve for the scientist, namely, as the source of facts which provide us the objective truth about nature (science) or God (theology).

Holy Communion — Sacrament or ordinance of bread and wine. This term for the sacrament emphasizes the communion between the recipient and Christ; it is also known by other names such as the Lord's Supper, Mass, and Eucharist.

Holy Spirit — The Spirit of God and/or Christ, conceived in Scripture through the images of wind or breath or fire, who is seen as effective throughout the whole of creation from beginning to end, in the creation and maintenance of the church, and through gifts to individuals. Dogma defines the Holy Spirit as God in the sense of being the Third Person of the triune identity of God.

homiletics — The preaching of the church, or, in the more technical sense, the study of the art of preaching.

homoousia — Greek word translated as "substance," such that Jesus as the incarnate Word is "of the same substance" as the Father (and the Spirit). *Homoousia* is the word used in the Nicene and Chalcedonian Creeds to refer to the divine essence ("one substance in three Persons"), in contrast to *homoiousia*, which means "of a similar substance."

hypostasis — Greek word translated as "substance" but which refers to the essence of something and which was used by the early church in the doctrine of the Trinity to refer to the three "Persons" of the Godhead, each as an individual identity.

hypostatic union — Theological phrase referring to the union of the two natures, divine and human, in the one person of Jesus Christ. It affirms both the personal unity and the two natures.

idealism — A philosophical view which holds that mind, ideas, and spiritual values are fundamental in the world as a whole. It rejects the view that mind and spiritual values have emerged from or are reducible to material things and processes. Plato was an idealist in the sense that he believed ideas or forms were eternal and existed in an eternal realm prior to their being embodied in the material world.

ideology — The ideas which create the basis from which one thinks about and approaches issues; often the term is used to indicate that these ideas are rigidly held and imposed.

image of God — The condition in which humans were created, such that we share and represent some quality or qualities of God, such as immortality, freedom, transcendence, language, or relationality. Sometimes it is thought of as the condition of relationship in which Adam and Eve originally existed and to which we will be restored. Jesus Christ is the full image of God.

immanence — The nearness of God; God is related to, involved with, and present in the world.

immortal/immortality — Not liable to the finitude and death which are characteristic of things in time. The soul is often conceived as intrinsically immortal in the sense that it has always existed or is a special creation that was created to be immortal and goes to the eternal realm once it has escaped its entrapment in the material realm.

imputed righteousness — The transfer of the righteousness of Christ, based on his obedience and sacrifice, to us. God looks at us through the lens of Christ to see us as if we were righteous, although we remain sinners as we are united with Christ in faith.

incarnation — The doctrine that God is with us in Jesus Christ, that God became or came to us in flesh or human form in Jesus Christ.

inclusivism — The belief that all are included in the work of Christ, either potentially (to the extent that they respond in faith to Christ) or actually (in the sense that God objectively redeemed the whole world in Christ and the benefits of his work are extended to the whole creation through the various forms of faith).

inerrancy — A term applied by fundamentalists to Scripture, which claims that the Bible does not and cannot lead us to any errors of any kind of knowledge, including scientific and historical facts. The Bible is free of any of the errors which result from finite and historical limitations of perception, language, or knowledge.

infallibility — A term applied by Christians to Scripture to indicate that it is a completely trustworthy guide to the life of faith and will not fail to accomplish its purpose. Roman Catholics also apply the term to papal pronouncements made *ex cathedra* (from the chair); according to this understanding of papal infallibility, adopted at Vatican Council I, when the pope speaks officially on certain matters, his teachings will not err.

infralapsarianism — The milder form of the doctrine of predestination which holds that God's election is after the fall; after the fall God elects to save a few out of the mass of perdition who otherwise would have been lost. Stands in contrast to supralapsarianism.

inspiration — To be "in-breathed" by the Spirit of God. Also an adjective applied to Scripture to indicate that God or the Holy Spirit has motivated, guided, protected, or, some believe, dictated the words of the Bible.

Irenaeus (115-190) — Second-century bishop in Lyon (France), who was an enemy of Gnosticism. He was known primarily for his recapitulation theory of atonement, according to which Christ recapitulates the human journey and thereby takes all men and women up into salvation. He had a less strenuous view of sin and evil than Augustine had.

Jesus — The name refers variously to (1) the Jesus of history prior to the resurrection and the church's preaching, which is reconstructed by modern scholarship from the New Testament texts and/or noncanonical texts; (2) the Jesus of history who is the object of faith confessed to be the Christ, an understanding not dependent on modern historical reconstruction; (3) the Jesus of the kerygma of the church contained in the apostolic witness of the New Testament; (4) the Jesus of the New Testament narrative itself apart from any effort to locate "the real Jesus" behind the texts. Many Christians use the name Jesus as a convertible term for Christ, or assume the name and title of Christ in using the name of Jesus alone.

justification/justifying grace — The act of God in restoring humans to a right relationship with God by imputing the righteousness of Christ to the sinner and thereby forgiving our sins; the divine favor and power by which this relationship is accomplished and we are united with Christ through faith.

Kant, Immanuel (1724-1804) — German philosopher who undermined the metaphysical foundations of orthodox theology and rationalist philosophy by his teaching that the human mind cannot know "the thing in itself" but, rather, constructs the phenomenal world through the categories of the mind which we impose upon the world. He relocated the foundations of religion and theology in the moral consciousness ("practical reason") instead of in "pure reason," and provided the philosophical framework and strategy of thinking for most forms of liberal Protestant theology. His emphasis on the construction of the world through the categories of the mind has been carried even further in much postmodern thought.

kerygma — The church's proclamation, preaching, or message about the significance of Jesus Christ for salvation.

kingdom of God — The rule or reign of God to which Christians look forward. Christians differ on whether the reign of God is the end of history and beyond history (in heaven) or whether the reign of God is the establishment of the time of the justice and love of God on earth.

liberal/liberalism — The root of the term means "to free," and a liberal can be seen as one who advocates greater freedom of thought and action. Theological liberalism is an effort to establish Christian faith on some other grounds of authority than the grounds of tradition. Theological liberalism locates the grounds of theology within the framework of human experience, either in the world of pure reason or in moral consciousness or in religious experience. "Liberalism" also refers to a set of modern beliefs in contrast to orthodox beliefs as embodied in the creeds; these beliefs are typically shaped in accord with modern scientific and historical assumptions and methods.

liberation theology — A form of postmodern theology that, through a hermeneutics of suspicion, recognizes and describes the ideological and therefore the repressive and oppressive character of much of the Christian tradition, including modern liberal theology and culture. It entails primarily a turn to the marginalized "other" (as in feminist theology, North American black theology, and Latin American liberation theology), with a focus on the significance of oppression and institutional violence for theology and with social, political, and economic liberation from oppression as the meaning of salvation. Liberation theology draws on many postliberal and postmodern sensibilities, emphasizes the liberating dimension of the gospel as primary, and attempts to bring the experience and voice of oppressed and ignored communities to the theological discussion.

linguistic philosophy — A twentieth-century movement in philosophy in which "the linguistic turn" made language the subject of philosophy. Specifically, it contends that the purpose of philosophy is not to determine the truth of ideas or propositions but is, rather, to uncover the meaning of language by a critical analysis of the context, usage, and function of words and sentences within the "language games" we use. The major figure in this movement was Ludwig Wittgenstein.

liturgy — Literally means "service," and so it is the work of Christians as their service to God through worship. In common use, the term refers to the rituals of worship, and most especially to the pattern or order of the worship service of a congregation or denomination.

Logos — Greek for "word" or "reason," which is a rich concept referring to the order, structure, pattern, or rationality of the world. In theology the assumption has been that there is some relationship between our own reason and the structure of the world which reflects the reason of the mind of God. The term can also refer to the Second Person of the Trinity, Jesus Christ.

Lord's Supper — The most general designation for the sacrament of bread and wine in which the presence of Christ is mediated to the believer through the ritual.

Luther, Martin (1483-1546) — Sixteenth-century German Reformer who criticized the medieval Catholic church for many of its beliefs and practices and finally broke with the church. He returned to the Bible as the Word of God as the grounds, content, and norm for Christian belief and practice, and especially emphasized justification by grace through faith as the meaning of salvation and the essence of the gospel.

Marxism — A social analysis of the class structure of modern capitalism based on the work of Karl Marx (1818-1883). Marxism attempts to show the contradictions, false consciousness, and ideological character of many beliefs which reflect and maintain the economic interests, especially social class interests, of those who hold them. Many of the various liberation theologians today employ a Marxist analysis of social class structure, or other forms of repressive and exploitive structures. Marxist analysis is not identical to the communism of Lenin and Stalin that grew out of his analysis.

Mass — A Roman Catholic term for the Lord's Supper which denotes an understanding that in the sacrament the sacrifice of Christ on the cross is repeated.

means of grace — Items or elements from the everyday world which serve as vehicles through or by which the presence of God or Christ is mediated to the believer, such as water, bread, and wine. Means of grace may also include, among other things, prayer, fasting, reading of Scripture, and other acts of piety.

Messiah — The promised deliverer who, according to Hebrew and Jewish thought, would come and establish the kingdom of God. Christians see Jesus as the fulfillment of this promise; the translation of the term into Greek is *Christos* or Christ.

metanarrative — A comprehensive story or perspective that includes and explains the origins, meaning, and purpose of the cosmos or the whole world and history. Scripture and its story of creation, fall, redemption, and eschatology forms a metanarrative for Christians; science forms the metanarrative for much of modernity.

metaphysical/metaphysics — Literally means "beyond the physical." Metaphysics is a type of philosophy which attempts to analyze what is real; it asks about the basic character, principles, and structure of reality as such apart from any particular examples.

Methodism — A religious renewal movement in eighteenth-century England and the United States led by John and Charles Wesley which eventually became a family of Methodist churches throughout the world. The renewal focused primarily on "the religion of the heart" (the experiential appropriation of God's love and mercy) and on "holiness" (being made perfect in the love of God and neighbor).

millennialism — Views about the thousand-year rule of Christ on the earth with peace and justice (the millennium; Rev. 20:1-7). In some contemporary apocalyptic thought, the millennium belongs to the last period in the division of creation into seven eras, which consists of a thousand-year rule of Christ with his saints before the final judgment and punishment of all sinners.

ministry — The work or service of each Christian in carrying out the mission of Christ to the world. In the narrower sense, the work or service of those who are ordained to a special ministry of the church, notably to Word and sacrament.

Minjung theology — A type of theology from Asian, and specifically Korean, theologians which makes the poor a resource and subject matter of theology. *Han* is a central concept in Minjung theology, whose major contemporary representative is Andrew Sung Park.

miracle — A sign of the work or power of God. Definitions of the term vary and range from, on the one extreme, a suspension of natural law by God and a divine intervention to accomplish what God wants done (such as the elimination of a tumor), to, on the other extreme, a natural event that has religious significance to the observer (such as the birth of a baby).

mission — The purpose and goal of a person or community. The mission of Jesus Christ is to preach and embody the kingdom of God; the mission of the church is to carry on and carry out the ministry of Jesus by preaching God's kingdom of justice and peace, by preaching the gospel to the whole world in word and deed.

modalism — The belief that the three "persons" of the Trinity are not distinct persons but rather three modes of the one divine being. Modalism is usually tied up with the notion that these modes are temporally sequential.

modernity/modernism — The ethos, culture, and beliefs derived from Enlightenment assumptions and epistemology, specifically, from science, industry, technology, and culture. In modernism community and tradition are seen primarily as constraints, and the modernist seeks to be free from oppressive tradition and authority. Modernism as a theological movement is a form of liberalism that took a highly critical and skeptical attitude toward traditional Christian doctrines and adopted a positive attitude toward biblical criticism; it stressed the need to reinterpret doctrine in a modern context, which means stressing the ethical in contrast to the theological significance of Christian faith. Representatives of modernism include late-nineteenth-century and early-twentieth-century Catholic theologians Alfred Loisy and George Tyrrell and the early-twentieth-century "Chicago School of Theology" at the Divinity School of the University of Chicago, whose proponents included Shirley Jackson Case and Shailer Mathews.

Moltmann, Jürgen (b. 1926) — German Reformed theologian who was a prison survivor of World War II and an early major advocate of a theology of hope grounded in biblical eschatology. Moltmann argues that theology does not end with eschatology but begins with eschatology and that eschatology shapes all Christian doctrine. He has made a major contribution to post-Holocaust Christian theology in his focus on "the crucified God" as the key to understanding the Trinitarian concept of God and of christology.

monism — The belief that the world or reality is of one kind, essence, substance, or being.

Monophysitism — A theory about the person of Christ according to which Christ had only one nature (rather than a divine and human nature united in one person), and which thus emphasized the divinity of Christ to the exclusion of his humanity.

mystery — From the Greek and Latin for "secret." In theology *mystery* refers primarily to the claim that God's essential nature or inner being is unknown and unknowable by us, either until it has been revealed to us or forever.

mystic — One who experiences the divine reality by direct apprehension through an immediate intuition that results in spiritual ecstasy. Some mystics speak of direct union with the godhead or absorption into the godhead, while others speak of communion with God either through direct, unmediated experience of God or through Christ (Christ mysticism).

myth — In common usage, prescientific stories and views of the world that are false. In theology, stories that embody and convey spiritual, religious, and theological truths. Myths must be interpreted but cannot be reduced or eliminated from religious language and usage since these truths cannot be conveyed adequately outside this language.

narrative theology — A twentieth-century movement in theology that stresses the essential narrative or story quality of biblical language, of the gospel, of all human experience, and of theology; the truth of the biblical language and of theology is not philosophical or even propositional but rather is the power of the Bible, its stories and language, to shape the consciousness, framework, perceptions, character, style of life, and purposes of those who learn it and inhabit the world it creates.

natural theology — Theology based in an appeal to nature, reason, or general human experience prior to and apart from any appeal to special revelation. Roman Catholic and liberal Protestant theology has appealed to natural theology, either in conjunction with revealed theology (Catholic) or as the foundation for and preparation for specific Christian doctrines (Protestant). Neo-orthodox theology, and Barth in particular, along with postliberal theology, has led to a resounding rejection of the appeal to any sources or norms for theology apart from special revelation.

naturalism — The belief that the natural world of space and time which is available to our senses (or to our reason) constitutes all that is real. The term also refers to a way of knowing this world, that is, to the knowledge that is available through empirical investigation by employing scientific principles and method.

neo-orthodoxy — Twentieth-century theological movement initiated and shaped by the theology of Karl Barth in which God is thought of as the Wholly Other who comes to us through the special revelation of Jesus Christ. The movement was "orthodox" in the sense that, in opposition to liberal theology, it returned to many of the primary myths, symbols, and doctrines of Scripture and the catholic church, and especially to traditional Protestant themes such as the Word of God, revelation, christology, sin, redemption, and eschatology. It was "neo" (new) in the sense that it accepted much of the framework of modern Protestant theology, such as the concepts of myth, science, historical criticism, and existential interpretation.

Nestorius (d. 451) — Syrian preacher and theologian and bishop of Constantinople who opposed the designation of Mary as the mother of God *(theotokos)* and was believed to have taught that Jesus Christ was two separate persons as well as possessing two separate natures (dualism; Nestorianism). He was condemned as a heretic by the Council of Ephesus in 431.

new birth — Regeneration or rebirth that occurs at the moment of justification through faith, either by baptismal regeneration or by a personal decision to accept Jesus Christ as Savior. Evangelical Christians emphasize the new birth as meaning that one has a "born-again experience."

Nicene Creed — The Christian creed adopted by the Council of Nicea in 325 and revised in Constantinople in 381, it formulates the orthodox Trinitarian doctrine of the church.

Niebuhr, Reinhold (1892-1971) — American theologian born in Missouri, pastor of a church in Detroit deeply involved in the social gospel movement, and a professor of ethics at Union Theological Seminary in New York at the beginning of the Great Depression. Niebuhr led a critical reaction to liberal Protestant theology, while remaining a liberal in his commitment to prophetic religion. He was an important neo-orthodox theologian in his recovery of major Protestant doctrines, most especially his re-appropriation and re-interpretation of the doctrines of sin, original sin, and grace both in its personal dimensions (forgiveness) and especially its social dimensions (justice).

norm — Rule, pattern, or model used to evaluate beliefs and practices. In theology the *norma normans* means "the ruling rule" and refers, for Protestants, to Scripture as the sole authority for belief and practice; *norma normata,* "the rule having been ruled," means normative beliefs or practices that have been tested by Scripture.

omnibenevolence — The divine attribute which describes God as all-loving. There is disagreement about whether this divine love is pure agape or includes eros, and about whether or how divine love includes anger, judgment, and wrath.

omnipotence — The divine attribute which describes God as all-powerful. Christians disagree about whether this means God is literally the direct cause of everything that happens ("nothing happens that is not the will of God"), is the hidden but ultimate cause of all that happens (through secondary causes), is sovereign over the direction of nature and history *(telos),* is provisionally self-limited within the span of history (free-will theism), or is the maximal power consistent with other centers of power in the world (process theism).

omniscience — The divine attribute which describes God as all-knowing. Christians disagree about whether this means that God knows everything — past, present, and future (foreknowledge) — or whether this means that God knows everything as it is, the past as past, the present as it is being experienced, and the future as a full range of real possibilities.

ontological argument — The argument for the existence of God based on reason alone. Anselm, the best-known advocate of this "proof," argued that God is "that than which nothing greater can be conceived"; the greatest being that could be conceived would exist, so, therefore, God must necessarily exist. Charles Hartshorne has developed a revision of this argument which has had some appeal among philosophers of religion and theologians.

oppressed, the — Term used in liberation theology for those who have been treated unjustly and are living without freedom. In black, Latin American, and Minjung theology it refers to the unjust and marginalized situation of those who lack freedom and live in wretched conditions brought about by the injustices of the upper classes or nations. In feminist theology it refers to the subordinate status and role of women in a patriarchal society.

ordinances — The term applied by the Anabaptist traditions to the rites of baptism and the Lord's Supper. The term is used to indicate that these rituals are not sacraments and do not have sacramental meaning or efficacy.

ordination — The rite (or, in Roman Catholic theology, sacrament) by which a person is set apart (by God, the church, a bishop, a denomination, or a congregation) to represent, in a way specified by this body, the ministry of Christ and the ministry of the church.

Origen (184-254) — Greek theologian born in Egypt and educated in Alexandria who led a catechetical school and was the first systematic theologian of the church. He wrote *De Principiis,* and he is best known for his view that the Bible has three levels of meaning, literal, moral, and allegorical, with the latter being the most important. He was finally declared a heretic because he taught the doctrine of *apokatastasis,* the belief that the whole creation (including the Devil) would finally be restored to God.

original righteousness — The state of Adam and Eve before their fall in which they lived in perfect obedience and harmony with the will of God.

original sin — The corruption of human nature which occurred as a result of the fall and which is now shared by all persons, who inevitably recapitulate the original sin. In much contemporary theology the term refers to the depth and universality of the brokenness of each person before God.

orthodox — That which is considered to be correct belief and practice, as defined by the dogmas and creeds of the church, especially the creeds affirmed by the first seven ecumenical councils of the church.

Orthodox Church, the — One of the major branches of Christianity, to be distinguished from the Roman Catholic Church and the Protestant churches. The Russian and Greek Orthodox Churches are two of the many in the Orthodox family.

orthopathy — Right passions or feelings as a norm for authentic Christian life. Some in the Methodist tradition have included this along with orthodoxy and orthopraxis as norms for the Christian life.

orthopraxis — Right practice or behavior (ranging from obedience to the Law to the demand for justice and the call to live in peace) as a norm for authentic Christian life.

panentheism — The doctrine that God is *in* the world and the world is *in* God; that is, there is an internal relationship between God and the world so that there is a mutuality between God and the world in the sense that God affects the world and the world affects God. To be distinguished from pantheism.

Pannenberg, Wolfhart (b. 1928) — German Protestant theologian who became a Christian while studying philosophy in Berlin and Göttingen. He has stressed throughout his career that revelation is mediated through history, and has made apocalyptic central to theology, arguing that the resurrection of Jesus is a historical event in which the eschatological future is present proleptically (is anticipated).

pantheism — The doctrine that the concept "God" and the concept "the world" (as the cosmos or nature conceived in its broadest sense) are convertible terms (God is the world and the world is God). To be distinguished from panentheism.

Parousia — A term referring to the coming of Christ, and generally to the "second coming of Christ" in the future. In contemporary theology the Parousia is often tied up with a millennialist theology of one sort or another.

patripassionism — The view that the First Person of the Trinity, the Father, actively suffered on the cross in the death of the Second Person, Jesus Christ. The church condemned this as heresy in the third century on the grounds that it was a form of modalism. The idea has been revived and revised today by Jürgen Moltmann in his concept of "the crucified God."

Pelagius (d. 410) — British theologian active in Rome who was the nemesis of Augustine. He argued that human beings are free by nature to choose the good and that divine grace is bestowed in relation to human merit. Though he did not deny any doctrine of original sin, he has been associated with that teaching because of his controversy with Augustine. Pelagianism was condemned at the Council of Ephesus in 431. Today "Pelagian" is used as a perjorative adjective to refer to any theology that emphasizes the role of freedom and choice in its understanding of salvation.

Pentecost — The day of the birth of the church in the New Testament (fifty days after Passover during the Festival of Weeks) when the Holy Spirit descended as fire on the gathered followers of Jesus fifty days after the resurrection.

Pentecostalism — Movements that experience the baptism or gifts of the Holy Spirit primarily through charismatic gifts, including speaking in tongues. There have been several denominations in the twentieth century formed around a pentecostal emphasis which teach a special experience of the Holy Spirit following the experience of conversion.

perfectionism — The teaching that the Christian will some day be perfected. There is debate about whether the state or condition of being made perfect happens only after death (Calvin) or can happen in this life (Wesley). Wesley taught that the Christian can be made perfect in this life in the sense that the love of God and the love of the neighbor can increase until that love motivates and dominates the passions and behavior of the Christian.

personalism — A metaphysical view which posits that the human self or personhood is the clue to the whole structure and meaning of the cosmos.

perspectival — Term emphasizing that every experience, perception, and conception of the world is shaped by the situation or context of the person, and therefore that that context, which differs from every other context, provides the perspective from which the world is perceived and described. A perspectival understanding stands counter to the teaching that there is one objective and universal point of view — whether derived from revelation, reason, a common human nature, or universal experience — by which we can know the truth about the world.

phenomenology — A type of philosophy engaged in a description and analysis of the phenomenal world as it appears in the subjective processes of our experience ("what appears"); philosophy is a depth description of that phenomena, instead of a construction of the world through speculative reason.

philosophical theology — A type of theology that depends upon philosophy to provide either the foundations or the framework by which and through which we can talk about the meaning and the truth of Christian symbols, myths, and doctrines. It stands in contrast to theologies that depend on special revelation or revealed dogmas as the content of theology independent of any other foundations.

philosophy — Literally the "love of wisdom." An attempt to gain knowledge or wisdom about the world, whether it be ultimate reality or the world of our everyday experience, through critical analysis, that is, through the use of logic, intuition, moral consciousness, and analytical description. Philosophy's great questions are, "What is real?" (ontology) and, "How do we know what we know?" (epistemology).

philosophy of religion — An analysis of religious symbols, myths, and concepts from the point of view of critical philosophy. It begins with a standpoint of neutrality in regards to the meaning and truth of these ideas, and asks what we can say about the meaning or the truth of the idea from the point of view of reason alone or at least from critical reflection.

Pietism/pietism — A renewal movement in German Lutheranism led by Philipp Jacob Spener during the seventeenth century which emphasized personal communion with God and the life of devotion. In modern times, the term has been used to refer to the importance of religious experience in the Christian life, and has been mediated to American religion primarily through Puritanism and through John Wesley's idea of "the religion of the heart," according to which the experiences of regeneration (the born-again experience) and assurance (the witness of the Spirit to our spirit) are the center of the Christian life.

Plato (428-348 BC**)** — Greek philosopher who taught that there is an eternal realm of ultimate reality in which ideals (ideas) or forms exist, and that these are embodied in the empirical or physical phenomena of this world. Platonism has had an enormous impact on Christian theology throughout history, beginning with Plotinus's Neoplatonism.

pluralism — The doctrine that the world is in its very character plural, composed of many things. (This is to be contrasted with monism.) In contemporary theology, the idea of pluralism has played itself out most significantly in pluralistic views of salvation, according to which God has provided a diverse number of ways for persons to know God and to be saved.

pneumatology — The doctrine of the person and work of the Holy Spirit. Christian theology teaches that the Holy Spirit is the Third Person of the triune God and that the work of the Holy Spirit is as the bringer of the grace of God the Creator and Redeemer to us. In ecclesiology, the Holy Spirit is the creator and sustainer of the church and brings the grace that incorporates the believer into the church, sustains the believer's life, and brings the believer to fulfillment.

polity — Form of church government, such as episcopal, presbyterial, or congregational forms of governance.

polytheism — Belief in many gods.

postliberal theology — One form of the postmodern approach to theology, it refers to intellectual and cultural movements since the 1960s which represent a break with modern Enlightenment liberal culture. It is highly critical of what it perceives to be the illusions, delusions, and repressive character of modern liberal culture and has abandoned the modern quest for certainty founded in a common human experience or reason in favor of a pluralism which acknowledges the linguistic and communal basis of all beliefs and practices; since beliefs are local and constructed, the language and practices of specific communities provide the basis for religious practices and theological beliefs. Postliberal theology is linguistically rather than experientially oriented, so that being a Christian is learning the language of the Bible and tradition rather than grounding theology in and expressing the religious experience of an autonomous individual.

postmodernism — An amorphous term which, since the mid 1960s, has referred to a sense that we live at the end of, or in transition from, the modern era and are beginning to create a new culture based on something different from that built on the assumptions and agenda of modernity. Postmodernism emphasizes that all knowledge is situated in a cultural tradition and questions whether there are any "foundations" or "essences" or "selves" beyond the language which has shaped them.

practical theology — An approach to theology as critical reflection based upon the inauguration, formation, and living out of the Christian life instead of speculative testing of beliefs; an approach to theology which tests and judges the Christian faith more in terms of the dispositions or character that its symbols create than in terms of philosophical speculation. Sometimes in the past the phrase was used to refer to the church disciplines or arts of preaching, worship, pastoral care, and religious education.

pragmatism — A movement in late-nineteenth-century and early-twentieth-century American philosophy, begun by Charles Sanders Peirce and developed in its classical forms by William James and John Dewey, in which the meaning of words and the truth of ideas, concepts, and beliefs are determined not by speculation but by their use in the conduct of life, which is determined by experimentation or experimentalism; the truth of beliefs is determined by how beliefs function in resolving practical problems of how to live. Pragmatism does not mean we are permitted to believe anything that works or makes us feel good but rather that the truth of beliefs lies in their capacity to resolve practical problems of life.

praxis — Greek for "practice." In theology the term is used to refer to the dialectic which works back and forth from practice to theory and theory to practice as revisions are made in each.

premodern — Coming before (or still unaffected by) the Enlightenment and its stress on deductive or inductive analysis as how we know what we know. In everyday terms, "premodern" refers in theology to the study of the Bible as if the questions and answers posed by modern historical critical study are irrelevant or contrary to the right way to understand the Scriptures, and as if any of the questions posed by modern critical ways of thinking are irrelevant to theology. Postmodern thinking differs in that postmoderns have been through modernity and have concluded that there are so many liabilities to modern criteria that they search for new ways to think about the meaning of Christian beliefs.

predestination — The idea that God has chosen or elected a few from the beginning of time to be saved from the punishments of hell and for the enjoyment of heaven. Often the term is used to mean foreordination, the idea that before the creation of the world God determined all that would come to pass in it. For Calvin, the idea primarily addresses the question of why and how some people are part of the church and others are not.

premillennialism — In contemporary apocalyptic theory, the belief that Jesus will return to earth prior to the period of his one-thousand-year reign to lead his armies at Armageddon.

prevenient grace — The grace of God which "comes before" whatever we believe, say, and do in Christ.

priesthood of all believers — A theological view associated with Martin Luther which emphasized that Christians have direct access to God and do not need to go through any priest or intermediary other than Christ.

process theology — A type of theology that employs the philosophy of Alfred North Whitehead and Charles Hartshorne to interpret Christian symbols and doctrines. It is a dynamic and relational philosophy which emphasizes the doctrines that God and the world are interdependent, that God is affected by the world as well as affecting the world, and that God changes in certain ways while not changing in others. Among evangelicals, free-will theism shares many of the beliefs of process theology, but is critical of it in the sense that it holds to the traditional doctrines of creation *ex nihilo* and the (ultimate) omnipotence of God.

prolegomena — Those things in a systematic theology which precede the exposition of specific doctrines and through which foundational issues are addressed as preparation for what is to follow.

prolepsis — An anticipation of a future event. The resurrection of Jesus Christ is the first fruits of the final consummation, an anticipation of our own fulfillment and the promise of the fulfillment of the whole creation, and is thus proleptic. This is a central theme in the theology of Wolfhart Pannenberg and Jürgen Moltmann.

providence — The continuation of the doctrine of creation in which God continues to create, sustain, guide, and govern the world toward the fulfillment of the purposes and will of God for persons, history, and the cosmos.

purgatory — An intermediate place or state where the souls of the faithful dead go following death while their souls are cleansed or purified before the final judgment and heaven. Emphasized in medieval Catholic theology, it completes sanctification.

Puritanism — A religious movement in sixteenth- and seventeenth-century England and seventeenth-century America which sought to purify the Church of England through a kind of Calvinism represented in Presbyterian and Congregational reforms. Emphasis was placed on the study of Scripture, ethical action, discipline, humility, moderation, modesty, thrift, preaching, providence, and obedience. Puritanism was strongly influential in American Christianity and culture through the Puritan immigration to the colonies and through the work of the Methodists.

rapture — In much contemporary apocalyptic thought, the moment when Jesus suddenly and unexpectedly returns on the clouds of heaven to remove his faithful followers from the earth before the tribulation occurs.

rationalism — The view that reality and truth are known through reason alone. In theology rationalists seek logically necessary truths that are undeniable, from which they then construct a logically coherent view of God and of the world.

real presence — Belief that Christ is really present in the sacrament of bread and wine. Church traditions have differed on the way this real presence — as opposed to a figurative or symbolic presence — is to be understood, but theories include a spiritual rather than a corporeal presence, consubstantiation (bodily presence with or alongside the bread and wine), and transubstantiation (bread and wine miraculously become the body and blood of Christ).

realism, theological — A conception of God which holds that the concept of God refers to something that exists independent of our perceptions and conceptions.

redemption — Literally, "buying back." An understanding of the work of Christ based on the notion of exchanging something in one's possession for something possessed by another. The human need for redemption is based on the assumption that we are in some kind of bondage (slavery, subjugation, condemnation), from which we can be delivered. In the strictest sense, redemption refers to being bought back through a ransom; in the broader sense, to being liberated whether or not a payment was involved.

Reformation, Protestant — Sixteenth-century movement of theological, liturgical, and moral reforms of the medieval church in Europe led by Hus, Zwingli, Luther, Calvin, and others, which resulted in the formation of various Protestant churches, originally in Europe, subsequently in North America, and now throughout the world.

Reformed — The Christian tradition associated with Zwingli and Calvin and represented today in the Presbyterian and Congregational churches, among others.

regeneration — The work of God in which we are born again, our lives renewed by our being in Christ.

relativism — The belief that there are no absolute, unconditioned ideas, moral teachings, or theological doctrines, but that all ideas and beliefs are relative in the sense that their meaning and truth depend upon the context in which they exist. In the larger sense the term refers to the belief that all reality is relative in the sense that all beings are dependent on their relationships in order to exist.

religion/religious — Terms about which there is almost no agreement today either among scholars or in popular usage. Typically "religion" is defined as a set of beliefs regarding the origin, nature, and purpose of the universe and life, while "religious" indicates belief in God or the gods or an unseen world. "Religious" is also sometimes used to indicate a certain attitude or sensibility, such as a sense of the sacred, awe, deep feeling, or moral commitment. The emphasis today is more on the rituals, myths, and social practices of groups of people, and the term is used pejoratively by many to identify people with institutions and in distinction from the more favored term, "spirituality."

religious studies — An academic discipline within the college or university in which religion is the subject matter. It uses scientific methodologies of various sorts in order to study objectively or at least in a detached way the function of religion for individuals and in social groups. The question of the truth of religious practices or beliefs is considered to be at least inappropriate if not a meaningless question in religious studies, and there is almost no agreement in this field on the origin, nature, or function of religion.

resurrection — God's raising of Jesus from the dead, as well as the future raising of all people before the final judgment. Resurrection is to be distinguished from resuscitation (to get up and start walking around again, as in the case of Lazarus). Christ's resurrection entails the idea that God transformed him into a new mode of being or existence following his death, a mode of being indicative of the life of the world to come; this entailed a spiritual body and not merely the release of his soul to heaven.

revelation — Literally, an uncovering or unveiling. The disclosure of something previously unknown, or at least inadequately known. In theology "revelation" refers to the movement of God to us in which God takes the initiative to reveal Godself to us, either in a general way through creation or in a specific way through the incarnation of God in Jesus Christ. In traditional theology doctrines were considered to be revealed, but in much contemporary theology the emphasis is upon God's presence, or character and purpose, revealed in Jesus Christ through the story of Jesus in the New Testament.

revelation, general — God's self-disclosure in the creation. According to the concept of general revelation, there is a knowledge of God that all human beings, to one degree or another, do (or can) have on the basis of their experience and knowledge of the natural world; it is knowledge about God apart from any special and specific revelation given by God in addition to this general knowledge through the revelation in Christ.

revelation, special — Divine revelation through a particular medium or person. In Christian theology, Jesus Christ is the special revelation of God.

revival/revivalism — In the broader sense, the work of the Holy Spirit among people or churches to bring a new sense of vitality and devotion. The term also refers to periods of church history of spiritual renewal and revitalization, such as the monastic movements or the ecumenical movement. In American usage, it typically refers to periodic attempts through mass meetings or short periods in local churches either to convert non-Christians to Christ through a personal decision and public display of decision or to revive the fervor of Christians whose commitment has waned.

Sabellianism — Teaching of Sabellius in the early third century that God is one person and one nature who reveals himself as Creator and then projects himself into the Son as Redeemer and then into the Spirit as sanctifier; these changes occurred sequentially, so the viewpoint is also known as modalism or Modalistic Monarchianism. Sabellianism was declared heretical by the church, which taught that God exists in three Persons, and that he does so eternally, not sequentially.

sacrament — An outward sign, channel, or means (water, bread, wine, Trinitarian formula) of an invisible grace through which God conveys God's presence and power to the recipient. Protestants believe there are two sacraments authorized by Christ (dominical institution), while Roman Catholics believe there are seven sacraments.

salvation — The process by which humans are saved from the guilt and power of sin and saved for freedom and life lived in the kingdom of God.

sanctification — The process by which the believer is made holy, either by an instantaneous work of God of through the process of growth in which the love of God and neighbor comes to dominate the Christian's intentions and actions.

satisfaction theory of the atonement — A theory of atonement in which the offended honor of God has been restored by someone (Jesus) paying the penalty for the offense and thereby fulfilling divine justice and restoring the offender to God.

Schleiermacher, Friedrich (1768-1834) — German theologian who was raised a Pietist and became the father of modern liberal Protestant theology. He appealed to our universal sense of absolute dependence on the Infinite, locating religion and theology in religious experience, namely, a feeling *(gefuhl)*. Theology, then, is the description and explication of this feeling of absolute dependence as it is mediated to the church and the believer through Jesus Christ. Schleiermacher provided a way forward for Protestants after Kant's *Critiques* and was central to the development of liberal Protestant theology in the modern period.

second coming — The time when Christ will return to judge all humanity. Some Christians speculate about the details of this return, while others do not speculate on when or how the end will occur.

secular — In common usage the term refers to the worldly, earthly, and temporal in contrast to the spiritual or religious. In a more technical sense, it refers to those not bound by monastic vows, rules, or church authority. Secular Christianity is the twentieth-century attempt to adapt Christianity to beliefs and practices compatible with the secular world. Secular humanism is the claim that all beliefs, values, practices, and institutions are determined by humans apart from any reference to a dimension beyond the secular world.

shame — The feeling of inadequacy or failure to live up to the societal ideals of what people should be able to do, be, know, feel, or look like. This feeling of unworthiness or worthlessness should be contrasted with guilt, where some objective law or rule has been violated.

sin/sins — The condition or acts in which or through which human beings are alienated, separated, or estranged from God.

social location — The context(s) of the believer and thinker. In particular, the term refers to the perspective or biases stemming from a person's race, gender, and class. In the larger sense it refers to all of the limits on thought created by the finite location of every thinker.

social gospel — A type of Protestant theology which arose in the late nineteenth and early twentieth centuries in industrial and urban America. Its proponents were critical of the individualistic ideas of sin or salvation and sought, in the midst of the social disruptions and inequalities of industrialization, to expand the social meaning of the gospel to economic and political justice, believing that social institutions and practices were also redeemable.

sola Scriptura — Latin for "Scripture alone." The claim that Scripture is the only source and norm for theology and practice. Most famous as the rallying cry of the Protestant Reformation.

sophia — The Greek word for wisdom; the Hebrew word is *chokma* (grammatically feminine). A power or agent of God, typically personified as a female, who is active in the creation.

soteriology — The doctrine of salvation, or the doctrine of the reconciling work of Christ. Specifically, it deals with the means of accomplishing salvation. It continues the work of christology by focusing on the work of Christ, specifically, the atoning work of Christ on the cross, and so includes such terms as justification, regeneration, sanctification, and the kingdom of God.

soul — An element or aspect of the human being, usually thought of as the seat of the reason and will, which either exists eternally or is a special creation of God for each person. The soul is thought to be independent of the body as a spiritual entity which survives death either because it is inherently immortal or as a gift of God.

special revelation — *See* revelation, special.

spirit/Spirit — A being that does not have a material substance. The term is also used to refer to the part of the human being that has a relationship with God. Capitalized, it refers to the Holy Spirit, the Third Person of the triune God.

spirituality — The spiritual capacities and sensibilities of each individual. Many today use the term positively, contrasting it with religion, which they use as a pejorative term for any institutionalized form of religious life. ("I am spiritual but I am not religious!"). Christian spirituality is centered on the relation of the believer to God and Christ and the way the spiritual capacities and sensibilities of the Christian are derived from, shaped by, and measured by life in Christ.

subordinationism — The teaching that God the Son (Christ) is subordinate to God the Father, or that the Son and the Spirit are subordinate to the Father, or that the Spirit is subordinate to the Son. These positions are considered to be heresy by orthodox Trinitarian doctrine, which teaches that all three Persons are eternal and equal within the godhead.

substitutionary theory of the atonement — A theory of the atonement, especially widespread in Protestantism, according to which Jesus died on the cross as our substitute as the punishment for our sins, thereby paying the debt we owe to God, who then transfers his righteousness to us.

supralapsarianism — The starker form of the doctrine of predestination which holds that before the creation and the fall *(lapsus)* God willed to save some without consideration of their merits. Stands in contrast to infralapsarianism.

supernaturalism — The belief that there is some kind of reality, realm, or being that exists above, beyond, or outside the cosmos or the natural world and intervenes occasionally in this world and the way this world usually works.

symbol — An image or idea which represents or stands for something else; it participates in or expresses the reality to which it points but is not identical with it.

systematic theology — The attempt of theologians to be as comprehensive in the range of Christian doctrines they interpret and as coherent or consistent in their interpretation of one doctrine in relation to another as is possible.

Tertullian (160-220) — An African theologian who forms a bridge between the Greek and Latin churches, especially in his writings against the heretics, such as Marcion. He is also well known for his claim that he believes "because it is absurd" or impossible to believe, and for saying, "What has Athens to do with Jerusalem?" — that is, what has reason to do with faith?

theism — Belief in the monotheistic concept of God. The term also refers to the classical formulation of the concept of God in the West which resulted from the marriage between the biblical God and the God of Greek philosophy, in which the ultimate reality is identified with the absolute, the changeless, the immutable. In classical theism God is defined as a supernatural person without a body who is creator, present everywhere, able to do anything, knows everything, is perfectly good, the source of moral obligation, holy, loving, and worthy of our worship.

theodicy — Narrowly defined, the task of holding together as logically consistent the claim that the all-powerful, all-loving God (the theistic God) can be said to exist even while there is genuine evil in the world. More broadly defined, the task of understanding the origins, nature, and extent of, and the response to, the reality of evil within the context of one's view of the nature of God, regardless of whether one has a theistic, pantheistic, free-will theistic, panentheistic, or Trinitarian view of God.

Thomas Aquinas (1225-1274) — The greatest medieval theologian, who continued to dominate Catholic theology up to Vatican II. He is known as the one who appropriated Aristotle as a source for theology and produced one of the greatest systematic theologies in the history of the church, reconciling the Christian faith with Aristotle's philosophy. He remains known for his "five ways" proof of the existence of God, and for his claim that natural theology is true as far as it can go but needs to be supplemented with revealed theology in order to complete our knowledge of God. The philosophical and theological viewpoint taken from his writings is known as Thomism.

Tillich, Paul (1886-1965) — The most influential Protestant theologian, along with Karl Barth, in the twentieth century. Tillich was a philosophical theologian who continued many themes of the liberal tradition in theology, primarily through his appropriation of existentialist philosophy, while he at the same time embodied some of the major themes of dialectical and neo-orthodox theology, such as revelation and the Word of God. He interpreted God as Being-itself or the power of being, and saw Jesus Christ as revelatory through his transparency to the ground of being.

Torah — The first five books of the Hebrew Bible and the first five books of the Christian Old Testament.

total depravity — The doctrine that sin affects every aspect of human existence. It does not mean humans are capable only of evil and incapable of any good, but rather that everything humans do, including their practice of religion, is corrupted by sinfulness.

tragic structure — The idea that some of the sources of suffering and evil are rooted in the very structure of the creation itself. Not all suffering and evil can be accounted for on the basis of free will and sin; some is caused by the way the world operates in its very structure (finite limitations) and by the choices we are sometimes forced to make (between two evils or two goods).

transcendence — The divine attribute which describes God as beyond, above, other than, or more than the finite world. This can be conceived of vertically, as God existing in a realm or dimension above and beyond the world, or horizontally, as God within but more than or other than the human equation or the finite. world.

transubstantiation — The Roman Catholic doctrine that in the Eucharist, through a miracle, the bread and the wine literally become the body and blood of Christ, though through another miracle the "properties" or "accidents" appear to our senses to be bread and wine.

tribulation — In contemporary apocalyptic theories, the seven years of calamities predicted in the book of Revelation which will end in Christ's victory over the antichrist at Armageddon.

Trinity, doctrine of the — The Christian church's teaching, established by the Council of Nicea in 325, that God is triune, that the Godhead exists as three equal and eternal persons (Father, Son, and Holy Spirit), and that these three persons share one substance or essence.

tritheism — Belief in three gods. Some non-Christians hold that Christians are tritheists in their doctrine of the Trinity because of the three persons within the Godhead.

ultimacy — The notion that there is an ultimate, unconditioned, timeless reality or realm upon which the finite world depends and which casts its shadow or is apparent in the finite world in experience.

universalism — The belief that all have been elected by the loving God and/or have been redeemed by Jesus Christ; the belief that all humanity over the stretch of time, including all non-Christians, will be saved, either through Christ or through some other means that God has provided.

Vatican Council II (1962-1965) — The twenty-first council of the Roman Catholic Church, summoned by Pope John XXIII, which enacted many reforms and recast many doctrines — such as revelation, biblical interpretation, salvation, and ecclesiology — in a new light.

via negativa — Literally, by way of negation. A way of speaking about God based on the idea that God is so transcendent, such a different kind of reality, that we can talk about God only by saying what we cannot say about God, such as that God is not finite, temporal, dependent (so is infinite, timeless, and exists in aseity).

virtualism — An understanding of the sacraments in which God is present through the power of the Spirit either to bring Christ down to us or us up to Christ.

Wesley, John (1703-1791) — Eighteenth-century founder of Methodism as a result of a revival movement within the Church of England. His distinctive theological work focuses almost wholly on soteriology, specifically, on an understanding of the nature of and the relation between justification and sanctification. His most distinctive teaching was focused on the idea of Christian perfection or holiness, the claim that we could be made perfect in love in this life. In terms of theological method, he made a distinctive contribution to the role of experience in Christian life and thought.

Whitehead, Alfred North (1861-1947) — Twentieth-century metaphysician who taught that all reality is processive and relational, from "the most trivial puff of smoke in the universe" to God. Whitehead understood God and the world to be internally related, and he introduced the idea of change into the concept of God's consequent nature, in contrast to classical theism, which taught that God is timeless, changeless, and unaffected by the world.

Wittgenstein, Ludwig (1889-1951) — One of the most important philosophers in modern philosophy, who was the impetus for "the linguistic turn" in modern philosophy. He was important for his discussion of the limits of language, and the majority of his later work was devoted to his analysis of "language games" and how the meaning of language is determined by the different rules by which languages are used in different contexts. He has had enormous influence on postmodern and postliberal theologies.

Word of God/word of God — Jesus Christ is the Word *(Logos)* of God incarnate. The Bible is the Word of God in the sense that it is the witness to, the proclamation of, and the record about Jesus as the incarnate Word of God. Some Christians hold that the Bible is the Word of God in the sense that the words of the Bible are the words of God either dictated by or controlled by God so that everything the Bible teaches is inerrant or infallible.

works righteousness — The idea that we are saved by God as a reward for our good works, that our good works — such as deeds of justice, mercy, and love — make us righteous in the sight of God. This concept stands in conflict with the idea that we are saved by grace through faith alone.

worldview — The large meta-picture (big picture) out of which we operate in seeing the world as a whole. Our worldview describes how we understand the basic character, structure, processes, and purpose of the creation, cosmos, or world. Some postmodern worldviews hold that there is no world as a whole (Richard Rorty, "there is no big picture").

Index